Environmental Quality and Health
Edited by Miryha Gould Runnerstrom Ph.D.

Second Edition

JONES & BARTLETT
LEARNING

World Headquarters
Jones & Bartlett Learning
5 Wall Street
Burlington, MA 01803
978-443-5000
info@jblearning.com
www.jblearning.com

Jones & Bartlett Learning books and products are available through most bookstores and online booksellers. To contact Jones & Bartlett Learning directly, call 800-832-0034, fax 978-443-8000, or visit our website, www.jblearning.com.

This book is produced through PUBLISH – a custom publishing service offered by Jones & Bartlett Learning. For more information on PUBLISH, contact us at 800-832-0034 or visit our website at www.jblearning.com.

Disclaimer
This publication is sold with the understanding that the publisher is not engaged in rendering medical, legal, accounting, or other professional services. If medical, legal, accounting, or other professional service advice is required, the service of a competent professional should be sought. The authors, editor, and publisher have designed this publication to provide accurate information with regard to the subject matter covered. However, they are not responsible for errors, omissions, or for any outcomes related to the use of the contents of this publication and make no guarantee and assume no responsibility or liability for the use of the products and procedures described, or the correctness, sufficiency, or completeness of stated information, opinions, or recommendations. Treatments and side effects described in this publication are not applicable to all people; required dosages and experienced side effects will vary among individuals. Drugs and medical devices discussed herein are controlled by the Food and Drug Administration (FDA) and may have limited availability for use only in research studies or clinical trials. Research, clinical practice, and government regulations often change accepted standards. When consideration is being given to the use of any drug in the clinical setting, the health care provider or reader is responsible for determining FDA status of the drug, reading the package insert, and reviewing prescribing information for the most current recommendations on dose, precautions, and contraindications and for determining the appropriate usage for the product. This is especially important in the case of drugs that are new or seldom used. Any references in this publication to procedures to be employed when rendering emergency care to the sick and injured are provided solely as a general guide; other or additional safety measures might be required under particular circumstances. This publication is not intended as a statement of the standards of care required in any particular situation; circumstances and the physical conditions of patients can vary widely from one emergency to another. This publication is not intended in any way to advise emergency personnel concerning their legal authority to perform the activities or procedures discussed. Such local determination should be made only with the aid of legal counsel. Some images in this publication feature models; these models do not necessarily endorse, represent, or participate in the activities represented in the images.

Cover Image: © argus/ShutterStock, Inc.

6048
Printed in the United States of America
23 22 21 20 19   10 9 8 7 6 5 4 3 2 1

Contents

Introduction:
The Environment At Risk

LEARNING OBJECTIVES

By the end of this chapter the reader will be able to:

- Describe how environmental health problems influence our lives.
- Discuss the potential impacts of population growth upon the environment.
- State a definition of the term *environmental health*.
- List at least five major events in the history of environmental health.
- Summarize employment opportunities in the environmental health field.

▶ Introduction

This chapter will illustrate how the environment impacts the health of people and survival of every living being on the planet. You will learn about key terms used in environmental health and the scope of the field. The focus will be on distinguishing features of the field and the basic concepts, which are essential to this discipline. For example, one of these concepts is the relationship between world population growth and the environment. Another concept relates to historically significant environmental events and how they influenced the topics that are of current importance to the environmental health field. An additional topic involves employment classifications, career roles, and opportunities for environmental health workers. The chapter will conclude with an overview of the textbook: the roles of **environmental epidemiology** and **toxicology**, policy aspects of environmental health, examples of environmentally related agents and diseases, and specific content areas of environmental health such as air quality, water quality, food safety, and waste disposal.

▶ Progress and Challenges in Protecting Our Environment

Although much progress has been made in protecting our environment, many lingering challenges confront humanity. Maintaining environmental quality is a pressing task for the 21st century. Often achievements in environment quality are limited primarily to the developed world, which has the financial wherewithal to address environmental health.

Improvement in environmental quality is an official goal of the US government, as articulated in *Healthy People 2020*. This goal (number 8, Environmental Health) is formatted as follows: "Promote health for all through a healthy environment."[1] A list of environmental objectives is shown in **TABLE 1**.

TABLE 1 Objectives for *Healthy People 2020*—Environmental Health Goal: Promote Health for All through a Healthy Environment
Outdoor Air Quality
EH-1 Reduce the number of days the Air Quality Index (AQI) exceeds 100, weighted by population and AQI.
EH-2 Increase use of alternative modes of transportation for work.
EH-3 Reduce air toxic emissions to decrease the risk of adverse health effects caused by mobile, area, and major sources of airborne toxics.
Water Quality
EH-4 Increase the proportion of persons served by community water systems who receive a supply of drinking water that meets the regulations of the Safe Drinking Water Act.
EH-5 Reduce waterborne disease outbreaks arising from water intended for drinking among persons served by community water systems.
EH-6 Reduce per capita domestic water withdrawals with respect to use and conservation.
EH-7 Increase the proportion of days that beaches are open and safe for swimming.
Toxics and Waste
EH-8 Reduce blood lead levels in children.
EH-9 Minimize the risks to human health and the environment posed by hazardous sites.
EH-10 Reduce pesticide exposures that result in visits to a health care facility.
EH-11 Reduce the amount of toxic pollutants released into the environment.
EH-12 Increase recycling of municipal solid waste.
Healthy Homes and Healthy Communities
EH-13 Reduce indoor allergen levels.
EH-14 Increase the proportion of homes with an operating radon mitigation system for persons living in homes at risk for radon exposure.
EH-15 Increase the proportion of new single-family homes (SFH) constructed with radon-reducing features, especially in high-radon-potential areas.
EH-16 Increase the proportion of the Nation's elementary, middle, and high schools that have official school policies and engage in practices that promote a healthy and safe physical school environment.
EH-17 (Developmental) Increase the proportion of persons living in pre-1978 housing that has been tested for the presence of lead-based paint or related hazards.

EH-18 Reduce the number of U.S. homes that are found to have lead-based paint or related hazards.

EH-19 Reduce the proportion of occupied housing units that have moderate or severe physical problems.

Infrastructure and Surveillance

EH-20 Reduce exposure to selected environmental chemicals in the population, as measured by blood and urine concentrations of the substances or their metabolites.

EH-21 Improve quality, utility, awareness, and use of existing information systems for environmental health.

EH-22 Increase the number of States, Territories, Tribes, and the District of Columbia that monitor diseases or conditions that can be caused by exposure to environmental hazards.

EH-23 Reduce the number of public schools located within 150 meters of major highways in the United States.

Global Environmental Health

EH-24 Reduce the global burden of disease due to poor water quality, sanitation, and insufficient hygiene.

Modified from US Department of Health and Human Services. Office of Disease Prevention and Health Promotion. *Healthy People 2020*: Environmental Health. Available at: https://www.healthypeople.gov/2020/topics-objectives/topic/environmental-health/objectives. Accessed January 17, 2017.

According to *Healthy People 2020*:

Humans interact with the environment constantly. These interactions affect quality of life, years of healthy life lived, and health disparities…. Maintaining a healthy environment is central to increasing quality of life and years of healthy life. Globally, nearly 25 percent of all deaths and the total disease burden can be attributed to environmental factors. Environmental factors are diverse and far reaching…. Poor environmental quality has its greatest impact on people whose health status is already at risk. Therefore, environmental health must address the societal and environmental factors that increase the likelihood of exposure and disease.[1]

Protecting the environment means creating a world in which the air is safe to breathe, the water is safe to drink, the land is arable and free from toxins, wastes are managed effectively, infectious diseases are kept at bay, and natural areas are preserved. **FIGURE 1** illustrates a beautifully maintained natural area in the United States. Crucial environmental dimensions also include the impacts of disasters, the built environment, and availability of nutritious foods.[1]

The requirements of a growing world population need to be balanced against the demands for environmental preservation. Although developed countries such as the United States have made substantial progress in clearing the air and reducing air pollution,

significant challenges to the environment and human health remain. For example, among the current and persistent threats to the environment in the United States are the following: trash that fouls our beaches, hazardous wastes (including radioactive wastes) leaching from disposal sites, continuing episodes of air pollution, exposures to toxic chemicals, destruction of the land through deforestation, and global warming.

The hallmarks of environmental degradation are not difficult to find: Warning signs posted on beaches advise bathers not to enter ocean water that is unsafe because of sewage contamination. In some areas of the United States, drinking water is threatened by toxic chemicals

FIGURE 1 A natural ecosystem in the United States. Maintaining environmental quality is a pressing task for the 21st century.

that are leaching from disposal sites. Too many factories continue to belch thick, black smoke or emit unseen pollutants. Avoidance of air pollution, which at best insults our aesthetic senses and at worst endangers our health, is often impossible. Society's appetite for lumber and new housing to satisfy the burgeoning population has resulted in clear-cutting of forests and destruction of wildlife habitats in order to accommodate new habitations for humans. Continued use of fossil fuels contributes to poor air quality and climate change.

Pollution and population growth, often associated with adverse economic circumstances, are closely connected with environmental health. In his classic article, the late Professor Warren Winkelstein wrote that "the three P's—pollution, population, and poverty—are principal determinants of health worldwide. . . ."[2(p932)] The three P's are interrelated: Population growth is associated with poverty, and both poverty and population growth are associated with pollution.

An example of the first "P" is pollution from combustion of fossil fuels (e.g., petroleum and coal), which disperses greenhouse gases along with other pollutants into the atmosphere. This process is believed to be a cause of global warming that in turn may have wide-ranging adverse effects. One such effect is to advance the range of disease-carrying insects, bringing them into new geographic areas; for example, mosquito-borne diseases such as the West Nile virus and dengue fever may appear in areas that previously were free from these conditions. (Refer to the chapter on zoonotic and vector-borne diseases for more information.) The second "P" is population, which is growing exponentially in many parts of the world, especially the less-developed areas, and may result in a worldwide population of up to 10 to 12 billion people during the 21st century; the presence of so many people may exceed the carrying capacity (defined later in the chapter) of the earth by a factor of two. The third "P," poverty, is linked to population growth; poverty is one of the well-recognized determinants of adverse health outcomes.

A recent environmentally related adverse health outcome may be attributed, at least in part, to one of the three P's: population growth (which is associated with urban crowding). As a result of known and unknown environmental and other factors, threats to the human population periodically arise from infectious disease agents. (This topic is discussed in the chapter on zoonotic and vector-borne diseases.) For example, influenza viruses threaten the world's population from time to time. Environmental factors that are likely to advance the spread of influenza viruses include intensive animal husbandry practices needed to supply food to the world's growing population. These practices create extremely crowded conditions among food animals coupled with their close residential proximity to humans. Often such farm animals are treated with antibiotics that contribute to the proliferation of antibiotic resistant strains of bacteria.

Several years ago, public health officials became concerned about the possible occurrence of a human pandemic of avian influenza, caused by the avian influenza A (H5N1) virus. Large outbreaks of avian influenza occurred on poultry farms in Asia. Apparently, some transmission of the virus from birds to humans also occurred. The disease (called bird flu) produces a severe human illness that has a high fatality rate. Health officials were concerned that the virus might mutate, enabling human-to-human transmission; if human-to-human transmission of the virus erupted, a pandemic might result. Contributing to the possible epidemic transmission of influenza (and other communicable diseases) is the ability of human beings to travel rapidly from one area of the globe to another.

An example of a global outbreak of influenza was the pandemic caused by swine flu (H1N1 influenza). In 2009, swine flu spread through North America to other parts of the globe. The World Health Organization (WHO) declared a pandemic of influenza was underway.

Another example of a condition that threatens the human population as well as all life on earth is global climate change. **EXHIBIT 1** presents a case study of global climate change. More information on this topic appears in the chapter on air quality. Refer to **FIGURE 2** for ways climate change threatens your health.

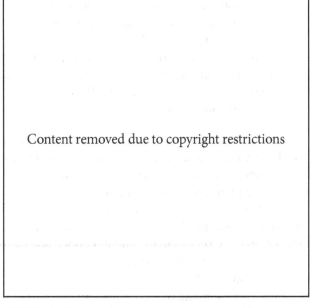

Content removed due to copyright restrictions

FIGURE 2 Climate change threatens your health.

EXHIBIT 1

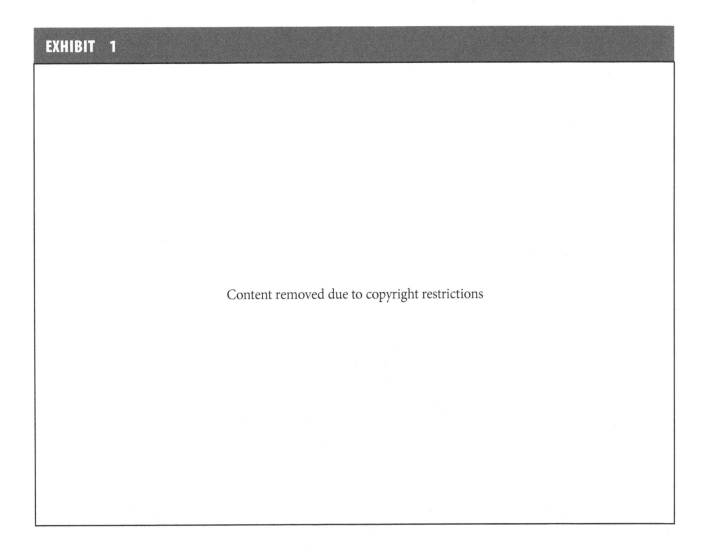

Content removed due to copyright restrictions

▶ Significance of the Environment for Human Health

The environment is intimately connected with human health, illness, and mortality. For example, although figures on the role of environmental factors in global mortality vary considerably, the environment is undoubtedly a salient influence on human deaths. Some estimates from the 1990s placed the toll of the world's deaths caused by environmental factors at around 40%.[3] World Health Organization data from 2012 suggested that almost one-quarter of global deaths result from an unhealthy environment. Exposures to potentially hazardous agents such as microbes, toxic chemicals and metals, pesticides, and ionizing radiation account for many of the forms of environmentally associated morbidity (acute and chronic conditions, allergic responses, and disability) and mortality that occur in today's world. These environmentally related determinants are believed to be important for the development of chronic diseases such as cancer, although most chronic diseases are thought to be the result of complex interactions between environmental and genetic factors.[4] All human beings are affected in some way by exposure to environmental hazards associated with lifestyle: at work, at home, during recreation, or while traveling on the expressway. TABLE 2 provides examples of the scope of disease burden associated with exposure to environmental hazards.

Vulnerable Subgroups of the Population

The elderly, persons with disabilities and chronic diseases, pregnant women, and children are more likely to be affected by environmental hazards than are members of the general population. With respect to age, research from WHO underscored the differential effects of environmental influences across the life course.[5] Age groups most likely to be impacted are children younger than 5 years, children as old as 10 years to a lesser degree, and older adults from 50 to 75 years.

TABLE 2 The Scope of Environmental Health Problems in the World and the United States

- The World Health Organization (WHO) estimated that in 2012, approximately 12.6 million deaths across the globe (23% of all deaths) were linked to environmental sources.[a]
- The US Environmental Protection Agency reported that in 2015, industry released 881 million pounds (400 million kilograms) of toxic chemicals into the air and water (690 million pounds [313 million kilograms] into the air and 191 million pounds [87 million kilograms] into the water). On the positive side, a declining trend in the release of these chemicals occurred between 2005 and 2015.[b]
- Elevated blood levels of lead continue to be an important problem in the United States, with children living in at least 4 million households that expose them to excessive amounts of lead.[c]
- The number of people with asthma in the United States increased to 8% of the population in 2009; environmental factors such as tobacco smoke and air pollution are asthma triggers.[d]
- "Strong evidence exists that industrial chemicals widely disseminated in the environment are important contributors to… the global, silent pandemic of neurodevelopmental toxicity."[e]
- "Using air quality standards established by WHO, experts have estimated that 1.3 billion of the world's urban inhabitants breathe air that exceeds these quality standards."[f]
- Environmental factors are thought to contribute significantly to various forms of cancer, including cervical cancer, prostate cancer, and breast cancer.

Data from:

[a]Prüss-Üstün A, Wolf J, Corvalan CF, et al. Preventing disease through healthy environments. Geneva, Switzerland: World Health Organization; 2016.

[b]US Environmental Protection Agency. Introduction to the 2015 TRI national analysis. Available at: https://www.epa.gov/sites/production/files/2017-01/documents/tri_na_2015_complete_english.pdf. Accessed June 29, 2017.

[c]Centers for Disease Control and Prevention. Lead home page. Available at: https://www.cdc.gov/nceh/lead. Accessed June 30, 2017.

[d]Centers for Disease Control and Prevention. Vital signs. Asthma in the US. Available at: https:// www.cdc.gov/vitalsigns/asthma/index.html. Accessed June 30, 2017.

[e]Grandjean P, Landrigan PJ. Neurobehavioural effects of developmental toxicity. *Lancet Neurol.* 2014;13(3):330-338.

[f]Butterfield PG. Upstream reflections on environmental health: An abbreviated history and framework for action. *Advances in Nursing Science.* 2002;25:34.

Children represent an especially vulnerable group with respect to exposure to hazardous materials, including pesticides and toxic chemicals. Their immune systems and detoxifying organs are still developing and are not fully capable of responding to environmental toxins.[6] Children may be exposed more often than adults to toxic chemicals in the ambient outdoor air and in the soil because they spend more time outside.[7,8]

Environmental Health and the Developing World

Residents of developing countries suffer far more from problems associated with environmental degradation than do those who live in developed countries; this observation holds true despite the fact that developed countries are highly industrialized and disseminate vast quantities of pollutants into the environment from industrial processes and motor vehicles. In comparison with developing countries, wealthy nations provide better access to medical care and are better able to finance pollution controls.

In the developing world, the pursuit of natural resources has caused widespread deforestation of tropical rain forests and destruction of wildlife habitat. Although these two issues have been the focus of much publicity, less widely publicized environmental hazards such as water contamination, air pollution, unsanitary food, and crowding take a steep toll in both morbidity and mortality in developing countries.[9]

One region of the world that at present confronts serious environmental threats is Asia. Many of the countries in this region are experiencing declines in the amount of forest land, unintentional conversion of arable land to desert, and rising levels of pollution. In order to meet the demands of the rapidly increasing populations of South Asia, rural farmers clear forests and cultivate land that erodes easily and eventually becomes useless for agriculture.[10] **Runoff** from the land contributes to water pollution. The world's most populous country, China, faces many challenging environmental problems including water shortages in the northwest; severe air pollution in major cities, such as Beijing; and increasing desertification.[11]

Environmental Risk Transition

The term **environmental risk transition** has been used to characterize changes in environmental risks that happen as a consequence of economic development in the less-developed regions of the world. Environmental risk transition is characterized by the following circumstances:

In the poorest societies, household risks caused by poor food, air, and water quality tend to dominate. The major risks existing in developing countries today are of this type—diarrhea is attributable to poor water/sanitation/hygiene, acute respiratory diseases to poor housing and indoor air pollution from poor quality household fuels, and malaria to poor housing quality, although all are of course influenced by other factors as well (malnutrition in particular). . . . As these problems are brought under control, a new set tends to be created at the regional and global level through long-term and long-range pollutants, such as acid rain precursors, ozone-depleting chemicals, and greenhouse gases.[12(p38)]

▶ Population and the Environment

Currently increasing at a geometric rate, the human population threatens to overwhelm available resources; some areas of the world face periodic food scarcity and famine. A number of factors have contributed to population growth, including increases in fertility and reductions in mortality. One of the consequences of population growth has been to encourage the conversion of large rural and forested areas of the earth into cities. Urbanization is linked to numerous adverse implications for the health of populations, including increasing rates of morbidity and mortality. Refer to the following text box, which discusses the consequences of continued population growth.

HOMO SAPIENS—A SUICIDAL SPECIES?

Largely as a result of human action, profound changes are occurring in our environment. . . . The basic cause of almost all of these problems is the world's large and growing human population, which consumes so much energy and produces such large quantities of toxic wastes. . . . Environmental changes, if accompanied by economic and political instability, could lead to the collapse of organized health services. In an era of scarcities of food, water, and other resources, and of a threat to survival, priorities should be reassessed.[13(pp121,123)]

Population Growth Trends

The human population has grown exponentially over the past 200 years and reached 6 billion in June 1999.[14] By 2017, this number reached 7.5 billion. The current trend is for world population growth to continue at a high rate, as noted in the following passage:

> Every day we share the earth and its resources with 250,000 more people than the day before. Every year there are another 90 million mouths to feed. That is the equivalent of adding a city the size of Philadelphia to the world population every week; a Los Angeles every two weeks; a Mexico every year; and a United States and Canada every three years.[15(p30)]

FIGURE 3 characterizes this burgeoning growth for a single year—2002. During that year the world population increased by 2⅓ persons per second, or 141 persons per minute. This annual growth rate would be equivalent to a Boeing 737 jetliner carrying a new group of 141 passengers each minute.

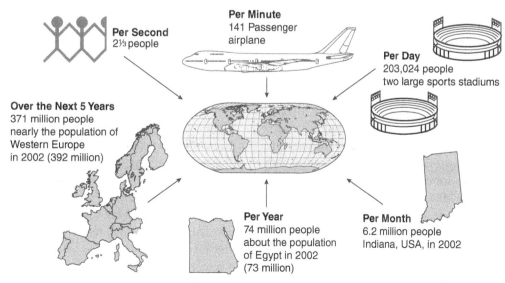

Per Second
2⅓ people

Per Minute
141 Passenger
airplane

Per Day
203,024 people
two large sports stadiums

Over the Next 5 Years
371 million people
nearly the population of
Western Europe
in 2002 (392 million)

Per Year
74 million people
about the population
of Egypt in 2002
(73 million)

Per Month
6.2 million people
Indiana, USA, in 2002

FIGURE 3 Net additions to the world: 2002. In 2002, the world gained 2⅓ people per second.
Modified from US Census Bureau. International Population Reports WP/02. *Global Population Profile: 2002.* Washington, DC: US Government Printing Office; 2004:14.

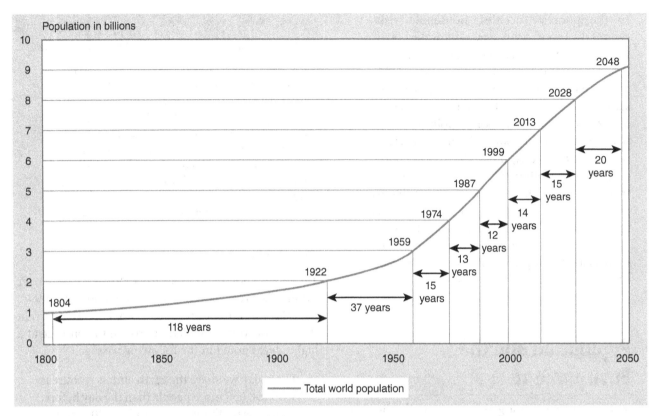

FIGURE 4 Time to successive billions in world population: 1800 to 2050.
Reproduced from US Census Bureau, International Population Reports WP/02. *Global Population Profile: 2002.* Washington, DC: US Government Printing Office; 2004:11.

From the origin of the species *Homo sapiens* (assumed to be about 250,000 years ago) to CE 1800, the population of the world grew by 1 billion individuals.[16] From 1800 to 1922 (122 years), the population added another 1 billion persons. Since 1922, the population has increased at a phenomenal rate: Another billion persons were added after 37 years, 15 years, and 13 years, respectively. Only 12 years elapsed before an additional billion persons were added between 1987 and 1999. See **FIGURE 4**.

Another perspective on population growth is the time that it takes for the population to double. From 1931 to 1974 (a 43-year interval), the earth's population doubled; it is projected to double again during approximately the same interval (1974 to 2018).[17] Estimates suggest that the world's population will reach 8 billion persons between the years 2018 and 2028.

In 1950, the world's five most populous countries were China, India, the United States, Russia, and Japan; at the turn of the 21st century, Russia and Japan were replaced by Indonesia and Brazil. In 2050, India will become the world's most populous country; China will fall to second place, the United States will remain in third place, Indonesia will be in fourth place, and Brazil will be replaced by Nigeria.

Around the 1960s, annual rates of population increase topped out at slightly more than 2% (an 81 million absolute increase annually since the 1980s).[18] Demographers project that the human population eventually may stabilize at a size—about 10 billion persons—that is about three quarters larger than it was around 2000.

Population Dynamics

The term **population dynamics** refers to the ever-changing interrelationships among the set of variables that influence the demographic makeup of populations as well as the variables that influence the growth and decline of population sizes. Among the factors that relate to the size as well as the age and sex composition of populations are fertility, death rates, and migration.

Fertility

One of the measures of fertility is the **completed fertility rate (total fertility rate)**, which is the "[n]umber of children a woman has given birth to when she completes childbearing."[19(p2)] In the United States, the completed fertility rate in 2012 was around 2.0 children per woman;[19] the natural population replacement rate is estimated to be around 2.1. (See the breaking news box about the decline in fertility).

During the baby boom era at the end of the 1950s, the US fertility rate exceeded 3.5 births per woman. Presently, western European countries have low fertility rates; also, the rates are declining in most regions of the developing world.[20] The United States, Canada, Japan, South Korea, Thailand, China, and many countries in populations in these countries will continue to increase because of births among the large cohort of persons of childbearing age who were born when fertility rates were high. Those individuals form a substantial proportion of the population in China and other rapidly industrializing countries. However, the overall trend is for the world's population to age and be composed of increasing numbers of older individuals.

Europe are at or below the replacement rate for fertility. Despite the declines in fertility rates in some Asian countries to levels approaching replacement rates, the

In comparison with the developed world, the fertility rates are considerably higher (at about 4.0 births per woman) in many Asian countries, Latin American countries, and African countries. In the future, their relatively higher fertility rates will enable these regions of the developing world to claim the largest population sizes. (See **FIGURE 5**.)

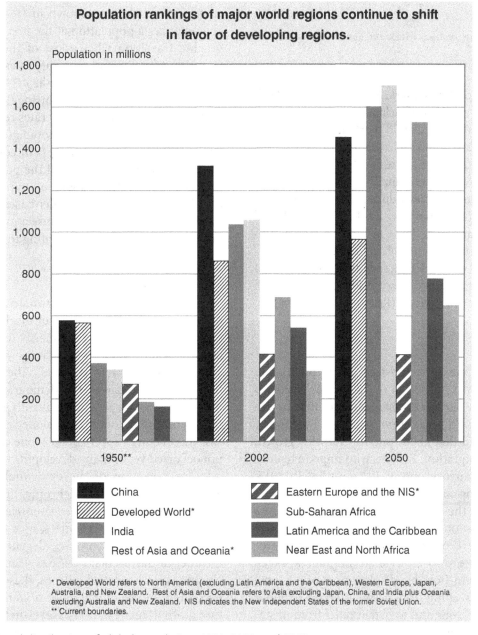

FIGURE 5 Regional distribution of global population: 1950, 2002, and 2050.

Reproduced from US Census Bureau. International Population Reports WP/02. *Global Population Profile: 2002.* Washington, DC: US Government Printing Office; 2004:12.

Mortality

Mortality has declined markedly over time in both industrialized and less-developed countries. Adult mortality and infant and child mortality have demonstrated downward trends. Declining mortality in the developed world began approximately 200 years ago; in the developing world, substantial declines in mortality have occurred more recently during the past 50 years or so. The reduction in mortality has been accomplished through measures that have included public health improvements, famine control, and increased availability of drugs and vaccines. Some additional terms related to mortality are burden of disease, life expectancy, and disability-adjusted life years. (Refer to the text box.)

Migration

Migration has continued to feed global population growth; more than 1 billion of the world's residents are migrants. Census estimates indicate that by the year 2050, the US population will grow by another 100 million and that about one-third of this growth will be from migration. Persons who migrate tend to cluster in a limited group of 10 countries. In 2015, the three leading countries for receiving international migrants were the United States, Germany, and the Russian Federation.[21] Reasons for migration include the search for economic betterment; a large proportion of those who relocate are migrant workers. Forced migration (forcible displacement of persons) is a means of escaping from persecution for religious and political reasons and to obtain relief from unstable conditions in one's home country. Toward the conclusion of 2015, more than 65 million persons were displaced. Many were refugees from Syria, Afghanistan, and Somalia.[21]

Demographic Transition

Demographic transition is the alteration over time in a population's fertility, mortality, and makeup.[14] (Note that demographic transition theory does not include the effects of migration upon the age and sex composition of a population.) According to the demographic transition theory, developed societies have progressed through three stages that have affected their age and sex distributions.

The three phases can be demonstrated by hypothetical population pyramids, which are graphs that show the distribution of a population according to age and sex. Examples of the population pyramids at stages 1 through 3 are shown in **FIGURE 6**. Stage 1 characterizes a population at the first stage of demographic transition when most of the population is young and fertility and mortality rates are high; overall, the population remains small. Stage 2 shows a drop in mortality rates that occurs during the demographic transition; at this stage fertility rates remain high, and there is a rapid increase in population, particularly among the younger age groups. In comparison with the narrow triangular shape of the population distribution at stage 1, this population pyramid also is triangular in shape but has a wider base. Stage 3 reflects dropping fertility rates that cause a more even distribution of the population according to age and sex.

Epidemiologic Transition

The term **epidemiologic transition** is used to describe a shift in the pattern of morbidity and mortality from causes related primarily to infectious and communicable diseases to causes associated with chronic, degenerative diseases. The epidemiologic transition accompanies the demographic transition. The epidemiologic transition already has taken place in the populations of most developed countries (a process that required approximately one century) but has not occurred yet in many developing countries.

One reflection of the epidemiologic transition is the growing burden of chronic, degenerative diseases, especially in developed countries and to a lesser extent in developing countries, as a consequence of population aging. Chronic, degenerative diseases include cardiovascular diseases, cancer, neuropsychiatric conditions, and injuries; these conditions are becoming the major causes of disability and premature death in many nations. Nevertheless, in developing countries communicable and infectious diseases remain the leading causes of morbidity and mortality.

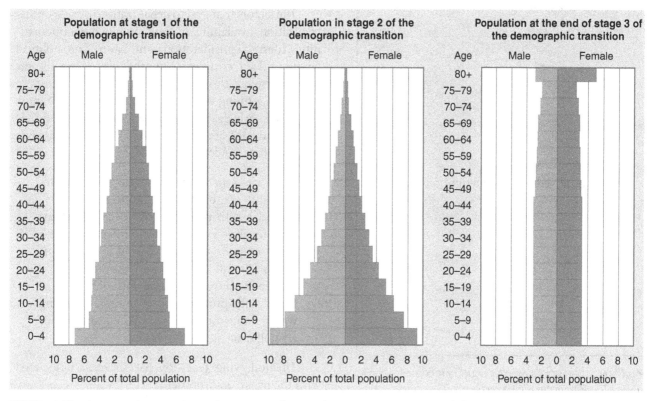

FIGURE 6 The demographic transition in three stages of age and sex composition: stage 1 (left), stage 2 (middle), and stage 3 (right).

Reproduced from Kinsella K, He W. US Census Bureau. International Population Reports P95/09-1. *An Aging World: 2008*. Washington, DC: US Government Printing Office; 2009:20.

Consequences of Population Increases

Rapid growth of the world's population contributes to the deterioration of the environment through widespread depletion of natural resources and by causing the levels of air, water, and other forms of pollution to increase. Also, the resources available per person decrease as the total number of individuals on the planet continues to increase geometrically. Consequently, population growth is a determinant of the number of persons who live in poverty. In already crowded regions, an even larger population means that the size of most people's living spaces must decline and population density must increase. Population density and associated urban crowding are dimensions of environmental degradation associated with increases in the spread of infectious and communicable diseases.

Unless significant technological innovations can be introduced, merely feeding the world's hungry population will become problematic. Many developing countries, where population growth rates are among the highest in the world, are reaching the limit of their abilities to provide for the economic and social needs of their citizens. The United Nations Secretariat states that:

> …excessive population pressure in specific geographical areas can pose serious ecological hazards, including soil erosion, desertification, dwindling supplies of firewood, deforestation

and the degradation of sources of fresh water. Often the link between population pressure and those types of environmental stress is the growth in the relative and absolute number of persons living in poverty. The result is marginalization of small-scale farmers and pressure on larger numbers to migrate from distressed areas. In many cases the result is also the prevalence of environmentally related diseases.[22(p32)]

The effects of rapid growth of the world's population include:

- Urbanization
- Overtaxing carrying capacity (defined later in this chapter)
- Food insecurity
- Loss of biodiversity

Urbanization and the Environment

The past two centuries have seen a rapid increase in the number of cities over the entire globe.[23] The proportion of urban residents has increased from about 5% in 1800 to 50% in 2000 and is expected to reach about 66% by 2030.[22] **FIGURE 7** illustrates the growth of the world's urban population between 1975 and 2015 for low- and middle-income countries in comparison with high-income countries. Although the

Content removed due to copyright restrictions

FIGURE 7 Urban population by country income level, 1975-2015 (1.84% total annual urban population growth between 2015 and 2020).

proportion of urban residents has increased in both categories, a relatively larger growth in the number of urban residents is projected to occur among low-income countries. This trend is apparent in the figure and is forecast to continue into the future. On average, the total urban population will grow by 1.84% annually between 2015 and 2020. (See Figure 7.)

The factors that lead to urbanization include industrialization, availability of food, employment opportunities, lifestyle considerations, and escape from political conflict.[23] Tied to increases in urbanization are numerous adverse health impacts, particularly in developing countries. Among the most important causes of morbidity and early death in urban environments of developing countries are environmentally related diseases and accidents.[24] According to McMichael:

> Large cities in the least developed countries typically combine the traditional environmental health problems of poverty, particularly respiratory and enteric infections, with those of poor quality housing and unregulated industrialization. Residents therefore are often at **risk** from diseases and injuries associated with poor sanitation, unsafe drinking water, dangerous roads, polluted air, indoor air pollution and toxic wastes.[23(p1119)]

The following text box lists hazards associated with the urban environment.

Megacities

The term **megacity** denotes an urbanized area that has 10 million or more inhabitants; in 2016, there were 31 megacities that contained slightly more than 6.8% of the world's population.[25] Examples of megacities and their respective 2016 populations (in millions) are Tokyo (38.1), Shanghai (24.5), Mumbai (formerly known as Bombay; 21.4), Sao Paulo (21.3), and Mexico City (21.2). The two megacities in the United States are New York (18.6) and Los Angeles (12.3).

HAZARDS TO HEALTH WITHIN THE URBAN ENVIRONMENT

Content removed due to copyright restrictions

FIGURE 8 Street scene in a crowded megacity (Mexico City).

Megacities have major influences upon the environment in a number of ways (e.g., demands for energy, potable water, construction materials, food, sewage processing, and solid waste disposal). **FIGURE 8** shows street life in a crowded megacity.

Carrying Capacity

Carrying capacity is "[t]he maximum number of individuals that can be supported sustainably by a given environment."[26] Both human and nonhuman populations may be threatened with disastrous consequences when available resources are exhausted. "Like a bacterial colony in a culture medium, we are susceptible to depletion of nutriments and to poisoning by our own waste products."[15(p123)]

Animal Populations

In the animal kingdom, the carrying capacity of an environment governs population size. In nature, the factors of food availability, reproductive behavior, and infectious diseases tend to keep animal populations in check. An example of an animal population kept in check by food availability follows: The U.S. Coast Guard shipped 29 reindeer to St. Matthew Island in the Bering Sea during the World War II era.[26] The deer were intended as a source of meat for personnel on the island; however, no deer were ever culled and all 29 remained when the war ended. An abundance of deer fodder was available on the island. By the early 1960s, the original deer population had swelled to 6,000 animals. Soon afterward, as a result of overgrazing and depletion of food sources for the deer, the population—having declined to fewer than 50 animals in 1966—faced extinction.

In a given area, the growth of animal populations appears to be sequenced according to the following characteristic patterns:

"Logistic growth, responding to immediate negative feedback, as carrying capacity is approached

Domed or capped growth, responding to deferred negative feedback but necessitating a period of excess mortality

Irruptive growth, with a chaotic post-crash pattern."[18(p978)]

Human Populations

The factors that lead to the crash of animal populations are similar to those that could threaten the survival of the human race. Human life is not possible without adequate food, breathable air, and safe water. Agricultural land must continue to be arable. There needs to be a diversity of plant and animal species. If these components of the human life support system are disrupted by overpopulation of the planet, the species *Homo sapiens* could suffer a population crash. This outcome would be in line with Malthusian predictions.

In 1798, Thomas Malthus authored *First Essay on Population*, which theorized that the human population had the potential to grow exponentially.[16] According to this scenario, the population could outstrip available resources. Malthus suggested that "positive checks" for excessive population growth rates were epidemics of disease, starvation, and population reduction through warfare. The growth of the population could be constrained also through "preventive checks" such as not allowing people to marry.

Endangerment of the human population through ecological damage is not far fetched: Previous history has recorded incidents of decimation and collapse of civilizations that were associated with disruption of the environment. It is believed that approximately 5,000 years ago, Mesopotamia, a renowned ancient civilization, declined as a result of agricultural practices that caused soil erosion, buildup of salt in the soil, and the filling of irrigation channels with silt.[27] During medieval times, crowded cities of Europe were devastated by plague and other infectious diseases. In the interval between the 13th and 16th centuries, global temperatures declined by approximately 1°C (1.8°F), contributing to the decimation of societies that were located in the far north (e.g., Viking settlements in Greenland).

Food Insecurity and Famine

The term **food insecurity** refers to a situation in which supplies of wholesome foods are uncertain or may have limited availability. Food insecurity and famine may occur when the carrying capacity in a particular geographic area is exceeded. An illustration of the effect of exceeding the carrying capacity in a local geographic area is the occurrence of a local subsistence crisis, which follows when the ability of land and available water to produce food are overtaxed.[18] In theory, low nutritional levels that accompany local subsistence crises may cause population mortality to increase so that mortality is brought into balance with fertility, stabilizing the population size. Periodically, food insecurity is a reality in some developing regions. For example, food insecurity endangers as much as one-third of Africa, and the prognosis for increasing the food supply in some African countries is poor.[27]

Loss of Biodiversity

The word *biodiversity* is formed from the combination of *biological* and *diversity*. An adequate definition of biodiversity is not readily available. Nevertheless, the term **biodiversity** generally refers to the different types and variability of animal and plant species and ecosystems in which they live.[28] With respect to a particular geographic area, biodiversity involves diversity in the genes of a population of a given species, diversity in the number of species, and diversity in habitats. Biodiversity is considered to be an essential dimension of human health.[29]

The dramatic human population growth during the past few decades and concomitant increases in urbanization and industrialization have caused the physical environment to be degraded substantially; one of the consequences of unchecked population growth is hypothesized to be accelerated loss of biodiversity. Human activities are thought to be related to the spread of harmful insect vectors, extinctions of species, and loss of flora; some of these plants and trees could be the source of valuable commodities such as new pharmaceuticals. Ultimately, loss of biodiversity may pose a danger to food production as a result of the growth in numbers of invasive species and the eradication of helpful plants and insects. An example of the loss of biodiversity is the destruction of tropical rain forests that has culminated in the extinction of some flowering plants that may have had future medical value.[29]

▶ Definitions Used in the Environmental Health Field

The Environment

The term **environment** refers to "the complex of physical, chemical, and biotic factors (as climate, soil, and living things) that act upon an organism or an ecological community and ultimately determine its form and survival."[30] This definition pertains to the physical environment. Examples of physical environmental factors (as noted previously) that affect human health include toxic chemicals, metallic compounds, ionizing and nonionizing radiation, and physical and mechanical energy. These factors will be discussed in more detail later in the text.

The term *environment* captures the notion of factors that are external to the individual, as opposed to internal factors such as genetic makeup. In contrast to the physical environment, described in the foregoing definition, the **social environment** encompasses influences upon the individual that arise from societal and cultural factors. Among the major determinants of health are the environment (physical and social), personal lifestyle factors, constitutional factors such as heredity and human biology, and healthcare systems dimensions such as access to and quality of medical care and methods for organization of healthcare systems.[31] A model that describes these aspects of health is the **ecological model**, which proposes that the determinants of health (environmental, biological, and behavioral) interact and are interlinked over the life course of individuals. (Refer to **FIGURE 9**.) From the model it may be inferred that the environment is one component of many interacting dimensions that affect the health of populations.

Ecological System (Ecosystem)

Ecosystems are one of the important dimensions of life in the biosphere. All life on earth survives in the biosphere, which consists of the atmosphere and the earth's surface and oceans. The biosphere covers a narrow range from about 6 miles (9.6 kilometers) above the earth to the surface of the earth to the deepest ocean trenches, some of which are 36,000 feet deep (about 11,000 meters). One of the crucial aspects of the earth's biosphere is energy flow; the ultimate source of energy for all living beings on earth is the sun. Energy flows from the sun in the form of electromagnetic radiation (e.g., ultraviolet radiation, infrared radiation, and visible light). Only a small percentage of the energy produced by the sun impinges upon the earth. Plants absorb some portions of the sun's electromagnetic radiation and convert them into nutrients and oxygen via the process known as photosynthesis. This energy is then transferred to other life forms through the food chain, for example, via herbivores that eat the plants themselves or carnivores that eat other animals.

"An ecosystem is a dynamic complex of plant, animal, and microorganism communities and the nonliving environment interacting as a functional

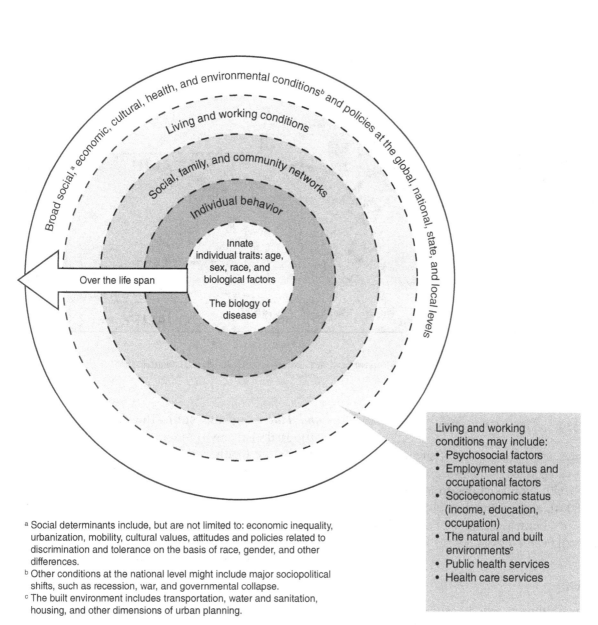

The ecological model of population health diagram with concentric circles from center outward:

Innate individual traits: age, sex, race, and biological factors / The biology of disease

Individual behavior

Social, family, and community networks

Living and working conditions

Broad social,[a] economic, cultural, health, and environmental conditions[b] and policies at the global, national, state, and local levels

Over the life span

Living and working conditions may include:
- Psychosocial factors
- Employment status and occupational factors
- Socioeconomic status (income, education, occupation)
- The natural and built environments[c]
- Public health services
- Health care services

[a] Social determinants include, but are not limited to: economic inequality, urbanization, mobility, cultural values, attitudes and policies related to discrimination and tolerance on the basis of race, gender, and other differences.

[b] Other conditions at the national level might include major sociopolitical shifts, such as recession, war, and governmental collapse.

[c] The built environment includes transportation, water and sanitation, housing, and other dimensions of urban planning.

FIGURE 9 The ecological model of population health.

Modified and reproduced with permission from *Who Will Keep the Public Healthy? Educating Public Health Professionals for the 21st Century*, © 2003 by the National Academy of Sciences, courtesy of the National Academies Press, Washington, D.C., p. 33; and from Dahlgren G, Whitehead M. *Policies and Strategies to Promote Social Equity in Health*. Stockholm, Sweden: Institute for Futures Studies; 1991.

unit. Humans are an integral part of ecosystems. Ecosystems vary enormously in size: a temporary pond in a tree hollow and an ocean basin can both be ecosystems."[32(p3)] The interconnected components of an **ecosystem** are in a steady state; disrupting one of the components can disrupt the entire ecosystem. **FIGURE 10** suggests that the health of the ecosystem is associated with the health of human beings as well as that of domestic animals and wildlife.

Survival of the human population depends upon ecosystems, which aid in supplying clean air and water as part of the earth's life support system.[33] Ecosystems are being degraded with increasing rapidity because of human environmental impacts such as urbanization and deforestation. Degradation of ecosystems poses environmental dangers such as loss of the oxygen-producing capacity of plants and loss of biodiversity.

Environmental Health

The field of **environmental health** has a broad focus and includes a number of subspecializations. For example, occupational health often is regarded as a topic that is closely allied with environmental health and is a subset of broader environmental health concerns. Consequently, in view of its broad reach, the term *environmental health* does not have a single definition, nor is it easy to define. According to the World Health Organization:

Environmental health addresses all the physical, chemical, and biological factors external to a person, and all the related factors impacting behaviours. It encompasses the assessment and control of those environmental factors that can potentially affect health. It is targeted towards preventing disease and creating health-supportive environments.[34]

15

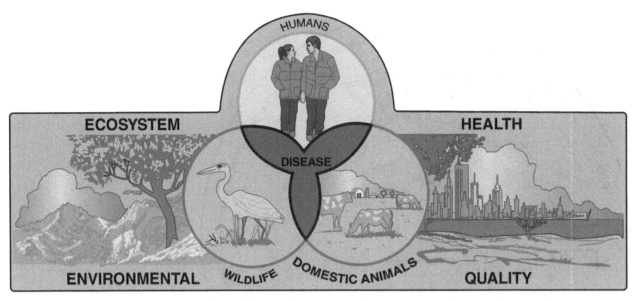

FIGURE 10 Ecosystem health.

Reproduced from Friend M. *Disease Emergence and Reemergence. The Wildlife-Human Connection.* Reston, VA: US Geological Survey, Circular 1285, p. 131. Illustration by John M. Evans.

▶ Historical Background

This section presents a brief review of environmental health history, categorized as follows: ancient history, occupational health (contributions from about 1500 to the mid-1800s), and environmental history post-1800. **FIGURE 11** summarizes some of the highlights in environmental health history.

Ancient History

Negative human impacts on the environment are thought to have begun many thousands of years ago. One of the initial targets of human activity was forests, which were cut down for use as timber and burned to clear land for agriculture and human settlements. Deforestation subsequently led to soil erosion that caused rivers and bays to be fouled with silt.

The observations, insights, and writings of the ancient Greeks are noteworthy for the history of environmental health.[35] Around the 5th century BCE, the ancient Greek philosophers had developed the concept of the relationship between environmental factors and human health; instead of advocating for the workings of supernatural factors and the belief that magic potions would have curative powers, their philosophical position linked the influence of environment to disease.

Hippocrates, who lived between 460 and 370 BCE, often is referred to as "the father of medicine." (See **FIGURE 12**.) Hippocrates emphasized the role of the environment as an influence on people's health and health status in his work titled *On Airs, Waters,* *and Places* (ca 400 BCE). The Greek philosopher proposed that environmental and climatic factors such as the weather, seasons, and prevailing winds; the quality of air, water, and food; and one's geographic location were influential in causing changes in human health. He espoused the doctrine of maintaining equilibrium among the body's four humors, known as yellow bile, black bile, phlegm, and blood; imbalance among the four humors caused by environmental influences led to the onset of infectious diseases.

Many of the principles identified by Hippocrates regarding the impact of the environment on human health and disease remain credible despite the great increases in medical knowledge that have occurred since Hippocrates' time.[35] For example, now it is known that polluted water is associated with many types of waterborne infections (e.g., cholera and cryptosporidiosis [discussed later in this text]). Consistent with the belief that air is a factor in diseases is the origin of the term *malaria* (bad air), a disease that is carried by airborne mosquitoes that dwell in standing pools of water.

For many years, people have known about the harmful effects of heavy metals.[36] Hippocrates identified the toxic properties of lead.[37] The toxic properties of sulfur and zinc were pointed out by the Roman scholar Pliny the Elder (CE 29–79) during the 1st century CE; Pliny invented a mask constructed from the bladder of an animal for protection against dusts and metal fumes. During the 2nd century CE, the renowned Greek physician Galen (CE 129–200) outlined the pathological aspects of lead toxicity and

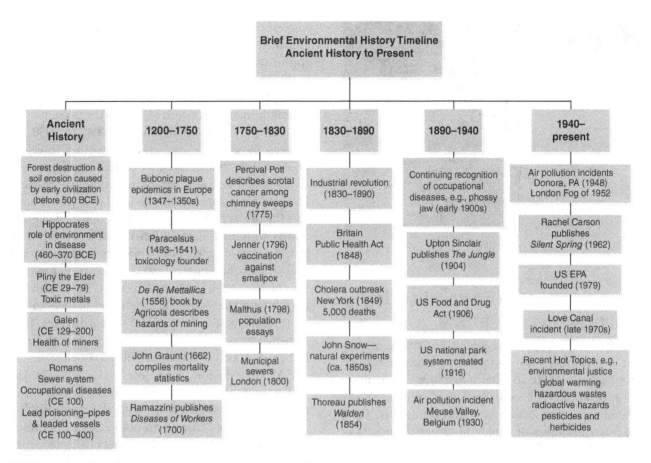

Brief Environmental History Timeline Ancient History to Present

Ancient History	1200–1750	1750–1830	1830–1890	1890–1940	1940–present
Forest destruction & soil erosion caused by early civilization (before 500 BCE)	Bubonic plague epidemics in Europe (1347–1350s)	Percival Pott describes scrotal cancer among chimney sweeps (1775)	Industrial revolution (1830–1890)	Continuing recognition of occupational diseases, e.g., phossy jaw (early 1900s)	Air pollution incidents Donora, PA (1948) London Fog of 1952
Hippocrates role of environment in disease (460–370 BCE)	Paracelsus (1493–1541) toxicology founder	Jenner (1796) vaccination against smallpox	Britain Public Health Act (1848)	Upton Sinclair publishes *The Jungle* (1904)	Rachel Carson publishes *Silent Spring* (1962)
Pliny the Elder (CE 29–79) Toxic metals	*De Re Mettallica* (1556) book by Agricola describes hazards of mining	Malthus (1798) population essays	Cholera outbreak New York (1849) 5,000 deaths	US Food and Drug Act (1906)	US EPA founded (1979)
Galen (CE 129–200) Health of miners	John Graunt (1662) compiles mortality statistics	Municipal sewers London (1800)	John Snow— natural experiments (ca. 1850s)	US national park system created (1916)	Love Canal incident (late 1970s)
Romans Sewer system Occupational diseases (CE 100) Lead poisoning–pipes & leaded vessels (CE 100–400)	Ramazzini publishes *Diseases of Workers* (1700)		Thoreau publishes *Walden* (1854)	Air pollution incident Meuse Valley, Belgium (1930)	Recent Hot Topics, e.g., environmental justice global warming hazardous wastes radioactive hazards pesticides and herbicides

FIGURE 11 Brief environmental history time line: ancient history to the present.

FIGURE 12 Hippocrates.
Courtesy of US National Library of Medicine, National Institutes of Health. History of medicine division. Available at: http://ihm.nlm.nih.gov/luna/servlet/view/search?q=B014553. Accessed July 1, 2017.

suggested that mists from acids could endanger the health of copper miners.[37]

The ancient Romans developed the first infrastructure for maintaining public health. Among their innovations were systems for the transport of water and sewage, heating devices for water and for rooms, and communal baths.[38,39] Beginning about 500 BCE, the Etruscans constructed a sewer called the Cloaca Maxima in Rome. As the city grew, a system of aqueducts that supplied fresh water and a web of sewers called cloacae were installed.

The Romans brought many of these innovations to their settlements all over Europe. Roman aqueducts and baths can been seen today in many parts of Europe. An example of the Roman baths at Baden-Baden, Germany is shown in **FIGURE 13**. The Romans used lead pipes to supply the homes of the affluent, who probably suffered from chronic lead poisoning. After the decline of their empire (possibly due, in part, to chronic lead poisoning), many of the hygiene-related contributions of the Romans were forgotten; for several centuries, the European world endured the abhorrent sanitary conditions of the medieval era, with its periodic outbreaks of epidemics of plague, cholera, and other pestilence.

FIGURE 13 Roman baths at Baden-Baden, Germany.

Occupational Health (Contributions from About 1500 to the Mid-1800s)

The field of occupational health has made numerous contributions to environmental health history. From about 1500 to the mid-1800s, recognition grew regarding the contribution of occupationally related exposures to adverse health conditions. There are many examples of explorations of the impacts of unsafe and hazardous working environments on the health of workers, especially the effects of exposures to toxic metals and hazards that occurred among miners. Among the historically important figures in occupational health were Paracelsus (1493–1541), Agricola (1494–1555), Bernardino Ramazzini (1633–1714), Percival Pott (1714–1788), and Alice Hamilton (1869–1970). See the chapter on environmental toxicology for information on Paracelsus, the chapter on environmental epidemiology for information about Percival Pott, and the chapter on occupational health for a discussion of Agricola, Ramazzini, and Hamilton; the chapter on occupational health also provides information on other historically important individuals in the field of occupational health.

Although his contributions were not limited specifically to occupational health, John Graunt (one of the early compilers of vital statistics data) published *Natural and Political Observations Made upon the Bills of Mortality* in 1662. Sometimes Graunt is referred to as the Columbus of statistics because his book made a fundamental contribution by attempting to demonstrate the quantitative characteristics of birth and death data.

Environmental History Post-1800

Just before the commencement of the 1800s, Jenner (in 1796) devised a method for vaccinating against smallpox; in 1798, Malthus wrote his well-known essays on population, mentioned earlier in this chapter. The

history of environmental health since 1800 may be classified into three major eras:[40] the first wave of environmental concern (19th century to mid-20th century), the second wave of environmental awareness (mid-20th century to the 1980s), and the third period of environmental concern (1980s to the present).

The period of approximately 1850 to 1950 was marked by growing awareness of existing threats to public health from unsanitary conditions, detrimental social conditions, and hazardous work environments. For example, a common employment practice in Europe was the use of child labor. This era coincided approximately with the Industrial Revolution and marked the introduction of public health reforms to improve environmental conditions. In 1800, construction began on sewers that served the city of London. The British Parliament enacted the Public Health Act in 1848 to promote clean water and control infectious diseases. There were major outbreaks of cholera, including an outbreak in New York City in 1849 that killed 5,000 people.

About the same time, John Snow hypothesized that sewage-contaminated water was associated with cholera and conducted a "natural experiment" to demonstrate the cause of an outbreak in the present Soho district of London. John Snow (1813–1858) was an English anesthesiologist who innovated several of the key epidemiologic methods that remain valid and in use today. In Snow's time, the mechanism for the causation of infectious diseases was largely unknown. The Dutchman Anton van Leeuwenhoek (1632–1723) had used the microscope to observe microorganisms (bacteria and yeast). However, the connection between microorganisms and disease had not yet been ascertained. During Snow's time, one of the explanations for infectious diseases such as cholera was the miasmic theory of disease, which alleged that illnesses were caused by clouds of noxious matter. Snow rejected the miasmatic theory and showed the connection between polluted water and cholera. Because of his pioneering work, Snow is regarded as an icon in the history of public health and continues to be influential during the 21st century. (More information about Snow's work is provided in the chapter on environmental epidemiology.)

In the United States, Lemuel Shattuck published the 1850 *Report on the Sanitary Conditions of Massachusetts*. Shattuck argued for the creation of a state health department and local health boards. Among other issues, Shattuck's report dealt in detail with the topic of environmental sanitation and its connection with health. Although not implemented by the state legislature at the time, Shattuck's proposed recommendations were extremely farsighted and innovative and became a major influence in the development of subsequent public health practice. Ultimately, years later, many of Shattuck's proposals were adopted by public health departments and are in use today.

Several additional developments marked the late 19th century and early 20th century. Henry David Thoreau published *Walden* in 1854; this book extolled the virtues of a simple life in a beautiful natural environment. Thoreau suggested that nature enriched the lives of human beings and therefore should be respected.

Beginning in 1900, Walter Reed, who was a US Army medical officer, investigated the causes of yellow fever, which was a scourge of US troops in the Caribbean. He showed that yellow fever was a mosquito-borne affliction. Following this discovery, Major William Gorgas was dispatched to Havana, Cuba, where he implemented a highly successful mosquito eradication program. This action led to a drastic reduction in yellow fever cases in Havana; later Gorgas conducted a mosquito control program in the Panama Canal Zone, making possible the construction of the canal.

In *The Jungle* (1906), Upton Sinclair described the deplorable conditions in the meat processing industry in Chicago. Sinclair's exposé was instrumental in passage of the first Food and Drug Act that was instituted in the United States in 1906. (Some of the US laws regarding food safety are described in the chapter on food safety.) One other development that reflected the public's concern for the environment was creation of the US National Park System in 1916.

During the second wave of environmental concern, defined approximately from the middle of the 1950s to the 1980s, environmental issues continued to come to the forefront. The period witnessed the occurrence of several noteworthy air pollution incidents, including the fatal 1930 incident in the Meuse Valley, Belgium; an air pollution episode that caused numerous deaths in Donora, Pennsylvania, in 1948; and the deadly London fog of 1952.[41] (More information on these incidents is presented in the chapter on air quality.)

Awareness increased regarding the potential health hazards of toxic chemicals. In the United States, efforts were made to protect ecologically sensitive areas from toxic hazards and from overdevelopment. Additional legislation in the United States modified food and drug laws designed to regulate toxins and the use of additives in food. Rachel Carson published *Silent Spring* in 1962, which highlighted the potential dangers of pesticides. In 1970, the Environmental Protection Agency (EPA) was founded to address environmental concerns at the federal government level (more information on this topic is presented in the chapter on environmental policy and regulation).

The topic of toxic waste disposal also was the focus of much attention during the 1970s. For example, when residents discovered that their homes had been constructed on a former toxic waste site referred to as the Love Canal, they became alarmed about possible adverse health effects that might be linked to the waste site. Love Canal became a cause célèbre for environmental activists. (This topic is covered in more detail in the chapter on solid and liquid waste.)

The most recent period in environmental history (the third wave of environmental concern—1980s to the present) has been marked by high population growth rates, industrialization, and urbanization. Specific concerns have continued regarding the effects of toxic chemicals in the environment.

A new topic has been the emission of greenhouse gases and their possible contribution to global warming. **TABLE 3** presents a compilation of some of the contemporary issues that are relevant to environmental health. Although this list is not exhaustive, it identifies several of the major "hot topics" in the environmental health field.

The topics shown in Table 3 will be covered in this text. However, let us select four of the issues—global climate change, pesticides and herbicides, air quality, and war and terrorism—and consider them briefly. For example, one issue that commands our attention (and that has generated extensive coverage in the media) is the prospect of global climate change including global warming (and production of greenhouse gases). Refer back to Exhibit 1. Among the outcomes believed to be associated with global warming are changes in the distribution of insect vectors that can carry diseases such as malaria and the West Nile virus. Elsewhere in this text, in the chapter on air quality, global warming—its hypothesized causes, extent, and effects—will be considered in more detail.

The impact of toxic pesticides and toxic chemicals is a major issue for environmental health. For example, toxic materials have been introduced into the drinking water supplies of some communities. In November 2005, an explosion at a factory in northeastern China caused about 100 tons (about 91 metric tons) of benzene and other hazardous chemicals to be released into the Songhua River. This incident led Chinese officials to shut off the water taps in Harbin because of potential contamination of the water supply in that city. A noteworthy incident in the United States was contamination of municipal water in Flint, Michigan in 2015, when the EPA detected lead contamination in the water used by households there. The events in China and Michigan, as well as many other similar occurrences in which toxic chemicals

TABLE 3 Examples of Hot Topics in Environmental Health

Air quality	Nuclear power
Conservation	Oceans
Endangered species/Wildlife impacts	Pesticides and herbicides
Energy resources	Pollution
Environmental justice	Radioactive waste
Environmental protection	Recycling
Forests	Solid waste
Global warming/Global climate change	War and terrorism
Greenhouse gases	Water resources
Hazardous wastes	Wetlands
Land use	

Partial data from LexisNexis, Environment issues. Copyright 2002, LexisNexis, a division of Reed Elsevier Inc. All Rights Reserved.

have intruded into the public water supply, raise the issue of what can be done to prevent and abate such hazards.

A related issue concerns the runoff of rainwater that overtaxes sewage processing facilities and results in pollution of public beaches and groundwater. Carelessly discarded solvents and other toxic chemicals pose dangers to aquifers; the author will provide more information on toxic pesticides and toxic chemicals in the chapter on pesticides and other organic chemicals.

Still another issue is the impact of air quality on human health, including the role of air pollution in causing cancer and lung diseases as well as aggravating chronic conditions such as heart disease. Some regions face a continuing and growing threat to the environment from air pollution. Several US cities, such as those located in the Los Angeles basin of southern California, face occasional episodes of significant air pollution. Fortunately, air quality has shown improvement in southern California and elsewhere in the United States during the past few decades. In contrast, many cities in the rapidly industrializing nations of the developing world are experiencing declines in air quality due to the increasing use of fossil fuels.

Finally, war and terrorism can have devastating impacts upon the environment. Some of these potential impacts include the destruction of fauna and flora,

exposure of the population to hazardous radiation from spent munitions, and water pollution caused by the manufacture of nuclear weapons. (Refer to the chapter on ionizing and nonionizing radiation.) Recently, health officials and the public have been concerned about threats to the environment from the intentional release of infectious biological agents such as the agent that causes anthrax. (Refer to the chapter on zoonotic and vector-borne diseases.)

▶ Careers in the Environmental Health Field

The field of environmental health provides numerous career roles and possible occupations. Private industry, government units, universities, and private research organizations employ environmental health workers in diverse functions. **TABLE 4** gives a detailed, although not exhaustive, list of occupations that have a connection with environmental health. Following is a description of some of these occupations.

Hygienist

In the work environment, professional industrial hygienists are responsible for control of hazards that

20

TABLE **4** Professions Involved in Environmental Health

Content removed due to copyright restrictions

(continues)

TABLE 4 Professions Involved in Environmental Health
(continued)

Content removed due to copyright restrictions

may affect the workers as well as hazards that may impact the community. They are involved with the design and installation of control systems for hazards in the occupational and environmental setting. They require training in the epidemiologic and biologic aspects of environmental hazards and also in toxicology. Industrial hygienists work closely with engineers who design and maintain industrial processes.[42]

Toxicologist

As a general description of the field, it may be said that toxicology concerns the effects of poisons. Among the many subspecializations in the field of toxicology are medical, veterinary, forensic, and environmental applications. The field of environmental toxicology specializes in the effects of toxic chemicals upon the environment and living creatures such as human beings and wildlife. Occupational and industrial toxicologists investigate the effects of chemicals found in the workplace upon the health of workers. Toxicologists are employed in academia as professors and researchers, by government agencies, by hospitals, and in various private industry settings. (See **FIGURE 14.**)

FIGURE 14 Researchers in a toxicology laboratory.
Courtesy of Dr. Arezoo Campbell, Department of Community and Environmental Medicine, University of California, Irvine.

Environmental Health Inspector

Public health departments provide many job opportunities for environmental health workers. Environmental health inspectors, who work mainly for state and local governments, are responsible for monitoring and enforcing government regulations for environmental quality. This employment category includes pollution inspectors, noise inspectors, and water quality inspectors. Such personnel help to monitor the treatment and disposal of sewage, refuse, and garbage. They also may visit toxic waste dumps, factories, and other sources of pollution in order to collect air, water, and waste samples for testing. They may be sent out to follow up on complaints from the community, attempt to determine the sources and nature of environmental pollution, and provide necessary background data for enforcement actions.

Food Inspector/Food Safety Specialist

Food inspectors and food safety specialists are involved with the cleanliness and safety of foods and beverages consumed by the public. They inspect restaurants, dairies, food processing plants, and other food preparation venues in order to control biological hazards from sources such as *Escherichia coli*, *Salmonella*, and other foodborne agents. Their purview of responsibility also may extend to hospitals and other institutional settings. They may be responsible for examining the methods for handling, processing, and serving of food so that these procedures are in compliance with sanitation rules and regulations. **FIGURE 15** demonstrates a food safety inspector examining a batch of food.

Vector Control Specialist

Vector control specialists (not listed in Table 4) are responsible for the enforcement of various public health laws, sanitary codes, and other regulations related to the spread of disease by vectors. Examples of vectors are insects such as mosquitoes and flies, rodents, and other animals and arthropods that carry disease organisms. Vector control specialists are involved with controlling rabies, mosquito-borne encephalitis, tick-borne diseases, and zoonotic diseases. At the local government level, vector control specialists may be responsible for conducting community education programs, monitoring animal bites, collecting specimens for testing, and developing other procedures for control of diseases carried by vectors. **FIGURE 16** illustrates a vector control specialist at work.

Researcher/Research Analyst

In universities and research units, individuals who have specialized training in environmental health conduct basic research on the risks associated with exposures to certain specific hazards and conduct statistical analyses of the impact of such exposures on human populations. Although this category is

FIGURE 15 Public health inspector checking a kitchen's sanitary conditions.
Courtesy of CDC/Amanda Mills

FIGURE 16 Vector control specialist spraying insecticidal dust for control of plague, 1993.
Courtesy of CDC

not listed in Table 4, examples of employment titles found in research settings are laboratory scientist and technician, epidemiologist, and statistician.

Occupational Health Physician/ Occupational Health Nurse

These professionals are involved with the prevention and treatment of occupationally related illnesses and injuries. They investigate hazards in the work environment and develop procedures for their abatement. They also conduct health education programs for the prevention of work-related diseases.

Environmental Lawyer

Beyond the research environment, there is an active field known as environmental health law. Closely linked with environmental health law are environmental policies. Specialists in this field provide input to government agencies, assist in the formulation of environmental policies, and may be involved in litigation concerning environmental health problems.

▶ Conclusion and Overview of the Text

The study of environmental health is crucial to one's understanding of the hazards and potential adverse effects posed by environmental agents and the extent to which environmental factors play a role in human disease. This foundation is essential for being an effective advocate for preventing environmentally caused diseases and for more advanced study of environmental health issues. This chapter has provided an introduction to the environmental health field: definitions, terminology and concepts, historical background, and career opportunities. The field of environmental health draws heavily upon **epidemiology** and toxicology.[43] As a result, environmental health makes abundant use of terminology from these disciplines. Epidemiologic aspects of environmental health include such well-known methods as case ascertainment, continuous surveillance of hazards, and development of tools for evaluation of intervention programs. Epidemiologic studies have been crucial for delineating the health effects of exposure to pollutants at the population level.

One of the contributions of toxicology to the environmental health field is in assessing **dose–response relationships**, which describe the responses of organisms to exposures to toxic substances. A dose–response relationship can be illustrated by an S-shaped curve known as a dose–response curve.[44] An additional concern of toxicology is exposure assessment, which involves procedures for determining what levels of specific hazards (e.g., a toxic chemical such as DDT) produce symptoms, disease, or other adverse effects.

Study Questions and Exercises

1. Define the following terms:
   a. Population dynamics
   b. Completed fertility rate (total fertility rate)
   c. Environmental health
   d. Environmental risk transition
   e. Environment, physical and social
   f. Demographic transition
   g. Epidemiologic transition
2. Discuss three of the six major objectives (Outdoor Air Quality) for goal number 8, environmental health, as described in *Healthy People 2020*. What steps can be taken in your community to accomplish the objectives you have selected?
3. Describe the three P's that are principal determinants of health worldwide. Discuss how the three P's could be considered interrelated characteristics. Can you think of other

consequences of the three P's that are not discussed in the text?

4. This chapter discussed how environmental exposures affect our daily lives.
   a. Illustrate the types of environmental health problems that you have in your own community.
   b. Review and summarize at least three articles on environmental health that you have seen in the media, e.g., on the web or in a newspaper, during the past week. Are any of these articles relevant to the community where you live?
   c. Why is maintenance of environmental quality important for human health?
5. Discuss the role of population growth in human health. How might recent outbreaks of diseases such as the bird flu or pandemic H1N1 be linked to population growth? In addition to population growth, what other environmental factors could lead to pandemics such as those associated with influenza viruses?
6. Describe the types of environmental health problems that prevail in the developing world. Give at least three examples.
7. Demonstrate population growth trends over the past two centuries. What is the likelihood that current exponential population growth rates will continue? Take a stand for or against population growth at present high levels.
8. Describe variables that affect the size of a population. What countries or regions of the world are projected to experience stable or declining population sizes? What areas are expected to have the greatest increases in population size?
9. Define and discuss the following terms:
   a. Ecological model of population health
   b. Ecosystem
10. Summarize the contributions of the early Greeks to environmental health. How do Hippocrates' explanations of disease etiology compare with current beliefs about the role of the environment in human illness?
11. List and discuss five of today's most pressing environmental health issues ("hot topics"). In addition to the material presented in the text, you also may use your own ideas.
12. Explain why environmental health is an important field of employment. List specific employment roles in environmental health. Consult the World Wide Web for employment listings (e.g., published by state, local, and federal government agencies) and summarize the requirements and functions of three job titles.

For Further Reading

The Population Bomb, Paul R. Ehrlich, 1968
Walden, Henry David Thoreau, 1854
The Jungle, Upton Sinclair, 1906.

References

1. HealthyPeople.gov. 2020 Topics & Objectives: Environmental Health. *Healthy People 2020*. Available at: https://www.healthypeople.gov/2020/topics-objectives/topic/environmental-health. Accessed January 17, 2017.
2. Winkelstein W Jr. Determinants of worldwide health. *Am J Public Health*. 1992;82:931–932.
3. National Institute of Environmental Health Sciences. Forum: killer environment. *Environ Health Perspect*. 1999;107:A62–A63.
4. Butterfield PG. Upstream reflections on environmental health: an abbreviated history and framework for action. *Adv Nurs Sci*. 2002;25(1):32–49.
5. Prüss-Üstün A, Wolf J, Corvalán CF, et al. Preventing disease through healthy environments: a global assessment of the burden of disease from environmental risks. Geneva, Switzerland: World Health Organization; 2016.
6. World Health Organization. WHO to highlight specific health risks to children from environmental dangers. Available at: http://www.who.int/mediacentre/news/notes/note04/en/. Accessed June 27, 2017.
7. Carlson JE. Children's Environmental Health Network, Emeryville, California. *Environ Health Perspect*. 1998;106(Suppl 3):785–786.
8. Goldman LR, Koduru S. Chemicals in the environment and developmental toxicity to children: a public health and policy perspective. *Environ Health Perspect*. 2000;108(Suppl 3):443–448.
9. Chukwuma C Sr. Environmental health concepts and issues—a viewpoint. *Intern J Environ Studies*. 2001;58:631–644.
10. Mellor JW. The intertwining of environmental problems and poverty. *Environ*. 1988;30:8–30.
11. Camp SL. Population pressure, poverty and the environment. *Integration*. June 1992;24–27.
12. Smith KR. Environment and health: issues for the new U.S. administration. *Environ*. 2001;43:34–41.
13. Last JM. *Homo sapiens*—a suicidal species? *World Health Forum*. 1991;12:121–126.
14. US Census Bureau. *Global Population Profile: 2002*. International Population Reports WP/02. Washington, DC: US Government Printing Office; 2004.
15. Hinrichsen D. The decisive decade: what we can do about population. *Amicus J*. 1990;12(1):30–33.
16. Raleigh VS. World population and health in transition. *BMJ*. 1999;319:981–984.
17. Brown LR. Feeding six billion. *World Watch*. September/October 1989;32–40.
18. McMichael AJ, Powles JW. Human numbers, environment, sustainability, and health. *BMJ*. 1999;319:977–980.
19. Monte LM, Ellis RR. Fertility of women in the United States: 2012. *Current Population Reports*, P20-575. Washington, DC: US Census Bureau; 2014.
20. Gelbard A, Haub C. Population "explosion" not over for half the world. *Popul Today*. 1998;26:1–2.
21. International Organization for Migration. 2015 Global Migration Trends. Factsheet. Available at: https://publications.iom.int/system/files/global_migration_trends_2015_factsheet.pdf. Accessed July 6, 2017.

22. United Nations Environment Programme. Population and the environment. *Popul Bull UN*. 1987;(21–22):32–44.

23. McMichael AJ. The urban environment and health in a world of increasing globalization: issues for developing countries. *Bull World Health Organ*. 2000;78:1117–1126.

24. Satterthwaite D. The impact on health of urban environments. *Environ Urban*. 1993;5:87–111.

25. United Nations, Department of Economic and Social Affairs, Population Division (2016). The World's Cities in 2016—Data Booklet (ST/ESA/SER.A/392).

26. Population Matters. Carrying capacity; 2011. Available at: https://populationmatters.org/wp-content/uploads/D20Carrying capacity.pdf Accessed June 27, 2017.

27. McMichael AJ. Ecological disruption and human health: the next great challenge to public health [editorial]. *Aust J Public Health*. 1992;16:3–5.

28. Congress of the United States. Office of Technology Assessment. Technologies to maintain biological diversity. OTA Brief Report; March 1987. Available at: http://ota.fas.org/reports/RB-Technologies%20To%20Maintain%20Biological%20Diversity.pdf. Accessed June 28, 2017.

29. Marwick C. Scientists stress biodiversity-human health links. *JAMA*. 1995;273:1246.

30. Merriam-Webster Online dictionary. Environment. Available at: https://www.merriam-webster.com/dictionary/environment. Accessed June 28, 2017.

31. The National Academies, Institute of Medicine. *Who Will Keep the Public Healthy? Educating Public Health Professionals for the 21st Century*. Washington, DC: The National Academies Press; 2003.

32. Millennium Ecosystem Assessment. *Ecosystems and Human Well-Being: A Framework for Assessment*. Washington, DC: Island Press; 2003.

33. World Health Organization. Damage to ecosystems poses growing threat to human health [press release]. March 29, 2005.

34. Available at: http://www.who.int/globalchange/publications/masynthesis/en/. Accessed June 27, 2017.

34. World Health Organization. Health topics: environmental health. Available at: http://www.searo.who.int/topics/environmental_health/en/. Accessed June 28, 2017.

35. Franco DA, Williams CE. "Airs, Waters, Places" and other Hippocratic writings: inferences for control of foodborne and waterborne disease. *J Environ Health*. 2000;62(10):9–14.

36. Järup L. Hazards of heavy metal contamination. *British Medical Journal*. 2003;68:167-182.

37. US Department of Labor, Occupational Safety and Health Administration Office of Training and Education. Industrial hygiene. Available at: https://www.osha.gov/dte/library/industrial_hygiene/industrial_hygiene.pdf. Accessed June 28, 2017.

38. Environmentalhistory.org. Environmental history timeline. Classical 1000 BCE–500 CE. Ancient Rome. Available at: http://environmentalhistory.org/ancient/classical-1000-bce-500-ce/. Accessed June 27, 2017.

39. History on the net.com. The Romans—public health. Available at: http://www.historyonthenet.com/the-romans-public-health/. Accessed June 27, 2017.

40. Yassi A, Kjellström T, de Kok T, et al. *Basic Environmental Health*. New York, NY: Oxford University Press; 2001.

41. Bell ML, Davis DL. Reassessment of the lethal London fog of 1952: novel indicators of acute and chronic consequences of acute exposure to air pollution. *Environ Health Perspect*. 2001;109(Suppl 3):389–394.

42. Sherwood RJ. Cause and control: education and training of professional industrial hygienists for 2020. *Am Ind Hyg Assoc J*. 1992;53:398–403.

43. Goldstein BD. Environmental risks and public health. *Ann NY Acad Sci*. 2001;933:112–118.

44. Friis RH, Sellers TA. *Epidemiology for Public Health Practice*. 5th ed. Burlington, MA: Jones & Bartlett Learning; 2014.

Environmental Epidemiology

LEARNING OBJECTIVES

By the end of this chapter the reader will be able to:

- Define the term environmental epidemiology.
- Describe three major historical events in environmental epidemiology.
- Provide examples of epidemiologic tools used in environmental health.
- Identify types of associations found between environmental hazards and health outcomes.
- Compare study designs used in environmental epidemiology.

▶ Introduction

In this chapter you will learn that epidemiology is one of the fundamental disciplines used in the study of environmental health. For example, by using epidemiology it may be possible to connect environmental hazards such as air pollution or toxic chemicals with cancer and other adverse health outcomes. The launching point for our discussion will be a definition of the term *environmental epidemiology*. You will acquire information about the scope of this discipline and be able to define several of the special quantitative measures used to study the occurrence of environmental health problems in populations.

Next, we will trace the key historical developments in environmental epidemiology. Some of these historical benchmarks include concerns of the ancient Greeks about diseases caused by the environment, the observations of Sir Percival Pott on scrotal cancer among chimney sweeps in England (including Pott's clever public health recommendation for prevention

of scrotal cancer), the work of John Snow on cholera, and later work on the role of toxic substances in the etiology of cancer. Closely linked to quantitative measures used by environmental epidemiology are the major study designs described in this chapter. See **FIGURE 1**.

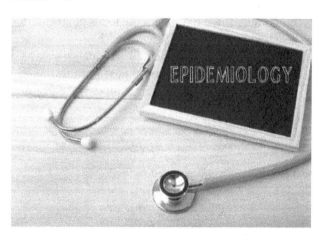

FIGURE 1 Epidemiology and environmental health.
© shahreen/Shutterstock

Research Topics for Environmental Epidemiology

Environmental epidemiology is a complex field that in some cases provides keen insights into environmentally caused diseases and in others provides unclear results that must be followed up by other types of studies. A special concern of the discipline is causality—whether research findings represent cause-and-effect associations. In order to explore such associations, the field employs experimental, quasi-experimental, and observational study designs. The latter (i.e., observational designs) include cross-sectional, ecologic, case-control, and cohort studies. More information on causality and epidemiologic study designs is provided later in this chapter.

Epidemiology is one of the research fields that seeks answers to crucial environmental questions, such as those that pertain to the domains of air pollution, chemicals, climate change, and water pollution.[1] Refer to the infographic presented in **FIGURE 2**.

- Air pollution continues to be a global public health issue. Associated with increasing urbanization of developing regions of the world are increasing levels of air pollution. Epidemiologic research has helped to identify adverse health effects of air pollution among vulnerable groups such as children and the elderly. A related concern pertains to the health impacts of exposure to environmental tobacco smoke.
- Potentially toxic chemicals such as pesticides, asbestos, lead, and mercury have been implicated in cancer, adverse reproductive outcomes, nervous system impacts, and numerous other health outcomes. These have been the focus of an extensive body of epidemiologic research.
- Scientists have documented gradual increases in global temperatures over past decades. Such changes have been accompanied by extreme climatic events, for example, high heat disasters in cities and flooding in coastal areas. Epidemiologic investigations will help to document adverse outcomes linked to global warming and inform policy decisions in response to climate change.
- Potable water has become increasingly scarce in the arid regions of the globe, depriving many of the world's inhabitants of safe water. In some parts of the United States, water supplies have also become compromised. An example is the intrusion of lead into the public drinking water supply from aging pipelines, as seen in Flint, Michigan in 2105. Pollution from urban runoff harms the nation's beaches and adversely affects marine life and seafood. Epidemiologic investigations have been instrumental in identifying the adverse health effects associated with such water pollution.
- As the sophistication of methodology in genetics, data analysis, and other cutting-edge disciplines has grown, the capacity of epidemiologic research to explore a panoply of intriguing issues has been enhanced. Some of these involve possible environmental concomitants of neurologic conditions such as Alzheimer's disease, interaction of environmental exposures with our genetic makeup, and exposure to radiation from nuclear power plants.

In summary, epidemiology is the method of choice to address issues such as the foregoing ones. Refer to the following text box for a further discussion of epidemiology and environmental health.

Definition of Environmental Epidemiology

Epidemiology is concerned with the study of the distribution and determinants of health and diseases, morbidity, injuries, disability, and mortality in populations.[2] Epidemiologic studies are applied to the control of health problems in populations. Epidemiology is one of the core disciplines used to examine the associations between environmental hazards and health outcomes. The term *environmental epidemiology* refers to the study of diseases and health conditions (occurring in the population) that are linked to environmental factors.[3,4] The exposures, which most of the time are outside the control of the individual, usually may be considered involuntary and stem from ambient and occupational environments.[5] According to this conception of environmental

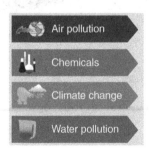

FIGURE 2 Environmental topics for epidemiology.
Reproduced from National Institutes of Health, National Institute of Environmental Health Sciences. What is environmental health? Available at: https://kidsenvirohealth.nlm.nih.gov. Accessed April 3, 2017.

EPIDEMIOLOGY'S UNIQUE CONTRIBUTION TO ENVIRONMENTAL HEALTH

Epidemiology makes a special contribution to environmental health through its focus on entire populations and by its use of descriptive and analytic methodologies. Clinical observations help to identify and diagnose individual patients who are afflicted by environmental hazards. However, this information may not be sufficient to discern how adverse health effects of environmental exposures are distributed in the community.

The chain of research often begins when local public health departments receive complaints of diseases such as asthma from people living in the departments' jurisdictions. When these individual case reports are collated, epidemiologists may be able to develop hypotheses regarding how these outcomes are related to environmental factors. Epidemiologists may then decide to conduct a broader investigation of the entire community in order to delineate specific groups of persons who are being affected as well as their location in relation to the presence of hazardous environmental exposures.

The findings of epidemiologic research can aid in controlling environmental exposures and developing health policies for protecting the public. For example, epidemiologic studies of air pollution conducted during the 20th century showed that people exposed to high levels of air pollution experienced increased mortality in comparison with those whose air was less polluted. More recent findings suggested a relationship between living in proximity to a heavily traveled motorway and adverse health effects connected with emissions from passing vehicles.

In response to findings such as these, government agencies and stakeholders introduced regulations to clean the air. These measures included reductions of "smokestack" emissions from factories and adoption of air quality standards for automobile exhaust. Without epidemiologic research, the ties between air pollution and specific adverse health effects might not have been obvious. Epidemiology has also uncovered connections between other forms of environmental pollution such as exposures to toxic chemicals and adverse health outcomes. For these reasons, epidemiology makes a unique contribution to the study of environmental health issues.

epidemiology, standard epidemiologic methods are used to study the association between environmental factors (exposures) and health outcomes. Examples of topics studied include air and water pollution, the occupational environment with its possible use of physical and chemical agents, and the psychosocial environment.[6]

As noted previously, for an environmentally associated health outcome to be considered a topic of environmental epidemiology, exposure factors must lie outside the individual's immediate control. Hazards associated with smoking can be explored as an exposure dimension that is either under or not under the control of the individual. As an example of the former, studies of the health effects of smoking among individuals who smoke would not be a usual concern of environmental epidemiology. However, exposure of populations to secondhand cigarette smoke would be a concern because nonsmokers and vulnerable groups such as children cannot control whether they are exposed to environmental tobacco smoke.

Thus, traditionally, environmental epidemiology has tended to focus on health effects linked to degradation of the air we breathe, the water we drink, and the food we eat.[7] With the advances achieved during the 20th century in environmental sanitation and control of disease-causing biological organisms, attention to chemical and physical impacts upon the environment has increased. Some of the agents and environmental factors being focused on are lead toxicity, particulates from diesel exhaust, and exposures to pesticides and halogenated compounds (a compound that is a combination of a halogen such as chlorine or iodine and one or more elements). Halogenated compounds include **polychlorinated biphenyls (PCBs)**, which through biological processes can become increasingly concentrated in foodstuffs, can pose hazards as potential carcinogens, and can impact the reproductive system. More recent concerns of environmental health include the reemerging infectious diseases (see the chapter on zoonotic and vector-borne diseases) and the effects of climate changes due to global warming.

Although the relationship between environmental exposures and their unknown hazards remains a concern of environmental epidemiology, the field has evolved to include a broader approach: identification of previously unrecognized exposures to known hazardous agents and the quantification of such risks, estimation of the amount of exposures that individuals have to environmental hazards, assessment of risks associated with exposures (discussed in the chapter on environmental toxicology), and evaluation of procedures to prevent exposures.[4] Similarly, in the related field of occupational health, the goals of epidemiologic research encompass the description of exposure–response gradients, discovery of how occupational hazards may cause harmful effects, characterization of vulnerable workers, and input into programs for the prevention of occupationally related diseases.[8]

This discussion regarding the definition of environmental epidemiology leads to the issue of the types of work performed by epidemiologists. **FIGURES 3** and **4** highlight two of several of the diverse settings where epidemiologists work. As indicated by Figure 3, a cadre of epidemiologists is situated primarily in a laboratory where they research disease agents such as the Zika virus. Others—as demonstrated by the team in Figure 4—analyze research data that may reveal patterns and associations with respect to the occurrence of adverse and other health outcomes.

FIGURE 3 Exploring the Zika virus epidemic.
© zaozaa19/Shutterstock

FIGURE 4 Epidemiologic data analysis.
© goodluz/Shutterstock

▶ Contributions of Epidemiology to Environmental Health

Epidemiology aids the environmental health field through:

- Concern with populations
- Use of observational data
- Methodology for study designs
- Descriptive and analytic studies

Epidemiology is important to the study of environmental health problems because (1) many exposures and health effects associated with the environment occur at the population level; (2) the epidemiologic methods of natural experiments and observational techniques are appropriate; (3) the study designs used in epidemiologic research can be applied directly to the study of environmental health issues; and (4) epidemiology aids in the development of hypotheses and the study of causal relationships.

Concern with Populations

In contrast with clinical medicine's traditional focus on the individual, a unique characteristic of epidemiology is that it studies the entire population and hence is sometimes called population medicine. Refer to **FIGURE 5.** For example, epidemiologic studies of lung disease may examine the occurrence of lung cancer mortality across counties or among regional geographic subdivisions known as census tracts. Investigators may want to determine whether lung cancer mortality is higher in areas with higher concentrations of "smokestack" industries in comparison with areas that have lower levels of air pollution or are relatively free from air pollution. The alternative approach of the clinician would be to concentrate on the diagnosis and treatment of lung cancer among specific individuals.

Use of Observational Data

In examining the occurrence of health and disease in human populations, researchers often are prohibited

FIGURE 5 Epidemiology's population focus.
© Tom and Kwikki/Shutterstock

from using experimental methods because of ethical issues such as potential dangers to subjects. Studies of the population's health present a challenge that is partially met by epidemiology because epidemiology is primarily an observational science that takes advantage of naturally occurring situations in order to study the occurrence of disease.

Methodology for Study Designs

In the realm of environmental health, epidemiologic research generally aims to portray the frequency of disease occurrence in the population or to link disease outcomes to specific exposures.[9] In order to research environmentally caused disease in the population, the field of environmental epidemiology uses characteristic study designs: cross-sectional, ecologic, case-control, and cohort. For example, these methods are useful in and linked closely to the field of risk assessment (discussed in the chapter on environmental toxicology). Professor A.H. Smith writes, "The epidemiologic input to environmental risk assessment involves the interpretation of epidemiological studies and their application to estimating the potential health risks to populations from known or estimated environmental exposures."[10(p124)]

Two Classes of Epidemiologic Studies: Descriptive and Analytic

The term **descriptive epidemiology** refers to the depiction of the occurrence of disease in populations according to classification by person, place, and time variables. Examples of person variables are demographic characteristics such as sex, age, and race/ethnicity. Place variables denote geographic locations including a specific country or countries, areas within countries, and regions where localized patterns of disease may occur. Illustrations of time variables are a decade, a year, a month, a week, or a day. Descriptive studies, regarded as a fundamental approach by epidemiologists, aim to delineate the patterns and manner in which disease occurs in populations.[11]

An example of a pattern derived from descriptive studies is disease clustering, which refers to "…a closely grouped series of events or cases of a disease or other health-related phenomena with well-defined distribution patterns in relation to time or place or both. The term is normally used to describe aggregation of relatively uncommon events or diseases (e.g., leukemia, multiple sclerosis)."[12]

Clustering may suggest common exposure of the population to an environmental hazard; it also may be purely spurious—due to the operation of chance. One cause of spurious clustering is called the Texas Sharpshooter Effect, discussed in the text box.

In the field of occupational health—which in many respects is emblematic of the general field of environmental health—"*descriptive studies* provide information for setting priorities, identifying hazards, and formulating hypotheses for new occupational risk."[13(p944)] A historical example (discussed later in this chapter) is William Farr's work showing that Cornwall metal miners had higher mortality from all causes than the general population.[13]

Analytic epidemiology examines causal (etiologic) hypotheses regarding the association between exposures and health conditions. "Etiologic studies are planned examinations of causality and the natural history of disease. These studies have required increasingly sophisticated analytic methods as the importance of low-level exposures is explored and greater refinement in exposure-effect relationships is sought."[13(p945)] The field of analytic epidemiology proposes and evaluates causal models that employ both outcome variables and exposure variables.

The exposure variables in epidemiologic research include contact with toxic substances, potential carcinogens, or air pollution. In other cases, exposure may be to biological agents or to forms of energy such as ionizing and nonionizing radiation, noise, and

31

A traveler passing through a small town in Texas noted a remarkable display of sharpshooting. On almost every barn he passed there was a target with a single bullet hole that uncannily passed through the center of the bull's-eye. He was so intrigued by this that he stopped at a nearby gas station to ask about the sharpshooter. With a chuckle, the attendant told him that the shooting was the work of Old Joe. Old Joe would first shoot at the side of a barn and then paint targets centered over his bullet holes so that each shot appeared to pass through the center of the target. . . . In a random distribution of cases of cancer over a geographic area, some cases will appear to occur very close together just on the basis of random variation. The occurrence of a group of cases of a disease close together in time and place at the time of their diagnosis is called a cluster.

Reproduced from Grufferman S. Methodologic approaches to studying environmental factors in childhood cancer. *Environ Health Perspect*. 1998;106(suppl 3):882.

extremes of temperature. For an environmental epidemiologic research study to be valid, the level of exposure in a population must be assessed validly.

The outcome variable in epidemiologic studies is usually a specific disease, cause of mortality, or health condition. Accurate clinical assessments of an outcome such as lung cancer are vitally important to the quality of epidemiologic research.

One approach of analytic epidemiology is to take advantage of naturally occurring situations or events in order to test causal hypotheses. These naturally occurring events are referred to as **natural experiments**, defined as "naturally occurring circumstances in which subsets of the population have different levels of exposure to a hypothesized causal factor in a situation resembling an actual experiment."[12] An example is the work of John Snow, discussed later in this chapter. Many past or ongoing natural experiments are relevant to environmental epidemiology. For example, in some regions of the United States, health legislation prohibits smoking in public areas in order to prevent exposure to secondhand smoke. At the same time, this activity may be considered a natural experiment that impacts human health and that can be studied by environmental epidemiologists.

Measures of Disease Frequency Used in Epidemiology

A number of quantitative terms, useful in environmental epidemiology, have been developed to characterize the occurrence of disease, morbidity, and mortality in populations. Particularly noteworthy are the two terms **prevalence** and **incidence**, which can be stated as frequencies or raw numbers of cases. In order to make comparisons among populations that differ in size, statisticians divide the number of cases by the population size. Several examples follow.

The term *prevalence* refers to the number of existing cases of or deaths from a disease or health condition in a population at some designated time. More specifically, **point prevalence** refers to all cases of or deaths from a disease or health condition that exist at a particular point in time relative to a specific population from which the cases are derived. Prevalence measures are used to describe the scope and distribution of health outcomes in the population. By revealing a snapshot of disease occurrence in the population, prevalence data contribute to the accomplishment of two of the primary functions of descriptive epidemiology: to assess variations in the occurrence of disease in populations and to aid in the development of etiologic hypotheses.

Comparisons among populations that differ in size cannot be accomplished directly by using frequency or prevalence data. In order to make such comparisons, prevalence (usually referring to point prevalence) may be expressed as a proportion formed by dividing the number of cases that occur in a population by the size of the population in which the cases occur.

$$\text{Point prevalence} = \frac{\text{Number of persons ill}}{\text{Total number in the group}} \text{ at a point in time}$$

The term *incidence* refers to the occurrence of new disease or mortality within a defined period of observation (e.g., a week, month, year, or other time period) in a specified population. Those members of the population who are capable of developing the disease or condition being studied are known as the **population at risk**.

The **incidence rate** denotes "[t]he RATE at which new events occur in a population."[12] The new events may be cases of disease or some other outcome of interest. Statistically speaking, the incidence rate is a rate because of the specification of a time period during which the new cases occur. (Several variations of incidence rates exist, but a discussion of all of them is beyond the scope of this chapter.) The incidence rate used most often in public health is formed by dividing the number of new cases that occur during a time period by the average number of individuals in the population at risk.

$$\text{Incidence rate} = \frac{\text{Number of new cases over a time period}}{\text{Average population at risk during the same time period}} \times \text{multiplier (e.g., 100,000)}$$

Incidence measures are central to the study of causal mechanisms with regard to how exposures affect health outcomes. Incidence measures are used to describe the risks associated with certain exposures; they can be used to estimate in a population "the probability of someone in that population developing the disease during a specified period, conditional on not dying first from another disease."[9(p23)]

One additional measure covered in this section is known as the case fatality rate (CFR). (Note that the chapter on zoonotic and vector-borne diseases will refer to the CFR.) The CFR, which provides a measure of the lethality of a disease, is defined as the number of deaths due to a specific disease within a specified time period divided by the number of cases of that disease during the same time period multiplied by 100. The formula is expressed as follows:

$$CFR(\%) = \frac{\substack{\text{Number of deaths} \\ \text{due to disease "X"}}}{\substack{\text{Number of cases} \\ \text{of disease "X"}}} \times \substack{100 \text{ during a} \\ \text{time period}}$$

The numerator and denominator refer to the same time period. For example, suppose that 45 cases of hantavirus infection occurred in a western US state during a year of interest. Of these cases, 22 were fatal. The CFR would be:

$$CFR(\%) = \frac{22}{45} \times 100 = 48.9\%$$

▶ Brief History of Environmental Epidemiology

Hippocrates

Environmental epidemiology has a long history that dates back 2,000 or more years.[14] For example, in about 400 BC the ancient Greek authority Hippocrates expounded on the role of environmental factors such as water quality and the air in causing diseases.[14] He produced the well-known book *On Airs, Waters, and Places*. Experts in the field confirm that these writings form the historical cornerstone of environmental epidemiology. Hippocrates' work and the writings of many of the ancients did not delineate specific known agents involved in the causality of health problems, but referred more generically to air, water, and food. In this respect, early epidemiology shares with contemporary epidemiology the frequent lack of complete knowledge of the specific agents of environmentally associated diseases.

Sir Percival Pott

Sir Percival Pott, a London surgeon, was significant to the history of environmental epidemiology because he is thought to be the first individual to describe an environmental cause of cancer. (See **FIGURE 6**.)

In 1775, Pott made the astute observation that chimney sweeps had a high incidence of scrotal cancer (in comparison with male workers in other occupations). He argued that chimney sweeps were prone to this malady as a consequence of their contact with soot.[15] (See **FIGURE 7**.)

In a book entitled *Chirurgical Observations Relative to the Cataract, the Polypus of the Nose, the Cancer of the Scrotum, the Different Kinds of Ruptures, and the Mortification of the Toes and Feet*, published in London in 1775, Pott developed a chapter called

PERCIVALL POTT Efq.r

Engraved by Heath, from a Picture of Sir Joshua Reynolds.

Publish'd March 10th 1790, by J.Johnson, St Paul's Church Yard.

FIGURE 6 Percival Pott, F.R.S., 1714–1788.

FIGURE 7 A chimney sweep.
© Annamaria Szilagyi/Shutterstock

"A Short Treatise of the Chimney Sweeper's Cancer." This brief work of only 725 words is noteworthy because

> ... it provided the first clear description of an environmental cause of cancer, suggested a way to prevent the disease, and led indirectly to the synthesis of the first known pure carcinogen and the isolation of the first carcinogenic chemical to be obtained from a natural product. No wonder therefore that Pott's observation has come to be regarded as the foundation stone on w[h]ich the knowledge of cancer prevention has been built![15(p521)]

In Pott's own words,

> [E]very body . . . is acquainted with the disorders to which painters, plummers, glaziers, and the workers in white lead are liable; but there is a disease as peculiar to a certain set of people which has not, at least to my knowledge, been publickly noteced; I mean the chimney-sweepers' cancer. . . . The fate of these people seems singularly hard; in their early infancy, they are most frequently treated with great brutality, and almost starved with cold and hunger; they are thrust up narrow, and sometimes hot chimnies, where they are

bruised, burned, and almost suffocated; and when they get to puberty, become peculiary [*sic*] liable to a noisome, painful and fatal disease. Of this last circumstance there is not the least doubt though perhaps it may not have been sufficiently attended to, to make it generally known. Other people have cancers of the same part; and so have others besides lead-workers, the Poictou colic, and the consequent paralysis; but it is nevertheless a disease to which they are particularly liable; and so are chimney-sweepers to the cancer of the scrotum and testicles. The disease, in these people . . . seems to derive its origin from a lodgment of soot in the rugae of the scrotum.[15(pp521–522)]

Following his conclusions about the relationship between scrotal cancer and chimney sweeping, Pott established an occupational hygiene control measure—the recommendation that chimney sweeps bathe once a week.

John Snow

During the mid-1800s, English anesthesiologist John Snow (see **FIGURE 8**) linked a cholera outbreak in London to contaminated water from the Thames River. His methodology for investigating the cholera outbreak of

FIGURE 8 John Snow.
© National Library of Medicine.

A section of London, designated the Broad Street neighborhood (now part of the Soho district), became the focus of Snow's detective work. Two water companies, the Lambeth Company and the Southwark and Vauxhall Company, provided water in such a manner that adjacent houses could receive water from two different sources. One of the companies, the Lambeth Company, relocated its water sources to a section of the Thames River that was less contaminated. During a later cholera outbreak in 1854, Snow observed that a higher proportion of residents who used the water from the Southwark and Vauxhall Company developed cholera than did residents who used water from the Lambeth Company. Snow's efforts to show a correspondence between changes in the water supply and occurrence of cholera became known as a natural experiment.

Here is Snow's graphic description of the cholera outbreak that occurred in 1849.

The most terrible outbreak of cholera which ever occurred in this kingdom, is probably that which took place in Broad Street, Golden Square, and the adjoining streets, a few weeks ago. . . . The mortality in this limited area probably equals any that was ever caused in this country, even by the plague; and it was much more sudden, as the greater number of cases terminated in a few hours. . . . Many houses were closed altogether, owing to the death of the proprietors; and, in a great number of instances, the tradesmen who remained had sent away their families: so that in less than six days from the commencement of the outbreak, the most afflicted streets were deserted by more than three-quarters of their inhabitants.[16(p38)]

Snow's pioneering approach illustrated the use of both descriptive and analytic epidemiology. One of his first activities was to plot the cholera deaths in relation to a pump that he hypothesized was the cause of the cholera outbreak. Each death was shown on the map (**FIGURE 9**) as a short line. An arrow in the figure points to the location of the Broad Street pump. "As soon as I became acquainted with the situation and the extent of this irruption of cholera, I suspected some contamination of the water of the much-frequented street-pump in Broad Street, near the end of Cambridge Street. . . . On proceeding to the spot, I found that nearly all the deaths had taken place within a short distance of the pump."[16(pp38–39)] The handle of the pump was later removed—a public health measure to control the outbreak. In Snow's time, many European cities took water for domestic use directly from rivers, which often were contaminated with microorganisms.

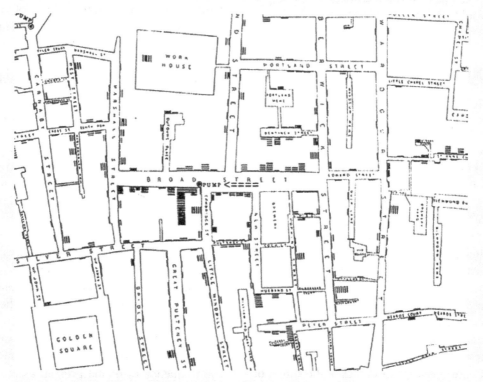

FIGURE 9 Map of cholera cases in the Broad Street area. Each case is indicated by a short line.

1849 was known as a "natural experiment," a methodology used currently in the study of environmental health problems. Refer to the text box for more information.

In addition to utilizing the method of natural experiment, John Snow provided expert witness testimony on behalf of industry with respect to environmental exposures to potential disease agents.[17] Snow attempted to extrapolate from the health effects of exposures to high doses of environmental substances what the effects of low doses would be. On January 23, 1855, the Nuisances Removal and Diseases Prevention Amendments bill was introduced in the British Parliament. This bill was a reform of Victorian public health legislation that followed the 1854 cholera outbreak described in the foregoing paragraph.[17] The intent of the bill was to control release into the atmosphere of fumes from operations such as gas works, silk-boiling works, and bone-boiling factories. Snow contended that these odors were not a disease hazard in the community.[18] The thesis of Snow's argument was that deleterious health effects from the low levels of exposure experienced in the community were unlikely, given the knowledge about higher-level exposures among those who worked in the factories. Snow argued that the workers in the factories were not suffering any ill health effects or dying from the exposure. Therefore, it was unlikely that the much lower exposures experienced by the members of the larger community would affect the latter's health.

▶ Strategies of Environmental Epidemiology

Study designs used in environmental epidemiology are similar to those developed for general epidemiologic research. Study designs can be arranged on a continuum ranging from hypothesis-generating designs that provide limited information to complex hypothesis-testing designs.[8] Purely observational study designs include case series and cross-sectional, ecologic, case-control, and cohort studies. Nonobservational and partly observational designs that are used include experimental and quasi-experimental designs.

For the particular problem being investigated, some designs are better than others, depending upon what is to be achieved, the availability of study populations, the disease or health outcome studied, and the need to uncover disease etiology.[8] Examples of the subset of observational designs that are used for hypothesis generation include cross-sectional studies, case series, some types of ecologic correlations, and proportionate mortality comparisons.[8] The subset of observational designs that are used for hypothesis testing includes cohort and

case-control studies. One of the distinguishing characteristics of study designs is whether they involve the individual or group as the unit of analysis. With the exception of ecologic studies, all the designs presented in this chapter use the individual as the unit of analysis.

Experimental Studies

Consider the use of experimental studies in environmental health research; in epidemiology, experimental studies are implemented as intervention studies. An **intervention study** is "[a]n investigation involving intentional change in some aspect of the status of the subjects, e.g., introduction of a preventive or therapeutic regimen or an intervention designed to test a hypothesized relationship. . . ."[12]

Two intervention study designs are clinical trials (randomized controlled trials) and quasi-experiments (community trials). A simple illustration of the former is a classic experimental design in which there is manipulation of an exposure variable and random assignment of subjects to either a treatment group or a control group. The exposure variable might be a new drug or other regimen. Some uses of randomized controlled trials are to test the efficacy of new medications, medical regimens, and vaccines. Among the many examples of a clinical trial is the Medical Research Council Vitamin Study, which examined the efficacy of folic acid supplementation during pregnancy in preventing congenital malformations (e.g., neural tube defects).[2]

A quasi-experimental study is one in which manipulation of an exposure variable occurs, but individual subjects are not randomly allocated to the study conditions. An example used in epidemiology is called a community trial, which tests an intervention at the community level. In some quasi-experimental designs, study units (e.g., communities, counties, or schools) may be assigned randomly to study conditions. However, in other research, assignment of study units may be arbitrary.

An example of a quasi-experimental study was a trial that tested the efficacy of fluoridation of drinking water in preventing tooth decay.[9] During the 1940s and 1950s, two comparable cities in New York State—Newburgh and Kingston—were contrasted for the occurrence of tooth decay and related dental problems among children. Newburgh had received fluoridated water for about a decade and Kingston had received none. In Newburgh, the frequency of dental problems decreased by about one half and increased slightly in Kingston.[9] In this quasi-experimental design, individual subjects were not randomized to the study conditions.

For several reasons, the use of experimental methods in environmental epidemiology is difficult to achieve; consequently, observational methods are usually more feasible to implement. Rothman points out:

> Randomized assignment of individuals into groups with different environmental exposures generally is impractical, if not unethical; community intervention trials for environmental exposures have been conducted, although seldom (if ever) with random assignment. Furthermore, the benefits of randomization are heavily diluted when the number of randomly assigned units is small, as when communities rather than individuals are randomized. Thus, environmental epidemiology consists nearly exclusively of non-experimental epidemiology. Ideally, such studies use individuals as the unit of measurement; but often environmental data are available only for groups of individuals, and investigators turn to so-called ecologic studies to learn what they can.[6(p20)]

Consequently, in order to study the effects of environmental exposures when dealing with human populations, researchers must use observational methods, and, in fact, the majority of research on health outcomes associated with the environment uses observational methods.[19]

Case Series

A **case series study** is one in which information about patients who share a disease in common is gathered over time. Although this type of study is among the weakest for making causal assertions, a case series can be useful for developing hypotheses for further study. Usually information from a case series study is considered to be preliminary and a starting point for more complex investigations. However, some astute clinicians have used information from series of cases to make important observations. An example comes from the work of Herbst and Scully, who were the first to describe the association between exposure to diethylstilbestrol (DES) during mothers' pregnancies and risk of clear-cell cervicovaginal cancer among six female adolescents and young adults.[20] (Refer to **FIGURE 10** for an advertisement for diethylstilbestrol [DES, des*PLEX*®], which was administered to "prevent abortion, miscarriage and premature labor.")

Cross-Sectional Studies

A **cross-sectional study** is defined as one

> …that examines the relationship between diseases (or other health outcomes) and other

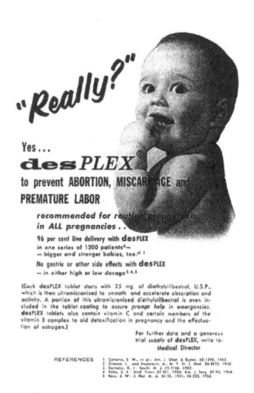

FIGURE 10 Advertisement promoting diethylstilbestrol (DES).

Available at: https://desinfo411.wordpress.com/tag/massachusetts-general-hospital/. Accessed April 3, 2017.

variables of interest as they exist in a defined population at one particular time. The presence or absence of disease and the presence or absence of the other variables … are determined in each member of the study population or in a representative sample at one particular time.[12]

Thus, a cross-sectional study is a type of prevalence study in which the distribution of disease and exposure are determined, although it is not imperative for the study to include both exposure and disease. A cross-sectional study may focus only on the latter.[2] Cross-sectional designs make a one-time assessment of the prevalence of disease in a sample that in most situations has been sampled randomly from the parent population of interest.[9] Cross-sectional studies may be used to formulate hypotheses that can be followed up in analytic studies.

Here is an example of a cross-sectional study: As part of an asthma reduction program conducted in Passaic, New Jersey during the 1998 through 1999 school year, investigators conducted a survey of a community in which all third graders were targeted.[21] The study children and their parents were given self-report symptom questionnaires. A total of 976 children and 818 parents returned the questionnaire. A respiratory therapist collected spirometry (lung function)

37

TABLE 1 Population Distribution and Percentage of Physician-Interpreted Abnormal Spirometry Readings (n = 455)

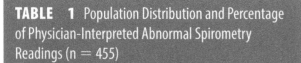

Content removed due to copyright restrictions

readings from 615 children (approximately 58% of the target population). The study demonstrated that about half the children experienced self-reported asthma-related symptoms. However, because self-reports were not associated closely with the results of the spirometry tests, the investigators concluded that the self-reported data from children were not good predictors of asthma risk. From the spirometry results, about 22% of the children had abnormal results, with significant differences occurring by race and ethnicity. More abnormal evaluations were found for blacks and Asians in comparison with other groups. **TABLE 1** reports the results of the spirometry evaluation.

Ecologic Studies

Ecologic studies are different from most other types of epidemiologic research in regard to the unit of analysis. An **ecologic study** (also called an ecological study) is "a study in which the units of analysis are populations or groups of people rather than individuals."[12] For example, the occurrence of an outcome of interest (e.g., a disease, mortality, health effect) might be assessed over different geographic areas—states, census tracts, or counties. To illustrate, one could study "the relationship between the distribution of income and mortality rates in states or provinces."[12] The assumption is made that outcome rates would be comparable in exposed and nonexposed groups if the exposure did not take place in the exposed group. In the foregoing example, if the outcome were mortality from cancer, researchers might hypothesize that

persons living in lower-income areas have greater exposure to environmental carcinogens than those who live in higher-income areas, producing differences in cancer mortality.

Ecologic analyses have been used to correlate air pollution with adverse health effects such as mortality. Instead of correlating individual exposure to air pollution with mortality, the researcher measures the association between average exposure to air pollution within a census tract and the average mortality in that census tract. Other types of geographic subdivisions besides census tracts may be used as well. This type of study attempts to demonstrate that mortality is higher in more polluted census tracts than in less polluted census tracts.

A major problem of the ecologic technique for the study of air pollution (and for virtually all ecologic studies) stems from uncontrolled factors. Examples relevant to air pollution include individual levels of smoking and smoking habits, occupational exposure to respiratory hazards and air pollution, differences in social class and other demographic factors, genetic background, and length of residence in the area.[8] Nonetheless, ecologic studies may open the next generation of investigations; the interesting observations gathered in ecologic studies may provide the impetus for more carefully designed studies. The next wave of studies that build on ecologic studies then may attempt to take advantage of more rigorous analytic study designs.

Ecologic studies have examined the association between water quality and both stroke and coronary diseases. A group of studies has demonstrated that hardness of the domestic water supply is associated inversely with risk of cerebrovascular mortality and cardiovascular diseases. However, a Japanese investigation did not support a relationship between water hardness and cerebrovascular diseases. In the latter ecologic study, the unit of analysis was municipalities (population subdivisions in Japan that consisted of from 6,000 to 3 million inhabitants). In analyzing the 1995 death rates from strokes in relationship to the values of water hardness, the researchers did not find statistically significant associations across municipalities.[22]

Other ecologic studies have examined the possible association between use of agricultural pesticides and childhood cancer incidence. For example, a total of 7,143 incident cases of invasive cancer diagnosed among children younger than age 15 were reported to the California Cancer Registry during the years 1988 to 1994. (Note that a registry is a centralized database for collection of information about a disease.) In this ecologic study, the unit of analysis was census blocks, with average annual pesticide exposure estimated per square mile. The study showed no overall association between pesticide exposure determined by this method and childhood cancer incidence rates. However, a significant increase of childhood leukemia rates was linked to census block groups that had the highest use of one form of pesticide, called propargite.[23]

Case-Control Studies

In a **case-control study**, subjects who participate in the study are defined on the basis of the presence or absence of an outcome of interest. The cases are those who have the outcome or disease of interest, and the controls are those who do not. In a case-control study, cases and controls generally are matched according to criteria such as sex, age, race, or other variables. Exposure to a factor is determined retrospectively, meaning that exposure has already occurred in the past. One method to determine past exposure is for the investigator to interview cases and controls regarding their exposure history. An advantage of case-control studies is that they can examine many potential exposures. For example, subjects may be queried about one or more exposures that they may have had in the past; in some variations of this approach, it may be possible to conduct direct measurements of the environment for various types of exposures. A disadvantage of case-control studies is that, in most circumstances, they can examine only one or a few outcomes.[8]

Researchers have a variety of sources available for the selection of cases and controls. For example, they may use patients from hospitals, specialized clinics, or medical practices. Sometimes, advertisements in media solicit cases. Cases may be selected from disease registries such as cancer registries. Controls can be either healthy persons or those affected by a disease that is etiologically unrelated to the outcome of interest. For example, investigators may identify as controls patients from hospitals or clinics; however, these control patients must not have been affected by the outcome of interest. In other studies, controls may be friends or relatives of the cases or be from the community.

The measure of association between exposure and outcome used in case-control studies is known as the **odds ratio (OR)**. A particular form of OR, the exposure-odds ratio, refers to "the ratio of the odds in favor of exposure among the cases [A/C] to the odds in favor of exposure among non cases [the controls, B/D]."[12] **TABLE 2** illustrates the method for labeling cells in a case-control study. This table is called a 2 × 2 table.

The OR is defined as $\dfrac{A/C}{B/D}$, which can be expressed as $\dfrac{AD}{BC}$.

TABLE 2 Table for a Case-Control Study

		Disease Status—Outcome of Interest	
		Yes (Cases)	No (Controls)
Exposure Status	Yes	A	B
	No	C	D
	Total	A + C	B + D

An odds ratio of more than 1 suggests a positive association between the exposure and disease or other outcome (provided that the results are statistically significant—a concept that will not be discussed here).

Calculation example: Suppose we have the following data from a case-control study: A = 9, B = 4, C = 95, D = 88. The OR is calculated as follows:

$$OR = \frac{AD}{BC} = \frac{(9)(88)}{(4)(95)} = 2.08$$

In this sample calculation, the OR is greater than 1, suggesting that the odds of the disease are higher among the exposed persons than among the nonexposed persons.

Case-control studies are very common in environmental epidemiologic research. For example, environmental health researchers have been concerned about the possible health effects of exposure to electromagnetic fields (EMFs). A case-control study among female residents of Long Island, New York examined the possible association between exposure to EMFs and breast cancer.[24] Eligible subjects were those who were younger than age 75 years and who had lived in the study area for 15 years or longer. Cases (n = 576) consisted of women diagnosed with in situ or invasive breast cancer. Controls (n = 585) were selected from the same community by random digit-dialing procedures. Several types of measurement of EMFs were taken in the subjects' homes and by mapping overhead power lines. The investigators reported that the odds ratio between EMF exposure and breast cancer was not statistically significantly different from 1; thus, the results suggested that there was no association between breast cancer and residential EMF exposure.

In comparison with cross-sectional study designs, case-control studies may provide more complete exposure data, especially when the exposure information is collected from the friends and relatives of cases who died of a particular cause. Nevertheless, some unmeasured exposure variables as well as methodological biases (a term discussed later in this chapter) may remain in case-control studies. For example, in studies of health and air pollution, exposure levels are difficult to quantify precisely. Also, it may be difficult to measure unknown and unobserved factors, including smoking habits and occupational exposures to air pollution, which affect the lungs.[8]

Cohort Studies

A **cohort study** design classifies subjects according to their exposure to a factor of interest and then observes them over time to document the occurrence of new cases (incidence) of disease or other health events. Cohort studies are a type of longitudinal design, meaning that subjects are followed over an extended period of time. Using cohort studies, epidemiologists are able to evaluate many different outcomes (causes of death) but few exposures.[8]

Cohort studies may be either prospective or retrospective. At the inception of a prospective cohort study, participating individuals must be certified as being free from the outcome of interest. As these individuals are followed into the future, the occurrence of new cases of the disease is noted. A retrospective cohort study (historical cohort study) is "conducted by reconstructing data about persons at a time or times in the past. This method uses existing records about the health or other relevant aspects of a population as it was at some time in the past and determines the current (or subsequent) status of members of this population with respect to the condition of interest."[12] An example of a retrospective cohort study would be one that examined mortality among an occupational cohort such as shipyard workers who were employed at a specific naval yard during a defined time interval (e.g., during World War II).

The measure of association used in cohort studies is called **relative risk (RR)**, the ratio of the incidence rate of a disease or health outcome in an exposed group to the incidence rate of the disease or condition in a nonexposed group. As noted previously, an incidence rate may be interpreted as the risk of occurrence of an outcome that is associated with a particular exposure. The RR provides a ratio of two risks—the risk associated with an exposure in comparison with the risk associated with nonexposure.

Mathematically, the term *relative risk* is defined as A/(A + B) (the rate [incidence] of the disease or condition in the exposed group) divided by C/(C + D) (the rate [incidence] of the disease or condition in the nonexposed group). A 2 × 2 table for the elements used in the calculation of a relative risk is shown in **TABLE 3**.

		Disease Status		
		Yes	**No**	**Total**
Exposure Status	Yes	A	B	A + B
	No	C	D	C + D

TABLE 3 Table for a Cohort Study

$$RR = \frac{A/(A+B)}{C/(C+D)}$$

Calculation example: Suppose that we are researching whether exposure to solvents is associated with risk of liver cancer. From a cohort study of industrial workers, we find that three persons who worked with solvents developed liver cancer (cell A of Table 3) and 104 did not (cell B). Two cases of liver cancer occurred among nonexposed workers (cell C) in the same type of industry. The remaining 601 nonexposed workers (cell D) did not develop liver cancer. The RR is:

$$RR = \frac{3/(3+104)}{2/(2+601)} = 8.45$$

We may interpret relative risk in a manner that is similar to that of the odds ratio. For example, a relative risk greater than 1 (and statistically significant) indicates that the risk of disease is greater in the exposed group than in the nonexposed group. In other words, there is a positive association between exposure and the outcome under study. In the calculation example, the risk of developing liver cancer is eight times greater among workers who were exposed to solvents than among those who were not exposed to solvents.

Sometimes a relative risk calculation yields a value that is less than 1. If the relative risk is less than 1 (and statistically significant), the risk is lower among the exposed group. This level of risk (i.e., less than 1) sometimes is called a protective effect.

Accurate disease verification is necessary to optimize measures of relative risk; disease misclassification affects estimates of relative risk. The type of disease and method of diagnosis affect accuracy of diagnosis.[8] To illustrate, death certificates are used frequently as a source of information about the diagnosis of a disease. Information from death certificates regarding cancer as the underlying cause of death is believed to be more accurate than the information for other diagnoses such as those for nonmalignant conditions. Nevertheless, the accuracy of diagnoses of cancer as a cause of death varies according to the particular form of cancer.

Cohort studies are applied widely in environmental health. For example, they have been used to examine the effects of environmental and work-related exposures to potentially toxic agents. One concern of cohort studies has been exposure of female workers to occupationally related reproductive hazards and adverse pregnancy outcomes.[25]

A second example is an Australian study that examined the health impacts of occupational exposure to insecticides.[26] The investigators selected a cohort of 1,999 outdoor workers known to be employed as field officers or laboratory staff for the New South Wales Board of Tick Control between 1935 and 1996. Only male subjects were selected for the study. A control cohort consisted of 1,984 men who worked as outdoor field officers at any time since 1935. Occupational monitoring programs demonstrated that members of the exposure cohort had worked with pesticides, including DDT. The investigators carefully evaluated exposure status and health outcomes such as mortality from various chronic diseases and cancer. They reported an association between exposure to pesticides and adverse health effects, particularly for asthma, diabetes, and some forms of cancer including pancreatic cancer.

Study Endpoints Used in Environmental Epidemiologic Research

In evaluating the health effects of occupational exposures to toxic agents, researchers may study various endpoints, including measures derived from self-report questionnaires, results of direct physical examinations, and mortality experience in a population. The endpoints also may be keyed to any of a number of stages in the natural progression of disease (e.g., presymptomatic, symptomatic, or permanent dysfunction).[27]

In some studies, self-reported symptom rates are used as a measure of the effects of low-level chemical exposure. Occupational health investigators can design and administer self-report questionnaires inexpensively. Self-reports to questionnaires, however, may not always be reliable, and although they correlate often with clinical diagnoses they also may differ markedly.[6]

Physiologic or clinical examinations are other means to evaluate adverse health effects. For example, in a study of respiratory diseases, pulmonary function tests, such as forced expiratory volume, may be an appropriate indicator. Although clinical examinations may provide "harder" evidence of health effects than self-reports, such examinations may be expensive or impractical to conduct in the case of workers who have left employment.

In other studies, mortality is the outcome of interest; research on mortality frequently uses a retrospective cohort study design.[7] Mortality experience in an employment cohort can be compared with the expected mortality in the general population (national, regional, state, or county) by using the standardized mortality ratio (SMR), which is defined as "the ratio of the number of deaths observed in the study group or population to the number that would be expected if the study population had the same specific rates as the standard population. Often multiplied by 100."[12] Typically the SMR is denoted by a percentage; when the percentage is greater than 100%, the SMR in the study population is elevated above that found in the comparison population. Conversely, when the SMR is less than 100%, the mortality experience in the study population is lower than that of the comparison population.

One also can contrast the mortality experience of exposed workers with the mortality rate of nonexposed workers in the same industry. For example, production workers might be compared with drivers or office workers. Another option is to identify a second industry or occupation that is comparable in terms of skill level, educational requirements, or geographic location but in which the exposure of interest is not present.

The use of mortality as a study endpoint has several advantages, including the fact that it may be relevant to agents that have a subtle effect over a long time period. Although any fatal chronic disease may be investigated, mortality from cancer often is studied as an outcome variable in occupational exposures. According to Monson, "Cancer specifically tends to be a fatal illness; its presence is usually indicated on the death certificate. Also, cancer is a fairly specific disease and is less subject to random misclassification than, say, one of the cardiovascular diseases."[28(p106)]

▶ Causality in Epidemiologic Studies

One of the fundamental models of causality used in epidemiologic studies is the **epidemiologic triangle**, which includes three major factors: agent, host, and environment. Although this model has been applied to the field of infectious disease epidemiology, it also provides a framework for organizing the causality of other types of environmental problems. Refer to **FIGURE 11** for an illustration.

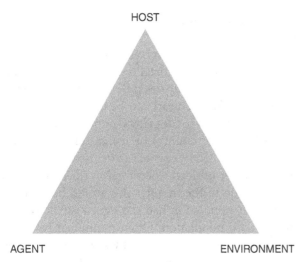

FIGURE 11 The epidemiologic triangle.

Reproduced from Friis RH, Sellers TA. *Epidemiology for Public Health Practice*. 5th ed. Burlington, MA: Jones and Bartlett Learning; 2014:493.

The term *environment* is defined as the domain in which disease-causing agents may exist, survive, or originate; it consists of "[a]ll that which is external to the individual human host."[12] The **host** is "[a] person or other living animal, including birds and arthropods, that affords subsistence or lodgment to an INFECTIOUS AGENT under natural conditions."[12] A human host is a person who is afflicted with a disease; or, from the epidemiologic perspective, the term host denotes an affected group or population. An **agent** (of disease) refers to

> … a factor (e.g., a microorganism, chemical substance, form of radiation, mechanical, behavioral, social agent or process) whose presence, excessive presence, or (in deficiency diseases) relative absence is essential for the occurrence of a disease. A disease may have a single agent, a number of independent alternative agents (at least one of which must be present), or a complex of two or more factors whose combined presence is essential for or contributes to the development of the disease or other outcome.[12]

In environmental health, agent factors can include (but are not limited to) particulate matter from pollution, toxic chemicals and pesticides, and microbes. Examples of agent factors covered in this text are:

- Microbial agents responsible for zoonotic diseases
- Microbial agents linked to foodborne illness
- Toxic chemicals including pesticides
- Toxic metals
- Airborne particulates and gases
- Radiation: ionizing and nonionizing

These agents are relevant to many of the environmental problems discussed in this text, including hazardous waste disposal, zoonotic illnesses, foodborne illnesses, unintentional injuries, occupational illnesses, and adverse health outcomes associated with water and air pollution.

Criteria of Causality

The epidemiologic triangle provides a framework for viewing hypothesized relationships among agent, host, and environmental factors in causation of disease. One of the central concerns of environmental epidemiology is to be able to assert that a causal association exists between an agent factor and a disease in the host. Hill pointed out that in the realm of occupational health, extreme conditions in the physical environment or exposure to known toxic chemicals should be invariably injurious.[29] More commonly the situation occurs in which weaker associations have been observed between certain aspects of the environment and the occurrence of health events. An example would be the development of lung diseases among persons exposed to dusts (e.g., miners who work in dusty, unventilated mines). Hill raised the question of how one moves from such an observed association to the verdict of causation (e.g., exposure to coal dust *causes* coal miner's pneumoconiosis). A second example is the perplexing question of the extent to which studies reveal a causal association between a specific environmental exposure and a particular form of cancer.[20]

Hill proposed a situation in which there is a clear association between two variables and in which statistical tests have suggested that this association is not due to chance. For example, data have revealed that smoking is associated with lung cancer in humans and that chance can be ruled out as being responsible for this observed association. The 1964 US government report *Smoking and Health* stated that "the evaluation of a causal association does not depend solely upon evidence from a probabilistic statement derived from statistics, but is a matter of judgment that depends upon several criteria."[30] Similarly, Hill listed nine causal criteria that need to be taken into account in the assessment of a causal association between factor A and disease B. For the purposes of this text, we will consider seven of the criteria, which are included in **TABLE 4.**

TABLE 4 Hill's Criteria of Causality	
Strength	Biological gradient
Consistency	Plausibility
Specificity	Coherence
Temporality	

Strength

Strong associations give support to a causal relationship between factor and disease. Hill provided the example of the very large increase in scrotal cancer (by a factor of 200 times) among chimney sweeps in comparison with workers who were not exposed occupationally to tars and mineral oils. Another example arises from the steeply elevated lung cancer mortality rates among heavy cigarette smokers in comparison with nonsmokers (20 to 30 times higher). Hill also cautioned that we should not be too ready to dismiss causal associations when the strength of the association is small, because there are many examples of causal relationships that are characterized by weak associations.[29] One example would be exposure to an infectious agent such as meningococcus that produces relatively few clinical cases of meningococcal meningitis.

Consistency

According to Hill, a consistent association is one that has been observed repeatedly "by different persons, in different places, circumstances and times. . . ."[29(p296)] An example of consistency comes from research on the relationship between smoking and lung cancer, a relationship that was found repeatedly in many retrospective and prospective studies.

Specificity

A specific association is one that is constrained to a particular disease–exposure relationship. In a specific association, a given disease results from a given exposure and not from other types of exposures. Hill gave the example of an association that "is limited to specific workers and to particular sites and types of disease and there is no association between the work and other modes of dying. . . ."[29(p297)] Returning to the smoking–lung cancer example, one may argue that the association is not specific, because "the death rate among smokers is higher than the death rate of non-smokers from many causes of death. . . ."[29(p297)] Nevertheless, Hill argued that one-to-one causation is unusual, because many diseases have more than one causal factor.

Temporality

This criterion specifies that we must observe the cause before the effect; Hill stated that we cannot put the cart before the horse. For example, if we assert that air pollution causes lung cancer, we first must exclude persons who have lung cancer from our study; then we must follow those who are exposed to air pollution to determine whether lung cancer develops.

Biological Gradient

A biological gradient also is known as a dose–response curve (discussed in the chapter on environmental toxicology), which shows a linear trend in the association between exposure and disease. An example arises from the linear association between the number of cigarettes smoked and the lung cancer death rate.

Plausibility

This criterion states that an association must be biologically plausible from the standpoint of contemporary biological knowledge. The association between exposure to tars and oils and the development of scrotal cancer is plausible in view of current knowledge about carcinogenesis. However, this knowledge was not available when Pott made his observations during the 18th century.

Coherence

This criterion suggests that "the cause-and-effect interpretation of our data should not seriously conflict with the generally known facts of the natural history and biology of the disease. . . ."[29(p298)] Examples related to cigarette smoking and lung cancer come from the rise in the number of lung cancer deaths associated with an increase in smoking, as well as lung cancer mortality differences between men (who smoke more and have higher lung cancer mortality rates) and women (who smoke less and have lower rates).

▶ Bias in Environmental Epidemiologic Studies

Epidemiologic studies may be impacted by **bias**, which is defined as the "[s]ystematic deviation of results or inferences from truth, or processes leading to such deviation. An error in the conception and design of a study—or in the collection, analysis, interpretation, reporting, publication, or review of data—leading to results or conclusions that are systematically (as opposed to randomly) different from truth."[12] There are many types of bias; particularly important for environmental epidemiology are those that impact study procedures. Examples of such bias are related to how the study was designed, the method of data collection, interpretation and review of findings, and procedures used in data analysis. For example, in measurements of exposures and outcomes, faulty measurement devices may introduce biases into study designs.

A complete discussion of all the kinds of bias is beyond the scope of the text; however, we will consider two types of bias, *recall bias* and *selection bias*. The former is particularly relevant to case-control studies. Recall bias refers to the fact that cases may remember an exposure more clearly than controls.[19] The consequence of recall bias is to reduce the reliability of exposure information gathered from control groups. Selection bias is defined as "bias in the estimated association or effect of an exposure on the outcome that arises from the procedures used to select individuals into the study or the analysis."[12] The effect of selection bias may be to cause systematic differences in characteristics between participants and nonparticipants in research. An example of selection bias is the **healthy worker effect**, which may reduce the validity of exposure data when employed persons are chosen as research subjects in studies of occupational health. Monson states that the healthy worker effect refers to the "observation that employed populations tend to have a lower mortality experience than the general population."[28(p114)] The healthy worker effect may have an impact on occupational mortality studies in several ways. People whose life expectancy is shortened by disease are less likely to be employed than healthy persons. One consequence of this phenomenon would be a reduced (or attenuated) measure of effect for an exposure that increases morbidity or mortality; that is, because the general population includes both employed and unemployed individuals, the mortality rate of that population may be somewhat elevated in comparison with a population in which everyone is healthy enough to work. As a result, any excess mortality associated with a given occupational exposure is more difficult to detect when the healthy worker effect is operative. The healthy worker effect is likely to be stronger for non-malignant causes of mortality, which usually produce worker attrition during an earlier career phase, than for malignant causes of mortality, which typically have longer latency periods and occur later in life. In addition, healthier workers may have greater total exposure to occupational hazards than those who leave the workforce at an earlier age because of illness.

Another example of study bias is **confounding**, which denotes "the distortion of a measure of the effect of an exposure on an outcome due to the association of the exposure with other factors that influence the occurrence of the outcome."[12] See **FIGURE 12**. Confounding factors are associated with disease risk and produce a different distribution of outcomes in the exposure groups than in the comparison groups. The existence

FIGURE 12 Confounding variables.

of confounding factors that occur in the exposed group may lead to invalid conclusions from a study.

An instance of confounding arises from the possible association between exposure of workers to occupational dusts and development of lung cancer. One of the types of dust encountered in the workplace is silica (e.g., from sand used in sandblasting). In a retrospective cohort study, one might compare the workers' mortality rates for lung cancer with those of the general population (by using SMRs). Suppose we find that the SMR for lung cancer of workers exposed to silica is greater than 100% (i.e., exceeds the rate of the nonexposed population). One conclusion is that the workers have a higher risk of lung cancer than the nonexposed population. However, the issue of confounding also should be considered: Employees exposed to silica are usually blue-collar workers who, as a rule, have higher smoking rates than the general population (that might be used as a comparison population). When smoking rates are taken into account, the strength of the association between silica exposure and lung cancer is reduced—suggesting that smoking is a confounder that needs to be considered in the association.[31]

▶ Limitations and Deficiencies of Environmental Epidemiology

According to Buffler, the three major requirements for the successful epidemiologic investigation of environmental exposures are: "(1) direct and accurate estimates of the exposures experienced by individual members of the study population, (2) direct and accurate determination of the disease status of individual members of the study population, and (3) appropriate statistical summarization and analysis of the individual data pertaining to disease and exposure."[14(p131)] To the extent that these requirements are not met, limitations are introduced into epidemiologic studies. Other limiting

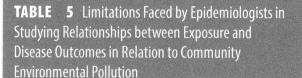

TABLE 5 Limitations Faced by Epidemiologists in Studying Relationships between Exposure and Disease Outcomes in Relation to Community Environmental Pollution

Content removed due to copyright restrictions

factors include the long latency periods and infrequent occurrence that characterize many environmentally associated diseases. (Refer to **TABLE 5**.)

Long Latency Periods

A consideration that limits one's ability to derive causal inferences from epidemiologic studies is the long **latency period** phenomenon.[9] The term *latency period* refers to the time interval between initial exposure to a disease-causing agent (e.g., environmental risk factor or exposure) and the appearance of a disease or its manifestations in the host.[12] Note that the occurrence of disease can be conceptualized in a number of different ways depending on the measure used, such as screening tests and observation of clinical signs and symptoms. Environmentally caused diseases, for example, some forms of cancer, have latency periods that span many years. These long latency periods reduce the epidemiologist's ability to ascertain definitively the outcomes of exposure.[9] Examples are asbestos-related diseases, which in many cases do not appear until many years after initial exposure.[32]

Low Incidence and Prevalence

Another limiting factor of studies concerns the infrequent occurrence of certain diseases that are the target of environmental epidemiologic studies.[9]

An example is the occurrence of childhood cancers, which have been examined in relation to environmental factors such as toxic chemicals.[11] The incidence of cancers among children is much lower than that of adults—17.0 per 100,000 among children aged 0 to 14 years and 436.6 per 100,000 for all ages (2014 data). When diseases are uncommon, one's ability to make precise estimates of exposure–disease associations is reduced. The researcher also may be dependent upon less powerful research designs—descriptive and case-control studies.

Difficulties in Exposure Assessment

Several authorities have stressed the requirement for accurate assessment of exposures in epidemiologic studies of environmental health. Rothman points out that "Atop the list of methodologic problems is the problem of exposure assessment, a problem that extends through all of epidemiologic research but is a towering obstacle in environmental epidemiology."[6(p19)] Gardner points out that "Epidemiological methods of investigation are incomplete without good quality exposure data to parallel information on health. The need for monitoring environmental and biological exposure is paramount to the successful interpretation of results and implementation of any required preventive programs."[33(p108)]

For high levels of exposures to toxic agents that produce clear and immediate effects, causation is clear cut.[34] Examples are the release of toxic gases in Bhopal, India, in 1984, and the 1986 Chernobyl nuclear reactor disaster in the former Soviet Union. Moreover, although earlier generations of studies led to the control of intense environmental exposures that were strongly correlated with disease outcomes, the focus of contemporary research has shifted. Modern studies examine low levels of exposure that potentially are associated with low levels of risk.[14]

Low-level environmental exposures challenge epidemiologic researchers who, when dealing with them, have difficulty applying standard laboratory methods used to determine exposure levels. Consequently, researchers are unable to establish definitively whether exposure to a particular agent has occurred. In the ambient environment, not only may several exposures be mixed, but also the levels of exposures may be uncertain.[34]

Examples of exposure measurements used in environmental epidemiology include the following: samples of toxic fumes in a manufacturing plant, ozone readings in the community, and distances of housing tracts from high-tension power lines that emit electromagnetic radiation. All of these measures are prone to error because they are indirect measures of exposure and do not provide direct information on the amount of exposure that an individual may actually receive.[6] As noted, a common method for approximating exposure is the use of proxies (substitutes for direct measures). An example of such a measure is the previously noted distance of a housing tract from the source of an environmental hazard. These proxy or surrogate measures are usually too diffuse to establish exposure definitively.

Nonspecific Effects

A specific health outcome is one that is usually associated with a particular exposure, and only that exposure. When an outcome is nonspecific, it can be associated with several or many different environmental exposures. The majority of diseases and conditions thought to be related to environmental exposures are influenced by many factors.[32] Consequently, any particular environmental exposure probably will not be associated with a specific outcome. Further complicating the picture of exposure determination is the fact that we are exposed to hundreds of chemicals in the environment; these chemicals often are mixed, clouding our knowledge of the level of exposure that took place. Exposures to any of these chemicals could produce outcomes that are similar to one another.

▶ Summary of Characteristics, Weaknesses, and Strengths of Environmental Epidemiology

Several of the key characteristics, weaknesses, and strengths of environmental epidemiology are shown in **TABLE 6**. One strength is the ability to deal with "real world" problems, for example community exposure to environmental contaminants; a second strength is the possibility of examining complex problems that involve multiple variables (e.g., exposure, demographic, and outcome variables); a third is the capability to impel environmental action, even though the level of exposure and etiologic mechanisms of health effects have not been ascertained definitively.

The weaknesses include the fact that exposure levels in environmental epidemiology studies are difficult to measure precisely; also, there may be many uncontrolled variables that can bias the results.[35] In the words of Grandjean, "The quality of environmental epidemiology research can be considered from two perspectives, one representing methodological issues, the other dealing with the usefulness of the work. These two views are connected, because a study of superior quality is likely to be of greater validity and therefore more useful. Still, an imperfect study can be of great relevance, and epidemiologists must therefore tackle the challenging balance between being an advocate for particular policies and being a skeptical ivory-tower scientist."[36(p158)] Nevertheless, these weaknesses do not negate the fact that environmental epidemiology has made, and will continue to make, important contributions to the environmental health field.

▶ Conclusion

Environmental epidemiology is one of the fields that research fundamental questions regarding the role of environmental exposures in human health. The discipline traces its history from the time of Hippocrates and from early studies of occupational cancer during the late 18th century. Also historically significant were Snow's investigations of cholera during the mid-19th century. Epidemiology, with its emphasis on observation as well as focus on populations, contributes important methodological tools—particularly with respect to study design.

Descriptive and analytic designs are the two major classes of epidemiologic studies. In order to infer causality among observed associations between environmental exposures and adverse health outcomes demonstrated by epidemiologic studies, one must

TABLE 6 Characteristics, Weaknesses, and Strengths of Environmental Epidemiology
Content removed due to copyright restrictions

apply the criteria of causality. Biases such as confounding can impact epidemiologic research. Although environmental epidemiology has yielded noteworthy insights, one needs to keep in mind the limitations of the discipline. For more information about epidemiology, consult Friis and Sellers[2] or one of the other introductory texts that is available.

Study Questions and Exercises

1. Define the following terms:
   a. Epidemiology
   b. Environmental epidemiology
   c. Descriptive epidemiology
   d. Natural experiments
   e. Prevalence
   f. Incidence
   g. Case fatality rate
   h. Odds ratio
   i. Relative risk

2. What is meant by a cause in environmental epidemiology? Apply Hill's criteria of causality to an example of an association between a specific environmental exposure and health outcome.

3. Explain the reason why studies of the health effects of smoking among individuals who smoke would not be a concern of environmental epidemiology. Explain the reason why exposure to secondhand cigarette smoke is a concern of this discipline.

4. Define the following terms and discuss how each affects the validity of epidemiologic study designs:
   a. Bias
   b. Confounding
   c. Latency period
   d. Exposure assessment

5. List the reasons why epidemiology is important to research studies of environmental health. What are some of the important limitations of the epidemiologic approach with respect to the study of environmental health problems?

6. Explain why epidemiology sometimes is called "population medicine." State how epidemiology contrasts with clinical medicine.

7. Explain the difference between descriptive and analytic epidemiology. Give examples of how both types of study design are utilized in the field of environmental health.

8. What does early epidemiology (e.g., Hippocrates) share in common with contemporary epidemiology in terms of examining the causality of health problems?

9. Describe the importance of the contributions of Sir Percival Pott to environmental health, particularly in the area of cancer prevention.

10. Explain the work of John Snow using the methodology of the natural experiment.

11. Name the study designs that are used for hypothesis testing and those that are used for generating hypotheses.

12. Explain why most studies conducted in the field of environmental epidemiology are nonexperimental.

13. Explain how ecologic analysis is used to study the health effects of air pollution. Give examples of uncontrolled factors that may affect ecologic study results.

14. Explain why cross-sectional studies are defined as prevalence studies. Give an example of a cross-sectional study.

15. Explain why cohort studies are an improvement over case-control studies with respect to measurement of exposure data.

For Further Reading

Snow on Cholera, John Snow, 1855.

References

1. U.S. National Library of Medicine, National Institutes of Health, National Institute of Environmental Health Sciences. What is environmental health? Available at: https://kidsenvirohealth .nlm.nih.gov. Accessed April 3, 2017.
2. Friis RH, Sellers TA. *Epidemiology for Public Health Practice.* 5th ed. Burlington, MA: Jones & Bartlett Learning; 2014.
3. Pekkanen J, Pearce N. Environmental epidemiology: challenges and opportunities. *Environ Health Perspect.* 2001;109:1–5.
4. Terracini B. Environmental epidemiology: a historical perspective. In: Elliott P, Cuzick J, English D, Stern R, eds. *Geographical and Environmental Epidemiology: Methods for Small-Area Studies.* New York, NY: Oxford University Press; 1992.
5. Acquavella JF, Friedlander BR, Ireland BK. Interpretation of low to moderate relative risks in environmental epidemiologic studies. *Ann Rev Public Health.* 1994;15:179–201.
6. Rothman KJ. Methodologic frontiers in environmental epidemiology. *Environ Health Perspect.* 1993;101 (suppl 4):19–21.
7. Hertz-Picciotto I, Brunekreef B. Environmental epidemiology: where we've been and where we're going. *Epidemiol.* 2001;12:479–481.
8. Blair A, Hayes RB, Stewart PA, Zahm SH. Occupational epidemiologic study design and application. *Occup Med.* 1996;11:403–419.
9. Morgenstern H, Thomas D. Principles of study design in environmental epidemiology. *Environ Health Perspect.* 1993;101 (Suppl 4):23–38.
10. Smith AH. Epidemiologic input to environmental risk assessment. *Arch Environ Health.* 1988;43:124–127.
11. Grufferman S. Methodologic approaches to studying environmental factors in childhood cancer. *Environ Health Perspect.* 1998;106(Suppl 3): 881–886.

12. Porta M, ed. *A Dictionary of Epidemiology*. 6th ed. New York, NY: Oxford University Press; 2014.
13. Wegman DH. The potential impact of epidemiology on the prevention of occupational disease. *Am J Public Health*. 1992;82:944–954.
14. Buffler PA. Epidemiology needs and perspectives in environmental epidemiology. *Arch Environ Health*. 1988;43: 130–132.
15. Doll R. Pott and the path to prevention. *Arch Geschwulstforsch*. 1975;45:521–531.
16. Snow J. *Snow on Cholera*. Cambridge, MA: Harvard University Press; 1965.
17. Lilienfeld DE. John Snow: the first hired gun? *Am J Epidemiol*. 2000;152:4–9.
18. Sandler DP. John Snow and modern-day environmental epidemiology. *Am J Epidemiol*. 2000;152:1–3.
19. Prentice RL, Thomas D. Methodologic research needs in environmental epidemiology: data analysis. *Environ Health Perspect*. 1993;101(Suppl 4):39–48.
20. DeBaun MR, Gurney JG. Environmental exposure and cancer in children. A conceptual framework for the pediatrician. *Pediatr Clin North Am*. 2001;48:1215–1221.
21. Freeman NCG, Schneider D, McGarvey P. School-based screening for asthma in third-grade urban children: the Passaic asthma reduction effort survey. *Am J Public Health*. 2002;92:45–46.
22. Miyake Y, Iki M. Ecologic study of water hardness and cerebrovascular mortality in Japan. *Arch Environ Health*. 2003;58:163–166.
23. Reynolds P, Von Behren J, Gunier RB, et al. Childhood cancer and agricultural pesticide use: an ecologic study in California. *Environ Health Perspect*. 2002;110:319–324.
24. Schoenfeld ER, O'Leary ES, Henderson K, et al. Electromagnetic fields and breast cancer on Long Island: a case-control study. *Am J Epidemiol*. 2003;158:47–58.
25. Taskinen HK. Epidemiological studies in monitoring reproductive effects. *Environ Health Perspect*. 1993;101(Suppl 3): 279–283.
26. Beard J, Sladden T, Morgan G, et al. Health impacts of pesticide exposure in a cohort of outdoor workers. *Environ Health Perspect*. 2003;111: 724–730.
27. Neutra R, Goldman L, Smith D, et al. Study, endpoints, goals, and prioritization for a program in hazardous chemical epidemiology. *Arch Environ Health*. 1988;43(2):94–99.
28. Monson RR. *Occupational Epidemiology*. Boca Raton, FL: CRC Press; 1990.
29. Hill AB. The environment and disease: association or causation? *Proc R Soc Med*. 1965;58:295–300.
30. US Department of Health, Education, and Welfare, Public Health Service, Centers for Disease Control. *Smoking and Health. Report of the Advisory Committee to the Surgeon General of the Public Health Service*. PHS Publication No. 1103. Washington, DC: US Government Printing Office; 1964.
31. Steenland K, Greenland S. Monte Carlo sensitivity analysis and Bayesian analysis of smoking as an unmeasured confounder in a study of silica and lung cancer. *Am J Epidemiol*. 2004;160:384–392.
32. Grandjean P. Epidemiology of environmental hazards. *Public Health Rev*. 1993–1994;21:255–262.
33. Gardner MJ. Epidemiological studies of environmental exposure and specific diseases. *Arch Environ Health*. 1988;43:102–108.
34. Health CW, Jr. Uses of epidemiologic information in pollution episode management. *Arch Environ Health*. 1988;43:75–80.
35. Goldsmith JR. Keynote address: improving the prospects for environmental epidemiology. *Arch Environ Health*. 1988;43: 69–74.
36. Grandjean P. Seven deadly sins of environmental epidemiology and the virtues of precaution. *Epidemiology*. 2008;19:158–162.

Environmental Toxicology

LEARNING OBJECTIVES

By the end of this chapter the reader will be able to:

- Illustrate two applications of toxicology in environmental health.
- Define three important terms used in the field of toxicology.
- State five factors that affect responses to a toxic chemical.
- Discuss the steps involved in risk assessment.
- Describe methods for human exposure assessment.

▶ Introduction

Did you know that toxicology—a.k.a. the science of poisons—helps scientists learn about the hazards associated with potentially harmful environmental chemicals? Toxicology aids in determining the safety of chemicals and their associated risks. You will learn why toxicology is a crucial discipline for environmental health research. This chapter will define terms used in toxicology, describe its relationships with other scientific disciplines, and provide an overview of the discipline as it applies to environmental health. Examples of how toxicology helps to delineate factors related to people's responses to toxic chemicals will be provided. An additional topic will be the links between toxicology and risk assessment. From this information you will be better equipped to explore the environmental health applications covered in the remainder of the text.

▶ Toxicology, a Cornerstone of Environmental Health

First, let us explore why toxicology is important to the environmental health field and the methods it uses to illuminate environmental health problems. The National Toxicology Program (NTP) emphasizes the central role of toxicology in identifying the potential hazards of the numerous chemicals in use in the United States. The NTP states:

> More than 80,000 chemicals are registered for use in the United States. Each year, an estimated 2,000 new ones are introduced for use in such everyday items as foods, personal care products, prescription drugs, household cleaners, and lawn care products. We do not know the effects of many of these chemicals

on our health, yet we may be exposed to them while manufacturing, distributing, using, and disposing of them or when they become pollutants in our air, water, or soil. Relatively few chemicals are thought to pose a significant risk to human health. However, safeguarding public health depends on identifying both what the effects of these chemicals are and at what levels of exposure they may become hazardous to humans—that is, understanding their toxicology.[1]

Toxicology overlaps other disciplines, including physiology, pharmacology, and pathology, and to some extent epidemiology, chemistry, and statistics. A basic assumption in toxicology is that "[a]ll substances are poisons; there is none that is not a poison. The right dose differentiates a poison from a remedy."[2(p2)] We can think of toxicology and epidemiology as working hand in hand, the latter concerned with the occurrence and etiology of disease, and the former studying dose–response relationships and mechanisms of action in order to better understand the adverse health effects linked to chemicals. The coupling of toxicology and epidemiology with genomic methods (employed in the study of genes) enables scientists to assess risks associated with toxic substances.[3]

Toxicology contributes to the armamentarium of tools that are crucial to the description and characterization of environmental chemicals and the responses of living organisms to these chemicals. Related to the functions of toxicology are assessment of exposure, risk, and hazards. **Exposure** is defined as "[p]roximity and/or contact with a source of a disease agent in such a manner that effective transmission of the agent or harmful effects of the agent may occur."[4] The terms **risk** and **hazard** are defined later in the chapter. In the following textbox, noted epidemiologist Douglas L. Weed describes how epidemiology and toxicology are compatible in delving into the complex nature of disease causation.[5]

EPIDEMIOLOGY, TOXICOLOGY, AND DISEASE CAUSATION

Content removed due to copyright restrictions

▶ Description of Toxicology

The field of toxicology has been in existence for many centuries, although in its early history the field may have operated under a rubric that is different from its current name. Also, modern toxicology has evolved a number of subspecializations.

Definition of Toxicology

According to its traditional definition, toxicology is the science of poisons. Refer to **FIGURE 1**. A more complete definition is "[t]he study of the adverse effects of chemicals on living organisms."[6(p6)] The science of toxicology is not confined to the study of humans, but can be applied

FIGURE 1 Toxicology: the science of poisons.
© Peter Nadolski/Shutterstock

to other species and organisms as well. Through in vivo (in living organisms) and in vitro (in "glass," e.g., cell culture) studies, toxicologists examine such health effects of chemical exposures as carcinogenesis (production of cancer), and damage to internal organs, to the developing fetus, and to the reproductive system. Several types of cancer have been tied to chemical exposure, including carcinoma of the lung, breast, and prostate gland, and some forms of skin cancer and leukemia.

History of Toxicology

Toxicology may be regarded as a field that, in some respects, has a venerable history, yet has a short history in the sense that much of the information regarding toxicology has been acquired in the last few decades. Since early history, human beings have been mystified by the nature of chemicals; they also became fascinated with the use of poisons. Ancient civilizations, early cave dwellers, and isolated primitive tribes were aware of the existence of toxic plants and animal venoms. In ancient Greece and Rome, poisons were used for suicides and executions, and to accomplish political aims. Socrates, who lived from 470 to 399 BCE, was executed by poison, as was Theophrastus (370–286 BCE).

FIGURE 2 Paracelsus (1493–1541).

Around the fourth century BCE, poisonings (especially by use of arsenic) grew more frequent in the Roman Empire; Nero was said to have used arsenic to poison Claudius in order to serve political ambitions.

Poisonings also were employed frequently during the Middle Ages to do away with rivals, including spouses and politicians. Beginning about the 17th century and onward, physicians and others developed a gradually increasing awareness of the toxic effects of exposure to industrial metals and chemicals that were then in common use.

Paracelsus (born Phillippus Theophrastus Aureolus Bombastus von Hohenheim) is considered to be one of the founders of modern toxicology.[7] His image is shown in **FIGURE 2**. Active during the time of da Vinci and Copernicus, Paracelsus contributed to the discipline during the early 16th century. Among his contributions were several important concepts, including the dose–response relationship, which refers to the observation that the effects of a poison are related to the strength of its dose, and the notion of target organ specificity of chemicals.

▶ Terminology Used in the Field of Toxicology

One aspect of toxicology is the examination of the mechanisms by which chemicals produce toxic effects on living organisms and their tissues. Virtually all known chemicals (even sodium chloride—common table salt) have the capacity to produce toxic effects, such as injury or death, depending upon the amount ingested. This wide spectrum of doses is related to a particular chemical in question, for example, from botulinum toxin (highly toxic in tiny doses) to ethyl alcohol (toxic in much larger doses than botulinum toxin).[6] Measures of lethality (discussed later in this chapter) may not describe fully a chemical's spectrum of toxicity; chemicals that have low acute toxicity may have other effects such as carcinogenicity or teratogenicity. This section introduces a number of terms that are used to describe toxic materials. It should be noted that some of the terms tend to overlap conceptually and are not always differentiated clearly in the literature.

Mathieu Orfila was another pioneer in the field of toxicology. In the 1800s, he authored a number of significant works, among them *Trait des poisons* (1813). This work described in great detail various types of poisons and their bodily effects, a development that contributed to the foundations of forensic toxicology.

Fields within Toxicology

What type of work does a toxicologist perform and what are the specializations within toxicology? A **toxicologist** is a scientist who has received extensive training in order to investigate in living organisms "the adverse effects of chemicals . . . (including their cellular, biochemical, and molecular mechanisms of action) and assess the probability of their occurrence."[6(p6)] The field of toxicology comprises several key areas, including regulatory matters (*regulatory toxicology*), medico-legal issues (*forensic toxicology*), and clinical manifestations of disease related to toxic substances (*clinical toxicology*).[6] In addition, the specializations known as *environmental toxicology*, *reproductive toxicology*, and *developmental toxicology* are particularly relevant to environmental health problems.

The field of **environmental toxicology** is defined as ". . .the study of the impacts of pollutants upon the structure and function of ecological systems."[8] For example, environmental toxicology examines how environmental exposures to chemical pollutants may present risks to biological organisms, particularly animals, birds, and fish. The field of **ecotoxicology** is concerned with the effects of pollutants on ecosystems. (Refer to the textbox, What Is Ecotoxicology?)

In several respects, the mission of environmental toxicology overlaps those of reproductive and developmental toxicology. *Reproductive toxicology* examines the association between environmental chemicals and adverse effects upon the reproductive system.[9] Exposure to chemicals may arise from a number of environmental sources including the workplace, the home, and the medications and foods that we consume. On the list of hazardous chemicals and other agents that are suspected of impacting human reproduction negatively are pesticides, drugs, heavy metals, and hormones.[10]

WHAT IS ECOTOXICOLOGY?

The field of *ecotoxicology* is ". . .the branch of Toxicology concerned with the study of toxic effects, caused by natural or synthetic pollutants, to the constituents of ecosystems, animal (including human), vegetable and microbial, in an integral context." This important subfield of environmental toxicology was proposed in 1969 at a scientific meeting in Stockholm, Sweden. Broadly speaking, ecotoxicology investigates dispersion of pollutants into the physical environment, their impact upon biological chains such as food chains, and their toxic effects within ecosystems.

Data from Truhaut R. Ecotoxicology: principles and perspectives. *Ecotoxicol Environ Saf.* 1977;1(2):151-173.

Developmental toxicology researches the effects of natural and man-made chemicals (some classified as teratogens—substances that cause birth defects) on prenatal development. Other chemicals that can produce developmental toxicity are included in the broad class known as **xenobiotics**, which are "[c]hemical substances that are foreign to the biological system. They include naturally occurring compounds, drugs, environmental agents, carcinogens, [and] insecticides. . . ."[11] Some specific examples of xenobiotics are antibiotics, dioxins, and polychlorinated biphenyls (PCBs).

Poison

The term **poison** is "defined as any agent capable of producing a deleterious response in a biological system."[6(p6)] Examples of deleterious responses are death or serious impairment of biological functioning. Some definitions of a poison affirm that it is an agent that produces immediate effects such as lethality or sickness even when present in small doses.[12]

Toxic Agent

The term **toxic agent** refers very generally to a material or factor that can be harmful to biological systems.[12] Examples are physical energy (e.g., heat and ionizing and nonionizing radiation), substances derived from biological sources (e.g., black widow spider venom), and almost all chemicals.

Toxicity

Toxicity is defined as "the degree to which something is poisonous."[13] Toxicity is related to a material's physical and chemical properties. Some chemicals have low innate toxicity (e.g., ethyl alcohol, sodium chloride); others have high toxicity (e.g., dioxins and botulinum toxin formed by the bacteria that cause botulism). Substances that have low toxicity must be ingested in large amounts in order for them to have toxic effects; the converse is true of chemicals that have high toxicity. For example, ingestion of large amounts of water (which has low toxicity) is necessary in order to produce water intoxication. In contrast, injection with a small amount of highly toxic insect venom such as spider venom may be sufficient to cause severe damage to the body or even death. The venom from the bite of a black widow spider shown in **FIGURE 3** can cause serious illness, but usually does not result in death.

Toxic Substance

A material that has toxic properties is called a **toxic substance**.[12] This substance can be a single toxic chemical (e.g., arsenic, lead) or a mixture of toxic chemicals

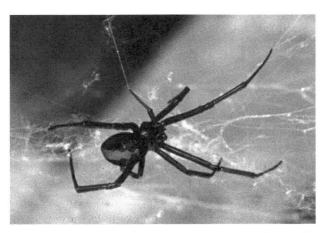

FIGURE 3 Black widow spider.
© Peter Waters/Shutterstock

INEDIBLE MUSHROOMS

Paxillus involutus   Amanita phalloides   Amanita muscaria   Boletus satanas

Galerina marginata   Lepiota cristata   Cortinarius orellanus   Clitocybe inversa

Amanita porphyria   Cortinarius sanguineus   Hygrocybe conica   Leucocoprinus brebissonii

FIGURE 4 Poisonous mushrooms.
© SkyPics Studio/Shutterstock

(e.g., gasoline). Toxic substances also can be categorized as organic toxins and inorganic toxins. Organic toxins denote substances originally taken from living organisms; such chemicals are carbon containing, frequently made up of large molecules, and capable of being synthesized. Inorganic toxins refer to specific chemicals, such as minerals, that have not been extracted from living organisms and do not follow the structure of a toxin derived from a living organism; such toxins generally are made up of small molecules.

Toxicant

Toxicants denote toxic substances that are man-made or result from human (anthropogenic) activity.[6] The toxic effect may occur directly or indirectly. The chemical potassium cyanide is directly toxic to the body; in contrast, methanol, a form of alcohol (wood alcohol) is indirectly toxic. Through the action of the liver, methanol is converted to formaldehyde and then to formic acid, a toxic metabolite.[14]

Toxin

A **toxin** usually refers to a toxic substance made by living organisms including reptiles, insects, plants, and microorganisms. To give one illustration, certain bacteria produce toxins that may act directly on the nervous or gastrointestinal system to produce symptoms of toxic effects. Foodborne botulism caused by the bacterium *Clostridium botulinum* is an environmental hazard associated with improperly canned foods and other unsafe practices in food preparation. Toxin production by microorganisms differs from disease causation in that the former involves actual invasion and multiplication of microorganisms and consequent organ and cell damage. *Systemic toxins* are those that affect the entire body or multiple organ systems; *target organ toxins* affect specific parts of the body.

Other toxins originate from plants. Some mushrooms (e.g., *Amanita phalloides*, "death cap") are highly poisonous. (See **FIGURE 4**.) There are many examples of plants that are toxic:

- Poison hemlock
- Foxglove
- Poison oak/poison ivy
- Rhubarb, especially the leaves, which have high levels of oxalates
- Some houseplants such as dieffenbachia

Refer to the following textbox for an example of poisonings caused by nicotine, a highly toxic substance derived from the tobacco plant, and by mushrooms.

CASE STUDY: CLASSIC EPISODES OF POISONINGS FROM PLANT-ORIGIN TOXINS

- **Nicotine poisoning from ground beef:** In Michigan during early 2003, some supermarket customers fell ill after consuming ground beef. The customers reported nausea, vomiting, dizziness, and—in one case—an irregular heartbeat. Samples of ground beef submitted by the supermarket were tested at a regional medical center and determined to have high levels of nicotine, which is a toxin derived from tobacco. Epidemiologic investigators interviewed the victims in order to examine the range of symptoms, their patterns, and their consistency with clinical presentations. A total of 92 persons among the interviewees demonstrated illnesses consistent with nicotine poisoning. A legal investigation led to the arrest of a store employee who was accused of putting a commercial insecticide that contained nicotine into 200 pounds of meat that was later purchased by unsuspecting customers.

- **Fatalities caused by ingesting "death caps":** The Centers for Disease Control and Prevention (CDC) have highlighted the dangers associated with popular interest in collecting mushrooms in the wild. Aficionados of wild mushrooms should observe the utmost caution in making certain that the fungi are safe for consumption; in some instances, one has extreme difficulty is distinguishing nontoxic from poisonous species. One of the species associated with poisonings is called *Amanita phalloides*. These mushrooms are also called "death cap" mushrooms for good reason; they cause about 90% of deaths from mushroom poisoning worldwide. Death caps, which can be confused with nontoxic species, do not have a distinct smell or taste. Cooking does not destroy their toxins. Consumption of these highly toxic mushrooms can result in severe hepatitis and even liver failure. Unfortunately, there is no antidote for this poison. (See Figure 4 for an illustration of poisonous mushrooms, including *A. phalloides*.)
- **1981: Mushroom poisoning among Laotian refugees:** During December 1981, a small group of Laotian refugees gathered mushrooms in Sonoma County in northern California. In Laos, a customary practice is to test the safety of mushrooms by boiling them with rice. If the rice turns red, the mushrooms are believed to be poisonous. As this was not the case in the Sonoma County incident, the refugees assumed the mushrooms were safe and consumed them. All of the seven mushroom hunters developed gastrointestinal distress; three required intensive care treatment. All recovered within a week.
- **1997:** The CDC reported two deaths in 1997 associated with eating *A. phalloides* mushrooms in northern California.
- **2016:** The California Poison Control System probed 14 poisoning cases suspected of being caused by eating wild *A. phalloides* mushrooms. The poisonings, which occurred in December in five northern California counties, necessitated three liver transplants; a child sustained permanent neurologic impairment. The remaining individuals recovered.

Data from Centers for Disease Control and Prevention. Nicotine poisoning after ingestion of contaminated ground beef—Michigan, 2003. *MMWR*. 2003;52:413–415; Centers for Disease Control and Prevention. Mushroom poisoning among Laotian Refugees—1981. *MMWR*. 1982;31:287-288; Centers for Disease Control and Prevention. Amanita phalloides mushroom poisoning—Northern California, January 1997. *MMWR*. 1997;46:489-492; Centers for Disease Control and Prevention. *Amanita phalloides* Mushroom Poisonings—Northern California, December 2016. *MMWR*. 2017;66:549-553.

▶ The Concept of a Dose and Related Terms

Dose

The term **dose** refers to "the amount of a substance administered at one time."[15] There are several ways of describing a dose such as exposure dose, absorbed dose, administered dose, total dose, external dose, internal dose, and effective dose. (Refer to **TABLE 1.**) In practice, dose often is expressed as a concentration of a substance in the body, for example, the concentration per milliliter (ml) of blood.

Toxicologists take into account the total dose, how often each individual dose occurs, and the time period during which the dosing occurs in order to describe the effects of a dose. When a dose is fractionated (broken up over a period of time), the effects may be different from those that transpire when a dose is administered all at one time. For example, poison that is fatal in a single, concentrated dose may no longer be fatal when the same dose is broken down into small units and given over time. Another consideration in the lethality or other effects of a dose relates to the body size of the subject. Young children, who have small body sizes, are more affected by a specific dose than are large adults who are given the same dose. For this reason, environmental exotoxins (those originating from external sources such as lead and mercury) at a given concentration may present a greater hazard to children than to adults.

Dose–Response Curves

The dose–response curve is a type of graph that is used to describe the effect of exposure to a chemical or toxic substance upon an organism such as an experimental animal. Toxicologists have devised two types of dose–response curves: one for the responses of an individual to a chemical and one for a population. For both types of curves, the dose is indicated along the x axis, and the response is shown along the y axis.

A typical dose–response curve for an individual exposed to ethyl alcohol is shown in **FIGURE 5**. The curve, which assumes a one-time exposure, shows a graded and increasing response as the dose of alcohol increases. The spectrum of effects can range from no effect when the dose is zero to death when the dose is increased to a toxic level.

With respect to the population, a dose–response relationship is "[t]he relationship of observed responses or outcomes in a population to varying levels of a beneficial or harmful agent."[4] The response could be measured as the percentage of exposed animals showing

TABLE 1 Ways to Describe a Dose

Term	Definition
Exposure dose	The amount of a xenobiotic encountered in the environment.[a]
External dose	A dose that results from contact with environmental sources, e.g., environmental contamination.
Absorbed dose	The actual amount of the exposed dose that enters the body.[a]
Internal dose	A synonym for absorbed dose.[a] 　　Various interpretations: The absorbed dose can reflect short-term exposure, previous day exposure, or long-term exposure.[b]
Administered dose	The quantity of a substance that is administered usually orally or by injection.[a]
Effective dose	Indicates the effectiveness of a substance. Normally, effective dose refers to a beneficial effect such as relief of pain. It may also stand for a harmful effect such as paralysis.[a]
Total dose	The sum of all individual doses.[a]

[a]National Library of Medicine. *ToxTutor*. Dose. Available at: https://toxtutor.nlm.nih.gov/02-001.html. Accessed March 10, 2017.
[b]Klaasen CD, Watkins JB III, eds. *Casarett & Doull's Essentials of Toxicology*. 3rd ed. New York, NY: McGraw-Hill, 2015.

Content removed due to copyright restrictions

FIGURE 5 Individual dose–response curve.

a particular effect, or it could reflect the effect in an individual subject.

The population dose–response curve, which has a sigmoid shape (S-shaped), is also a cumulative percentage response curve. (Refer to **FIGURE 6**.) This type of dose–response curve (i.e., population based) also is called a quantal curve.[6] The estimates of LD_{10}, LD_{50}, and LD_{90} appear in the figure. .

FIGURE 7 illustrates the threshold of a dose–response curve. At the beginning of the curve, there is a flat portion suggesting that at low levels an increase in dosage produces no effect; this is known as the subthreshold phase. After the threshold is reached, the curve rises steeply and then progresses to a linear phase, where an increase in response is proportional to the increase in dose. When the maximal response is reached, the curve flattens out. A dose–response relationship is one of the indicators used to assess a

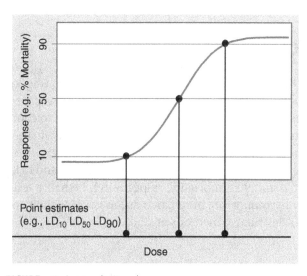

FIGURE 6 A population dose–response curve.

Modified from Guidelines for Ecological Risk Assessment. US Environmental Protection Agency, Risk Assessment Forum. Washington, DC, EPA/630/R095/002F; 1998:81.

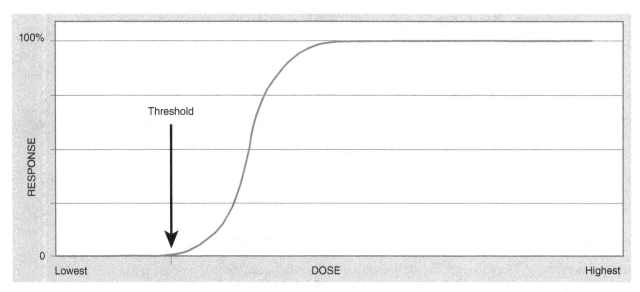

FIGURE 7 The threshold of a dose–response curve.

causal effect of a suspected exposure upon a health outcome.

The term **threshold** refers to the lowest dose at which a particular response may occur. It is unclear whether exposure to toxic chemicals at low (sub-threshold) levels may produce any health response. Although society's concern about the health effects of exposure to environmental pollutants has increased, it still remains unclear whether chronic exposures to toxic chemical agents in the environment occur at high enough doses to affect human health. Nevertheless, environmental scientists have had increasing concerns over the long-term effects of low-level exposures to toxic substances, exposures such as those that may take place in the workplace.

Lethal Dose 50 (LD$_{50}$)

To describe toxic effects, toxicologists use the symbol **LD$_{50}$ (lethal dose 50)**, which is "the dosage (mg/kg body weight) causing death in 50 percent of exposed animals."[6(p7)] One of the applications of LD$_{50}$ is to compare the toxicities of chemicals (i.e., to describe whether one chemical is more or less toxic than another). Other variations of the term *lethal dose* include LD$_{10}$ and LD$_{90}$ (10% and 90% mortality, respectively). Lethality tests are becoming rare in research due to the availability of less destructive methods of study.

Dose–Response Relationships

One of the most basic toxicologic concepts, a dose-response relationship, refers to a type of correlative relationship between "the characteristics of exposure to a chemical and the spectrum of effects caused by the chemical."[16(p61)] The existence of a dose–response relationship may be used to establish the following kinds of information[15]:

- Causal association between a toxin and biological effects
- Minimum dosages needed to produce a biological effect
- Rate of accumulation of harmful effects

▶ Factors that Affect Responses to a Toxic Chemical

Several factors determine whether an individual will respond to exposure to a toxic chemical and the type of response that occurs.[17] The nature of a toxic effect depends on the innate toxicity of the chemical, whether it is in sufficient concentration, and how it impinges upon a somatic location as a consequence of the route and site of exposure. In addition, exposure needs to take place for a sufficient time duration and frequency: The effects of a one-time exposure of short duration are usually different from those of an exposure that happens on several occasions over a long period of time. Other factors are related to a person's sensitivity to a chemical, for example, one's ability to metabolize the chemical (through biological processes that convert the chemical into either less harmful or more harmful substances). The concentration and toxicity of the chemical are affected by the following:

- Route of entry into the body
- Received dose of the chemical
  - Duration of exposure
  - Interactions that transpire among multiple chemicals
  - Individual sensitivity

Route and Site of Entry

The most frequent sites of exposure to environmental (i.e., xenobiotic) chemicals include the gastrointestinal tract, the respiratory system, and the skin. (Refer to **TABLE 2**.) With respect to route of exposure, chemicals may enter the body intentionally (as in the example of medical interventions) or unintentionally (through injuries or environmental exposures). Illustrations of the routes of exposure corresponding to the sites of entry are ingestion (e.g., consumption of contaminated food or drink), injections into the bloodstream, contact with the surface of the skin (topical mode), and inhalation. With respect to inhalation, when we breathe contaminated air (for instance, at work), potentially dangerous particles and gases may enter our bodies and be absorbed into the bloodstream by the alveoli of the lungs without producing any warning symptoms. These chemicals later may cause serious lung diseases, including lung cancer. In some cases the absorbed chemicals may affect other organs such as the brain.

As mentioned previously, other routes of exposure include skin contact, eye contact, and ingestion. The skin forms a protective barrier that can be compromised by dehydration, physical damage, caustic chemicals, and organic solvents; the result is that chemicals may bypass the barrier and enter the bloodstream. The eyes are particularly vulnerable to chemical exposure, especially when chemicals splash into the eye during an accident. Finally, employees who work with toxic chemicals may unwittingly ingest such chemicals when they smoke or eat on the job; in addition, workers unintentionally may transport them home on their clothing and skin.

How quickly a chemical produces acute and other effects depends on the site and route of exposure.[6] Among possible sites and routes, contact with the skin generally produces the slowest response, and direct injection into the bloodstream typically yields the fastest and strongest effects. (Refer to Table 2.)

Length and Duration of Exposure

Toxicologists describe the duration of exposure in a range from acute to chronic. Relevant terms are defined in the following box.

The duration of exposure is important from the toxicologic point of view because the effects of exposure to many chemicals may vary depending on whether the exposure is minimal and takes place on a single occasion for a short time period or is heavy and long-standing. Some workers (for example, agricultural workers) receive exposures to pesticides in greater concentrations and over much longer time periods than does the general population. Acute exposures may produce acute effects that disappear rapidly, although this outcome is not invariable. In comparison with short-term exposures, chronic exposures may allow for the buildup of effects over time with the resulting accumulation of biological damage. However, such accumulation may not occur if the chemical is excreted before the next exposure happens.

Effects of Chemical Mixtures

In the "real world" of environmental exposures, most exposures are to multiple chemicals rather than to a

TABLE 2 Ranking of the Relative Speed of Effect According to the Site and Route of Exposure		
Site	**Route**	**Relative Speed of Effect[a]**
Bloodstream	Intravenous	++++++++
Lungs	Inhalation	+++++++
Other	Intraperitoneal	++++++
Other	Subcutaneous	+++++
Other	Intramuscular	++++
Other	Intradermal	+++
Gastrointestinal	Ingestion (oral route)	++
Skin	Dermal	+

[a]The greater the number of plus signs (+), the faster the effect; e.g., when chemicals enter the bloodstream directly they usually have the fastest effect.
Data from Eaton DL, Gilbert SG. Principles of toxicology. In: Klaasen CD, Watkins JB III, eds. *Casarett & Doull's Essentials of Toxicology*. 3rd ed. New York, NY: McGraw-Hill, 2015:9.

> **LIST OF TERMS THAT DESCRIBE DURATION OF EXPOSURE**
>
> *Acute*—Usually a single exposure for less than 24 hours
> *Subacute*—Repeated exposure for 1 month or less
> *Subchronic*—Repeated exposure for 1 to 3 months
> *Chronic*—Repeated exposure for more than 3 months

Reproduced from Eaton DL, Gilbert SG. Principles of toxicology. In: Klaasen CD, Watkins JB III, eds. *Casarett & Doull's Essentials of Toxicology*. 3rd ed. New York, NY: McGraw-Hill, 2015;9.

single chemical. By way of example, the ambient air in a factory may contain a soup of chemicals that impinge upon the production workers. Toxicologists and others have observed that when chemicals mix, they may produce surprising effects—sometimes their combined effects may be greater and sometimes less than expected. When an organism is exposed to two or more chemicals, their combined effects may be additive, synergistic, antagonistic, or coalitive; some chemicals may cause potentiation. **Additive** means that the combination of two chemicals produces an effect that is equal to their individual effects added together. The term **synergism** (from the Greek word *synergos*—working together) indicates that the combined effect of exposures to two or more chemicals is greater than the sum of their individual effects.

There are many examples of synergism in the field of environmental health. One is the interaction between asbestos and smoking in causing lung cancer. The prominent medical researcher Irvine Selikoff and associates demonstrated that lung cancer mortality risk among asbestos insulation workers was much higher among those who smoked in comparison with those who did not smoke.[18] A second example pertains to the synergistic effects of solvents (e.g., n-hexane and methyl ethyl ketone [MEK]). These chemicals, when acting simultaneously on the nervous system, produce a much greater combined effect than would be expected from their simple additive individual effects.[19]

Another type of interaction between two chemicals is called **potentiation**, which happens when one chemical that is not toxic causes another chemical to become more toxic.[6] For example, isopropanol by itself is not toxic to the liver but has the capacity to increase the liver toxicity of carbon tetrachloride when exposure of the two chemicals occurs together. In a **coalitive interaction**, several agents that have no known toxic effects interact to produce a toxic effect.[20]

The term **antagonism** means that "two chemicals administered together interfere with each other's actions or one interferes with the action of the other. . . ."[6(p8)] In illustration, supplemental vitamins may reduce the effects of needed prescription medicines such as antibiotics; an example is the antagonistic relationship between calcium and tetracycline.

Individual Responses to Toxic Exposures

The responses of individuals to toxic substances can vary greatly, ranging from no apparent response to severe responses. Responses may vary according to age, sex, race, and health status. Other influences include the person's genetic background, use of medications, consumption of alcohol, and pregnancy

status. Some chemicals (e.g., bee venom) produce severe or life-threatening reactions in persons afflicted with allergies.

The term **chemical allergy** refers to "an immunologically mediated adverse reaction to a chemical resulting from previous sensitization to that chemical or to a structurally similar one."[6(p10)] Some of the alternative terms used to describe this response are hypersensitivity, allergic reaction, and sensitization reaction. After initial sensitization, small doses of a chemical may bring about an allergic reaction. Some genetically predisposed persons may be prone to *chemical idiosyncrasy*, meaning that they have either extreme sensitivity to low doses of a chemical or insensitivity to high doses.

Recall that the term *xenobiotics* refers to foreign chemicals that are introduced into the body. Although their effects may be beneficial, they also may produce adverse effects at the same time; these adverse effects may occur either directly or indirectly. A direct effect denotes an immediate impact upon the cells and tissues of the body or upon specific target organs. An indirect effect would be a change in the function of the body's biochemical processes. Examples of direct and indirect adverse effects are shown in **TABLE 3**.

Direct adverse effects of exposures to chemicals range from local effects to systemic effects to target organ effects. These terms are defined as follows:

Local effects—Damage at the site where a chemical first comes into contact with the body; examples are redness, burning, and irritation of the skin.

Systemic effects—Adverse effects associated with generalized distribution of the chemical throughout the body by the bloodstream to internal organs.

TABLE 3 Direct and Indirect Adverse Effects of Xenobiotics

Direct Adverse Effects	Indirect Adverse Effects
Cell replacement, such as fibrosis (buildup of scar tissue)	Modification of an essential biochemical function
Damage to an enzyme system	Interference with nutrition
Disruption of protein synthesis	Alteration of a physiological mechanism
Production of reactive chemicals in cells	
DNA damage	

Modified from National Library of Medicine, *Toxicology Tutor I. Basic Principles: Toxic Effects*. Available at: http://www.sis.nlm.nih.gov/enviro/toxtutor/Tox1/a31.htm. Accessed April 21, 2017.

Target organ effects—Some chemicals may confine their effects to specific organs; the most common organs affected by such chemicals are the liver, lungs, heart, kidneys, brain and nervous system, and the reproductive system.

FIGURE 8 differentiates between a systemic and organ toxicant.

Latency and Delayed Responses to Toxic Substances

The term *latency* refers to the time period between initial exposure and a measurable response. The latency period can range from a few seconds (in the case of acutely toxic agents) to several decades for agents that may be carcinogenic.

One example of a delayed effect of exposure to chemicals is carcinogenesis, the potential to induce cancerous growth of cells. The word **carcinogen** denotes a chemical (or substance) that causes or is suspected of causing cancer, a disease associated with unregulated proliferation of cells in the body. In fact, many forms of cancer are believed to have a latency period of 10 years up to 40 years (counting the time between first exposure to a carcinogen and the subsequent development of cancer). For example, mesothelioma (a rare form of thoracic or abdominal cancer) has a latency period as long as 40 years between first exposure to asbestos and subsequent development of the condition.

The long latency for many of the health events studied in environmental research makes detection of the effects of exposures to toxic substances a methodologically difficult problem. For human exposures, toxicologists may be unable to differentiate among exposures to multiple chemicals or to rule out the impacts of confounding factors (discussed in the chapter on environmental epidemiology) that may be implicated in carcinogenesis.

Methods of Testing for Toxicity

The subjects used for testing the toxicity of chemicals include the following[21]:

- Volunteers who have had normal or accidental exposures
- Animals exposed purposively (in vivo experiments)
- Cells derived from human, animal, or plant sources (in vitro experiments)

Toxicity testing that uses these categories of subjects may take the form of epidemiologic investigations (described in the chapter on environmental epidemiology), formal clinical trials, or animal studies.

In the United States, randomized controlled clinical trials are regulated by the Food and Drug Administration (FDA). They are used to evaluate the safety of new drugs in humans, following tests in animals. The trials are conducted in three phases, beginning with small groups of patients and gradually expanding to larger patient populations after an earlier phase has demonstrated the safety and efficacy of the drug in question. Before the advent of rigorous clinical trials, new drugs could enter the marketplace without the benefit of evaluation. A notorious example is the drug thalidomide, which, when administered to pregnant women outside the United States (e.g., in Europe, Japan, Australia, and Canada) was found to be a potent teratogen (a drug or other substance that causes birth defects). Not approved for use in the United States, thalidomide was prescribed during the late 1950s to treat morning sickness in pregnant women (refer to the following textbox). As a result, these women gave birth to more than 10,000 children who had severe birth defects, such as missing limbs.[22]

Even with the use of clinical trials, new drugs entering the marketplace still may have potential to cause harm. An example that occurred in 2005

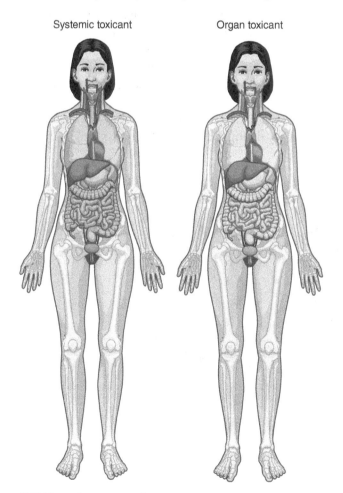

Systemic toxicant   Organ toxicant

FIGURE 8 Systemic and organ toxicant.

involved Vioxx (used to control pain among arthritis patients), which was thought to increase the risk of heart problems.

When highly controlled and standardized conditions are desired, animal models are used in toxicologic testing. Another purpose for the use of animals is in preliminary testing of pharmaceuticals, pesticides, and substances that may present toxic hazards to human subjects. Standard protocols using animals evaluate the acute effects of chemicals, as well as toxicity to specific organs. Another concern of animal assays for toxicity is damage to the reproductive system or offspring. Animal protocols also are applied to measure the carcinogenic potential of chemicals. Research and toxicity testing may require the use of multiple animal species, including rats, mice, rabbits, dogs, and monkeys. Animal studies aid in preventing highly toxic chemicals from being introduced into human populations. Often alternatives such as in vitro studies have been employed as a means of reducing experimentation with live animals.

One focus of evaluation is the role of chemicals in causing toxicity to nucleic acids; some results might be mutations, chromosomal abnormalities, and DNA damage. In these studies, tests may be conducted with bacteria, fruit flies, and cell lines from animals or humans.

▶ Links Between Toxicology and Risk Assessment

Once we have obtained toxicologic information regarding the nature and health effects of a chemical, we would like to be able to determine the risks to health that the chemical represents. Let us examine the concept of risk briefly. One can never be free from all risk to health and well-being. Even the most benign activities carry risk; for example, while riding on a busy street, a bicyclist may be struck by a car. Perhaps the person chose to ride a bicycle in order to avoid the financial risk of owning a car. Thus, many aspects of life involve weighing risks (e.g., buying versus renting a house, investing in stocks versus purchasing a certificate of deposit, or choosing a potential life partner) and then making a decision about what action to take. The concept of risk can be classified according to levels from low risk activities such as riding a bicycle (while wearing a protective helmet) to higher risk activities such as sky diving. Refer to **FIGURE 9**.

FIGURE 9 Risk levels.
© phoelixDE/Shutterstock

In simple terms, a risk involves the likelihood of experiencing an adverse effect. The term **risk assessment** refers to "a process for identifying adverse consequences and their associated probability."[23(p611)] Risk assessment is "[t]he process of determining risks to health attributable to environmental or other hazards."[4] "Risk research addresses the identification and management of situations that might result in losses or harm, immediate or delayed, to individuals, groups, or even to whole communities or ecosystems, often as a result of the interaction of human activities with natural processes."[24(px)] Risk assessment provides a qualitative or quantitative estimation of the likelihood of adverse effects that may result from exposure to specified health hazards or from the absence of beneficial influences. "Risk assessment uses clinical, epidemiologic, toxicologic, environmental, and any other pertinent data."[4]

The meaning of the term *risk* varies greatly not only from one person to another, but also between lay persons and professionals; the latter characterize risk mainly in terms of mortality.[25] In a psychometric study, psychology professor Paul Slovic reported that lay persons classified risk according to two major factors. His methods enabled risks to be portrayed in a two-dimensional space so that their relative positions could be compared. The two factors that Slovic identified were the following:

Factor 1, labeled "dread risk," is defined at its high (right-hand) end by perceived lack of control, dread, catastrophic potential, fatal consequences, and the inequitable distribution of risks and benefits. . . .

Factor 2, labeled "unknown risk," is defined at its high end by hazards judged to be unobservable, unknown, new, and delayed in their manifestation of harm.[25(p283)]

Refer to **FIGURE 10**, which maps the spatial relationships among a large number of risks according to the two major factors shown in the figure. For example, nuclear reactor accidents fall in the space that defines uncontrollable dread factors that are of unknown risk. In other words, nuclear reactor accidents fall in the quadrant defined by both high levels of unknown risk and high levels of dread risk. In contrast, home swimming pools are perceived as falling in the quadrant in which risks are not dread and are known to those exposed.

Risk assessment generally takes place in four steps: (1) hazard identification, (2) dose–response assessment, (3) exposure assessment, and (4) risk characterization.[26,27] Refer to **FIGURE 11** for an illustration of the four step risk assessment process. The term

risk management shown in the figure is discussed in the chapter on environmental policy and regulation.

Hazard Identification

Hazard identification (hazard assessment) "examines the evidence that associates exposure to an agent with its toxicity and produces a qualitative judgment about the strength of that evidence, whether it is derived from human epidemiology or extrapolated from laboratory animal data."[27(p286)] Evidence regarding hazards linked to toxic substances may be derived from the study of health effects among exposed humans and animals. These health effects may range from dramatic outcomes such as mortality or cancer to lower-level conditions such as developmental delays in children and reductions in immune status.[26]

A *hazard* is defined as the "[i]nherent capability of a natural or human-made agent or process to adversely affect human life, health, property, or activity, with the potential to cause a DISEASE, EPIDEMIC, ACCIDENT, or DISASTER."[4] Hazards may originate from chemicals, biological agents, physical and mechanical energy and force, and psychosocial influences. We have covered the toxic agents such as organic toxins and chemicals. Examples of other hazards will be covered in more detail elsewhere in the text. Some physical hazards arise from ionizing radiation from medical X-rays and naturally occurring background radiation.

Other hazards originate from nonionizing radiation—sunlight, infrared and ultraviolet light, and electromagnetic radiation from power lines and radio transmissions. In urban and work environments, mechanical energy is associated with high levels of noise that can be hazardous for hearing and for psychological well-being. Examples of psychosocial hazards are work-related stresses, combat fatigue, and posttraumatic stress disorder (topics not covered in this text).

Dose–Response Assessment

Dose–response assessment is the measurement of "the relationship between the amount of exposure and the occurrence of the unwanted health effects."[26(p38)] According to Russell and Gruber:

Dose-response assessment examines the quantitative relation between the experimentally administered dose level of a toxicant and the incidence or severity or both of a response in test animals, and draws inferences for humans. The presumed human dosages and incidences in human populations may also be used in cases where epidemiological studies are available.[27(p286)]

Content removed due to copyright restrictions

FIGURE 10 Location of 81 hazards on factors 1 and 2 derived from the relationships among 15 risk characteristics.

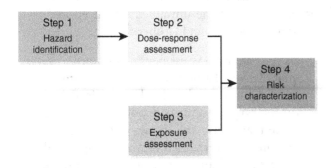

FIGURE 11 The four-step risk assessment process.

Modified from US EPA. Risk assessment. Human health risk assessment. Available at: https://www.epa.gov/risk/human-health-risk-assessment. Accessed February 8, 2017.

Exposure Assessment

Exposure assessment is defined as the procedure that "identifies populations exposed to the toxicant, describes their composition and size, and examines the roots, magnitudes, frequencies, and durations of such exposures."[27(p286)] **FIGURE 12** summarizes the three key steps in exposure assessment. The text box provides a more detailed overview of the steps involved in an exposure assessment.

The process of human exposure assessment is believed to be one of the weakest aspects of risk

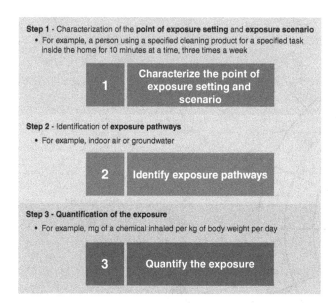

Step 1 - Characterization of the **point of exposure setting** and **exposure scenario**
- For example, a person using a specified cleaning product for a specified task inside the home for 10 minutes at a time, three times a week

1	Characterize the point of exposure setting and scenario

Step 2 - Identification of **exposure pathways**
- For example, indoor air or groundwater

2	Identify exposure pathways

Step 3 - Quantification of the exposure
- For example, mg of a chemical inhaled per kg of body weight per day

3	Quantify the exposure

FIGURE 12 The three-step process in exposure assessment.

Modified from ToxTutor. Available at: https://toxtutor.nlm.nih.gov/06-004.html. Accessed April 13, 2017.

assessment. Available methods are unable to provide adequate quantitative information regarding how much humans are exposed to toxic substances as well as the specific kinds and patterns of exposure.[28] The quality of exposure assessment data determines the accuracy of risk assessments and therefore is a limiting factor in the risk assessment process.[29]

When referring to a toxic substance, exposure assessment must take into account where the exposure occurs, how much exposure occurs, and how the substance is absorbed by the body. The process of human exposure assessment examines "the manner in which pollutants come into actual contact with the human body—the concentration levels at the points of contact and the sources of these pollutants making contact. The key word here is *contact*—the occurrence of two events at the same location and same time."[30(p449)] The methods by which human beings are exposed to toxic substances include encountering them in water,

WHAT IS AN EXPOSURE ASSESSMENT?

Suppose we would like to conduct an exposure assessment of an exposure to a toxic agent such as a chemical. For human populations, an exposure assessment with respect to toxic agents may be elucidated by the following components:

- **Magnitude:** How large is the exposure?
- **Frequency:** How often does an exposure take place?
- **Duration:** Over what time period has an exposure occurred?
- **Future exposures:** What is the estimate for future exposures?
- **Exposure pathways:** How does the agent move from its source to the individual?
- **Exposure routes:** How does the agent gain access to the body?

In addition, one needs to consider the characteristics of the population that is exposed. For example, how widespread is the exposure? And also, what are the exposed population's characteristics in terms of age, race, vulnerabilities, and related dimensions?

Exposure pathways include the processes for movement of substances from their sources to the people who are exposed. Exposure routes (concerned with contact with an agent) are modes of entry into the body. Examples of entry sites are through a body orifice (e.g., direct ingestion and inhalation) and via skin contact. Consider an employment-related example; workers might inadvertently ingest a toxic industrial chemical that has contaminated food or beverages brought to work. Community residents might inhale pesticides applied to agricultural fields. Another route is direct absorption of a toxic chemical through the skin when someone touches a toxic chemical.

An exposure assessment in the community could determine which people are being exposed as well as their varying levels of exposure. This procedure delineates the range of exposures. For example, let's assume that we would like to know a community's range of exposures to a toxic chemical at a factory. Hypothetically speaking, employees inside the factory might have the highest levels of exposure to the chemical. (It should be noted that most modern industrial concerns have developed protections for minimizing employee exposures.) The next highest levels of exposure would occur among persons who live or play downwind from the factory. Lower exposures would impinge upon residents in the geographic area surrounding the factory but not immediately downwind from the pollution source. (See **FIGURE 13**.)

Another crucial issue for exposure assessment is how to quantify exposures. One way this can be accomplished is by measuring exposures at their point of contact with the body; for example, by placing exposure measuring devices such as radiation monitors on the person of exposed individuals. Another method is to place monitoring devices strategically throughout the community. An example would be locating measuring devices for air pollution near sources of pollution, e.g., major highways. Also used are modeling techniques to predict exposures. Finally, at the individual level, one may also be able to quantify exposures by measuring biomarkers, excretions of chemicals from the body, and related methods that employ internal indicators of exposure. Internal indicators "reconstruct" exposures that have already happened.

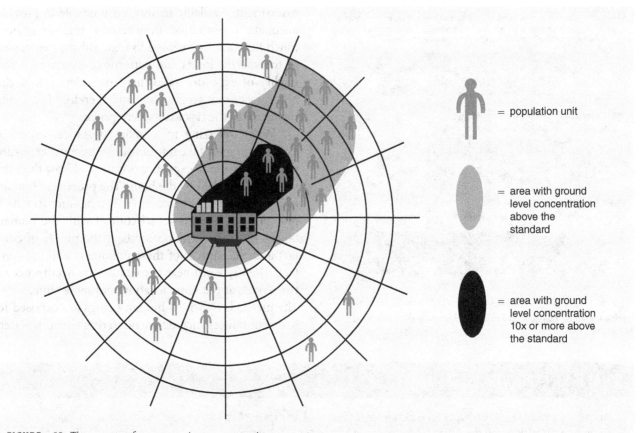

FIGURE 13 The range of exposure in a community.

Modified from US EPA. Risk assessment. Human health risk assessment. Available at: https://www.epa.gov/risk/human-health-risk-assessment. Accessed February 8, 2017.

Data from US Environmental Protection Agency. Conducting an exposure assessment. Step 3: Exposure Assessment. Available at: https://www.epa.gov/conducting-human-health-risk-assessment. Accessed March 14, 2017, and ToxTutor. Exposure Assessment. Available at: https://toxtutor.nlm.nih.gov/06-004.html. Accessed March 13, 2017.

air, food, soil, and various consumer products and medications.

As noted previously in the chapter on environmental epidemiology, high-quality data on exposure are necessary for making valid interpretations of a study's findings.[31] Several methods of exposure assessment (e.g., personal exposure monitoring and use of biological markers) are employed in toxicology, environmental epidemiology, and other environmental health disciplines. In some exposure assessments sampling devices may be placed in the community in order to determine the population's range of exposures. In tracking exposures to emissions from an industrial plant, researchers may find that the highest exposures occur downwind and closest to the plants. Figure 13 illustrates the range of exposure in a community. (Refer to the text box on exposure assessment for more information.)

During a review of records to assess exposure, the investigator may select a study population from personnel records maintained by a company. If the records of former and retired workers are retained by the company, a complete data set spanning long time periods may be available. Ideally, every previous and current worker exposed to the factor should be included. Selection bias may occur if some workers are excluded because their records have been purged from the company's database.[32] Data collected from employment records may include:

- Personal identifiers to permit record linkage to Social Security Administration files and retrieval of death certificates
- Demographic characteristics, length of employment, and work history with the company
- Information about potential confounding variables, such as the employee's medical history, smoking habits, lifestyle, and family history of disease

Some environmental studies use biomarkers that may be correlated with exposures to potential carcinogens and other chemicals. These biomarkers involve changes in genetic structure that are thought to be the consequence of an exposure.

One marker is called a **sister chromatid exchange (SCE)**. SCEs refer to reciprocal exchanges of deoxyribonucleic acid (DNA) between pairs of DNA molecules.[33] In a study of exposure to styrene gas (involved in boat building and plastics manufacture), researchers examined the utility of SCEs in comparison with environmental monitoring, and exhaled styrene levels as alternative measures of styrene exposure.[34] The use of biomarkers such as SCEs is growing in the environmental health field.

Risk Characterization

Risk characterization develops "estimates of the number of excess unwarranted health events expected at different time intervals at each level of exposure."[26(p38)] Risk characterization follows the three foregoing steps by integrating the information from hazard identification, dose–response assessment, and exposure assessment.[35] The process of risk characterization yields "[a] synthesis and summary of information about a hazard that addresses the needs and interests of decision makers and of interested and affected parties. Risk characterization is a prelude to decision making and depends on an iterative, analytic-deliberative process."[36(p216)] "Risk characterization presents the policy maker with a synopsis of all the information that contributes to a conclusion about the nature of the risk and evaluates the magnitudes of the uncertainties involved and the major assumptions that were used."[27(p286)]

Risk Management

Oriented toward specific actions, risk management "consists of actions taken to control exposures to toxic chemicals in the environment. Exposure standards, requirements for premarket testing, recalls of toxic products, and outright banning of very hazardous materials are among the actions that are used by governmental agencies to manage risk."[26(p37)] This topic is covered more fully in the chapter on environmental policy and regulation.

▶ Conclusion

Toxicology, the science of poisons, is a powerful and important discipline for protecting human health and the environment. Often, toxicologists work collaboratively with specialists in other, overlapping fields, such as epidemiology. Toxicology has a lengthy and distinguished history, beginning with ancient civilizations. This chapter has covered some of the important terminology used to characterize the effects of xenobiotics on biological systems. Two of these concepts are the lethal dose and dose–response curves.

Environmental chemicals have differing effects upon humans, depending upon a number of factors that include route of entry into the body, received dose, duration of exposure, interactions among chemicals, and individual sensitivity. Toxicology is an important component of risk assessment.

Despite the many helpful applications of toxicology, the field has some limitations as well. First, the laboratory models used (in vivo and in vitro) may not completely represent environmental conditions, which often are more complex than those conditions found in controlled settings. Also, toxicology, by looking only at adverse effects, ignores benefits important to human health and welfare that may also be present.

Study Questions and Exercises

1. Define environmental toxicology. Give an example of a study that would be relevant to this field.
2. What were the contributions of Paracelsus to toxicology?
3. Define the terms teratogen, xenobiotic, and carcinogen.
4. Explain the difference between toxins and toxicants. Give an example of each. How does a toxin differ from a poison?
5. State what is meant by the term LD_{50}.
6. What determines the toxicity of a chemical? To what extent do you agree with the assumption that "all substances are poisons"?
7. Describe methods for testing the toxicity of chemicals.
8. Explain the significance of duration of exposure from a toxicity point of view. What are the terms used to describe the different ranges of exposure?
9. What is latency? How does the issue of latency challenge environmental researchers who are trying to detect hazards associated with specific exposures?
10. Describe the typical shape of the population dose–response curve and explain why it is shaped this way.
11. Define the terms *dose* and *threshold*. Draw a figure to illustrate a threshold.
12. Explain the differences among synergism, antagonism, and potentiation. Give specific examples of each.
13. What is meant by the term *risk assessment*? Describe the steps that constitute risk assessment. Give an example of each step.
14. What is human exposure assessment? Describe some of the methods of exposure assessment.

For Further Reading

Newman C. 12 Toxic Tales, *National Geographic*, May 2005, 2-31.

References

1. US Department of Health and Human Services, Public Health Service, National Toxicology Program (NTP). About NTP. Available at: US Department of Health and Human Services, Public Health Service, National Toxicology Program. Accessed March 9, 2017.
2. Gallo MA. History and scope of toxicology. In: Klaasen CD, Watkins JB III, eds. *Casarett & Doull's Essentials of Toxicology*. 3rd ed. New York, NY: McGraw-Hill, 2015.
3. Henry CJ, Phillips R, Carpanini F, et al. Use of genomics in toxicology and epidemiology: findings and recommendations of a workshop. *Environ Health Perspect*. 2002;110:1047–1050.
4. Porta M, ed. *A Dictionary of Epidemiology*. 6th ed. New York, NY: Oxford University Press; 2014.
5. Weed DL. Environmental epidemiology basics and proof of cause-effect. *Toxicol*. 2002;181–182:399–403.
6. Eaton DL, Gilbert SG. Principles of toxicology. In: Klaasen CD, Watkins JB III, eds. *Casarett & Doull's Essentials of Toxicology*. 3rd ed. New York, NY: McGraw-Hill, 2015.
7. Borzelleca JF. Profiles in toxicology. Paracelsus: herald of modern toxicology. *Toxicol Sci*. 2000;53:2–4.
8. Landis WG, Sofield RM, Yu M-H. *Introduction to Environmental Toxicology*. 4th ed. Boca Raton, FL: CRC Press: 2010.
9. Briggs GB. Risk assessment policy for evaluating reproductive system toxicants and the impact of responses on sensitive populations. *Toxicol*. 1996;111:305–313.
10. Schwetz BA. Noncancer risk assessment: reproductive toxicology. *Drug Metab Rev*. 1996;28(1–2):77–84.
11. Online Medical Dictionary. Xenobiotics. Available at: http://www.online-medical-dictionary.org/definitions-x/xenobiotics.html. Accessed March 10, 2017.
12. National Library of Medicine. Welcome to ToxTutor. Available at: https://toxtutor.nlm.nih.gov/index.html. Accessed March 10, 2017.
13. Hyperdictionary. Meaning of toxicity. Available at: http://www.hyperdictionary.com/dictionary/toxicity. Accessed April 11, 2017.
14. Fox DA, Boyes WK. Toxic responses of the ocular and visual system. In: Klaasen CD, Watkins JB III, eds. *Casarett & Doull's Essentials of Toxicology*. 3rd ed. New York, NY: McGraw-Hill, 2015.
15. National Library of Medicine. *Toxicology Tutor I*. Basic principles: dose and dose response—dose. Available at: http://sis.nlm.nih.gov/enviro/toxtutor/Tox1/a21.htm. Accessed April 18, 2017.
16. National Institutes of Health, National Institute of Environmental Health Sciences. *Chemicals, the Environment, and You: Explorations in Science and Human Health*. Dose-response relationships. Available at: http://science.education.nih.gov/supplements/nih2/chemicals/guide/pdfs/lesson3.pdf. Accessed April 11, 2017.
17. Health Evaluation System and Information Service (HESIS), Occupational Health Branch, California Department of Public Health. Understanding toxic substances: an introduction to chemical hazards in the workplace. 2008 edition. Richmond, CA: HESIS; 2008.
18. Selikoff IJ, Hammond EC, Churg J. Asbestos exposure, smoking, and neoplasia. *JAMA*. 1968;204:104–112.
19. Australian Government, National Occupational Health and Safety Commission. Synergism and potentiation. Available at: http://www.safeworkaustralia.gov.au/sites/SWA/about/Publications/Documents/238/GuidanceNote_InterpretationOfExposureStandardsForAtmosphericContaminants_3rdEdition_NOHSC3008-1995_PDF.pdf. Accessed April 17, 2017.
20. Suk WA, Olden K. Multidisciplinary research: strategies for assessing chemical mixtures to reduce risk of exposure and disease. *Int J Occup Med Environ Health*. 2004;17:103–110.
21. National Library of Medicine. *Toxicology Tutor I*. Basic principles: toxicity testing methods. Available at: http://sis.nlm.nih.gov/enviro/toxtutor/Tox1/a51.htm. Accessed April 18, 2017.
22. Pannikar V. The return of thalidomide: new uses and renewed concerns. Available at: http://www.who.int/lep/research/Thalidomide.pdf. World Health Organization. Accessed April 17, 2017.
23. McKone TE. The rise of exposure assessment among the risk sciences: an evaluation through case studies. *Inhal Toxicol*. 1999;11:611–622.
24. Amendola A, Wilkinson DR. Risk assessment and environmental policy making. *J Hazard Mater*. 2000;78:ix–xiv.
25. Slovic P. Perception of risk. *Science*. 1987;236:280–285.
26. Landrigan PJ, Carlson JE. Environmental policy and children's health. *The Future of Children*. 1995;5(2):34–52.
27. Russell M, Gruber M. Risk assessment in environmental policy-making. *Science*. 1987;236:286–290.
28. US Department of Health and Human Services, National Toxicology Program. Human exposure assessment. Available at: http://webharvest.gov/peth04/20041020135705/ntp.niehs.nih.gov/index.cfm?objectid=06F6F41D-9B12-8FD0-63E4048B173CC36A. Accessed April 17, 2017.
29. Lippmann M, Thurston GD. Exposure assessment: input into risk assessment. *Arch Environ Health*. 1988;43:113–123.
30. Ott WR. Human exposure assessment: the birth of a new science. *J Expos Anal Environ Epidem*. 1995;5:449–472.
31. Gardner MJ. Epidemiological studies of environmental exposure and specific diseases. *Arch Environ Health*. 1988; 43:102–108.
32. Monson RR. *Occupational Epidemiology*. Boca Raton, FL: CRC Press; 1990.
33. Hyperdictionary. Meaning of sister chromatid exchange. Available at: http://www.hyperdictionary.com/dictionary/sister+chromatid+exchange. Accessed April 17, 2017.
34. Rappaport SM, Symanski E, Yager JW, et al. The relationship between environmental monitoring and biological markers in exposure assessment. *Environ Health Perspect*. 1995;103 (Suppl 3):49–54.
35. Duffus JH. Risk assessment terminology. *Chemistry International*. 2001;23(2):34–39.
36. Stern PC, Fineberg HV, eds. *Understanding Risk: Informing Decisions in a Democratic Society*. National Academy of Sciences' National Research Council, Committee on Risk Characterization. Washington, DC: National Academy Press; 1996.

Environmental Policy and Regulation

LEARNING OBJECTIVES

By the end of this chapter the reader will be able to:

- Contrast key environmental health regulatory agencies at three levels.
- State four principles that guide environmental policy development.
- Compare five major environmental laws.
- Describe environmental policies designed to protect vulnerable groups.
- Apply the steps in the policy-making process to a specific example.

▶ Introduction

In this chapter you will learn how governments, advocacy groups and other organizations, and stakeholders create environmental policies for the mitigation of environmental hazards and protection of the health of the planet. (See **FIGURE 1** for the major topic of this chapter.) We will present terminology and concepts related to the environmental policy process. Also described are some of the major US governmental and international agencies charged with the development, adoption, and enforcement of environmental policies and regulations. The chapter also will cite some of the US laws and regulations that have been developed to protect air and water quality and natural resources and to safeguard the public against hazards that originate from toxic substances and wastes. Throughout this discussion you will need to keep in mind how policy development is an imperfect process that often reflects the tension

that exists between political influences and scientific knowledge.

FIGURE 1 Environmental policy.

© Stuart Miles/Shutterstock

The Role of Policy and Environmental Challenges

During the current century, human illness and death linked to environmental exposures represent one of the most significant challenges to the world's inhabitants. To date, extensive resources have been expended in the implementation of public policies, regulations, and laws that are designed to protect the health of the public from environmentally caused diseases. Nevertheless, much more work needs to be completed. Referring specifically to the United States, Bailus Walker, the past president of the American Public Health Association, noted:

Despite these investments—which amount to billions of dollars—we have not at all completed the task of preventing environmentally provoked disease and of providing more protection for the ecological system. Even an abbreviated list will show how many problems remain to be solved: an epidemic of childhood lead poisoning, the increasing incidence of genetic diseases exacerbated by environmental stressors, pesticides in food and water, too much ozone at ground level and too little in the stratosphere, global temperature warming, slow implementation of national toxic waste policies, and flaws in the institutions and processes the nation relies on to reduce environmental risks. Obviously, environmental health activities cannot be narrowly focused but must recognize the critical interrelationships between environmental media and between policies and programs.[1(p1395)]

Increasingly, protection from environmentally associated health hazards is regarded as a fundamental human right; policy making will need to take into account the reduction of disparities in health status that result from environmental sources. Momentum is gathering for the development of policies that protect the health of vulnerable population groups such as children, who may be even more susceptible to the actions of environmental toxins than adults. For example, data have shown an increasing occurrence of childhood asthma, which may be linked to air pollution.

Overview of the Environmental Policy Process

This overview will define and explain the following terms and concepts related to the policy process:

- Environmental policy
- Principles of environmental policy development
- The policy cycle
- The interplay between the evaluation process and policy development

Some argue that a systems approach—holistic thinking—is essential for policy development in the arena of the environment, which may be thought of as a set of interconnected elements or subsystems.[2] These include scientific, economic, cultural, and political dimensions that are relevant to the formulation and implementation of particular environmental policies. An example relates to the problem of agricultural pollution, which poses health hazards from animal wastes, fertilizers, and pesticides. Farming practices are designed to maximize output, using economic, climatic, and land use criteria. In addition to taking into account the health consequences of agricultural pollution, environmental policies also need to consider economic factors such as market costs that influence agricultural practices.[3] Another economic factor concerns stakeholders' willingness to pay for the costs necessitated by policy programs. Good policy decisions can be made if data on the economic costs and benefits of the policy package and its components are available.[4]

The environmental policy process takes place within the political context and reflects tension between political considerations and scientific knowledge. In some instances, the public may reject environmental policies that are justified scientifically. In illustration, research has suggested that logging of the nation's forests contributes to increases in greenhouse gases; as a result, some municipalities may decide to prohibit logging in order to protect the natural environment. However, in communities supported by lumber production, residents may oppose restrictions on logging because such prohibitions cause widespread unemployment. Another example is the reactivation of coal mining and fossil fuel extraction in order to create employment opportunities for miners.

In other instances, politics may be instrumental in the adoption of environmental policies that might not be scientifically justified. For example, scientific findings may demonstrate that the low levels of some pollutants in the water supply are unlikely to have adverse human health impacts. Nevertheless, consumers may demand that such pollutants be removed completely from the water supply even if their removal is very costly.

Public demonstrations in support of environmental causes is another example of the political process in action. Groups have demonstrated against attempts to exploit parks, government lands, and sensitive areas for resource extraction. Other demonstrations have been in support of environmental justice and in response to disasters such as oil spills. (See **FIGURE 2.**)

FIGURE 2 Demonstration against British Petroleum and in support of environmental justice.
© Albert H. Teich/Shutterstock

Definition of Environmental Policy

An **environmental policy** is "[a] statement by an organization [either public, such as a government, or private] of its intentions and principles in relation to its overall environmental performance. Environmental policy provides a framework for action and for the setting of its environmental objectives and target."[5] The goal of environmental policy is "to reduce human risks or environmental damages resulting from pollution. Policy analysis facilitates social valuation of these risks and damages, by clarifying the costs of reducing environmental damages in terms of foregone economic returns."[3(pp244–245)] An example of an environmental policy in the United States is the National Environmental Policy Act of 1969, which sought to benefit the human population by preventing damage to the environment. The act is written, in part, as seen in the Congressional Declaration of National Environmental Policy box.

Principles of Environmental Policy Development

In the environmental health arena, a number of environmental principles or philosophies may guide the work of those who are charged with creation of policy (formal and informal policy actors, policy researchers, and policy analysts):

- The precautionary principle
- Environmental justice
- Environmental sustainability
- The polluter-pays principle

A significant ethical issue for policy developers involves setting an acceptable level of risk associated with a potential environmental hazard. There needs to be a "moral consensus regarding the level of risk that is sufficient to regard a substance in the environment as a potential threat to human and ecologic health."[7(p1786)]

Sec. 101 [42 USC § 4331].

(a) The Congress, recognizing the profound impact of man's activity on the interrelations of all components of the natural environment, particularly the profound influences of population growth, high-density urbanization, industrial expansion, resource exploitation, and new and expanding technological advances and recognizing further the critical importance of restoring and maintaining environmental quality to the overall welfare and development of man, declares that it is the continuing policy of the Federal Government, in cooperation with State and local governments, and other concerned public and private organizations, to use all practicable means and measures, including financial and technical assistance, in a manner calculated to foster and promote the general welfare, to create and maintain conditions under which man and nature can exist in productive harmony, and fulfill the social, economic, and other requirements of present and future generations of Americans.[6]

The **precautionary principle** states that "preventive, anticipatory measures . . . [should] be taken when an activity raises threats of harm to the environment, wildlife, or human health, even if some cause-and-effect relationships are not fully established."[8(p263)] The practice of risk assessment is a science of uncertainty, so environmental toxins often present risks that have not been ascertained completely. The precautionary principle suggests that policy makers should err on the side of "an ounce of prevention" and take protective measures even when full scientific certainty is lacking.

A specific case that could merit the application of the precautionary principle relates to endocrine disruptors. The term *endocrine disruptor* refers to "an exogenous substance or mixture that alters function(s) of the endocrine system and consequently causes adverse health effects in an intact organism, or its progeny, or (sub)populations."[9] For example, some chemicals are believed to have an estrogenic effect (acting as female hormones); two of the many varieties of these chemicals are DDT and the family of pesticides known as organochlorines. Scientists have speculated that endocrine-disrupting chemicals may be related to human sexual abnormalities such as low sperm counts in boys and animal abnormalities such as changes in the sexual functioning of aquatic animals.

The precautionary principle would advocate for the control of potential endocrine-disrupting chemicals, even though the focus of most research has been on whether or not they cause cancer (carcinogenesis). The absence of demonstrated carcinogenic effects does not rule out the possibility of other health hazards (e.g., endocrine disruption). Environmental research that focuses on risks of carcinogenic effects should not exclude from consideration other effects such as damage to the endocrine and immune systems; these health effects are overlooked frequently in environmental research. Further, exposures to such chemicals that occur early in life may pose greater health risks than exposures that occur later in life. Policies developed by the European Union adhere to the precautionary principle and advocate that preventive action be taken to reduce risks from potential environmental hazards.[10]

The principle is applied when the weight of scientific evidence suggests that a chemical is suspected of having adverse health consequences, even though such health effects have not been established definitively.

The concept of **environmental justice** denotes the equal treatment of all people in society irrespective of their racial background, country of origin, and socioeconomic status. (See **FIGURE 3**.) The presence of an environmental hazard may be the end product of disparities of power and privilege within a community. Consequently, unequal toxic exposures of adults and children from different racial, ethnic, or socioeconomic groups may occur. Children who reside in minority communities may receive especially high exposures to environmental toxins.

FIGURE 3 Environmental justice.
© Lightspring/Shutterstock

Here is a statement on environmental justice by the US Environmental Protection Agency (EPA):

Environmental Justice is the fair treatment and meaningful involvement of all people regardless of race, color, national origin, or income with respect to the development, implementation, and enforcement of environmental laws, regulations, and policies. Fair treatment means that no group of people should bear a disproportionate share of the negative environmental consequences resulting from industrial, governmental and commercial operations or policies. Meaningful involvement means that: (1) people have an opportunity to participate in decisions about activities that may affect their environment and/or health; (2) the public's contribution can influence the regulatory agency's decision; (3) their concerns will be considered in the decision-making process; and (4) the decision makers seek out and facilitate the involvement of those potentially affected. EPA has this goal for all communities and persons across this Nation. It will be achieved when everyone enjoys the same degree of protection from environmental and health hazards and equal access to the decision-making process to have a healthy environment in which to live, learn, and work.[11]

As a goal of environmental policy, **environmental sustainability** adheres to the philosophical viewpoint "that a strong, just, and wealthy society can be consistent with a clean environment, healthy ecosystems, and a beautiful planet."[12(p5383)] The three components of sustainable development are materials and energy use, land use, and human development. Environmental sustainability means that resources should not be depleted faster than they can be regenerated; the concept also specifies that there should be no permanent change to the natural environment. Critics of sustainable development argue that the definition of the term is not entirely clear and is open to interpretation.[13] Individuals are able to contribute to environmental sustainability through sustainable living, which is adoption of a lifestyle that minimizes demands upon the environment. An example is to lower one's carbon footprint through energy conservation. (See **FIGURE 4**.)

A crucial aspect of any environmental policy concerns who should bear the costs of eliminating environmental hazards. As defined by the Organisation for Economic Co-operation and Development (OECD), the **polluter-pays principle** "means that the polluter should bear the expenses of carrying out the pollution

FIGURE 4 Sustainable living.
© nnnnae/Shutterstock

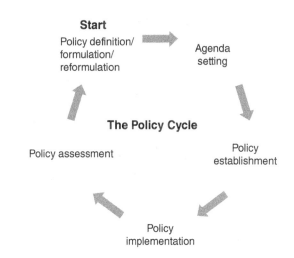

FIGURE 5 The policy cycle.

Modified from data presented in D@dalos, Policy Cycle: Teaching Politics. Available at: http://www.dadalos-d.org/politikdidaktik/politik/policy-zyklus.htm. Accessed February 14, 2017.

prevention and control measures introduced by public authorities in Member countries, to ensure that the environment is in an acceptable state."[14] The principle, implemented by the OECD in November 1974, applies to pollution that originates from a variety of sources including accidental releases during manufacturing processes and from installations that handle hazardous materials. The costs of controlling pollution generated during manufacturing and consumption are to be incorporated into the prices of associated goods and services.

The Policy Cycle

The **policy cycle** refers to the distinct phases involved in the policy-making process.[15] (Refer to **FIGURE 5**.) The policy cycle comprises several stages: (1) problem definition, formulation, and reformulation; (2) agenda setting; (3) policy establishment (i.e., adoption and legislation); (4) policy implementation; and (5) policy assessment.

The terms subsumed under the policy cycle are illustrated in **TABLE 1**.

Problem definition, formulation, and *reformulation* are terms that denote the processes of defining the problem for which the policy actors believe that policies are necessary. This early stage—problem definition and development of alternative solutions—often is regarded as the most crucial phase of the policy development process. The problems chosen should be significant for the health of the environment and have realistic and practical solutions. Poorly defined problems are unlikely to lead to successful policy implementation. Note that Figure 5 (the policy cycle) shows that following a process of assessment, problem definitions may need to be reformulated and the steps in the policy cycle repeated.

Agenda setting refers to setting priorities, deciding at what time to deal with the environmental problem,

and determining who will deal with the problem. Policy makers need to establish priorities in order to reconcile budgetary constraints, resource restrictions, and the complexity of environmental problems against the need to develop those policies that are most feasible, realistic, and workable. Public support for protecting the environment is strong; opinion polls suggest that environmental policies are likely to gain acceptance in many sectors of society.

Barriers and difficulties in establishing priorities stem from the lack of information on risks[16] and lack of coordination among government agencies.[17] When the nature of the risks associated with an environmental hazard or toxin is uncertain, planners are left in a quandary about what aspects of the exposure require policy interventions. In addition, a criticism levied against the US Congress, which is a crucial policy-formulating body for the government of the United States, is its inability to set priorities due to fragmentation of authority among numerous committees and subcommittees that are involved with environmental policy.

A successful approach in developing priorities (and environmental policies in general) is to involve the community and stakeholders. This statement is especially true for the development of policies that impact arctic native territories and tribal lands. For such policies to be successful, planners should respect the cultural traditions of potentially affected indigenous peoples.[18] An illustration of an environmental action that could affect indigenous peoples occurred at the Standing Rock Sioux reservation in the United States. The Dakota Access Pipeline, a $3.8 billion project that would transport 500,000 barrels of oil per day from North Dakota to Illinois, would pass near the reservation. The tribe opposed construction of the pipeline because it could endanger water supplies and

71

TABLE 1 Components of the Environmental Policy Cycle

Component	Problem Definition, Formulation, and Reformulation	Agenda Setting	Policy Establishment	Policy Implementation	Assessment/ Evaluation
What happens?	Define problems and alternatives.	Set priorities. Involve stakeholders.	Formally adopt public policy. Legitimization.	Put the policy into practice.	Assess or evaluate effectiveness.
Who performs the function?	Formal and informal policy actors	Formal and informal policy actors	Formal decision makers	Government agencies	Arm of government responsible for assessment
What factors influence policy?	Research and science Interest groups Public opinion Social and economic factors	Research and science Interest groups Public opinion Social and economic factors	Research and science Interest groups Public opinion Social and economic factors	Research and science Interest groups Public opinion Social and economic factors	Research and science Interest groups Public opinion Social and economic factors
What problems are encountered?	Poorly defined problems	Lack of information on risk Lack of coordination	Inability to coordinate and assess research information	Lack of government support	Lack of sound scientific data

disrupt sacred sites on the reservation. The pipeline was first proposed in 2014.

Policy establishment involves the formal adoption of policies, programs, and procedures that are designed to protect the public from environmental hazards. A factor that impedes policy establishment is the unavailability of empirical information on the scope of risks associated with environmental hazards. According to Walker, "Limitations on our ability to coordinate, assess, and disseminate research information hampers efforts to translate policy into programs and services designed to reduce environmental risk."[16(p190)]

Policy implementation is the phase of the policy cycle that "focuses on achieving the objectives set forth in the policy decision."[16(p186)] Often this phase of the policy cycle is neglected in favor of the earlier phases of policy development. Barriers to policy implementation can arise from the government administration in power. In the case of the United States, whatever administration is in power may choose to weaken policy prescriptions due to political considerations. Organizations such as environmental groups, trade associations, and professional

associations may stimulate public opinion and influence elected government officials with respect to environmental health policy.[19]

In order for a policy to be implemented successfully, policy developers may include economic incentives. For example, some policies for control of environmental pollutants use a market-based trading scheme.[20] This method assigns limits for pollution. Companies that fall below their assigned limits can accumulate credits for pollution control. These credits can be "banked" or resold to other companies that exceed their pollution limits.[21] The term *cap and trade* is used to describe a method for reducing greenhouse gas emissions from facilities such as electric generating plants.

In 2017, the state of California extended its unique cap-and-trade program, which aims to reduce greenhouse gases from facilities such as power plants and oil refineries. Each facility must obtain a permit for every metric ton of greenhouse gas that it emits. A certain number of these permits are available at no cost from the state. Other permits are available from state auctions. A facility that is successful in reducing its greenhouse gas emissions can sell its additional permits to other companies. The state proposes to use revenue generated by the cap-and-trade program to support projects (e.g., electric cars) for reducing greenhouse gases.

The political and social contexts may stimulate or impede the creation and implementation of environmental policy.[22] In many situations, public concern over a perceived hazard may provide the impetus to new environmental policies, regardless of whether scientific evidence supports their adoption. Research conducted in China has demonstrated the linkage among the social, environmental, and political elements as they affect policy goals and the implementation mechanisms for policy. (Refer to **FIGURE 6**.)

Assessment/evaluation, the final stage in the policy cycle, refers to assessment of the effectiveness of the policy. In order to facilitate assessment, environmental policies may incorporate **environmental objectives**, which "are statements of policy. . . intended to be assessed using information from a monitoring program. An environmental monitoring program has to be adequate in its quality and quantity of data so that environmental objectives can be assessed."[23(p144)] An example of an environmental objective is the statement that the amount of particulate matter in an urban area (e.g., Mexico City) will be reduced by 10% during the next 5 years.

Interplay between the Evaluation Process and Policy Development

Underlying the policy development cycle is environmental health research, which includes the identification of toxic substances and other hazards, assessment of mechanisms of environmental toxicity, and establishment of evaluations of interventions to mitigate hazards.[7] Some recent US governmental initiatives have emphasized the importance of research on pollutants as a specific component of environmental policies.[20]

Scientific data are linked closely to the policy cycle. "The creation of sound policy requires a foundation of sound data. It is through fundamental, mechanistically based research that environmental and public health officials can improve their understanding of risk and translate this knowledge into prevention strategies."[18(p118)] Epidemiologic studies provide the source of much valuable data for construction of environmental health policies. **FIGURE 7** demonstrates the interface between science and policy development.

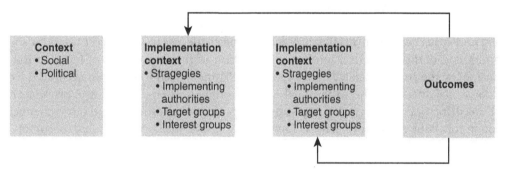

FIGURE 6 Relationships and interactions during policy implementation.

Data from Sinkule BJ, Ortolano L. *Implementing Environmental Policy in China*. Santa Barbara, CA: Praeger; 1995, p. 44.

Content removed due to copyright restrictions

FIGURE 7 The interface of science and health policy.

The linkage begins with creation of hypotheses, moves to review of scientific evidence, and proceeds to development of models of exposures and health effects, and assessments of risks associated with exposures. The linkage concludes with the decision-making process in setting priorities and, ultimately, with formulation of specific policies.

▶ Risk Assessment and Policy Development

In the chapter on environmental toxicology, risk assessment was defined as a process for determining health risks associated with environmental and other hazards. Risk assessment is closely aligned with the policy process through the balancing of economic and other costs with health and societal benefits that may accrue through specific policy alternatives. It should be obvious that the adoption of new environmental policies may involve the expenditure of considerable public and private funds, with potentially adverse economic consequences. For example, imagine the expense incurred when the United States and other countries implemented the policy decision to switch from leaded to unleaded gasoline. However, removal of lead from gasoline carried numerous health benefits that justified the high economic cost of this policy decision.

In some instances, the risks associated with exposure to hazardous substances may be so minimal as to obviate the need for policies to control exposure to them, although this issue is controversial. At some point the net economic and social costs of a policy may exceed the social benefits of pollution controls. An example is the presence of trace levels of pollutants in drinking water that has already undergone purification.

Policy adoption is difficult when an environmental issue is complex. An example comes from policies to control the potential environmental impacts of agricultural pesticide use.[24] Policy developers are confronted with several complex and often interrelated issues:

1. Pesticide use involves multiple contaminants that have differing characteristics.
2. Exposure of the population (both the general public and agricultural workers) to contaminants can arise from unspecified sources as well as clearly delineated sources; sometimes it is difficult to identify the sources of pesticide emissions.
3. The costs incurred to measure pesticide emissions are high.
4. There may be interactions among different types of pesticides.

The complicated nature of measuring pesticide exposures muddies the development of policies to limit the population's exposure to pesticides and to promote the appropriate uses of pesticides.

FIGURE 8 shows both a model of the four major factors connected with policy development and the interrelationships among them. The four components are hazard, risk, impacts, and social costs.[24] An example of their application is a scenario for the development of policies regarding the use of pesticides. The term *hazard* relates to chemical and physical properties (e.g., color, boiling point, volatility) of pesticides; *risk* refers to the probability of exposure; the term *impacts* pertains to the actual effects (e.g., harm) of pesticide usage; *social cost* refers to society's perception of the importance of harm to the environment. Planners need to take into account the entire panel of variables when developing appropriate environmental policies for pesticides and other chemicals.

Risk assessment should occur at the inception of the environmental policy-making process.[25] Risk assessment should be "a participatory procedure, in which the different stake-holders are involved early in the risk analysis process to 'characterize' risks, even before they are given a formal assessment."[10(px)] An example would be incorporating community-based participatory methods designed to assess biomarkers of contaminant exposures in children and adults. A biomarker is "[a] specific biochemical in the body which has a particular molecular feature that makes

Content removed due to copyright restrictions

FIGURE 8 The links between hazard, risk, impacts, and social cost.

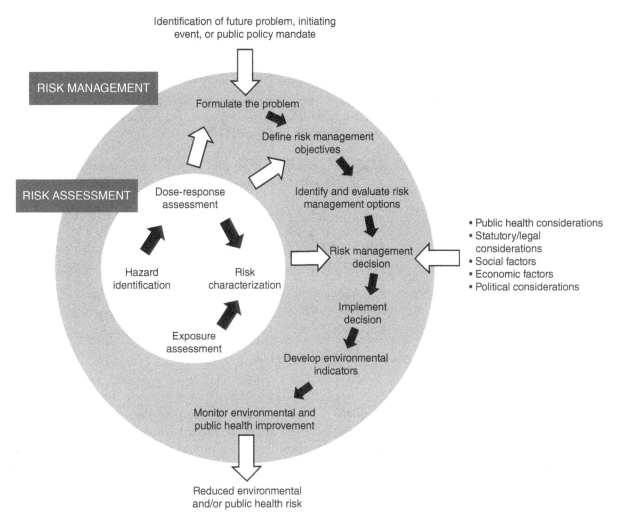

FIGURE 9 Risk assessment/risk management paradigm.

Reproduced with permission from National Research Council. *Risk Assessment in the Federal Government: Managing the Process, 1983* by the National Academy of Sciences. Courtesy of the National Academies Press, Washington, D.C.

it useful for measuring the progress of disease or the effects of treatment."[26] The participatory process aims "at eliciting the 'values' and the perspectives of the community involved so that the multiple dimensions of risk can be taken into account early on in the assessment."[10(pxi)]

Risk Management

The process of risk management involves the adoption of steps to eliminate identified risks or lower them to acceptable levels (often as determined by a government agency that has taken into account input from the public).[25] After a risk assessment has been completed, public policy mandates may be adopted for the management of the identifiable risk. Suppose, for example, that a risk assessment shows that exposure to lead is harmful to children. A government agency has adopted a policy that states that children shall be protected from environmental exposures to lead. The risk management plan involves

the adoption and implementation of procedures that are designed to protect children from lead exposure. Refer to **FIGURE 9** for more information.

Other examples of risk management include the development of regulations that control the production, use, and disposal of toxic chemicals. In the United States, risk management of toxic substances is governed by the Toxic Substances Control Act (discussed later in this chapter). Methods of risk management include licensing laws, standard-setting laws, control-oriented measures, and monitoring.[25] (Refer to **TABLE 2**.)

Environmental Impact Assessment and Health Impact Assessment

An *environmental impact* is defined as "[a]ny change to the environment, whether adverse or beneficial, wholly or partially resulting from an organization's activities, products or services."[5] An **environmental impact assessment (EIA)** is a process that reviews

TABLE 2 Examples of Risk Management

Risk Management Procedure	Description
Licensing laws	Require licensing and registration for new and existing chemicals; include requirements for toxicity testing, including the Federal Insecticide, Fungicide, and Rodenticide Act (FIFRA).
Standard-setting laws	Establish standards of exposure for chemicals used in specific situations; an example is the Clean Air Act.
Control-oriented measures	Deal with explicitly identified chemicals, groups of chemicals, or chemical processes; an example is the design of packages so that they are childproof and prevent young children's access to harmful substances.
Monitoring	Measures of the level of an environmental toxin so that regulations can be enforced. Monitoring programs are in place for ozone and smog and for pesticide levels in foods, to name several examples.

Data from Landrigan PJ, Carlson JE. Environmental policy and children's health. *The Future of Children*. 1995;5(2):41–43.

the potential impact of anthropogenic (human-related) activities (e.g., a proposed construction project) with respect to their general environmental consequences. To give an example, an EIA might consider whether a proposed residential development would increase water and air pollution beyond acceptable limits or endanger threatened species of animals and plants. An EIA seeks abatement measures for pollution before it is produced; procedures for control of pollution should be feasible and cost effective.[22] An example of an abatement procedure is the construction of catch basins for containment of water runoff from new housing developments in order to prevent polluted water from reaching the ocean.

Although it is similar to an environmental impact assessment, a **health impact assessment (HIA)** refers to "a method for describing and estimating the effects that a proposed project or policy may have on the health of a population."[27(p198)] Refer to **TABLE 3** for a list of the types of projects that may require an HIA. Major construction projects can have a damaging effect upon the health of human populations and, accordingly, should require an HIA. An example would be the construction of a giant water reservoir in a densely populated, tropical country that has high levels of tropical diseases. The large body of standing water created by the reservoir could encourage the multiplication of disease-causing vectors such as mosquitoes.

Six stages have been identified for the completion of an HIA.[28] Two of these stages include review of research evidence and evaluation. An HIA makes

an in-depth appraisal of data relevant to a project. The appraisal should consider how a project affects health-related and sociodemographic variables (e.g., population displacement). The HIA incorporates a plan for the meticulous evaluation and continuous monitoring of possible adverse outcomes such as increases in poverty, undue damage to the environment, detriments to the social fabric, and increases in morbidity from infectious and other diseases.[27]

▶ Case Studies: Environmental Policies to Protect Human Health

The 2014–2018 EPA Strategic Plan

The mission of the US EPA is "To Protect Human Health and the Environment."[29] In order to support its mission, the EPA has developed a strategic plan that, according to the requirements of the Government Performance and Results Act of 1993, must be updated periodically. The FY 2014-2018 strategic goals and priorities include:

- "Addressing climate change and improving air quality;
- Reinvigorating water-quality-improvement efforts, including support for green infrastructure;
- Taking action on toxics and strengthening chemical safety;

TABLE 3 Applications of Health Impact Assessment

Content removed due to copyright restrictions

- Enhancing the livability and economic vitality of neighborhoods in and around brownfield sites;
- Aligning and incentivizing partnerships that spur technological innovations, reducing costs and pollution; and
- Advancing research efforts to provide relevant, robust and transparent scientific data to support the agency's policy and decision-making needs." [29(p1)]

Protection of the Arctic and Antarctic Environments

Significant contamination of the arctic environment with organic materials, toxic metals, and radioactivity has occurred as a result of pollution that originates in the industrialized areas of the world. The list of contaminants found in the traditional foods used by indigenous arctic peoples (and in their tissue samples) is extensive. (See **TABLE 4**
)

In view of the future potential health impacts of toxic substances in the arctic environment, policies will need to be developed to protect this region.

The use of a community advisory board working in conjunction with environmental scientists to protect the arctic environment has been recommended. The Arctic Monitoring and Assessment Program, with the input of community advisory boards, will aid in the development of appropriate policies. The Antarctic environment is also at risk and requires protection from pollution generated by military activities, tourism, and scientific exploration.[30]

Water Policy Reform in South Africa

South Africa has developed new policies—the National Water Act (1998) and the Water Services Act (1997)—to increase the equitability of water distribution and to protect aquatic ecosystems in the country.[31] Historically, before the introduction of these acts, water rights were held almost exclusively by large landowners. The purposes of the acts are to bring water rights under the control of the South African central government, to ensure that all citizens have sufficient water supplies to meet their basic needs, to make water affordable, to introduce controls over pollution, and to make sufficient water available for the maintenance of the aquatic environment.

Environmental Policies in Economies in Transition

In the Baltic and nearby regions of Central and Eastern Europe, former Soviet economies have changed to market economies as a result of the collapse of the Soviet Union. (Estonia, Poland, Hungary, and the Czech Republic are examples.) Previously, emphasis in these economies was placed on heavy industries that contributed greatly to the burden of pollution. Environmental protections were not enforced vigorously, resulting in heavy pollution of some regions. These economies inherited barriers to implementation of

TABLE 4 Environmental Contaminants Detected in Traditional Food Items and Human Tissue Samples

Industrial chemicals and by-products (e.g., dioxins, polychlorinated biphenyls, flame retardants)

Pesticides (e.g., DDT)

Polycyclic aromatic hydrocarbons (e.g., benzo(a)pyrene)

Heavy metals (e.g., mercury, lead)

Products of nuclear radiation

Modified and reproduced with permission from Suk WA, Avakian MD, Carpenter D, et al. Human exposure monitoring and evaluation in the Arctic: the importance of understanding exposures to the development of public health policy. *Environmental Health Perspectives.* 2004;112:115.

environmental policies that included economic and governmental inefficiencies and absence of environmental policy principles. New and effective environmental policies have been implemented that gradually have brought pollution under control. These policies include adoption of the polluter-pays principle and reduction in subsidies to inefficient heavy industries that cause pollution. Consequently, many of these countries have had substantial remediation of stationary sources of pollution such as those related to the coal mining industry.[32]

Control of Pollution across International Boundaries

Environmental impacts caused by the release of greenhouse gases such as carbon dioxide are global in scope. Control of such problems may not necessarily be confined to a single country but may involve actions at the international level. The New York Convention (1992) and Kyoto Protocol (1997) are two multilateral agreements that set forth international policies to reduce the emission of so-called greenhouse gases into the atmosphere. Other examples of environmental problems that have an international scope are climate change, ozone layer depletion, loss of **biodiversity**, and radioactive emergencies. Thus, international cooperation should be a feature of a single country's environmental policy. For example, three Baltic countries—Estonia, Latvia, and Lithuania—have designed multinational environmental agreements to control pollution in this region.[33]

Industrialization of Rural China

The shift from an agricultural economy to rapid industrialization, with consequential environmental quality degradation, is an increasingly common feature of rural China. Some of the causes of pollution are use of low-quality coal, energy inefficiencies, and lack of wastewater treatment facilities. Although strong environmental policies exist in China, numerous social, political, and economic barriers (e.g., insufficient funding) restrict their implementation or prevent their enforcement. Awareness is increasing among the general public regarding the adverse consequences of pollution. Nevertheless, environmental degradation remains a compelling issue in China.[22]

Protecting the Rights of Children and Special and Vulnerable Populations

Those who may be especially sensitive to environmental hazards include children, persons with genetic vulnerability, and minority groups such as blacks and American Indians. Although efforts are under way to intervene in childhood asthma, birth defects, and lead poisoning, increased attention needs to be given to other environmental issues such as exposure to carcinogens, neurotoxins, and endocrine disruptors.[34] Despite this need, according to some experts, the United States lacks a coherent policy to assure that the environment is free from children's exposure to environmental toxicants. Blacks in many cases reside in urban centers where they are exposed to high levels of air pollution and toxic metals such as lead. Many American Indians live on sovereign lands that have serious environmental problems. American Indian groups sometimes face difficulty in reaching consensus about the appropriate action steps needed to reduce environmental hazards on their lands.

Landrigan and Carlson state that "[u]nderstanding the differences in the effects of environmental contamination on children and adults is an important part of environmental policymaking; however, unless environmental health policies reflect the differences between adults and children, this knowledge will have little practical effect."[25(p34)] Children's vulnerability to environmental toxins is related to their reduced ability to metabolize and excrete toxicants, rapid growth and development that increase vulnerability to toxicants, and the fact that children have more time to develop chronic diseases than do adults.[35]

Nowadays children are exposed to thousands of new chemicals. As a result of medical advances, infectious diseases are taking a reduced toll in the developed world. Consequently, chronic diseases of noninfectious origin are replacing infectious diseases as major causes of death among children in the developed world. (This shift is known as the epidemiologic transition.) Long-term exposure to environmental toxicants may play a role in causing some of these chronic conditions. Note that asthma and lead poisoning are increasingly important examples of the new morbidity among children. Some researchers believe that asthma may be associated with factors such as outdoor and indoor air pollution and insect contamination; lead poisoning is associated with exposure to environmental lead from painted surfaces in older buildings and from leaded fuels (which presently are banned from use in the United States and most developed countries).

One method for controlling and intervening in children's exposures to environmental hazards is known as the lifecycle approach to identifying exposure pathways.[34] (See **FIGURE 10**.) Environmental policies can be directed toward the various lifestyle exposure pathways shown in the figure (e.g., prevention of children's oral, dermal, and inhalation exposures to toxicants in the home and outdoor environments).

Prenatal

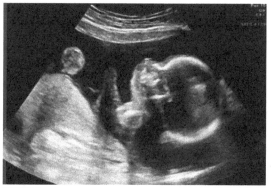

© PEDRE/E+/Getty

A stage when the developing fetus is very susceptible to the effects of pollutants; exposures can be transplacental and external.

Neonatal (birth to < 3 months)

© Olga Max/Shutterstock

Oral and dermal exposures: breast and bottle feeding; hand-to-mouth activity.

Inhalation exposures: time spent sleeping; time spent in sedentary activities.

Infant/Crawler (3 to 12 months)

© Konstantin Chagin/Shutterstock

Oral and dermal exposures: consumption of solid food, increased floor mobility, hand-to-mouth activity.

Inhalation exposures: breathing close to floor; development of personal dust clouds.

Toddler (1 to < 2 years)

© NARONGRIT LOKOOLPRAKIT/Shutterstock

Oral and dermal exposures: consumption of range of solid foods; increased play activity and curiosity.

Inhalation exposure: time spent sleeping; time spent in sedentary activities.

Preschool (2 to < 6 years)

© FamVeld/Shutterstock

Oral and dermal exposures: wearing adult-style clothing; decreased hand-to-mouth activities.

Inhalation exposures: increased time spent outdoors.

School-Age (6 to < 11 years)

© Knot. P. Saengma/Shutterstock

Oral and dermal exposures: decreased oral contact with hands and objects; decreased contact with surfaces.

Inhalation exposures: time spent in school environments; participation in sports.

FIGURE 10 Pathways of children's exposure to environmental pollutants and hazards vary according to stage of development.

Data from United States Environmental Protection Agency. *A Decade of Children's Environmental Health Research: Highlights from EPA's Science to Achieve Results Program.* EPA/600/S-07/038. December 2007.

Turning from the developed world, consider the less-developed regions such as parts of Southeast Asia and the Pacific, where numerous environmental threats confront children. These regions comprise the most rapidly industrializing areas of the world and contain half the world's children.[35] The quantity and severity of threats are increasing due to rapid industrialization and the epidemiologic transition. Examples of environmental hazards are smoke from wood used in home cooking and heating, arsenic in ground water, pesticides, lead emissions, and methyl isocyanate.[35] (Methyl isocyanate is a highly poisonous chemical used in the manufacture of pesticides. On December 3, 1984, 40 tons (36.3 metric tons) of the gas was released in Bhopal, India, causing many fatalities.)

The Built Environment

The term **built environment** refers to urban areas and structures (e.g., roads, parks, and buildings) constructed by human beings, as opposed to undeveloped, rural areas. From the world perspective, the built environment is increasing dramatically as formerly rural and agricultural economies transition to industrialized economies. FIGURE 11 shows a highly urbanized section of Caracas, Venezuela in 2006. Regarding the developed world, for example, in many sections of the United States, cities have taken over farmland and forests as metropolitan areas have expanded.

Policies for design of the built environment have great potential for influencing public health.[36] Examples of design features with implications for health consequences are land development, community design, and transportation patterns. Some land development methods inadvertently cause people to drive cars by increasing the distances that people must

FIGURE 11 Built environment example: Caracas, Venezuela; 2006.

travel. Encouraging the use of cars by making them affordable and installing free parking lots may have the indirect consequences of increasing air pollution and a sedentary lifestyle. Adoption of innovative public policies may stimulate people to walk more and use public transportation. An example is the colocating of business facilities, shopping centers, and residences so that city inhabitants are able to walk to work, ride bicycles, or take public transportation. Other innovations include available bicycles and vehicles for sharing by the public. Finally, development policies should foster the protection of open space and the creation of public parks.

▶ Agencies Involved in the Adoption, Implementation, and Enforcement of Environmental Policies

A constellation of international, national, state or territorial, and local agencies maintain responsibility for development and enforcement of environmental health regulations, and for investigation of incidents that affect environmental health.

FIGURE 12 shows a flow chart of some of the agencies involved with environmental health regulations.

Referring to Figure 12, you can see that the World Health Organization (WHO) is a major international agency that is responsible for environmental health at the global level. WHO provides leadership in minimizing adverse environmental health outcomes associated with pollution, industrial development, and related issues. Although WHO's primary mission is to control and prevent disease, its reach extends to environmental health, which is closely related to disease prevention. More information about WHO is presented later in this chapter.

At the national level, many countries have a federalist system of government. The concept of federalism implies a type of government "that is structured around a strong central (i.e., federal) government, with specified authorities retained by lower levels of government, such as states and local governments."[19(p34)] This situation characterizes the United States, where the legislative and judicial branches of government perform important functions in environmental policy formulation. The Congress of the US government (Senate and House of Representatives) retains significant responsibility for creation of environmental laws. Judicial bodies in the United States (i.e., the court system) support interpretation, strengthening, and

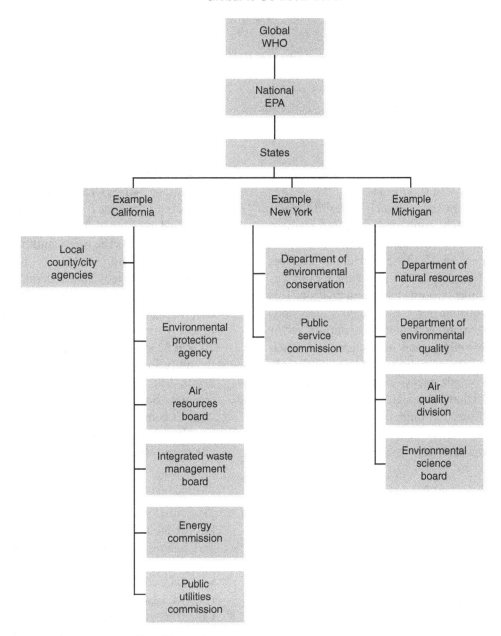

Global to US Local Level

FIGURE 12 Overview of environmental health regulation agencies.

enforcement of environmental laws; an example is the interpretation of relevant environmental policies that are the focus of lawsuits.

At the national level, many government agencies regulate environmental health hazards in their respective countries. For example, in the United States, the EPA is responsible for protecting human health and safeguarding the natural environment, including air, land, and water. The EPA develops and enforces environmental regulations, which bring about cleaner air and purer water as well as protect the land. In addition, other national agencies (discussed later in this chapter) are charged with the responsibility of protecting the environment.

Within the United States, individual states and local governments also maintain responsibility for control of environmental health issues. Figure 12 shows some examples of agencies involved in environmental health regulation in three representative states—California, New York, and Michigan. As an example of one state agency's function, California's Air Resources Board (ARB) states as its mission: "To promote and protect public health, welfare and ecological resources through the effective and efficient reduction of air pollutants while recognizing and considering the effects on the economy of the state."[37] In large urban areas such as California's major cities, air pollution has continued to be a significant health and

TABLE 5 Some Major Environmental Regulatory Agencies: US and Other

United States	Other
US Environmental Protection Agency (EPA)	European Environment Agency (EEA)
National Institute for Occupational Safety and Health (NIOSH)	World Health Organization (WHO)/Regional Office for
Agency for Toxic Substances and Disease Registry (ATSDR)	Europe
National Institute of Environmental Health Sciences (NIEHS)	

aesthetic issue. The ARB has had a significant role in reducing air pollution in California.

Local government agencies such as health departments also are closely connected with enforcement of environmental laws. For example, the City of Long Beach Department of Health and Human Services (DHHS), one of the city health departments in California, operates an environmental health division. This division is responsible for water quality, hazardous materials management, community sanitation, vector control, lead poisoning, food inspection, and housing quality (e.g., through lead abatement). County and local government agencies in other states perform similar functions, although their exact organizational configurations may differ from one another. The remainder of this section identifies some of the agencies in the US that are responsible for environmental regulation. (Refer to **TABLE 5**.)

US Environmental Protection Agency (EPA)

"The EPA's purpose is to ensure that . . . all Americans are protected from significant risks to human health and the environment where they live, learn and work[.]"[38] Among its activities, EPA implements the best available scientific information for environmental risk reduction, enforces federal environmental laws fairly and effectively, supports dissemination of accurate information regarding human health and environmental risks, and maintains a leadership role with respect to protecting the global environment. Other functions of the EPA are to:

- "Give Grants . . .
- Study Environmental Issues . . .
- Sponsor Partnerships . . .
- Teach People About the Environment . . .
- Publish Information . . ."[38]

National Institute for Occupational Safety and Health (NIOSH)

The National Institute for Occupational Safety and Health (NIOSH) is the U.S. federal agency that conducts research and makes recommendations to prevent worker injury and illness. NIOSH research is key to these efforts and provides practical solutions to identified problems. The Institute's work in this area protects the safety and health of the nation's 155 million workers. . . . NIOSH provides the only dedicated federal investment for research needed to prevent the societal cost of work-related fatalities, injuries and illnesses in the United States, estimated in 2007 at $250 billion in medical costs and productivity losses alone. . . . These safety and health risks take huge tolls on workers, their families, businesses, communities, and the nation's economy; NIOSH works to promote a healthy, safe and capable workforce that can rise to the challenges of the 21st Century. . . .

NIOSH Mission

[The mission of NIOSH is] [t]o develop new knowledge in the field of occupational safety and health, and to transfer that knowledge into practice. . . . . Headquartered in Washington, D.C. and Atlanta, Georgia, NIOSH has research labs and offices in Anchorage, Alaska; Cincinnati, Ohio; Denver, Colorado; Morgantown, West Virginia; Pittsburgh, Pennsylvania; and Spokane, Washington.

About NIOSH

The Occupational Safety and Health Act of 1970 established NIOSH. NIOSH is part of the U.S. Centers for Disease Control and Prevention, in the U.S. Department of Health and Human Services. It has the mandate to assure "every man and woman in the Nation safe and healthful working conditions and to preserve our human resources." NIOSH has more than 1,300 employees from a diverse set of fields including epidemiology, medicine, nursing, industrial hygiene, safety, psychology, chemistry, statistics, economics, and many branches of engineering. NIOSH works closely with the Occupational

Safety and Health Administration (OSHA) and the Mine Safety and Health Administration (MSHA) in the U.S. Department of Labor to protect American workers and miners.[39]

Agency for Toxic Substances and Disease Registry (ATSDR)

The Agency for Toxic Substances and Disease Registry (ATSDR) is the nation's public health agency for chemical safety. The agency's mission is to use the best science, take responsive action, and provide trustworthy health information to prevent and mitigate harmful exposures [to] toxic substances and related disease.

The discovery of contamination in New York State's Love Canal during the 1970s first brought the problem of hazardous wastes to national attention. Similarly, the health threat from sudden chemical releases came into focus in December 1984, when a cloud of Methyl isocyanate gas released from a Union Carbide facility in Bhopal, India, seriously injured or killed thousands of people.

Both events represent the kinds of issues at the core of ATSDR's congressional mandate. First organized in 1985, ATSDR was created by the Comprehensive Environmental Response, Compensation, and Liability Act (CERCLA) of 1980, more commonly known as the Superfund law. In 1986, Congress passed the Superfund Amendments and Reauthorization Act (SARA). Through these and other pieces of legislation, Congress responded to the public's demand for a more complete accounting of toxic chemicals and releases. In addition, Congress was—and remains—concerned by other pathways of potential exposure, including food, water, air, and consumer goods.

Since the creation of ATSDR, thousands of hazardous sites have been identified around the country. The Superfund program remains responsible for finding and cleaning up the most dangerous hazardous waste sites in the country. ATSDR has also been at the forefront in protecting people from acute toxic exposures that occur from hazardous leaks and spills, environment-related poisonings, and natural and terrorism-related disasters.

Under its CERCLA mandate, ATSDR's work falls into four functional areas:

- Protecting the public from toxic exposures;
- Increasing knowledge about toxic substances;

- Delivering health education about toxic chemicals; and
- Maintaining health registries.

Through our work in these areas, ATSDR continues to prevent and mitigate exposures and related health effects at hazardous waste sites across the nation.[40(p9)]

National Institute of Environmental Health Sciences (NIEHS)

The National Institute of Environmental Health Sciences (NIEHS) is one of 27 institutes and centers of the National Institutes of Health (NIH), which is a component of the U.S. Department of Health and Human Services (HHS). NIEHS is located in Research Triangle Park (RTP), North Carolina. NIEHS's broad focus on the environmental causes of disease makes the institute a unique part of the NIH. NIEHS is home to the National Toxicology Program (NTP), the nation's premier program for testing and evaluation of agents in our environment. . . .

NIEHS supports a wide variety of research programs directed toward preventing health problems caused by our environment.

Grants programs. The largest portion of the NIEHS budget goes to fund laboratory research, population-based studies, and training programs that are conducted at universities, hospitals, businesses, and organizations around the country and in other lands. This research is being supported through the NIH grants program — also known as the extramural program.

In-house laboratories. In-house, or intramural research, is done by scientists employed by the federal government who have laboratories at NIEHS. Research conducted at NIEHS includes epidemiology, biostatistics, molecular genetics, signal transduction, reproductive and developmental toxicology, respiratory biology, molecular carcinogenesis, and other environmental research areas. Our in-house scientists collaborate extensively with partners in other institutes, agencies, and academia. NIEHS also has a clinical research unit on site, to help translate basic research findings into human health gains.

National Toxicology Program. NTP is a federal, interagency program, headquartered at NIEHS, whose goal is to safeguard the public, by identifying substances in the environment that may affect human health. Current NTP initiatives are examining the effects of cell phone radiation, endocrine disruptors, and nanomaterials, as well as developing new approaches to advance high-throughput (high speed and high quantity) screening of chemicals, to reduce the number of animals used in research. NTP also conducts health hazard evaluations, such as the Report on Carcinogens, that are used by federal, state, and local health regulatory research agencies for decision-making.[41]

European Union (EU) and European Environment Agency (EEA)

The European Union (EU)'s environment program supports the development of environmental policies for protecting the health and quality of life for its residents of its vast geographic area. The European Environment Agency (EEA), which is located in Copenhagen, Denmark, is an arm of the European Union. The EEA is tasked with the mission of supplying information to 33 member countries regarding the environment. This information is used for environmental policy development, adoption, implementation, and evaluation. For more information about the EEA, consult https://www.eea.europa.eu/downloads/c10100ed9b3ec24746afc41b75a1c277/1502186235/who-we-are.pdf?direct=1.

Environmental Action Programs (EAPs) help to direct EU environmental policy and establish priority objectives. In 2013 the European Parliament and the Council of the European Union adopted the seventh Environmental Action Program, which extended until 2020. The nine priority objectives of the EAP are as follows:

1. "to protect, conserve and enhance the Union's natural capital.
2. to turn the Union into a resource-efficient, green, and competitive low-carbon economy.
3. to safeguard the Union's citizens from environment-related pressures and risks to health and wellbeing.
4. to maximise the benefits of the Union's environment legislation by improving implementation.
5. to increase knowledge about the environment and widen the evidence base for policy.
6. to secure investment for environment and climate policy and account for the environmental costs of any societal activities.
7. to better integrate environmental concerns into other policy areas and ensure coherence when creating new policy.
8. to make the Union's cities more sustainable.

9. to help the Union address international environmental and climate challenges more effectively."[42]

World Health Organization (WHO)/ Regional Office for Europe

WHO attributes up to 25% of the global burden of disease to environmental factors; according to WHO, a total of 20% of all deaths result from environmental factors (2007 data). Environmental determinants are manifested differentially across regions, demographic groups, and socioeconomic groups in a manner that demonstrates complex interactions with the environment.[43] The following passage describes WHO's Regional Office for Europe:

The WHO Regional Office for Europe supports the efforts of its Member States and partners to understand and navigate this complexity and to identify policies and actions that can benefit the environment and human health, using the best available evidence to guide national and international decision-making in different sectors....In 1989, concerned about the growing evidence of the impact of hazardous environments on human health, the WHO Regional Office for Europe initiated the first-ever international environment and health process, developing a broad-based primary prevention public health approach for addressing environmental determinants of health.

The European Environment and Health Process (EHP) is steered by ministerial conferences that are unique for bringing together different sectors and stakeholders to identify environment and health challenges, set priorities, agree on commitments and shape shared European policies and actions on environment and health.

Representatives of WHO European Member States, the Commission of the European Union and their partners adopted the European Charter on Environment and Health at the first Ministerial Conference in Frankfurt in 1989, committing to basic principles, mechanisms and priorities for future action....The conference also called on WHO to establish the European Centre for Environment and Health, which remains the key institution of the EHP to this day.[43]

Beyond the Regional Office for Europe, WHO's global environmental health activities cover a broad range of issues in many countries. These public health and environmental topics include:

- Air pollution, including indoor air pollution
- Children's environmental health
- Environmental health impact assessment
- Climate change and human health
- Environmental health in emergencies
- Quantifying environmental health impacts
- Water, sanitation, and health

For more information, refer to the WHO website: http://www.who.int.

Environmental Advocacy Organizations

Although they are not components of government, environmental advocacy organizations constitute an important part of the fabric of environmental policy formulation and are a significant force in influencing public policy. Environmental advocacy organizations help to educate people and seek to mold public opinion regarding the organizations' positions on specific topics, including global warming, reduction of air pollution, and protection of consumers from potential carcinogens in food, water, and cosmetics. One of the recent concerns of environmental advocacy groups is the development of alternative and green energy sources. Refer to FIGURE 13, which shows the use of wind turbines for generation of electric power.

Many organizations lobby local, state, and federal governmental bodies in support of particular environmental causes such as protection of endangered species and purchase of wilderness areas for public access. In the United States and worldwide, numerous organizations function at various levels (from grassroots to national and international) to promote environmental

causes. Some examples of the multitude of environmental advocacy groups are the following:

- Environmental Working Group
- Greenpeace
- National Resources Defense Council
- National Wildlife Federation
- The Nature Conservancy
- Sierra Club
- Union of Concerned Scientists

▶ Major US Environmental Health Laws

Several of the major environmental health laws adopted by the United States are presented in TABLE 6.

Clean Air Act (42 U.S.C. § 7401 et seq. [1970])

The Clean Air Act (CAA) is the comprehensive federal law that regulates air emissions from stationary and mobile sources. Among other things, this law authorizes EPA to establish National Ambient Air Quality Standards (NAAQS) to protect public health and public welfare and to regulate emissions of hazardous air pollutants.

One of the goals of the Act was to set and achieve NAAQS in every state by 1975 in order to address the public health and welfare risks posed by certain widespread air pollutants. The setting of these pollutant standards was coupled with directing the states to develop

TABLE 6 Major US Environmental Health Laws	
Name of Law	Date Enacted
Clean Air Act	1970
Clean Water Act	1977, and later amendments
Safe Drinking Water Act	1974
National Environmental Policy Act (NEPA)	1969
Federal Insecticide, Fungicide, and Rodenticide Act (FIFRA)	1996
Toxic Substances Control Act (TSCA)	1976
Comprehensive Environmental Response, Compensation, and Liability Act (CERCLA-Superfund)	1980
Resource Conservation and Recovery Act (RCRA)	1976
Occupational Safety and Health Act	1970
Endangered Species Act	1973

FIGURE 13 Wind turbine for generation of electric power.

state implementation plans (SIPs), applicable to appropriate industrial sources in the state, in order to achieve these standards. The Act was amended in 1977 and 1990 primarily to set new goals (dates) for achieving attainment of NAAQS since many areas of the country had failed to meet the deadlines. [See **FIGURE 14**.]

Section 112 of the Clean Air Act addresses emissions of hazardous air pollutants. Prior to 1990, CAA established a risk-based program under which only a few standards were developed. The 1990 Clean Air Act Amendments revised Section 112 to first require issuance of technology-based standards for major sources and certain area sources. "Major sources" are defined as a stationary source or group of stationary sources that emit or have the potential to emit 10 tons (9 metric tons) per year or more of a hazardous air pollutant or 25 tons (23.7 metric tons) per year or more of a combination of hazardous air pollutants. An "area source" is any stationary source that is not a major source.

For major sources, Section 112 requires that EPA establish emission standards that require the maximum degree of reduction in emissions of hazardous air pollutants. These emission standards are commonly referred to as "maximum achievable control technology" or "MACT" standards. Eight years after the technology-based MACT standards are issued for a source category, EPA is required to review those standards to determine whether any residual risk exists for that source category and, if necessary, revise the standards to address such risk.[44]

Clean Water Act (33 U.S.C. § 1251 et seq. [1972]) (Comprises Several Related Acts)

The Federal Water Pollution Control Act of 1948 was the first major US law to address water pollution. Growing public awareness and concern for controlling water pollution led to sweeping amendments in 1972. As amended in 1972, the law became commonly known as the Clean Water Act (CWA). The 1972 amendments:

> Established the basic structure for regulating pollutant discharges into the waters of the United States.
>
> Gave EPA the authority to implement pollution control programs such as setting wastewater standards for industry.
>
> Maintained existing requirements to set water quality standards for all contaminants in surface waters.
>
> Made it unlawful for any person to discharge any pollutant from a point source into navigable waters, unless a permit was obtained under its provisions.
>
> Funded the construction of sewage treatment plants under the construction grants program.
>
> Recognized the need for planning to address the critical problems posed by nonpoint source pollution.

Subsequent amendments modified some of the earlier CWA provisions. Revisions in 1981 streamlined the municipal construction grants process, improving the capabilities of treatment plants built under the program. Changes in 1987 phased out the construction grants program, replacing it with the State Water Pollution Control Revolving Fund, more commonly known as the Clean Water State Revolving Fund. This new funding

strategy addressed water quality needs by building on EPA-state partnerships.

Over the years, many other laws have changed parts of the Clean Water Act. Title I of the Great Lakes Critical Programs Act of 1990, for example, put into place parts of the Great Lakes Water Quality Agreement of 1978, signed by the U.S. and Canada, where the two nations agreed to reduce certain toxic pollutants in the Great Lakes. That law required EPA to establish water quality criteria for the Great Lakes addressing 29 toxic pollutants with maximum levels that are safe for humans, wildlife, and aquatic life. It also required EPA to help the States implement the criteria on a specific schedule.[45]

Safe Drinking Water Act (42 U.S.C. § 300f et seq. [1974])

The Safe Drinking Water Act (SDWA) was established to protect the quality of drinking water in the U.S. This law focuses on all waters actually or potentially designed for drinking use, whether from above ground or underground sources.

The Act authorizes EPA to establish minimum standards to protect tap water and requires all owners or operators of public water systems to comply with these primary (health-related) standards. The 1996 amendments to SDWA require that EPA consider a detailed risk and cost assessment, and best available peer-reviewed science, when developing these standards. State governments, which can be approved to implement these rules for EPA, also encourage attainment of secondary standards (nuisance-related). Under the Act, EPA also establishes minimum standards for state programs to protect underground sources of drinking water from endangerment by underground injection of fluids.[46]

Refer to the text box for provisions of the Safe Drinking Water Act as amended in 1996.

National Environmental Policy Act (42 U.S.C. § 4321 et seq. [1969])

The National Environmental Policy Act (NEPA) was one of the first laws ever written that establishes the broad national framework

for protecting our environment. NEPA's basic policy is to assure that all branches of government give proper consideration to the environment prior to undertaking any major federal action that significantly affects the environment.

NEPA requirements are invoked when airports, buildings, military complexes, highways, parkland purchases, and other federal activities are proposed. Environmental Assessments (EAs) and Environmental Impact Statements (EISs), which are assessments of the likelihood of impacts from alternative courses of action, are required from all Federal agencies and are the most visible NEPA requirements.[47]

Federal Insecticide, Fungicide, and Rodenticide Act (7 U.S.C. § 136 et seq. [1996])

The Federal Insecticide, Fungicide, and Rodenticide Act (FIFRA) provides for federal regulation of pesticide distribution, sale, and use. All pesticides distributed or sold in the United States must be registered (licensed) by EPA. Before EPA may register a pesticide under FIFRA, the applicant must show, among other things, that using the pesticide according to specifications "will not generally cause unreasonable adverse effects on the environment."

FIFRA defines the term "unreasonable adverse effects on the environment" to mean: "(1) any unreasonable risk to man or the environment, taking into account the economic, social, and environmental costs and benefits of the use of any pesticide, or (2) a human dietary risk from residues that result from a use of a pesticide in or on any food inconsistent with the standard under section 408 of the Federal Food, Drug, and Cosmetic Act."[48]

Toxic Substances Control Act (15 U.S.C. § 2601 et seq. [1976])

The Toxic Substances Control Act of 1976 provides EPA with authority to require reporting, record-keeping and testing requirements, and restrictions relating to chemical substances and/or mixtures. Certain substances are generally excluded from TSCA, including, among others, food, drugs, cosmetics and pesticides.

TSCA addresses the production, importation, use, and disposal of specific chemicals including polychlorinated biphenyls (PCBs), asbestos, radon and lead-based paint.

Various sections of TSCA provide authority to:

- Require, under Section 5, pre-manufacture notification for "new chemical substances" before manufacture.
- Require, under Section 4, testing of chemicals by manufacturers, importers, and processors where risks or exposures of concern are found.
- Issue Significant New Use Rules (SNURs), under Section 5, when it identifies a "significant new use" that could result in exposures to, or releases of, a substance of concern.
- Maintain the TSCA Inventory, under Section 8, which contains more than 83,000

chemicals. As new chemicals are commercially manufactured or imported, they are placed on the list.[49]

[Note: The foregoing list is abstracted from a list of nine items.]

Comprehensive Environmental Response, Compensation, and Liability Act (Superfund) (42 U.S.C. § 9601 et seq. [1980])

The Comprehensive Environmental Response, Compensation, and Liability Act—otherwise known as CERCLA [pronounced "SIR-cla"] or Superfund—provides a Federal "Superfund" to clean up uncontrolled or abandoned hazardous-waste sites as well as accidents, spills, and other emergency releases of pollutants and contaminants into the environment. Through CERCLA, EPA was given power to seek out those parties responsible for any release and assure their cooperation in the cleanup.

EPA cleans up orphan sites when potentially responsible parties cannot be identified or located, or when they fail to act. Through various enforcement tools, EPA obtains private party cleanup through orders, consent decrees, and other small party settlements. EPA also recovers costs from financially viable individuals and companies once a response action has been completed.

EPA is authorized to implement the Act in all 50 states and U.S. territories. Superfund site identification, monitoring, and response activities in states are coordinated through the state environmental protection or waste management agencies.[50]

Resource Conservation and Recovery Act (42 U.S.C. § 6901 et seq. [1976])

The Resource Conservation and Recovery Act (RCRA) [pronounced "rick-rah"] gives EPA the authority to control hazardous waste from the "cradle to grave." This includes the generation, transportation, treatment, storage, and disposal of hazardous waste. RCRA also set forth a framework for the management of nonhazardous solid wastes. The 1986 amendments to RCRA enabled EPA to address environmental problems that could result from underground tanks storing petroleum and other hazardous substances.

HSWA—the Federal Hazardous and Solid Waste Amendments—are the 1984 amendments to RCRA that focused on waste minimization and phasing out land disposal of hazardous waste as well as corrective action for releases. Some of the other mandates of this law include increased enforcement authority for EPA, more stringent hazardous waste management standards, and a comprehensive underground storage tank program.[51]

Occupational Safety and Health Act (29 U.S.C. § 651 et seq. [1970])

Congress passed the Occupational Safety and Health Act to ensure worker and workplace safety. Their goal was to make sure employers provide their workers a place of employment free from recognized hazards to safety and health, such as exposure to toxic chemicals, excessive noise levels, mechanical dangers, heat or cold stress, or unsanitary conditions.

In order to establish standards for workplace health and safety, the Act also created the National Institute for Occupational Safety and Health (NIOSH) as the research institution for the Occupational Safety and Health Administration (OSHA). OSHA is a division of the U.S. Department of Labor that oversees the administration of the Act and enforces standards in all 50 states.[52]

Endangered Species Act (16 U.S.C. § 1531 et seq. [1973])

The Endangered Species Act (ESA) provides a program for the conservation of threatened and endangered plants and animals and the habitats in which they are found. [Endangered species are those at risk of extinction; threatened species are those at risk of becoming endangered in the future. See **FIGURE 15**.] The lead federal agencies for implementing ESA are the U.S. Fish and Wildlife Service (FWS) and the U.S. National Oceanic and Atmospheric Administration (NOAA) Fisheries Service. The FWS maintains a worldwide list of endangered species. Species include birds, insects, fish, reptiles, mammals, crustaceans, flowers, grasses, and trees. [Refer to **FIGURE 16**, which is a cartoon about endangered species selection.]

The law requires federal agencies, in consultation with the U.S. Fish and Wildlife Service and/or the NOAA Fisheries Service, to ensure that

FIGURE 15 Endangered species.
© Hung Chung Chih/Shutterstock

"We prefer to only protect the cutest animals."

FIGURE 16 Endangered species selection.
© Cartoon Resource/Shutterstock

actions they authorize, fund, or carry out are not likely to jeopardize the continued existence of any listed species or result in the destruction or adverse modification of designated critical habitat of such species. The law also prohibits any action that causes a "taking" of any listed species of endangered fish or wildlife. Likewise, import, export, interstate, and foreign commerce of listed species are all generally prohibited.[53]

▶ Conclusion

This chapter defined issues and principles that pertain to the development and implementation of public policies, regulations, and laws designed to protect the health of the public from environmentally caused diseases. The chapter presented terminology and concepts such as the policy cycle and risk assessment that are related to the environmental policy process. Also described were some of the major US and international agencies charged with the development, adoption, and enforcement of environmental policies and regulations.

Some of the specific US laws and regulations designed to reduce air pollution, maintain water quality, and protect natural resources also were reviewed. It was noted that a significant ethical issue for policy developers involves setting acceptable levels of risk associated with potential environmental hazards and balancing these risks against societal benefits that may accrue through specific policy alternatives. Despite the efforts made to develop and implement appropriate environmental policies, much more work is required in order to protect the population from environmental hazards. Particularly in need of greater protection from environmental hazards are vulnerable groups such as children, as well as residents of less-developed countries that do not have adequate environmental protections in place.

Although such efforts will be essential, promotion of human health in some cases may run counter to safeguarding the environment. Bioethicist David Resnik wrote that, "Policies that protect the environment, such as pollution control and pesticide regulation, also benefit human health. In recent years, however, it has become apparent that promoting human health sometimes undermines environmental protection. Some actions, policies, or technologies that reduce human morbidity, mortality and disease [e.g., increasing food production and draining swamps] can have detrimental effects on the environment. Since human health and environmental protection are sometimes at odds, political leaders, citizens, and government officials need a way to mediate and resolve conflicts between these values."[54(p261)]

Study Questions and Exercises

1. Define and give examples of the following terms:
   a. Risk assessment
   b. Risk management
   c. Environmental impact assessment
   d. Health impact assessment
   e. The built environment

2. What is meant by the term *environmental policy*? Give two examples of environmental policies that have been developed in the United States.

3. Discuss the precautionary principle. Describe the types of environmental situations to which this principle might apply.

4. Cite the EPA's statement on environmental justice. What does the term *fair treatment* mean?

5. List the components of meaningful involvement; indicate how they are correlated with equal access of communities to the decision-making process that leads to a healthful environment.

6. Define the term *environmental sustainability*. List the three components of sustainable development.

7. Describe the rationale for the polluter-pays principle.

8. List and define the stages of the policy cycle. Explain how environmental health research is a component of the policy cycle. How does environmental health research contribute to the implementation of sound environmental policies?

9. Explain how risk assessment aligns with policy development. Give an example.

10. Why is it important to incorporate community-based participatory methods into the process of environmental policy development?

11. Name some environmental problems that have an international scope. What policy initiatives have been developed to bring them under control?

12. Explain why children are more vulnerable to environmental toxins than adults. What types of policies are needed to protect vulnerable populations from environmental hazards?

13. Describe the role of each of the following agencies in policy formation and in protecting the environment:
    a. US Environmental Protection Agency (EPA)
    b. National Institute for Occupational Safety and Health (NIOSH)
    c. National Institute of Environmental Health Sciences (NIEHS)
    d. European Environment Agency (EEA)
    e. World Health Organization (WHO)

14. Define the following environmental acts and explain how they have helped to ensure a safe environment in the United States:
    a. Clean Water Act
    b. Safe Drinking Water Act
    c. National Environmental Policy Act
    d. Federal Insecticide, Fungicide, and Rodenticide Act
    e. Toxic Substances Control Act
    f. Comprehensive Environmental Response, Compensation, and Liability Act
    g. Resource Conservation and Recovery Act
    h. Occupational Safety and Health Act
    i. Endangered Species Act

For Further Reading

Johnson, BJ. The environmental health policy-making process. In Friis, RH, ed. *The Praeger Handbook of Environmental Health*, Volume 1. Santa Barbara, CA: ABC-CLIO, LLC, 2012, 305-332.

References

1. Walker B Jr. Environmental health and African Americans. *Am J Public Health.* 1991;81:1395–1398.
2. Edgens JG. Environmental policy through a systems approach. *J Med Assoc Georgia.* 1995;84:225–227.
3. House R, McDowell H, Peters M, et al. Agriculture sector resource and environmental policy analysis: an economic and biophysical approach. *Novartis Found Symp.* 1999;220:243–261.
4. Christie M. A comparison of alternative contingent valuation elicitation treatments for the evaluation of complex environmental policy. *J Environ Manage.* 2001;62:255–269.
5. Sturm A. The Global Development Research Center. Glossary of environmental terms. Available at: http://www.gdrc.org/uem/ait-terms.html. Accessed April 23, 2017.
6. Executive Office of the President of the United States. Council on Environmental Quality. *A Citizen's Guide to the NEPA: Having Your Voice Heard.* National Environmental Policy Act Sec. 101. Available at: https://energy.gov/sites/prod/files/nepapub/nepa_documents/RedDont/G-CEQ-CitizensGuide.pdf. Accessed April 23, 2017.
7. Sharp RR. Ethical issues in environmental health research. *Environ Health Perspect.* 2003;111:1786–1788.
8. Smith C. The precautionary principle and environmental policy: science, uncertainty, and sustainability. *Int J Occup Environ Health.* 2000;6:263–265.
9. EUROPA—European Commission. Endocrine disrupter research. What are endocrine disrupters? Available at: http://ec.europa.eu/environment/chemicals/endocrine/definitions/endodis_en.htm. Accessed April 23, 2017.
10. Amendola A, Wilkinson DR. Risk assessment and environmental policy making. *J Hazard Mater.* 2000;78:ix–xiv.
11. US Environmental Protection Agency. Environmental justice: basic information. Available at: https://www.epa.gov/environmentaljustice/learn-about-environmental-justice. Accessed April 24, 2017.
12. Thomas VM, Graedel TE. Research issues in sustainable consumption: toward an analytical framework for materials and the environment. *Environ Sci Technol.* 2003;37:5383–5388.
13. Maddox J. Positioning the goalposts: the best environmental policy depends on how you frame the question. *Nature.* 2000;403:139.
14. Organization for Economic Cooperation and Development. Recommendation of the council concerning the application of the polluter-pays principle to accidental pollution. July 7, 1989–C(89)88/Final. Available at: http://acts.oecd.org/Instruments/ShowInstrumentView.aspx?InstrumentID=38&InstrumentPID=305&Lang=en&Book=False. Accessed April 24, 2017.
15. Dadalos. Policy cycle: teaching politics. Available at: http://www.dadalos.org/politik_int/politik/policy-zyklus.htm. Accessed April 24, 2017.
16. Walker B Jr. Impediments to the implementation of environmental policy. *J Public Health Policy.* 1994;15:186–202.
17. Rabe BG. Legislative incapacity: the congressional role in environmental policy-making and the case of Superfund. *J Health Polit Policy Law.* 1990;15:571–589.
18. Suk WA, Avakian MD, Carpenter D, et al. Human exposure monitoring and evaluation in the Arctic: the importance of understanding exposures to the development of public health policy. *Environ Health Perspect.* 2004;112:113–120.
19. Johnson BJ. *Environmental Policy and Public Health.* Boca Raton, FL: Taylor & Francis Group, CRC Press; 2007.
20. Kaiser J. EPA gives science a bigger voice. *Science.* 2002;296:1005.
21. Schmidt CW. The market for pollution. *Environ Health Perspect.* 2001;109:A378–A381.
22. Swanson KE, Kuhn RG, Xu W. Environmental policy implementation in rural China: a case study of Yuhang, Zhejiang. *Environ Manage.* 2001;27:481–491.
23. Goudey R, Laslett G. Statistics and environmental policy: case studies from long-term environmental monitoring data. *Novartis Found Symp.* 1999;220:144–157.
24. Falconer K. Pesticide environmental indicators and environmental policy. *J Environ Manage.* 2002;65:285–300.
25. Landrigan PJ, Carlson JE. Environmental policy and children's health. *Future Child.* 1995;5(2):34–52.
26. Hyperdictionary. Meaning of biomarker. Available at: http://www.hyperdictionary.com/dictionary/biomarker. Accessed April 24, 2017.
27. Lerer LB. How to do (or not to do) . . . health impact assessment. *Health Policy Plan.* 1999;14(2):198–203.
28. Lock K, Gabrijelcic-Blenkus M, Martuzzi M, et al. Health impact assessment of agriculture and food policies: lessons learnt from the Republic of Slovenia. *Bull World Health Organ.* 2003;81:391–398.
29. US Environmental Protection Agency. *Fiscal Year 2014-2018 EPA Strategic Plan.* Washington, DC: U.S. Environmental Protection Agency; April 10, 2014.
30. Ensminger JT, McCold LN, Webb JW. Environmental impact assessment under the National Environmental Policy Act and the Protocol on Environmental Protection to the Antarctic Treaty. *Environ Manage.* 1999;24:13–23.
31. Tarmann A. South Africa's water policy champions rights of people and ecosystem. *Popul Today.* 2000;28(5):1–2.
32. Zylicz T. Environmental policy in economies in transition. *Scand J Work Environ Health.* 1999;25(suppl 3):72–80.
33. Kratovits A, Punning J-M. Driving forces for the formation of environmental policy in the Baltic countries. *Ambio.* 2001;30:443–449.
34. Goldman L, Falk H, Landrigan PJ, et al. Environmental pediatrics and its impact on government health policy. *Pediatrics.* 2004;113:1146–1157.
35. Suk WA, Ruchirawat KM, Balakrishnan K, et al. Environmental threats to children's health in southeast Asia and the western Pacific. *Environ Health Perspect.* 2003;111:1340–1347.
36. Pollard T. Policy prescriptions for healthier communities. *Am J Health Promot.* 2003;18(1):109–113.
37. California Air Resources Board. ARB mission and goals. Available at: http://www.arb.ca.gov/html/mission.htm. Accessed April 24, 2017.
38. US Environmental Protection Agency. About EPA. Available at: http://www.epa.gov/aboutepa/our-mission-and-what-we-do. Accessed April 24, 2017.
39. Centers for Disease Control and Prevention. National Institute for Occupational Safety and Health. Factsheet. DHHS(NIOSH) Publication No. 2013-140; October, 2015. Available at: https://www.cdc.gov/niosh/about/default.html. Accessed April 24, 2017.
40. US Department of Health and Human Services, Agency for Toxic Substances and Disease Registry. *FY 2008 ATSDR Annual Performance Report: Safer Healthier People.* Atlanta, GA: Agency for Toxic Substances and Disease Registry; 2008.
41. National Institutes of Health. National Institute of Environmental Health Sciences. NIEHS Priority Areas and

Programs. Available at: http://www.niehs.nih.gov/health/docs/niehs-overview.pdf. Accessed April 24, 2017.

42. European Commission. Living well, within the limits of our planet. 7th EAP—The new general Union Environment Action Program to 2020. Available at: http://ec.europa.eu/environment/pubs/pdf/factsheets/7eap/en.pdf. Accessed July 10, 2017.

43. WHO Regional Office for Europe. *Health and the Environment in the WHO European Region.* Copenhagen, Denmark: World Health Organization; 2013.

44. US Environmental Protection Agency. Summary of the Clean Air Act. Available at: https://www.epa.gov/laws-regulations/summary-clean-air-act. Accessed April 24, 2017.

45. US Environmental Protection Agency. History of the Clean Water Act. Available at: https://www.epa.gov/laws-regulations/history-clean-water-act. Accessed April 24, 2017.

46. US Environmental Protection Agency. Summary of the Safe Drinking Water Act. Available at: https://www.epa.gov/laws-regulations/summary-safe-drinking-water-act. Accessed April 24, 2017.

47. US Environmental Protection Agency. Summary of the National Environmental Policy Act. Available at: https://www.epa.gov/laws-regulations/summary-national-environmental-policy-act. Accessed April 24, 2017.

48. US Environmental Protection Agency. Summary of the Federal Insecticide, Fungicide, and Rodenticide Act. Available at: https://www.epa.gov/laws-regulations/summary-federal-insecticide-fungicide-and-rodenticide-act. Accessed April 24, 2017.

49. US Environmental Protection Agency. Summary of the Toxic Substances Control Act. Available at: https://www.epa.gov/laws-regulations/summary-toxic-substances-control-act. Accessed April 24, 2017.

50. US Environmental Protection Agency. Summary of the Comprehensive Environmental Response, Compensation, and Liability Act (Superfund). Available at: https://www.epa.gov/laws-regulations/summary-comprehensive-environmental-response-compensation-and-liability-act. Accessed April 24, 2017.

51. US Environmental Protection Agency. Summary of the Resource Conservation and Recovery Act. Available at: https://www.epa.gov/laws-regulations/summary-resource-conservation-and-recovery-act. Accessed April 24, 2017.

52. US Environmental Protection Agency. Summary of the Occupational Safety and Health Act. Available at: https://www.epa.gov/laws-regulations/summary-occupational-safety-and-health-act. Accessed April 24, 2017.

53. US Environmental Protection Agency. Summary of the Endangered Species Act. Available at: https://www.epa.gov/laws-regulations/summary-endangered-species-act. Accessed April 24, 2017.

54. Resnik DB. Human health and the environment: In harmony or in conflict? *Health Care Anal.* 2009;17:261–276.

© Jean-Luc Rivard/EyeEm/Getty Images

Zoonotic and Vector-Borne Diseases

LEARNING OBJECTIVES

By the end of this chapter the reader will be able to:

- Provide a rationale for environmental change and infectious disease occurrence.
- Indicate how a disease may be transmitted from an animal reservoir to humans.
- Define the terms vector-borne and zoonotic diseases, giving examples.
- Compare three human diseases transmitted by arthropod vectors.
- Discuss methods used to control vector-borne and zoonotic diseases.

▶ Introduction

Zoonotic and vector-borne diseases have substantial environmental components and contribute greatly to society's burdens of morbidity and mortality. Medicine and public health made great strides toward the control of infectious diseases during the late 19th century and the 20th century. In fact, by the mid-1960s, some health authorities proclaimed that society was moving toward the virtual elimination of infectious diseases as significant causes of morbidity and mortality.[1] Medical advances included immunizations, the use of antibiotics for the treatment of infectious diseases, declines in mortality from infectious and parasitic diseases, and the eradication of smallpox during the late 1970s. Public health achievements included improved environmental sanitation, disinfection of drinking water, and innovations in methods of food storage. Despite these notable accomplishments, infectious diseases once again have come to the forefront, especially with the occurrence of emerging and reemerging infections. In this chapter, you will learn about some of the notable examples of these conditions: malaria, dengue fever, and viral hemorrhagic fevers.

▶ Terminology Used in the Context of Zoonotic and Vector-Borne Diseases

The pathogenic agents for diseases in this category may involve prions, viruses, bacteria, protozoa, and helminths. For example, a total of more than 200 zoonotic pathogens may cause disease in human beings. Refer to **TABLE 1** for a list of some of the diseases in this category.

TABLE 1 Examples of Zoonoses and Vector-Borne Diseases
Bacterial
Anthrax
Cat scratch disease
Escherchia coli O157:H7 infection (discussed in Chapter)
Lyme disease
Plague
Psittacosis
Salmonellosis (discussed in Chapter)
Tularemia
Viral
Dengue fever
Encephalitis
Eastern equine encephalitis (EEE)
Japanese encephalitis (JE)
St. Louis encephalitis (SLE)
Tick-borne viral encephalitis
Venezuelan equine encephalitis (VEE)
Western equine encephalitis (WEE)
Hand, foot, and mouth disease
Hantavirus
Human monkeypox
Influenza
Avian influenza (discussed in Chapter)
Swine flu
Rabies
Rift Valley fever
West Nile virus
Yellow fever
Parasitic
Cryptosporidiosis (discussed in Chapter)
Cysticercosis and taeniasis (discussed in Chapter)
Giardiasis (discussed in Chapter)
Leishmaniasis
Malaria
Trichinellosis (discussed in Chapter)
Rickettsial
Q fever
Rocky Mountain spotted fever (RMSF)
Nonconventional (e.g., prions)
Variant Creutzfeldt-Jakob disease (v-CJD); mad cow disease (discussed in Chapter)

Zoonosis

The term **zoonosis** refers to "an infection or infectious disease transmissible under natural conditions from vertebrate animals to humans."[2] The definition of *zoonosis* varies to include several different situations.[3] In some cases a zoonosis may be a disease-causing pathogen that maintains an infection cycle in a host that is independent from humans, who can become inadvertent hosts. Other definitions refer to organisms that can infect both humans and animals during their life cycles. Conceptions of zoonotic agents may also include pathogens that cause disease in a nonhuman host or situations in which an infected animal remains free from symptoms of the disease. Contact with the skin, the bite or scratch of an animal, direct inhalation or ingestion (e.g., eating contaminated foods such as infected meat), or the bite of an arthropod vector are some of the methods for transmission of zoonotic pathogens. Note that immunocompromised persons, infants, and children younger than 5 years old may be at increased risk of morbidity from zoonotic diseases (e.g., toxoplasmosis) transmitted by cats and dogs. **TABLE 2** provides examples of zoonotic diseases and animals that are associated with those diseases.

Vector

In the context of infectious diseases, a **vector** is defined as "an insect or any living carrier that transports an infectious agent from an infected individual or its wastes to a susceptible individual or its food or immediate surroundings."[2] Part of the chain in transmission of infectious disease agents, vectors include various species of rodents (rats and mice) and arthropods (mosquitoes, ticks, sand flies, and biting midges).

Vector-Borne Infection

The term **vector-borne infection** refers to "[s]everal classes of vector-borne infections . . . each with epidemiological features determined by the interaction between the infectious agent and the human host on the one hand and the vector on the other. Therefore, environmental factors, such as climatic and seasonal variations, influence the epidemiologic pattern by virtue of their effects on the vector and its habits."[2] Vector-borne infections spread by biological transmission, which refers to "[t]ransmission of the infectious agent to [a] susceptible host by bite of blood-feeding (arthropod) vector, as in malaria, or by other inoculation, as in *Schistosoma* infection."[2]

TABLE 2 Examples of Zoonotic Diseases (and Associated Animals)

Name/Type of Animal	Zoonotic Disease
Domestic animals	
Cats	Rabies, toxocariasis (a parasitic disease from *Toxocara* roundworms), cat scratch disease (cat scratch fever), toxoplasmosis
Dogs	Rabies, parasites (e.g., dog tapeworm, hookworm, roundworm), campylobacteriosis
Farm animals (in general)	Anthrax, brucellosis, *Escherichia coli* O157:H7, Q fever, cryptosporidiosis
Horses	Salmonellosis, ringworm; less common: anthrax, cryptosporidiosis, rabies
Poultry (e.g., chickens and ducks)	Avian influenza, salmonellosis
Sheep and goats	Anthrax, Q fever
Reptiles (e.g., pet turtles and snakes)	Salmonellosis
Wild animals	
Bats	Rabies
Bears and wild hogs	Trichinosis
Birds	Cryptococcosis, histoplasmosis
Mammals (e.g., beavers, bison, deer, foxes, raccoons, skunks)	Rabies (raccoons, skunks, foxes), giardiasis (beavers, deer), brucellosis (bison)
Rodents	Hantavirus, plague, tularemia

Data from Centers for Disease Control and Prevention. Healthy Pets Healthy People. Available at https://www.cdc.gov/healthypets/pets/index.html. Accessed July 18, 2017.

▸ Examples of Vector-Borne Diseases

Names of diseases in this group are malaria, leishmaniasis, plague, Lyme disease, and Rocky Mountain spotted fever. Malaria is a disease of great significance for environmental health, even though it does not usually occur in developed regions such as North America, Europe, and Australia. Leishmaniasis affects residents of Middle Eastern countries, where it is endemic, and has been a particular concern of US military personnel stationed in endemic areas. The plague remains a serious threat to the world's population; during the Middle Ages, the "black death" (caused by plague) wiped out millions of people in Europe. Lyme disease, with an epidemic focus in the eastern and upper midwest United States and an expanding focus in the western United States, also occurs in other parts of the world.

Malaria

According to the Centers for Disease Control and Prevention (CDC), malaria is a disease that is found in more than 100 countries, with about 50% of the world's population at risk.[4] Typically, malaria is endemic to the warmer geographic areas of the globe. Endemic regions include Central and South America, Africa, South Asia, Southeast Asia, the Middle East, and Oceania. In 2015, the worldwide death toll for malaria was 438,000 persons, with an estimated 214 million clinical cases.[4]

The health impacts of malaria can be severe, as demonstrated by **FIGURE 1**, which shows a child who has developed edema (swelling) brought on by nephrosis associated with malaria. Nephrosis is a disease that impairs kidney function, resulting in a syndrome that produces edema, protein in the urine, and elevated levels of cholesterol in the blood.[5]

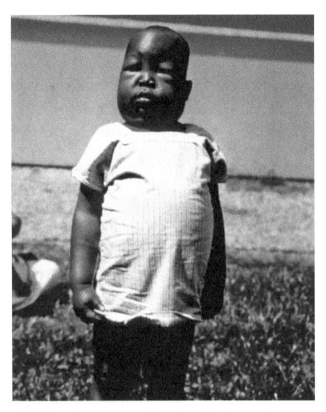

FIGURE 1 The edema exhibited by this African child was brought on by nephrosis associated with malaria (1975).
Courtesy of CDC/Dr. Myron G. Schultz

FIGURE 2 Ronald Ross, one of the discoverers of the malaria parasite.
Courtesy of CDC

Developing countries located in economically disadvantaged tropical and subtropical regions are especially affected by malaria. At greatest risk of dying are young children.[4] In addition to its human toll, malaria also exacts devastating economic impacts.[6] Sub-Saharan countries account for a disproportionate burden of morbidity and mortality from malaria.[7]

The average global, direct economic costs incurred by malaria are estimated to be $12 billion US annually.[6] The direct costs include those for treatment and prevention of the disease (e.g., medicine, hospitalization, and pesticide use). Other economic costs include lost productivity and earnings as well as negative impacts upon travel and tourism and agricultural labor.

The name *malaria* originates from the Italian *mala aria*, which referred to "bad air."[8] Originally, it was believed that malaria originated from the dank atmosphere around swamps. Now it is known that malaria is transmitted by mosquitoes that carry a unicellular parasite known as a plasmodium. Ronald Ross, an Indian Medical Service Officer (shown in FIGURE 2), is credited with discovering the malaria parasite in 1897 when he dissected mosquitoes and found the organism in their stomachs. He reported that he "saw a clear and almost perfectly circular outline before me of about 12 microns in diameter. The outline was much too sharp, the cell too small to be an ordinary stomach-cell of a mosquito. I looked a little further. Here was another, and another exactly similar cell."[9]

The four human forms of malaria are: *Plasmodium falciparum*, *P. vivax*, *P. ovale*, and *P. malariae*. Infection with plasmodia, the causative agent, can be life threatening; malaria symptoms include the occurrence of fever and flu-like symptoms such as headache, muscle aches, fatigue, and shaking chills. In some instances vomiting and diarrhea may accompany the disease. Another symptom of malaria is jaundice due to anemia, which is caused by the loss of red blood cells. *P. falciparum*, the most deadly type, may produce kidney failure, seizures, mental confusion, coma, and ultimately death.[4] *P. falciparum* is a very common variety of malaria in Africa south of the Sahara desert.

The *Anopheles* mosquito is the principal vector for malaria. The transmission of malaria involves the complex life cycle of mosquitoes (the vector) and human hosts (with human liver and human blood stages). The first stage in transmission involves the bite of an infected mosquito of the *Anopheles* type. (Refer to FIGURE 3.)

During the transmission cycle the malaria parasite (called the sporozoite form) is transferred to the human host when the mosquito takes a blood meal. In the human host the organism multiplies in the liver

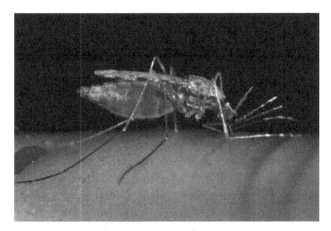

FIGURE 3 Female *Anopheles gambiae* mosquito feeding.
Courtesy of CDC/James Gathany

(exo-erythrocytic cycle) and red blood cells (erythrocytic cycle) and later develops into a form (gametocytic) that can be transmitted from the infected person to another host after a mosquito feeds on the infected host. In the sporogenic cycle in the mosquito, oocysts are produced that can be transmitted to a human host, continuing the life cycle of malaria. Symptoms of malaria occur approximately 9 to 14 days after the bite of an infected mosquito. **FIGURE 4** illustrates the cycle of transmission. (Malaria also may be transmitted by contaminated syringes or through blood transfusions.)

In the United States, malaria was endemic until the end of the 1940s. An antimalaria campaign was launched on July 1, 1947; one of the major activities consisted of spraying homes with DDT. By 1949, malaria was declared as having been brought under control as a major public health challenge in the United States.[10]

During the mid-20th century, efforts to control malaria by spraying with DDT and administering synthetic antimalaria drugs were found to be efficacious. Consequently, the World Health Organization (WHO) submitted a plan to the World Health Assembly in 1955 for the global eradication of malaria.[11] The plan

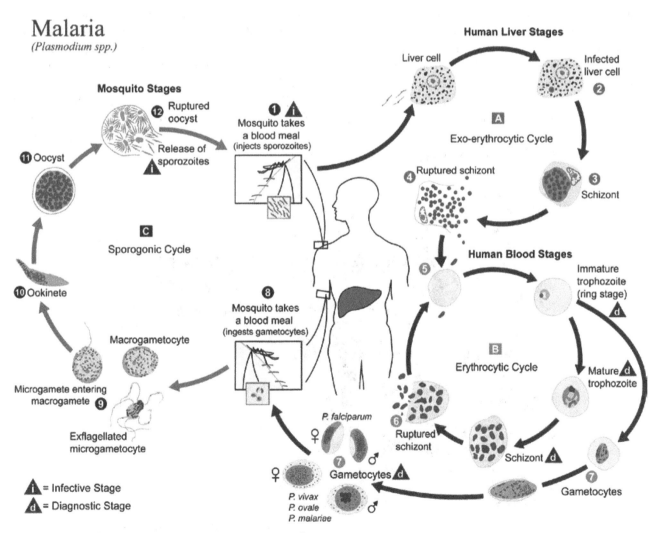

FIGURE 4 The life cycle of the malaria parasite (*Plasmodium* spp.).
Courtesy of CDC - DPDx/Alexander J. da Silva, PhD, Melanie Moser

FIGURE 5 A Stearman bi-plane spraying an insecticide during malaria control operations in Savannah, GA.
Courtesy of CDC

involved spraying, drug treatment, and surveillance. These efforts at eradication were successful in countries that had temperate climates and seasonal transmission of malaria but had limited success in other countries such as Indonesia, Afghanistan, Haiti, and Nicaragua.

DDT was highly effective in controlling the mosquito that can transmit malaria. For example, **FIGURE 5** and **FIGURE 6**, respectively, illustrate the use of bi-planes to spray for mosquitoes over wide areas and hand spraying methods to apply insecticide. At one time insecticides such as DDT were applied directly

to military personnel (**FIGURE 7**). Over a period of several decades, environmental observers began to gather suggestive evidence that DDT was harmful to bird species and other species of wildlife; the use of DDT was eventually opposed by many developed nations, especially the United States. This opposition led to withdrawal of funding for malaria spraying programs.

Discontinuance of outdoor DDT spraying and mosquitoes' development of insecticide resistance are among the factors that are believed to have contributed to the resurgence of malaria-bearing mosquitoes. As an alternative to outdoor spraying, South Africa has used annual spraying of DDT inside of homes, a procedure that appears to reduce the number of malaria cases.[12] Another means to control malaria is the use of bed nets that are impregnated with insecticides.

In addition to the use of insecticides, other methods of malaria control include the regular use of suppressive drugs in endemic areas and the avoidance of blood from donors who reside in endemic areas. Sanitary improvements such as the filling and draining of swamps and removal of standing water help to reduce the breeding areas for malaria-carrying mosquitoes. More information on the topic of mosquito control is provided later in the chapter.

The equatorial and southern areas of the continent of Africa form one of the endemic regions for malaria, as shown in **FIGURE 8**. In Africa, which accounts for a total of 91% of the world's malaria deaths,[6] evidence

FIGURE 6 In 1958, the National Malaria Eradication Program used an entirely new approach, implementing DDT for spraying of mosquitoes.
Courtesy of CDC

points to the movement of malaria from the low-lying areas where it is usually found to higher elevations where it is uncommon. In the late 1980s and early 1990s, Kenya experienced an upward movement of malaria cases, possibly due to small changes in climate that provided suitable conditions for malaria to survive.[13]

Malaria cases are not confined to endemic areas, because they may be imported into nonendemic areas by refugees and immigrants.[14] For example, the US state of Minnesota saw an increase in the number of reported cases of malaria from 5 in 1988 to 76 in 1998. The sources of these cases were persons native to Minnesota who had traveled to foreign areas and returned home as well as immigrants whose travel originated in a foreign country. In nonendemic areas, importation of cases of malaria presents a significant challenge to healthcare providers, who may not be familiar with the symptoms of diseases that they may not ordinarily see in clinical practice or during their training.

Leishmaniasis

Three forms of leishmaniasis are the visceral, mucocutaneous, and cutaneous varieties; the latter is the focus of this section. Cutaneous leishmaniasis is transmitted by the bite of an infected sand fly.[15,16] After being bitten by the fly, the human host develops a characteristic sore on the skin that forms after an incubation period of several weeks or months. **FIGURE 9** illustrates a lesion due to leishmaniasis. Near the site of the bite, a localized reaction occurs that forms a papule, which is "a small, raised, solid pimple or swelling, often forming part of a rash on the skin and typically inflamed."[17] Subsequently, ulceration, healing, and a scar form at the site.

Content removed due to copyright restrictions

FIGURE 8 Global number of reported cases of malaria, 2014.

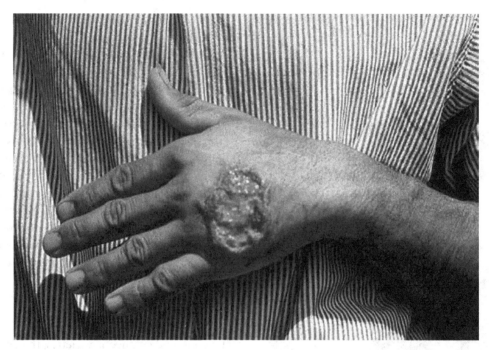

FIGURE 9 Skin ulcer due to leishmaniasis; hand of Central American adult.
Courtesy of CDC/Dr. D.S. Martin

The reservoir for the cutaneous form of leishmaniasis includes wild rodents, human beings, and carnivores (e.g., domestic dogs). The disease is transmitted from the reservoir to the human host by a sand fly known as the phlebotomus fly. (See **FIGURE 10**.)

FIGURE 11 shows the cycle of transmission from the sand fly to the human host and vice versa, during the sand fly and human stages. The causative agent for leishmaniasis is a protozoal organism, which exists in two forms—promastigotes and amastigotes. These two organisms are shown in Figure 11. Promastigotes are an extracellular form of the organism that has flagella (whip-like appendages that enable the organism to move), whereas amastigotes are nonflagellated intracellular forms. Following the bite of an infected sand fly, promastigotes are injected into the host. The promastigotes are phagocytized by macrophages; phagocytization refers to the process whereby the macrophages in bodily fluids scavenge for foreign materials and, in this case, capture the promastigotes. The promastigotes transform into amastigotes within the macrophages, multiply and later explode out of the macrophages, and then may be ingested by sand flies through a blood meal that contains infected macrophages. Subsequently, amastigotes are transformed in the gut of the sand fly into promastigotes, continuing the cycle of transmission.

The various forms of leishmaniasis, present in the countries surrounding the Mediterranean and endemic in another 82 countries, are showing an increasing incidence. For example, Syria, Tunisia,

FIGURE 10 This is a female *Phlebotomus sp.* sand fly, a vector of the parasite responsible for leishmaniasis.
Courtesy of CDC

and Israel have reported increasing numbers of cases. Among 350 million persons at risk for leishmaniasis, the annual incidence is approximately 600,000 cases. The environmental factors hypothesized to be responsible for increases in leishmaniasis include movement of the human population into endemic areas, increasing urbanization, extension of agricultural projects into endemic areas, and climate change due to global warming.

Cutaneous leishmaniasis is a concern of US military personnel stationed in endemic areas (e.g., Afghanistan, Iraq, and Kuwait). The condition has been subjected to

Leishmaniasis
(Leishmania spp.)

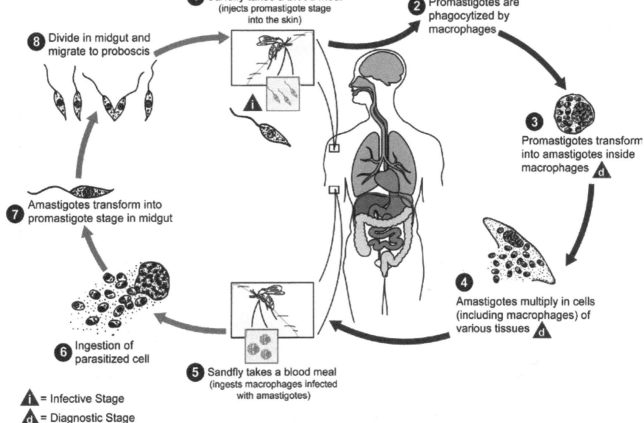

FIGURE 11 This is an illustration of the life cycle of *Leishmania* spp., the causal agents of leishmaniasis.

Courtesy of CDC- DPDx/Alexander J. da Silva, PhD

extensive epidemiologic investigations in Israel, where leishmaniasis affects both military personnel and the general population. **FIGURE 12** demonstrates that in 2013 reported endemic cases were concentrated primarily in the Middle East and South America.

Methods of control of leishmaniasis include the following:

- Periodic application of long-acting insecticides to dwelling units
- Use of screens to prevent sand flies from entering housing
- Elimination of breeding areas (e.g., rubbish heaps) for the phlebotomus fly
- Destruction of rodent burrows and control of domestic dogs

Plague

The bacterium *Yersinia pestis* is the infectious agent for plague, a condition that infects both animals and humans. Plague may be transmitted by the bite of a flea harbored by rodents (see **FIGURE 13**, an oriental rat flea). Historians believe that the plague epidemic during the Middle Ages (the "black death") was caused by fleas from infested rats.

Although morbidity and case fatality rates among persons infected with the disease remain high, prompt treatment with antibiotics is efficacious.[18] Nevertheless, human infections with *Y. pestis* remain a matter of great concern for authorities. **FIGURE 14** illustrates how plague may be transmitted from the environment to humans. Plague is distributed widely across the world, including the United States, South America, Asia, and parts of Africa (see **FIGURE 15**). In some regions, plague is a zoonotic disease.

One of the natural reservoirs for plague is wild rodents, such as the ground squirrels that are at home in the western United States. Pets, such as house cats and dogs, may bring the wild rodents' fleas into homes or may even transmit plague on rare occasions from their bites or scratches. The condition known as bubonic plague begins with nonspecific

FIGURE 12 Status of endemicity of cutaneous leishmaniasis, worldwide, 2013.

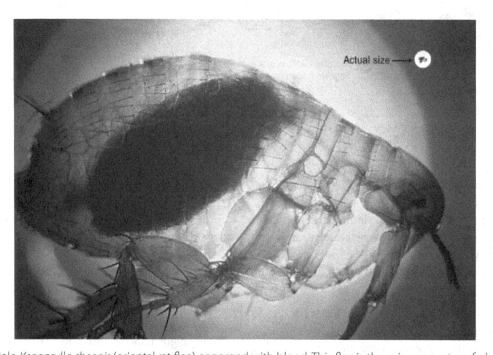

Actual size ⟶

FIGURE 13 Male *Xenopsylla cheopis* (oriental rat flea) engorged with blood. This flea is the primary vector of plague in most large plague epidemics in Asia, Africa, and South America.
Courtesy of CDC

symptoms such as fever, chills, and headache and then progresses into lymphadenitis (infected lymph nodes) at the site of the initial flea bite. There may be secondary involvement of the lungs, known as pneumonic plague. The epidemiologic significance of this form of plague is that respiratory droplets from an infected person can transfer *Y. pestis* to other individuals. The case fatality rate for untreated bubonic plague is high, ranging from about 50% to 60%. Patients who are infected with the disease need to be placed in strict isolation and their clothing and other personal articles disinfected. Persons who have had contact with the patient should be placed under quarantine.

FIGURE 14 Transmission of plague from the environment to humans.

Reproduced from Centers for Disease Control and Prevention. Protect yourself from plague. C5235098-A. Available at: https://www.cdc.gov/plague/resources/235098_plaguefactsheet_508.pdf
Accessed January 23, 2017.

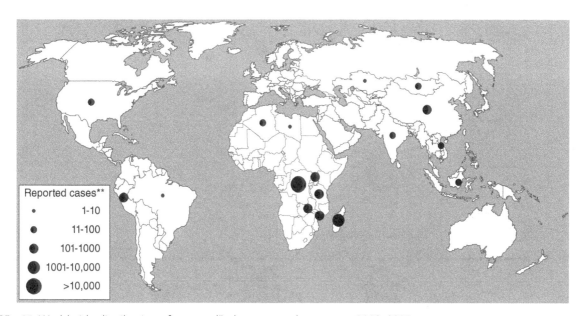

FIGURE 15 Worldwide distribution of reported* plague cases by country, 2000–2009.

Modified and reproduced from Centers for Disease Control and Prevention. Plague. Maps and statistics. Available at: https://www.cdc.gov/plague/maps/index.html.
Accessed January 29, 2017.
* Data reported to World Health Organization (WHO).
** Dot placed in center of reporting country.

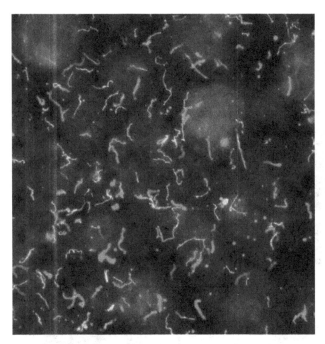

FIGURE 16 *Borrelia burgdorferi*, the spirochetal bacteria that cause Lyme disease.

Courtesy of National Institute of Allergy and Infectious Diseases (NIAID)

ignore posted warning signs in nature parks and risk contracting plague when they feed squirrels and chipmunks. Also, the number of rodents needs to be kept in check. Public health officials should inform the public of the importance of preventing rats from entering buildings and should encourage the removal of food sources that could enable rats to multiply. Shipping areas and docks need to be patrolled because rats can be transferred to and from cargo containers and ships. Hunters and persons who handle wildlife should take care to wear gloves.[19]

Lyme Disease

Lyme disease is a condition that was identified in 1977 when a cluster of arthritis cases occurred among children around the area of Lyme, Connecticut. The causative agent for the disease is a bacterium (bacterial spirochete) known as *Borrelia burgdorferi*, shown in **FIGURE 16**.

Transmission of Lyme disease to humans is associated with infected black-legged ticks (*Ixodes scapularis*) that ingest blood by puncturing the skin of the host. (Refer to **FIGURE 17**.) In the Pacific coastal region of the United States, the western black-legged tick (*Ixodes pacificus*) has been identified as the vector. Also shown in the figure are the Lone Star tick and the

Environmental control of the disease may be accomplished by encouraging the public to avoid enzootic areas, especially rodent burrows, and direct contact with rodents. Unfortunately, some people

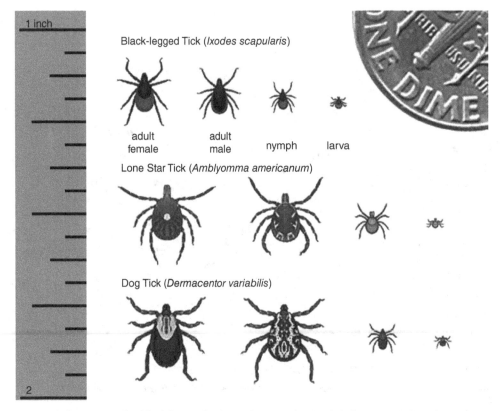

FIGURE 17 (Top) From left to right: The black-legged tick (*Ixodes scapularis*) adult female, adult male, nymph, and larva.

Modified and reproduced from Centers for Disease Control and Prevention. Lyme Disease. Available at: https://www.cdc.gov/ticks/life_cycle_and_hosts.html. Accessed January 25, 2017.

dog tick, which are not known to be transmitters of the Lyme disease bacterium to human beings.

A total of 28,453 confirmed cases were reported to the CDC in 2015.[20] From 2005 to 2014, the annual number of reported cases ranged from 19,931 (2006) to 29,959 (2009). Regarding the geographic distribution for Lyme disease, about 95% of cases in 2014 were concentrated in the northeastern, mid-Atlantic, and upper midwestern regions of the United States. (Refer to **FIGURE 18**.) The map in Figure 18 shows other geographic regions where Lyme disease occurred during that year.

Those at risk of developing Lyme disease include people who work in or come into contact with tick-infested areas. For example, persons who engage in recreational activities that take them outdoors into infested areas or who clear brush or landscape their own backyards may be at risk of infection with Lyme disease. Antibiotic therapy exists for successful treatment of most patients who are diagnosed in the early stages of the disease. Preventive measures are directed at reducing exposure to the ticks that carry the bacterium. For example, people who venture into endemic areas should be inspected for the presence of ticks. Wearing light-colored clothing helps to disclose the presence of ticks.

Rocky Mountain Spotted Fever

Rocky Mountain spotted fever (RMSF), among the most acute infectious diseases, is caused by *Rickettsia rickettsii*, a rickettsial agent. (Rickettsia are agents that are similar to viruses in that they reproduce within living cells and are similar to some bacteria in that they require oxygen and are susceptible to antibiotics.)

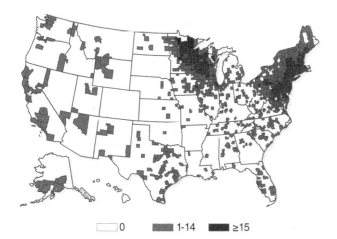

FIGURE 18 Incidence* of reported cases of Lyme disease by county—United States, 2014.

Modified and reproduced from Centers for Disease Control and Prevention. Summary of notifiable diseases—United States, 2014. *MMWR.* 2016;63(54):117.

* Per 100,000 population.

It is a febrile disease with sudden onset of moderate to high fevers that may last up to 3 weeks when untreated. Other symptoms include rash, headache, and chills. The case-fatality rate can range up to 25% among untreated patients, but drops dramatically when patients are treated with antibiotics early in the course of the disease. The bite of an infected tick (e.g., the American dog tick or the Rocky Mountain wood tick) is associated with transmission of RMSF. These species of ticks form the reservoir for *R. rickettsii*. Ticks also can transmit RMSF to wild animals and domestic animals such as dogs.

▶ Viral Hemorrhagic Fevers

According to the Centers for Disease Control and Prevention, viral hemorrhagic fevers (VHFs) denote

> …a group of illnesses that are caused by several distinct families of viruses. In general, the term "viral hemorrhagic fever [VHF]" is used to describe a severe multisystem syndrome.… Characteristically, the overall vascular system is damaged, and the body's ability to regulate itself is impaired. These symptoms are often accompanied by hemorrhage (bleeding); however, the bleeding is itself rarely life-threatening. While some types of hemorrhagic fever viruses can cause relatively mild illnesses, many of these viruses cause severe, life-threatening disease.[21]

Of particular interest to the field of environmental health are the characteristics that VHFs share. The viruses that cause most VHFs are zoonoses, referring to the fact that they require an animal or insect host as a natural reservoir; the viruses reside and multiply in their hosts and are dependent upon their hosts for survival. The principal reservoirs for VHFs are rodents and arthropods. Examples of rodents that form the animal host reservoir for VHFs include certain species of rats such as the cotton rat, mice including the deer mouse and house mouse, and field rodents. Mosquitoes and ticks serve as the main arthropod vectors, whereas other forms of VHFs have unknown hosts.

The causative viruses for VHFs can be found throughout much of the world. Nevertheless, many of the viruses responsible for VHFs tend to be localized to those geographic areas in which the host species reside. Humans may become infected when they encounter an infected host (e.g., through contact with excreta from rodents) or are bitten by an arthropod. Sometimes, person-to-person transmission of the viruses can occur; examples of viruses in this category are Ebola and Marburg viruses. In most instances, there are no known cures for viral hemorrhagic fevers with the exception of supportive therapy. Viruses that cause VHFs and are spread by arthropods are also classified as arboviruses (discussed in the next section).

Examples of VHFs discussed in this chapter are:

- Hantavirus pulmonary syndrome (see emerging zoonoses)
- Dengue hemorrhagic fever (covered in the section on emerging and reemerging infections)

▶ Arthropod-Borne Viral Diseases (Arboviral Diseases)

The term **arboviral disease** (abbreviated from arthropod-borne viral disease) denotes viral diseases that can be acquired when blood-feeding arthropod vectors infect a human host. Typically, the complex cycle of transmission involves a non-human vertebrate (reservoir host) and an arthropod vector. The arthropod vectors that transmit arboviruses include ticks, sand flies, biting midges, and mosquitoes; however, most arboviruses are spread by mosquitoes. A total of more than 100 viruses are known at present as arboviruses that produce disease in humans. For some arboviral diseases (e.g., West Nile virus and Japanese encephalitis virus), humans are not usually an important component of the cycle of infection; other arboviruses (e.g., dengue fever virus and yellow fever virus) involve humans in virus amplification and infection of vectors.[19] The four main clinical symptoms or illnesses caused by arboviruses are:

1. Acute central nervous system (CNS) illness ranging in severity from mild aseptic meningitis to encephalitis or flaccid paralysis.
2. Acute self-limited fevers, with and without exanthum (rash), and often accompanied by headache; some may give rise to more serious illness with CNS involvement or hemorrhages.
3. Hemorrhagic fevers, often associated with capillary leakage, shock, and high case-fatality rates (these may be accompanied by liver damage with jaundice, particularly in cases of yellow fever).
4. Polyarthritis and rash, with or without fever and of variable duration, self-limited or with

arthralgic sequelae lasting several weeks to years.[19(p34)]

Examples of diseases caused by arboviruses are arboviral encephalitides (e.g., mosquito-borne and tick-borne viral encephalitis) and West Nile virus.

Arboviral Encephalitides

This group of viral illnesses (encephalitis) is associated with acute inflammation of sections of the brain, spinal cord, and meninges. Generally of short duration, the majority of infections are asymptomatic. Other cases present as a mild illness with fever, headache, or aseptic meningitis. Severe illness also can occur, with headache; high fever; disorientation; coma; and, occasionally, convulsions, paralysis and death.[19]

Among the etiologic agents of viral encephalitis are the St. Louis encephalitis virus (SLEV), eastern equine encephalitis virus (EEEV), and LaCrosse encephalitis virus (LACV).[22] A form of viral encephalitis associated with West Nile virus is discussed in next section. St. Louis encephalitis occurs most commonly in the eastern and central states of the United States. Eastern equine encephalitis is found mostly in the Atlantic and Gulf Coast states. The geographic range for most cases of LaCrosse encephalitis spans the upper midwest, mid-Atlantic, and southeastern regions. Western equine encephalitis virus (WEEV) and Venezuelan equine encephalitis virus (VEEV) are two additional viral agents associated with encephalitis. An additional form of encephalitis known as Japanese encephalitis (JE) affects the western Pacific islands ranging from the Philippines to Japan, parts of eastern Asia including Korea and China, as well as India.[19]

Most arboviral encephalitides are transmitted by the bite of an arthropod vector—primarily mosquitoes, but other vectors include midges or sandflies.[19] The reservoir hosts for some forms of encephalitis viruses consist of nonhuman vertebrate hosts (e.g., wild birds and small animals). According to the Centers for Disease Control and Prevention, the cost of arboviral encephalitides is approximately $150 million per year, including vector control and surveillance activities. In the United States, the incidence of these forms of encephalitis varies from 150 to 3,000 cases per year.[22]

Tick-borne viral encephalitides refer to a group of viral encephalitides transmitted by ticks.[19] These forms of encephalitides, also caused by arboviruses, produce diseases that bear a similarity to mosquito-borne encephalitides; the geographic range for tick-borne encephalitides includes parts of the former Soviet Union, eastern and central Europe, Scandinavia, and the United Kingdom. They are found also in eastern Canada and the United States. The reservoir for this group of encephalitides consists of ticks, or ticks in combination with some mammalian species, rodents, and birds.

Other Mosquito-Borne Viral Fevers— West Nile Virus

The West Nile virus (WNV), an example of an arbo-viral disease, is classified as a type of mosquito-borne viral fever; the etiologic agent is a *Flavivirus*.[19] WNV has gained much notoriety in the United States

WEST NILE VIRUS (WNV) FACT SHEET

What Is West Nile Virus?

West Nile infection can cause serious disease. WNV is established as a seasonal epidemic in North America that flares up in the summer and continues into the fall.

What Can I Do to Prevent WNV?

The easiest and best way to avoid WNV is to prevent mosquito bites.

- When outdoors, use insect repellents containing DEET, picaridin, IR3535, some oil of lemon eucapyptus, or paramenthane-diol. Follow the directions on the package.
- Many mosquitoes are most active from dusk to dawn. Be sure to use insect repellent and wear long sleeves and pants at these times or consider staying indoors during these hours.
- Make sure you have good screens on your windows and doors to keep mosquitoes out.
- Get rid of mosquito breeding sites by emptying standing water from flower pots, buckets, and barrels. Change the water in pet dishes and replace the water in bird baths weekly. Drill holes in tire swings so water drains out. Keep children's wading pools empty and on their sides when they aren't being used.

What Are the Symptoms of WNV?

- **Serious symptoms in a few people.** About one in 150 people infected with WNV will develop severe illness [neuroinvasive disease]. The severe symptoms can include high fever, headache, neck stiffness, stupor, disorientation, coma, tremors, convulsions, muscle weakness, vision loss, numbness, and paralysis. These symptoms may last several weeks, and neurological effects may be permanent.
- **Milder symptoms in some people.** Up to 20% of the people who become infected will have symptoms that can include fever, headache, body aches, nausea, vomiting, and sometimes swollen lymph glands or a skin rash on the chest, stomach, and back. Symptoms can last for as short as a few days to as long as several weeks.
- **No symptoms in most people.** Approximately 80% of people who are infected with WNV will not show any symptoms at all.

How Does West Nile Virus Spread?

- **Infected mosquitoes.** WNV is spread by the bite of an infected mosquito. Mosquitoes become infected when they feed on infected birds. Infected mosquitoes can then spread WNV to humans and other animals when they bite.
- **Transfusions, transplants, and mother-to-child transmission.** In a very small number of cases, WNV also has been spread directly from an infected person through blood transfusions, organ transplants, breastfeeding, and during pregnancy from mother to baby.
- **Not through touching.** WNV is not spread through casual contact such as touching or kissing a person with the virus.

How Soon Do Infected People Get Sick?

People typically develop symptoms between 3 and 14 days after they are bitten by the infected mosquito.

How Is WNV Infection Treated?

There is no specific treatment for WNV infection. In cases with milder symptoms, people experience symptoms such as fever and aches that pass on their own, although illness may last weeks to months. In more severe cases, people usually need to go to the hospital where they can receive supportive treatment including intravenous fluids, help with breathing, and nursing care.

Reproduced from Centers for Disease Control and Prevention. West Nile virus (WNV) fact sheet. Available at: https://www.cdc.gov/westnile/resources/pdfs/wnvFactsheet_508.pdf. Accessed July 14, 2017.

West Nile virus transmission cycle

In nature, West Nile virus cycles between mosquitoes (especially *Culex* species) and birds. Some infected birds can develop high levels of the virus in their bloodstream and mosquitoes can become infected by biting these infected birds. After about a week, infected mosquitoes can pass the virus to more birds when they bite.

Mosquitoes with West Nile virus also bite and infect people, horses and other mammals. However, humans, horses and other mammals are 'dead end' hosts. This means that they do not develop high levels of virus in their bloodstream, and cannot pass the virus on to other biting mosquitoes.

Mosquito Vector

"Dead end" host

Bird amplifier host

"Dead end" host

Centers for Disease Control and Prevention

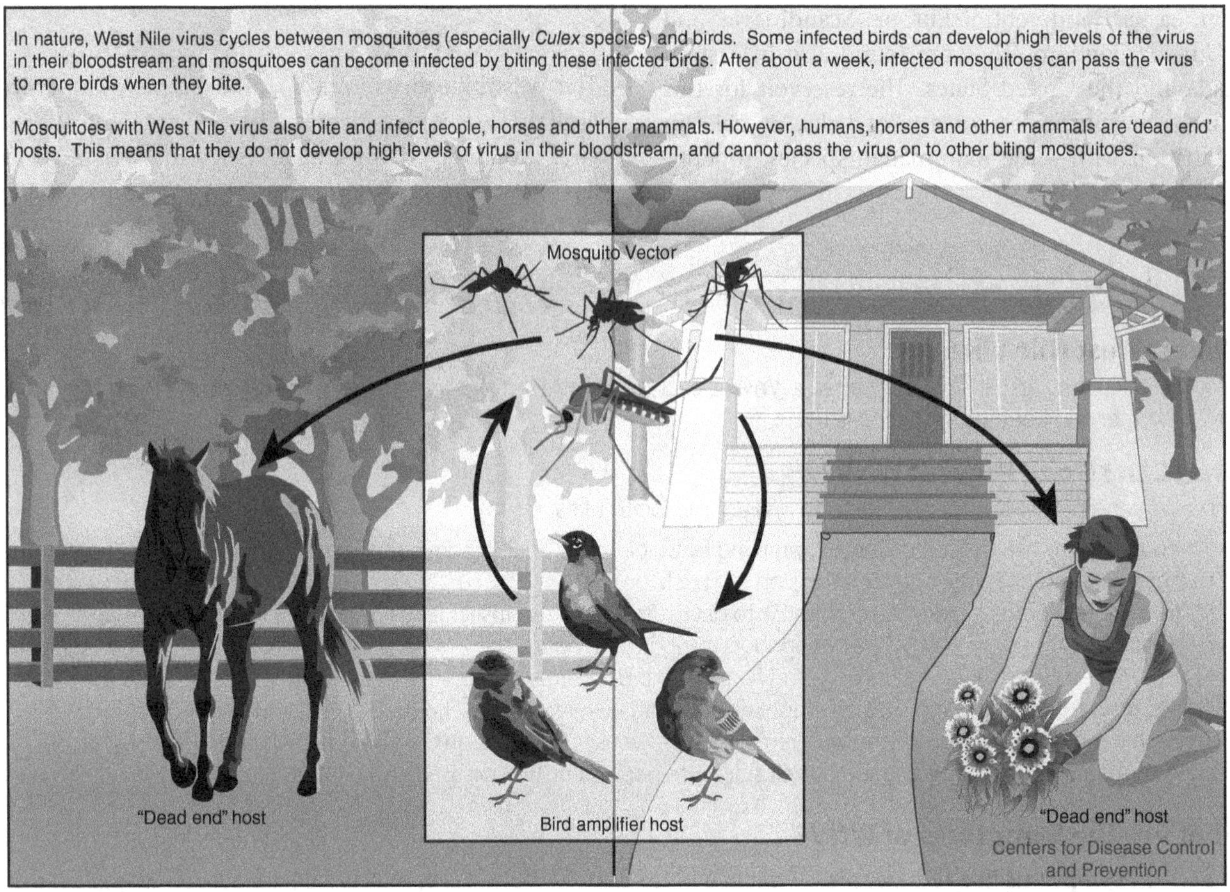

FIGURE 19 West Nile virus transmission cycle.

Reproduced from Centers for Disease Control and Prevention. West Nile virus transmission cycle. Available at: https://www.cdc.gov/westnile/resources/pdfs/13_240124_west_nile_lifecycle_birds _plainlanguage_508.pdf. Accessed July 14, 2017.

because of its ability to spread rapidly across wide geographic regions. In addition, WNV caused the deaths of many wild birds and some humans. During summer 2004, WNV spread to the US state of California, having been associated previously with outbreaks in New York and other areas of the eastern United States. People most at risk of contracting WNV are those who spend a great deal of time outdoors, where they could be bitten by infected mosquitoes. Older people (age 50+) are more likely than younger people to develop serious symptoms from WNV infection. Refer to the text box for more information.

FIGURE 19 presents the West Nile virus transmission cycle. Neuroinvasive disease is the most severe form of WNV and occurs in somewhat less than 1% of cases. **FIGURE 20** shows the incidence of reported cases of neuroinvasive disease associated with West Nile virus in United States and US territories during 2014. The states with the highest reported incidence of neuroinvasive disease were Nebraska, North Dakota, California, South Dakota, Louisiana, and Arizona.

▶ Emerging and Reemerging Infectious Diseases/Emerging Zoonoses

Emerging and reemerging infectious diseases include conditions that may have been unrecognized as well as those reappearing after a decline in incidence. The term **emerging zoonoses** refers to zoonotic diseases that are caused by either apparently new agents or by known agents that occur in locales or species that previously did not appear to be affected by these known agents.[23]

Several factors may have contributed to the resurgence of these conditions: migration of human populations within tropical and semitropical areas, increases in international travel, population growth with attendant crowding and urbanization, overuse of antibiotics and pesticides, lack of clean drinking water, and climate changes attributed to human activity.[1] In the northern hemisphere, rising temperatures

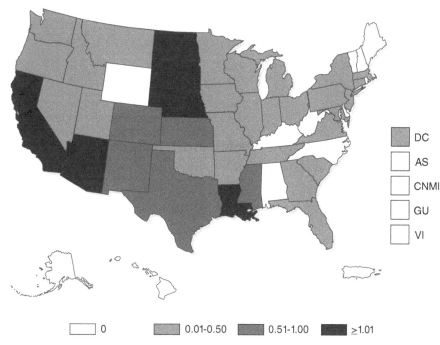

	DC
	AS
	CNMI
	GU
	VI

| | 0 | | 0.01-0.50 | | 0.51-1.00 | | ≥1.01 |

FIGURE 20 West Nile virus. Incidence* of reported cases of neuroinvasive disease—United States and US territories, 2014.

Modified and reproduced from Centers for Disease Control and Prevention. Summary of notifiable diseases—United States, 2014. *MMWR*. 2016;63(54):79.

* Per 100,000 population.

and increasing rainfall promote the growth and northward migration of mosquito populations, with corresponding increases in diseases transmitted by mosquitoes.

See **FIGURE 21** for the geographic locations where emerging and reemerging infections have been identified; note that the figure shows both zoonotic and nonzoonotic conditions. Among the most commonly identified factors associated with the rise of emerging zoonoses are ecological changes that result from agricultural practices (e.g., deforestation, conversion of grasslands, and irrigation).[23] Other factors include changes in the human population and human behavior (e.g., wars, migration, and urbanization). **TABLE 3** presents examples of emerging zoonoses and lists conditions that may be linked to their occurrence. In the following sections, some of these emerging zoonoses will be covered in more detail.

Hantaviruses and Hantavirus Pulmonary Syndrome

The hantavirus pulmonary syndrome (HPS) represents a very severe and sometimes fatal respiratory condition that is transmitted by rodent vectors.[24] The causative agent is the hantavirus, part of the bunyavirus family of viruses.[25] HPS may be transmitted when aerosolized (airborne) urine and droppings from infected rodents are inhaled. For example, vacationers who return to a mountain cabin after an extended absence may cause rodent droppings to be aerosolized when they sweep up in order to make the cabin habitable, or they may stir up virus particles when they walk across a floor contaminated with urine from rodents. The primary known vectors for transmission of the hantavirus are four species of rodents: the cotton rat, the rice rat, the white-footed mouse, and the deer mouse (shown in **FIGURE 22**). One of the most widely distributed vectors and the main host for the hantavirus is the deceptively cute deer mouse—*Peromyscus maniculatus*—which is found throughout North America.

Hantaviruses have existed for many years, yet they gained public attention in 1993 when a mysterious case (a so-called first outbreak) occurred. The CDC reports that "[i]n May 1993, an outbreak of an unexplained pulmonary illness occurred in the southwestern United States, in an area shared by Arizona, New Mexico, Colorado and Utah known as 'The Four Corners.' A young, physically fit Navajo man suffering from shortness of breath was rushed to a hospital in New Mexico and died very rapidly."[26] This case created an environmental health mystery in which an unknown causative agent also was believed to have caused the death of the man's fiancée and an

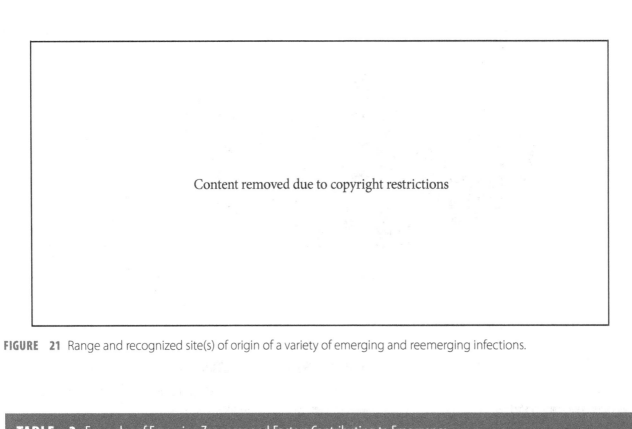

Content removed due to copyright restrictions

FIGURE 21 Range and recognized site(s) of origin of a variety of emerging and reemerging infections.

TABLE 3 Examples of Emerging Zoonoses and Factors Contributing to Emergence
Content removed due to copyright restrictions

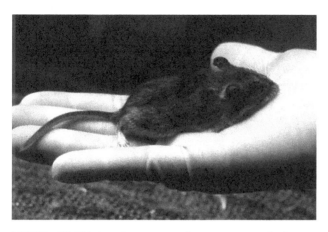

FIGURE 22 This is a deer mouse, *Peromyscus maniculatus*, a hantavirus carrier that becomes a threat when it enters human habitation in rural and suburban areas.
Courtesy of CDC/Brian W.J. Mahy, BSc, MA, PhD, ScD, DSc

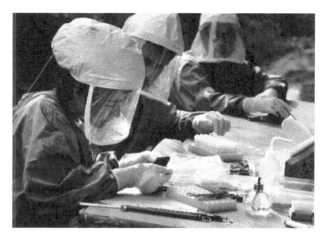

FIGURE 23 Three CDC health officials inspecting specimens suspected of being connected with a hantavirus outbreak.
Courtesy of CDC

additional five people. Epidemiologic investigations ruled out a new type of influenza or pesticide exposure. Eventually the deaths were linked to a heretofore unknown form of hantavirus, which was traced to the deer mouse via extensive rodent-trapping programs. To avoid a panic situation, the trappers did not wear protective devices. However, in the laboratory, researchers who dissected the trapped rodents wore special clothing, masks, and goggles as protection against biohazards (see **FIGURE 23**).

Further study suggested that rodents may have entered the households where the victims lived. During 1993, the deer mouse population increased to higher levels than normal. This population increase was attributed to heavy snows and rainfall in early 1993 that followed a lengthy drought in the Four Corners area. Because of the increased availability of food following the heavy precipitation, the mouse population increased by a factor of 10 between May 1992 and May 1993. Thus it was more likely that humans could contract hantavirus carried by the mice.

Although HPS is known to cause potentially deadly infections, fortunately the syndrome is rare. According to the CDC, "[t]hrough January 6, 2016, a total of 690 cases of hantavirus pulmonary syndrome have been reported in the United States. Of these, 659 cases occurred from 1993, onward, following identification of hantavirus pulmonary syndrome, whereas 31 cases were retrospectively identified."[27] The epidemiologic features of these cases in 35 states where the syndrome was reported were as follows: 63% male, 78% white, 18% American Indian, and mean age 38 years; the case-fatality rate for the disease was 36%.[27] (See **FIGURE 24**.) Among the states reporting the largest number of cases were New Mexico, Colorado, California, and Arizona.

Dengue Fever, Dengue Hemorrhagic Fever, and Dengue Shock Syndrome

Four related viruses (flavivirus serotypes) cause dengue infection, which produces a spectrum of illness that ranges from mild to severe. The mildest form of dengue causes a low-level illness with a nonspecific fever. Classic dengue fever (DF) is also a rather benign, self-limited disease; symptoms may include high fever, severe headache, eye pain, muscle pain, joint pain, rash, and mild bleeding. Dengue hemorrhagic fever (DHF) results in a life-threatening illness with fever (that lasts 2–7 days), abdominal pain, and bleeding phenomena. Dengue shock syndrome (DSS) includes the symptoms of DHF and is associated with shock (e.g., hypotension and rapid, weak pulse). DSS is a potentially fatal condition.[19,28]

As shown in **FIGURE 25**, the primary locations for dengue fever are the tropical and subtropical areas of the world, for example, southeast Asia, tropical Africa, and South America. The virus is thought to have existed among monkeys, and several centuries ago moved to humans in Africa and Asia. Dengue was uncommon until after the mid-20th century, with outbreaks occurring in the Philippines and Thailand in the 1950s and later in the Caribbean and Latin America.

The vector for transmission of the disease is a type of domestic day-biting mosquito known as the *Aedes aegypti*, a mosquito that prefers to feed on human hosts. (Refer to **FIGURE 26**.) The spread of the vector was linked to transport ships during World War II. At present, dengue is among the most significant mosquito-borne viral diseases that afflict humans. The CDC estimates that more than 100 million cases of dengue fever occur annually.[28]

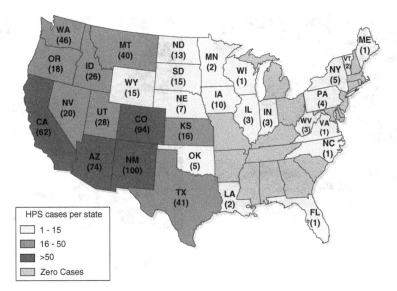

FIGURE 24 Hantavirus pulmonary syndrome (HPS) cases,* by state of residence: 1993—January 8, 2017.

Reproduced from Centers for Disease Control and Prevention. Hantavirus. Available at: https://www.cdc.gov/hantavirus/surveillance/state-of-exposure.html. Accessed January 26, 2017.

* N = 659 in 31 states.

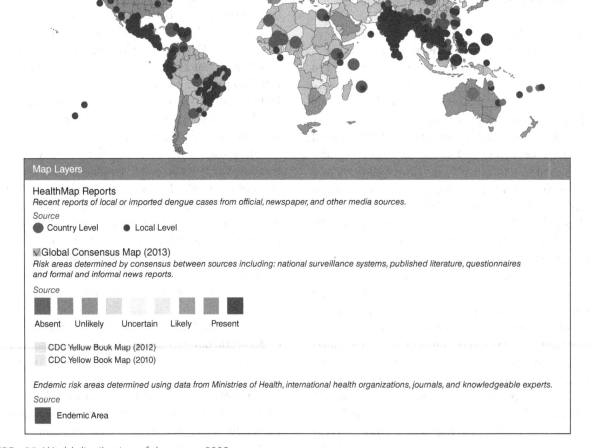

FIGURE 25 World distribution of dengue—2008.

Reproduced from Centers for Disease Control and Prevention. Dengue. Available at: http://www.healthmap.org/dengue/en/. Accessed October 19, 2017.

Courtesy of CDC/James Gathany

In the United States, most reported cases of dengue usually are imported by travelers who are returning from endemic areas or by immigrants. Although very uncommon, cases of dengue fever that originated in the continental United States have been documented. Southern Texas and the southeastern United States are at theoretical risk for transmission of dengue and for sporadic outbreaks.

Public health authorities have attributed the dramatic global emergence of dengue fever to lack of effective mosquito control in endemic areas, rapid population growth and urbanization, and poor or nonexistent systems for the treatment of water and human wastes. International travel is also thought to have contributed to increases in dengue fever by transmitting the viruses from endemic to nonendemic areas. Mosquito eradication programs that involved the use of DDT have been discontinued, causing the resurgence of *Aedes aegypti*. For example, between 1930 and 1970, the range of *A. aegypti* declined greatly in much of Central and South America; then, by 1998, the mosquito had reinvaded previous habitats.

Zika Virus

The mosquito-borne Zika virus, linked with development of a febrile rash, has been associated with adverse birth outcomes among pregnant women who become infected. The CDC asserts that congenital infection with the Zika virus is capable of producing microcephaly and abnormalities of the brain among infants born to infected pregnant women.[29] Since late 2014, health officials in Brazil observed increased Zika virus transmission that accompanied increased reports of microcephaly. As of January 2016, the total number of reports of suspected cases in Brazil reached 3,520.

Cases of Zika infection have also been reported in the US—279 reports as of early May 2016. Most of these were associated with travel to areas where local transmission of Zika had taken place. However, by mid-summer of 2016, cases also were related to local occurrence in the continental United States (e.g., Florida and California) and US territories. **FIGURE 27** shows how the Zika virus is spread. In addition to being mosquito borne, the virus was found to be transmitted sexually and through blood transfusions. Epidemiologic techniques, for example, surveillance programs, have helped to track the Zika virus and reduce risks of its transmission.

Ebola Viral Hemorrhagic Fever

This condition refers to a dramatic, highly fatal, and acute disease associated with infection with Ebola virus (shown in **FIGURE 28**). Ebola hemorrhagic fever (HF) is one of a group of viral diseases known as Ebola-Marburg viral diseases.[19] Symptoms of infection with the virus can include sudden onset of fever, headache, diarrhea, and vomiting and may also involve external and internal bleeding. Ebola disease was first recognized in 1976 in the Sudan and in Zaire (now called the Democratic Republic of Congo—DRC). In 1995, Kikwit, DRC experienced an outbreak of 315 cases that caused 244 deaths. Outbreaks associated with a subtype of Ebola virus have occurred among monkeys housed in quarantine facilities in the United States.

The largest outbreak in history descended upon west Africa in 2014. By April 13, 2016, a total of 28,652 cases had been reported in Africa. Approximately two out of five persons with Ebola died. When the Ebola outbreak exploded in 2014, public health officials scrambled to meet the challenge. Epidemiologic methods contributed to bringing this massive outbreak under control.

Rift Valley Fever

The causative agent for Rift Valley fever (RVF) is a virus from the genus *Phlebovirus* in the family *Bunyaviridae*.[30] **FIGURE 29** presents an electron micrograph of the virus.

RVF can produce epizootic or widespread disease among domestic animals including cattle, buffalo, sheep, goats, and camels. Mosquitoes transmit the disease to domestic animals that can then spread the disease to one another. The disease is transmissible to humans and can produce epidemics among human populations. Infected mosquitoes are able to transmit RVF to humans, who also may contract the disease if

PROTECT YOUR FAMILY AND COMMUNITY:

HOW ZIKA SPREADS

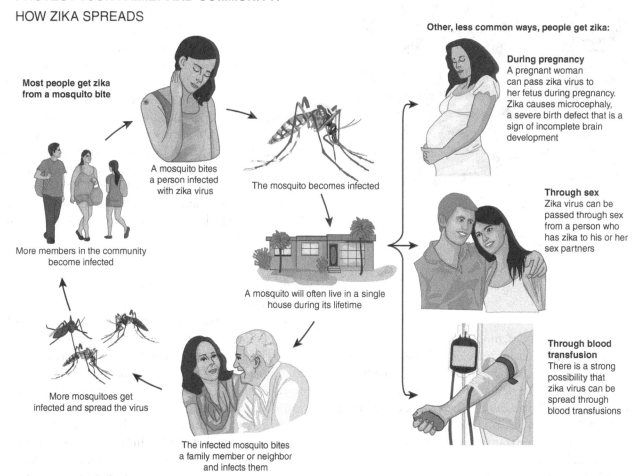

Most people get zika from a mosquito bite

A mosquito bites a person infected with zika virus

The mosquito becomes infected

A mosquito will often live in a single house during its lifetime

More members in the community become infected

More mosquitoes get infected and spread the virus

The infected mosquito bites a family member or neighbor and infects them

Other, less common ways, people get zika:

During pregnancy
A pregnant woman can pass zika virus to her fetus during pregnancy. Zika causes microcephaly, a severe birth defect that is a sign of incomplete brain development

Through sex
Zika virus can be passed through sex from a person who has zika to his or her sex partners

Through blood transfusion
There is a strong possibility that zika virus can be spread through blood transfusions

FIGURE 27 How Zika spreads.

Reproduced from Centers for Disease Control and Prevention. Protect your family and community: How Zika spreads. Available at: https://www.cdc.gov/zika/pdfs/Zika-Transmission-Infographic.pdf. Accessed July 14, 2017.

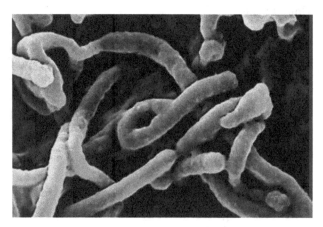

FIGURE 28 Scanning electron microscopic image of Ebola virus particles.

Courtesy of National Institute of Allergy and Infectious Diseases (NIAID)

they encounter the blood or body fluids of infected animals through slaughtering or handling infected meat. In humans, infection with RVF most typically produces either no obvious symptoms or mild illness characterized by fever and liver abnormality. Some patients may develop a more severe form in which they experience a hemorrhagic fever, encephalitis, or ocular diseases. An outbreak of Rift Valley fever in Kenya in 1950 through 1951 caused the death of approximately 100,000 sheep.

The endemic areas for RVF include southern Africa, most countries of sub-Saharan Africa, and Madagascar. (Refer to **FIGURE 30**.) Increases in Rift Valley fever follow periods of heavy rainfall when large numbers of mosquitoes develop. In west Africa in 1987, an outbreak of Rift Valley fever was linked to construction of the Senegal River project. This project modified the usual interactions between animals and humans when flooding occurred in the lower Senegal River area.

▶ Other Zoonotic Diseases

Monkeypox

Monkeypox derives its name from 1958 outbreaks that occurred in laboratory monkeys.[31] A rare disease

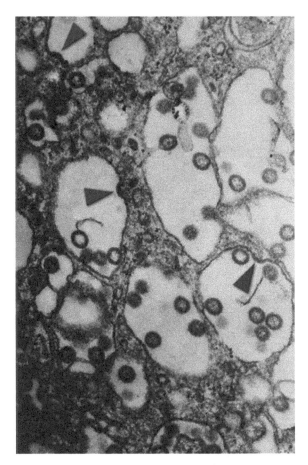

FIGURE 29 Electron micrograph of the Rift Valley Fever virus.
Courtesy of CDC/Dr. Fred Murphy

caused by the monkeypox virus, which is from the *Orthopoxvirus* genus in the family *Poxviridae*. This genus includes the smallpox virus (variola virus), the vaccinia virus (used for vaccinating against smallpox), and the cowpox virus. Endemic in the Democratic Republic of Congo, monkeypox has also occurred in other countries in central and west Africa. According to the CDC, "...symptoms of monkeypox are similar to but milder that the symptoms of smallpox. Monkeypox begins with fever, headache, muscle aches, and exhaustion. The main difference in symptoms of smallpox and monkeypox is that the latter causes lymph nodes to swell (lymphadenopathy) while smallpox does not."[31] Refer to the text box for a description of an outbreak that occurred in the midwestern United States during 2003—the only outbreak that has happened outside of Africa.

Tularemia

Also known as rabbit fever, tularemia is a bacterial disease associated with *Francisella tularensis*. The disease is broadly distributed in the United States, and occurs in all states except Hawaii. It is most often a disease of rural areas and is linked with wild animals such as rodents, rabbits, and hares. The bacterium may be transmitted in several ways, including the bite of an arthropod (e.g., tick or deer fly), coming into contact with infected animal carcasses, consuming food or water that has been contaminated with the bacterium, or even breathing in the bacterium.[32] The condition presents with a range of possible symptoms that are related to how the organism enters the body. Often, symptoms include skin ulcers, swollen lymph glands, painful eyes, and sore throat. Inhalation of the bacterium may cause sudden fever, chills, headaches, muscle aches, joint pain, dry cough, and progressive weakness; in some cases, pneumonia may occur.[19] Tularemia, which is treatable with antibiotics, may be a severe or fatal condition when untreated.

Rabies (Hydrophobia)

Rabies is an acute and highly fatal disease of the central nervous system caused by a virus transmitted most often through saliva from the bites of infected animals; globally, dog bites are the principal source of transmission of rabies to humans.[19] A disease that affects mammals, it causes encephalopathy and paralysis of the respiratory system. In the early stages of the disease, symptoms of rabies are nonspecific, consisting of apprehension, fever, headache, and

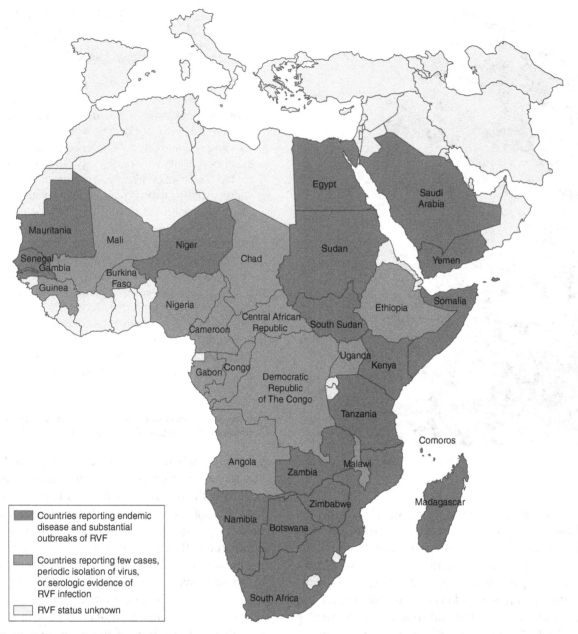

FIGURE 30 Rift Valley Fever distribution map.

Modified and reproduced from Centers for Disease Control and Prevention, National Center for Emerging and Zoonotic Infectious Diseases (NCEZID). Rift Valley Fever Distribution Map. Available at: https://www.cdc.gov/vhf/rvf/outbreaks/distribution-map.html. Accessed January 31, 2017.

malaise. The disease then progresses to paralysis, hallucinations, swallowing difficulties, and fear of water (called hydrophobia). Rabies is almost always fatal; only a few cases of survival from rabies have been documented worldwide. Once a person has developed clinical rabies, the current option for treatment consists of intensive medical care. However, vaccination (called postexposure prophylaxis [PEP]) can be administered to an individual who has been bitten by a suspected rabid animal in order to prevent clinical rabies. PEP should be given soon after the bite has occurred.

In the United States, human cases of rabies are rare. A case of abortive human rabies occurred in Texas beginning in early 2009. The case was termed "abortive" because that patient recovered without ever having received intensive care. The patient was a 17-year-old female who was seen in a hospital emergency room for symptoms that included severe headache, photophobia (sensitivity to light), neck pain, and fever. The patient was discharged after 3 days, when the symptoms resolved. Subsequently, after the headaches returned, she was rehospitalized and treated for suspected infectious encephalitis. During subsequent examinations, the patient revealed that while on a camping trip she had been bitten by flying bats. After serological tests were found to be positive for rabies, the patient was administered rabies

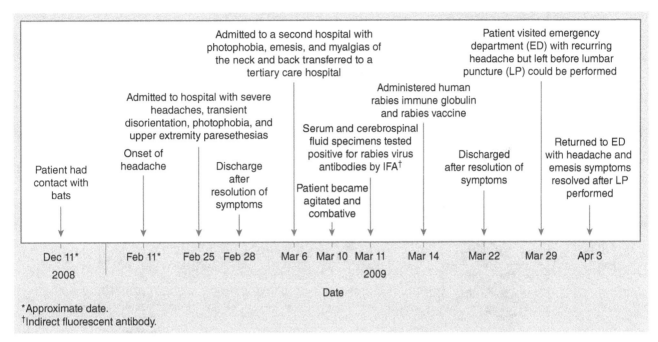

Admitted to a second hospital with
photophobia, emesis, and myalgias of
the neck and back transferred to a
tertiary care hospital

Patient visited emergency
department (ED) with recurring
headache but left before lumbar
puncture (LP) could be performed

Admitted to hospital with severe
headaches, transient
disorientation, photophobia, and
upper extremity paresethesias

Administered human
rabies immune globulin
and rabies vaccine

Onset of
headache

Serum and cerebrospinal
fluid specimens tested
positive for rabies virus
antibodies by IFA†

Returned to ED
with headache and
emesis symptoms
resolved after LP
performed

Discharge
after
resolution of
symptoms

Discharged
after resolution of
symptoms

Patient had
contact with
bats

Patient became
agitated and
combative

| Dec 11* | Feb 11* | Feb 25 | Feb 28 | Mar 6 | Mar 10 | Mar 11 | Mar 14 | Mar 22 | Mar 29 | Apr 3 |

2008   2009

Date

*Approximate date.
†Indirect fluorescent antibody.

FIGURE 31 Timeline of course for a patient with presumptive abortive human rabies—Texas, 2009.

Reproduced from Centers for Disease Control and Prevention. Presumptive abortive human rabies—Texas, 2009. *MMWR* 2010;59:187.

immune globulin and rabies vaccine. Following these steps, the young woman was given supportive care until the symptoms resolved and she was discharged. Refer to **FIGURE 31** for a time line of the patient's illness.

The hosts for rabies are wild animals—carnivores and bats. Before 1960, the majority of US rabies cases occurred among domestic animals—dogs, cats, and cattle—now most cases occur in the wild. The CDC estimates that more than 90% of rabies cases occur in wild animals (e.g., skunks, raccoons, foxes, and coyotes) and the remainder in domestic animals. The locations of wild animal rabies reservoirs in the United States are shown in **FIGURE 32. FIGURE 33** presents the number of reported cases of rabies that occurred among wild and domestic animals during 1983 to 2014 (in the United States and Puerto Rico). The two most commonly affected species were raccoons and bats. In the United States, vaccination programs for domestic animals, measures to control animals, and public health laboratories for conducting rabies tests have changed the prevalence of rabies.

Environmental health programs have prevented human cases of rabies very successfully through post-exposure prophylaxis (PEP). In the United States, one reason that fatal human rabies cases have declined from about 100 annually in the early 1900s to about 1 to 2 cases annually at the end of the 20th century has been the introduction of PEP, which is nearly 100% successful; the remaining fatal cases usually

can be attributed to failure to seek medical attention. PEP consists of a series of vaccinations that should be given as soon as possible after the occurrence of an animal bite from a suspected rabid animal. Outside the United States, rabid dogs—which cause 99% of human rabies deaths—constitute the most common source of rabies exposure. For this reason, an important component of rabies prevention is the control and vaccination of stray dogs. Within the United States, people are most likely to be exposed to rabies from bats.[19]

Anthrax

Anthrax gained notoriety in 2001 when it was distributed intentionally via the US mail system. Approximately one week after the September 11 terrorist attacks on the World Trade Center in New York City and the Pentagon in Washington, DC, letters containing anthrax spores were mailed to former NBC news anchor Tom Brokaw and to the editor of the *New York Post* in New York City, exposing employees to the spores. These exposures resulted in five confirmed cases of anthrax among media company employees or visitors. An isolated case was a 61-year-old hospital worker who subsequently died. Additional exposures also were reported in Washington, DC; Virginia, New Jersey, and Florida. Ultimately, there were a total of 22 confirmed cases of anthrax and 5 resulting deaths.[33–35]

The causative agent for anthrax, an acute infectious disease, is *Bacillus anthracis*, a spore-forming

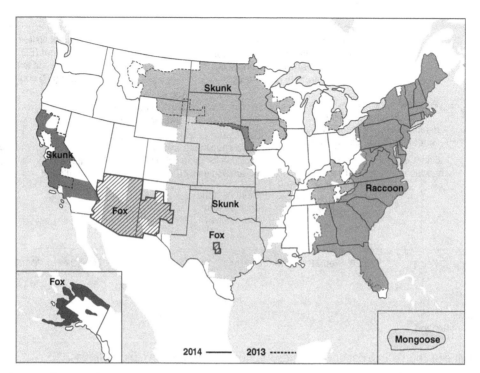

FIGURE 32 Distribution of major rabies virus variants among mesocarnivores* in the United States and Puerto Rico, 2008 to 2014.

Reproduced from Centers for Disease Control and Prevention. Rabies surveillance in the United States during 2014. March 2016. Available at: https://www.cdc.gov/rabies/pdf/2014-us-rabies-surveillance-508.pdf. Accessed January 25, 2017.

* An animal that consumes meat as 50% to 70% of its diet.
Black diagonal lines: fox rabies variants (Arizona gray fox and Texas gray fox).
Solid borders: 5-year rabies virus variant aggregates for 2009 through 2014.
Dashed borders: the previous 5-year aggregates for 2008 through 2013.

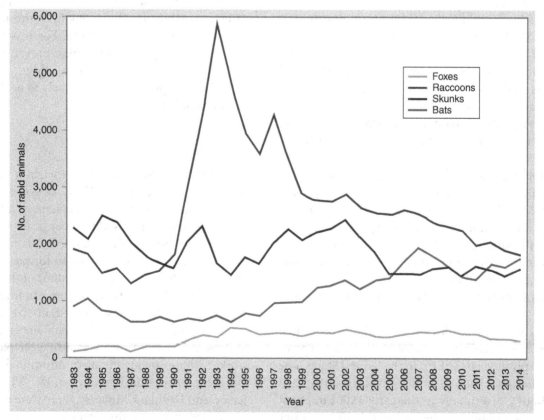

FIGURE 33 Cases of rabies among wildlife in the United States, by year and species, 1983 to 2014 (in thousands).

Reproduced from Centers for Disease Control and Prevention. Rabies surveillance in the United States during 2014. March 2016. Available at: https://www.cdc.gov/rabies/pdf/2014-us-rabies-surveillance-508.pdf. Accessed January 25, 2017.

bacterium. (Refer to **FIGURE 34.**) Anthrax is a disease that most commonly occurs among cattle, sheep, goats, and other herbivores.[36] Those normally at risk of anthrax are veterinarians, agricultural workers who come into contact with cattle, and those who are involved with the processing of animal products: hides, wool, and hair.[19] The general population is unlikely to become infected (with the exception of those who work on ranches or farms where livestock are present).

The three forms of anthrax are cutaneous, inhalational, and gastrointestinal. In humans, the cutaneous form is characterized by itching, skin lesions, development of a black eschar, and possible spread to lymph nodes. Although the case fatality rate for untreated cutaneous anthrax ranges from 5% to 20%, the disease can be treated effectively with antibiotics.[19]

The inhalational form of anthrax begins with nonspecific symptoms that mimic upper respiratory infections and then deepen into respiratory distress, fever, and shock. This form of anthrax is very severe and has a high case fatality rate.

The gastrointestinal form may be acquired from infected animals by eating contaminated meat that is undercooked. Gastrointestinal anthrax is the least common form of anthrax in the United States. Symptoms of gastrointestinal anthrax include nausea, anorexia, and abdominal pain; from 25% to 60% of cases are fatal. All three forms of anthrax are treatable with antibiotics that should be administered as soon as possible after suspected exposure. Anthrax infections can develop largely undetected until the patient becomes very ill

and nearly dies. When the case is very advanced, treatment with antibiotics is not likely to be effective.

Before the use of anthrax as a terrorist weapon, environmental health experts were concerned mainly about outbreaks of the disease among cattle and other herbivores and among people who have contact with these animals and their products. Subsequently, public health departments were spurred to action by the potential threat from a terrorist-incited anthrax epidemic. The anthrax bacterium has the capacity to spread across a wide area and cause many cases of illness and numerous deaths. A challenge to environmental health professionals will be the development of effective methods to recognize a terrorist attack, respond to it in an appropriate and timely manner, and bring the threat under control.

Psittacosis

Psittacosis, a disease associated with the bacterial agent *Chlamydia psittaci*, is conveyed by dried bird droppings (refer to the text box for a description).

Influenza: Animal to Human Transmission of Influenza A Viruses

Influenza A viruses associated with human influenza epidemics and pandemics are linked to animal reservoirs (especially birds and swine). An example of an influenza A pandemic was the "Spanish flu" pandemic of 1918 to 1920 (responsible for the deaths of more

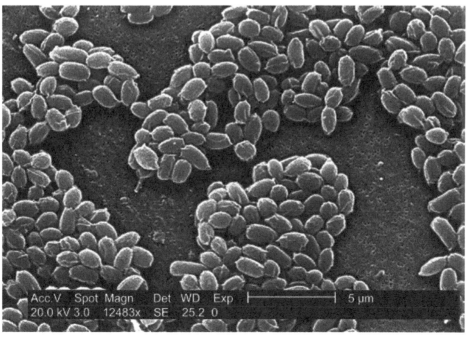

FIGURE 34 Spores from the Sterne strain of *Bacillus anthracis* bacteria.
Courtesy of CDC/Laura Rose

than 20 million people). Other influenza A pandemics were the outbreaks of the Asian flu in 1957 and the Hong Kong flu in 1968. Lesser outbreaks were the swine flu of 1976 and the chicken flu of 1997.

The three types of influenza viruses are A, B, and C, which have the following characteristics:

■ Influenza A viruses—wild and aquatic birds are considered to be the main natural reservoir. In addition to humans, influenza A viruses can infect a variety of animals such as ducks, chickens, pigs, whales, horses, and seals. "However, certain subtypes of influenza A virus are specific to certain species, except for birds, which are hosts to all known subtypes of influenza A. . . . Influenza A viruses that typically infect and transmit among one animal species sometimes can cross over and cause illness in another species."[37] Examples are the transfer of influenza viruses from humans to pigs or from horses to dogs. Influenza A viruses can be transmitted indirectly from pigs (intermediate hosts) to humans or directly from birds to humans.

Direct infection of humans with avian influenza A is unusual. Human infections with avian influenza A viruses have been linked to direct contact with infected poultry. The spread of these influenza viruses may be promoted by the close proximity of live animals such as poultry and swine to residents of densely populated areas. In order to prevent epidemics, environmental health authorities need to maintain surveillance programs and conduct routine investigations of influenza outbreaks in animals and humans.

PSITTACOSIS

Clinical Features	In humans, fever, chills, headache, muscle aches, and a dry cough. Pneumonia is often evident on chest X-ray.
Etiologic Agent	*Chlamydia psittaci*, a bacterium.
Incidence	Since 2010, fewer than 10 confirmed cases are reported in the United States each year. More cases may occur that are not correctly diagnosed or reported.
Sequelae	Endocarditis, hepatitis, and neurologic complications may occasionally occur. Severe pneumonia requiring intensive-care support may also occur. Fatal cases have been reported but are rare.
Transmission	Birds are the natural reservoirs of *C. psittaci* and infection is usually acquired by inhaling dried secretions from infected birds. The incubation period is 5 to 19 days. Although all birds are susceptible, pet birds (parrots, parakeets, macaws, and cockatiels) and poultry (turkeys and ducks) are most frequently involved in transmission to humans. Personal protective equipment (PPE), such as gloves and appropriate masks, should be used when handling birds or cleaning their cages.
Risk Groups	Bird owners, aviary pet shop employees, poultry workers, and veterinarians. Outbreaks of psittacosis in poultry processing plants have been reported.
Surveillance and Treatment	Psittacosis is a reportable condition in most states. Tetracyclines are the treatment of choice.
Trends	Annual incidence varies considerably because of periodic outbreaks. A decline in reported cases since 1988 may be the result of improved diagnostic tests that distinguish *C. psittaci* from more common *C. pneumoniae* infections.
Challenges	Diagnosis of psittacosis can be difficult. Serologic tests are often used to confirm a diagnosis, but antibiotic treatment may prevent an antibody response, thus limiting diagnosis by serologic methods. Infected birds are often asymptomatic. Tracebacks of infected birds to distributors and breeders often is not possible because of limited regulation of the pet bird industry.

Modified and reproduced from Centers for Disease Control and Prevention. Pneumonia. Psittacosis. Available at: https://www.cdc.gov/pneumonia/atypical/psittacosis.html. Accessed January 22, 2017.

Influenza A viruses are categorized into subtypes according to the arrangement of two proteins on the surface of the virus. An example of a subtype is the 2009 H1N1 influenza virus (discussed in Chapter); another example is the H5N1 avian influenza A virus that occurred as early as 1997 in Hong Kong (Special Administrative Region).

■ Influenza B viruses—confined to humans, who form the primary reservoir for these viruses.

■ Influenza C viruses—a cause of mild illnesses and sporadic outbreaks among humans; they are not considered to be responsible for widespread epidemics.

▶ Control and Prevention of Mosquito-Borne Diseases

One method to control mosquito-borne diseases is to monitor for the presence of viruses in sentinel chickens and birds. Some health departments position small flocks of chickens and other birds in strategic locations where mosquitoes may be active. These birds are tested periodically for the presence of viral antibodies. Examples of sentinel birds are shown in **FIGURE 35**.

Mosquitoes are dependent upon water to lead and complete their life cycle. Accordingly, one method for mosquito control consists of removing standing sources of water in which mosquitoes can multiply. Vector control experts advise homeowners to remove standing water from around their households, for example, water standing in buckets, old tires, or flowerpots. They also introduce mosquito-eating fish into small ponds and other bodies of standing water.

Other preventive efforts include wearing long clothing to prevent being bitten by mosquitoes, using insect repellent, closing open windows, and repairing broken screens.

▶ Conclusion

Zoonotic and vector-borne diseases represent a continuing and growing challenge. Among the recent conditions that have gained the attention of environmental health experts are the emerging and reemerging infections (e.g., dengue fever and hantavirus). In addition, scourges first observed and notorious during early historical times, such as plague, present hazards to modern society. Diseases brought under control during the mid-20th century (e.g., malaria) are showing resurgence. Several circumstances are responsible for the emergence of new diseases and the reemergence of formerly uncommon ones. Some of these factors are reduction in funding for environmental control programs, movement of human populations, increasing urbanization, and possible climatic changes. It is likely that zoonotic and vector-borne diseases will continue to challenge experts in the field of environmental health.

Study Questions and Exercises

1. Define the following terms:
    a. Emerging infectious disease
    b. Reemerging infectious disease
    c. Emerging zoonosis
    d. Zoonotic disease
    e. Vector
    f. Vector-borne infection

FIGURE 35 Sentinel birds used to monitor for mosquito-borne viruses.

2. State three factors that have contributed to the development of emerging infectious diseases. Give one example of an emerging disease and another example of a reemerging disease.

3. Give examples of three major zoonotic diseases and compare their modes of transmission. Using your own ideas, explain how transmission of these zoonotic diseases might be prevented.

4. Describe how vectors play a role in the transmission of disease.

5. List three characteristics of viral hemorrhagic fevers.

6. Discuss the impact of malaria on environmental health. Give an example of the economic impact this disease has on the developing world.

7. Summarize briefly the life cycle of malaria, describing the human and insect phases of the disease.

8. In what respects is leishmaniasis a vector-borne disease? Name some of the countries in the world where leishmaniasis is endemic and state why the disease is of particular concern to US military personnel.

9. Discuss the vector and agent factors involved in the transmission and causation of plague. Distinguish between bubonic and pneumonic plague. Describe procedures for control and prevention of plague.

10. What factors are involved in the chain of causation of Lyme disease? From the environmental health perspective, describe how the condition can be controlled and prevented.

11. What are arboviral encephalitides? Describe the reservoirs and modes of transmission of this group of diseases to humans.

12. What are the primary symptoms of West Nile virus (WNV)? List some of the ways that individuals can avoid being infected with WNV. Describe methods that environmental health officials might use to control the condition.

13. For the conditions listed below, provide the following information: (a) causative agent; (b) symptoms; (c) geographic distribution; (d) host factors; (e) responsible vectors, if any; (f) potential hazards to the human population; and (g) methods of control.

Dengue fever and dengue hemorrhagic fever

Rift Valley fever

Rabies

Anthrax

For Further Reading

The Great Influenza, John M Barry, 2005

References

1. Nicastri E, Girardi E, Ippolito G. Determinants of emerging and re-emerging infectious diseases. *J Biol Regul Homeost Agents*. 2001;15:212–217.

2. Porta M, ed. *A Dictionary of Epidemiology*. 6th ed. New York, NY: Oxford University Press; 2014.

3. Sellman J, Bender J. Zoonotic infections in travelers to the tropics. *Prim Care Clin Office Pract*. 2002;29:907–929.

4. Centers for Disease Control and Prevention. Malaria: frequently asked questions. The disease. What is malaria? Available at: https://www.cdc.gov/malaria/about/faqs.html. Accessed January 29, 2017.

5. Hyperdictionary. Meaning of nephrosis. Available at: http://www.hyperdictionary.com/search.aspx?define=nephrosis. Accessed January 29, 2017.

6. Centers for Disease Control and Prevention. Malaria. Impact of malaria. Available at: https://www.cdc.gov/malaria/malaria_worldwide/impact.html. Accessed January 29, 2017.

7. World Health Organization. Fact sheet: malaria. Available at: http://www.who.int/mediacentre/factsheets/fs094/en/. Accessed January 29, 2017.

8. *The American Heritage Dictionary of the English Language*. 4th ed. Boston, MA: Houghton Mifflin Company; 2000.

9. The Wellcome Trust. Ronald Ross and the treatment of malaria. Available at: https://wellcomecollection.org/articles/ronald-ross-and-treatment-malaria. Accessed April 24, 2017.

10. Centers for Disease Control and Prevention. Malaria: history. Elimination of malaria in the United States (1947–1951). Available at: https://www.cdc.gov/malaria/about/history/elimination_us.html. Accessed April 25, 2017.

11. Centers for Disease Control and Prevention. Malaria: history. Eradication efforts worldwide: success and failure (1955–1978). Available at: https://www.cdc.gov/malaria/about/history/. Accessed January 29, 2017.

12. Rosenberg T. What the world needs now is DDT. *The New York Times*; April 11, 2004;6:38.

13. Hay SI, Noor AM, Simba M, et al. Clinical epidemiology of malaria in the highlands of western Kenya. *Emerg Infect Dis*. 2002;8:543–548.

14. Seys SA, Bender JB. The changing epidemiology of malaria in Minnesota. *Emerg Infect Dis*. 2001;7:993–995.

15. Anis E, Leventhal A, Elkana Y, et al. Cutaneous leishmaniasis in Israel in the era of changing environment. *Public Health Rev*. 2001;29:37–47.

16. Wasserberg G, Abramsky Z, Anders G, et al. The ecology of cutaneous leishmaniasis in Nizzana, Israel: infection patterns in the reservoir host, and epidemiological implications. *Int J Parasitol*. 2002;32:133–143.

17. *The Oxford College Dictionary*. 2nd ed. New York, NY: Spark Publishing, by arrangement with Oxford University Press, Inc.; 2007.

18. Centers for Disease Control and Prevention. Plague: CDC plague home page. Available at: https://www.cdc.gov/plague/. Accessed January 30, 2017.

19. Heymann DL, ed. *Control of Communicable Diseases Manual*. 20th ed. Washington, DC: American Public Health Association; 2015.

20. Centers for Disease Control and Prevention. Lyme disease data tables. Reported cases of Lyme disease by state or locality, 2005–2015. Available at: https://cdc.goc/lyme/state/tables.html. Accessed April 25, 2017.

21. Centers for Disease Control and Prevention. Special Pathogens Branch. Viral hemorrhagic fevers. Available at: https://www.cdc.gov/vhf/index.html. Accessed January 30, 2017.

22. Centers for Disease Control and Prevention, Division of Vector-Borne Diseases. About Division of Vector-Borne Diseases. Available at: http://www.cdc.gov/ncezid/dvbd/about.html. Accessed July 15, 2017.

23. Chomel BB. Control and prevention of emerging zoonoses. *J Vet Med Educ*. 2003;30(2):145–147.

24. Centers for Disease Control and Prevention, National Center for Infectious Diseases, Special Pathogens Branch. Hantavirus. Hantavirus pulmonary syndrome (HPS). Available at: https://www.cdc.gov/hantavirus/hps/index.html. Accessed April 26, 2017.

25. Centers for Disease Control and Prevention, National Center for Infectious Diseases, Special Pathogens Branch. All about hantaviruses: hantaviruses. Available at: http://www.cdc.gov/ncidod/diseases/hanta/hps/noframes/hanta.htm. Accessed March 1, 2010.

26. Centers for Disease Control and Prevention, National Center for Infectious Diseases, Special Pathogens Branch. Hantavirus. Tracking a mystery disease: the detailed story of hantavirus pulmonary syndrome (HPS). Available at: https://www.cdc.gov/hantavirus/outbreaks/history.html. Accessed January 30, 2017.

27. Centers for Disease Control and Prevention. Hantaviruses. Reported cases of HPS. HPS in the United States. Available at: https://www.cdc.gov/hantavirus/surveillance/index.html. Accessed January 30, 2017.

28. Centers for Disease Control and Prevention. Dengue. Frequently asked questions. Available at: https://www.cdc.gov/dengue/faqfacts/index.html. Accessed April 26, 2017.

29. Centers for Disease Control and Prevention. Possible Zika virus infection among pregnant women—United States and territories, May 2016. *MMWR*. 2016;65(20):514–519.

30. Centers for Disease Control and Prevention. Rift Valley fever. https://www.cdc.gov/vhf/rvf/index.html. Accessed January 31, 2017.

31. Centers for Disease Control and Prevention. Monkeypox. Available at: http://www.cdc.gov/poxvirus/monkeypox/. Accessed January 31, 2017.

32. Centers for Disease Control and Prevention. Tularemia. Available at: http://www.cdc.gov/tularemia/. Accessed January 31, 2017.

33. Centers for Disease Control and Prevention. Update: investigation of bioterrorism-related anthrax, 2001. *MMWR*. 2001;50:1008–1010.

34. Jernigan DB, Raghunathan PL, Bell BP, et al. Investigation of bioterrorism-related anthrax, United States, 2001: epidemiologic findings. *Emerg Infect Dis*. 2002;8:1019–1028.

35. Hughes JM, Gerberding JL. Anthrax bioterrorism: lessons learned and future directions. *Emerg Infect Dis*. 2002;8:1013–1014.

36. Centers for Disease Control and Prevention. Anthrax. Basic information. Available at: https://www.cdc.gov/anthrax/basics/index.html. Accessed January 31, 2017.

37. Centers for Disease Control and Prevention. Influenza (flu). Information on avian influenza. Available at: https://www.cdc.gov/flu/avianflu/. Accessed January 31, 2017.

© Jean-Luc Rivard/EyeEm/Getty Images

Water Quality

LEARNING OBJECTIVES

By the end of this chapter the reader will be able to:

- Describe sources of potable water.
- Define what is meant by the hydrological cycle.
- List hazardous substances that may be found in drinking water.
- Describe how water is made safe for human consumption.
- Discuss hazards to the aquatic environment (oceans, lakes, and rivers) associated with environmental pollution.

▶ Introduction

This chapter covers the topics of water quality (e.g., freedom from waterborne diseases and hazards) and the water supply (e.g., sources and availability of water). Water quality is a crucial issue for environmental health, given that water is essential for life on earth. Residents of the United States and other developed countries assume that they will be able to turn on a faucet and draw a refreshing glass of water that is free from dangerous contaminants and microbial agents. (Refer to **FIGURE 1**.) In contrast, a safe water supply is not always available in the less developed regions of the world, where waterborne diseases represent a significant public health threat. In this chapter, you will learn about how water is treated to make it safe for residential consumption, microbial waterborne pathogens, chemicals in the water supply, and beach and costal pollution (for example, from oil spills).

▶ Water Quality and Public Health

Safe, high-quality drinking water is an essential aspect of public health. One of the most significant measures to protect the health of the public was the introduction of chlorination of drinking water. Since the early 20th century, drinking water chlorination has resulted in drastic reductions in waterborne infections (e.g., cholera and typhoid) in the United States.

Vulnerable groups such as children, the elderly, and immunocompromised patients (e.g., those who are undergoing chemotherapy, taking steroids, or afflicted with HIV/AIDS) are at special risk of diseases caused by water contamination.[1,2] In the United States, water quality regulations are designed to protect the public from contaminated drinking water and from other forms of water pollution. Two major water quality regulations are the Safe Drinking Water

FIGURE 1 A glass of pure water.
© Africa Studio/Shutterstock

Act and the Clean Water Act, both discussed elsewhere in the chapter on environmental policy and regulation.

The US Environmental Protection Agency (EPA) notes some interesting facts about water: Although it is possible for a human being to live up to a month without food, that same individual can survive for only about a week without water.[3] The average requirement for human consumption of water per day is approximately 2.5 liters (about 2.5 quarts). This level is necessary to maintain health and includes water from all sources, including food sources. It is also noteworthy that approximately two-thirds of the human body is made up of water; this amount increases to about three-quarters for human brain tissue.

In the United States the average person uses about 100 gallons (about 400 liters) of water per day, and the average residence uses over 100,000 gallons (about 400,000 liters) during a typical year. From 50% to 70% of this household water is used for outdoor purposes such as watering lawns and washing cars. **FIGURE 2** illustrates the relative percentage of

different types of residential uses for water in a southern California city in the United States. Because of its semiarid climate, this community uses more than half of its water for landscape maintenance; 5% is lost to system leaks.

In addition to its life-supporting role, water is required in immense quantities by agriculture and industry, such as new car manufacture, steel production, and production of canned foods. According to the EPA,[3] examples of the amounts of water required for industrial purposes are as follows:

- Manufacture of a new automobile and its four tires: 39,090 gallons (about 160,000 liters)
- Production of one barrel of beer: 1,500 gallons (about 6,000 liters)
- Production of one ton of steel: 62,600 gallons (about 250,000 liters)
- Processing one can of fruit or vegetables: 9.3 gallons (about 38 liters)

Despite the fact that water is a necessity of human life, about 20% of the world's population lacks safe drinking water. With the increasing world population, the problem of lack of access to safe drinking water is likely to worsen.[2] Although most developed nations treat industrial discharges and **sewage**, contamination of water supplies with chemicals such as arsenic and some microorganisms place public water supplies at risk. In the wealthier nations (e.g., Japan, western European countries, and the United States), the public water supplies, although generally safe, may carry organic chemicals, lead, and arsenic, as well as bacteria, viruses, and parasites from fecal contamination.

The problem of water quality is especially acute for developing nations. In these countries up to 90% of the cities discharge their untreated sewage into rivers and streams. (Refer to **FIGURE 3**.) These surface

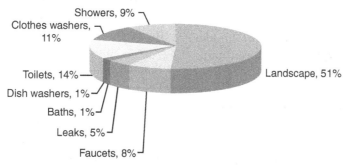

FIGURE 2 Residential uses for water in a southern California community.
Data from Irvine Ranch Water District, Irvine, California.

125

FIGURE 3 A slum in Ecuador that was heavily affected by cholera due to its proximity to unsafe water sources.
Courtesy of CDC

FIGURE 4 Examples of surface waters.

waters in turn may be used for drinking and personal sanitation purposes. In the developing world, there are several large urban areas known as megacities, defined as cities with 10 million or more people. The unsanitary water supplies found in many of these densely populated areas foster the spread of gastrointestinal illnesses and serious infectious diseases that contribute greatly to the burden of morbidity and mortality in these regions.

The lack of a safe water supply is compounded in some parts of the developing world by chronic water shortages. Regions that face a water shortfall include north Africa, the Middle East, and parts of sub-Saharan Africa. The residents of these areas are faced periodically with a chronic shortage of freshwater.

▶ The Water Supply

The two main sources of drinking water used by the human population are surface water and **groundwater**.[4] (Refer to the text box for definitions.) Surface waters are from rivers and lakes, as shown in **FIGURE 4**.

The second type of water available for human consumption is groundwater, which is stored naturally in underground aquifers. (See **EXHIBIT 1** for a definition of the term **aquifer** and other key hydrological terms.) Wastewater from human activities can find its way back into aquifers. In some regions of the world, communities treat wastewater and store it in percolation ponds so that it may recharge aquifers. Refer to **FIGURE 5**, which demonstrates that communities near the sea run the risk of saltwater

intrusion into the aquifer when excessive amounts of water are withdrawn. Saltwater intrusion eventually may render the water unsuitable for human consumption.

The field of water science is known as hydrology. Some of the terms that relate to hydrology are *aquifer*, the **hydrological cycle**, **water scarcity**, and **water stress**. Some of these terms are discussed later in the chapter.

The Hydrological Cycle

The hydrological cycle is akin to a pumping system, driven by the sun, which moves freshwater from the oceans to landmasses and then returns it to the ocean.[5] This cycle describes the process by which the

WATER DEFINITIONS USED BY FEDERAL AND STATE WATER AUTHORITIES

Finished water: the water (e.g., drinking water) delivered to the distribution system after treatment, if any.

Groundwater: water that is contained in the interconnected pores in an aquifer.

Groundwater system: a system that uses water extracted from an aquifer (i.e., a well or spring) as its source.

Groundwater under the direct influence of surface water: as defined by the US Environmental Protection Agency (EPA), any water beneath the surface of the ground with substantial occurrence of insects or other macroorganisms, algae, or large-diameter pathogens (e.g, *Giardia intestinalis* or *Cryptosporidium*), or substantial and relatively rapid shifts in water characteristics (e.g., turbidity, temperature, conductivity, or PH) that closely correlate with climatologic or surface water conditions. Direct influence must be determined for individual sources in accordance with criteria established by the state (where the source is located).

Source water: untreated water (i.e., raw water) used to produce drinking water.

Surface water: all water on the surface (e.g., lakes, rivers, reservoirs, ponds, and oceans) as distinguished from subsurface or groundwater.

Note: On December 16, 1998, the EPA's Interim Enhanced Surface Water Treatment Rule (IESWTR) appeared in the *Federal Register.* The purpose of the rule was to "[i]mprove control of microbial pathogens including specifically the protozoan *Cryptosporidium,* in drinking water"[a(p.69478)] as well as minimize risks associated with agents used to disinfect water. The control of *Cryptosporidium* applied both to surface waters and groundwater under the influence of surface water. The IESWTR mandated that "[s]tates are required to conduct sanitary surveys for all public water systems using surface water or ground water under the direct influence of surface water. . . Sanitary surveys are required no less frequently than every three years for community systems. . . ."[a(p69484)] EPA standards for evaluation and processing of groundwater under the influence of surface water are stricter than those applied to groundwater not under such influence.[b]

[a] Environmental Protection Agency. National Primary Drinking Water Regulations: Interim Enhanced Surface Water Treatment. *Federal Register.* December 16, 1998;63(241):69478–69521.

[b] Gostin LO, Lazzarini Z, Neslund, VS Osterholm MT. Water quality laws and waterborne diseases: *Cryptosporidium* and other emerging pathogens. *Am J Public Health.* 2000;90:847–853.

Water definitions modified and reproduced from Centers for Disease Control and Prevention, Surveillance Summaries. Surveillance for waterborne disease and outbreaks associated with drinking water and water not intended for drinking—United States, 2005–2006. *MMWR.* 2008;57(SS-9):64–65.

EXHIBIT 1

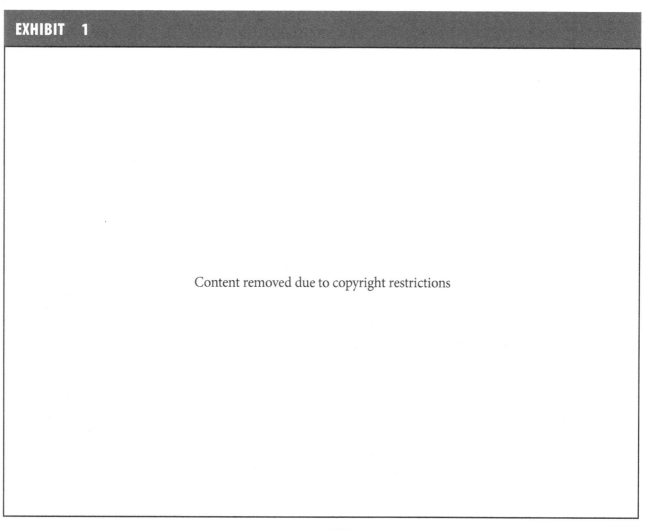

Content removed due to copyright restrictions

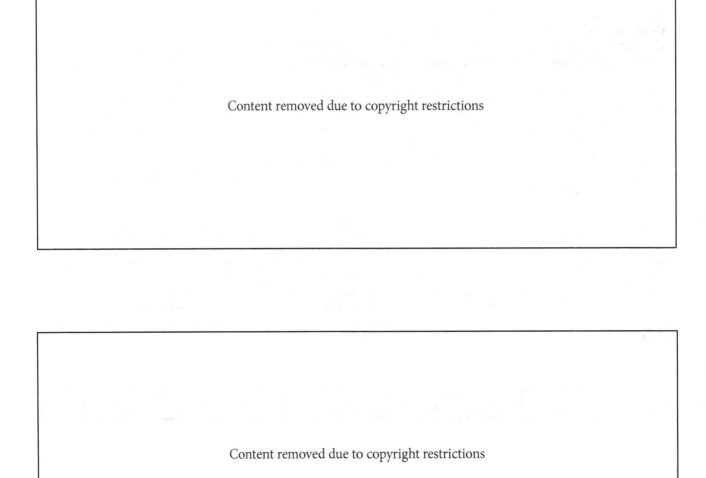

Content removed due to copyright restrictions

Content removed due to copyright restrictions

FIGURE 5 Types of aquifers, wells, and groundwater flow.

freshwater supply is continuously replenished. Refer to **FIGURE 6**.

The United Nations Environment Program provides the following description of the hydrological cycle:

Water is transported in different forms within the hydrological cycle or "water cycle." . . . [E]ach year about 502,800 km³ [120,600 mi³] of water evaporates over the oceans and seas, 90% of which (458,000 km³) [110,000 mi³] returns directly to the oceans through precipitation, while the remainder (44,800 km³) [10,700 mi³] falls over land. With evapo-transpiration totaling about 74,200 km³ [17,800 mi³], the total volume in the terrestrial hydrological cycle is about 119,000 km³ [28,500 mi³]. About 35% of this, or 44,800 km³ [10,700 mi³], is returned to the oceans as run-off from rivers, groundwater and glaciers. A considerable portion of river flow and groundwater percolation never reaches the ocean, having evaporated in internal runoff areas or inland basins lacking an outlet to the ocean. However, some groundwater that bypasses the river systems reaches the oceans. Annually the hydrological cycle circulates nearly 577,000 km³ [138,000 mi³] of water. . . .[6]

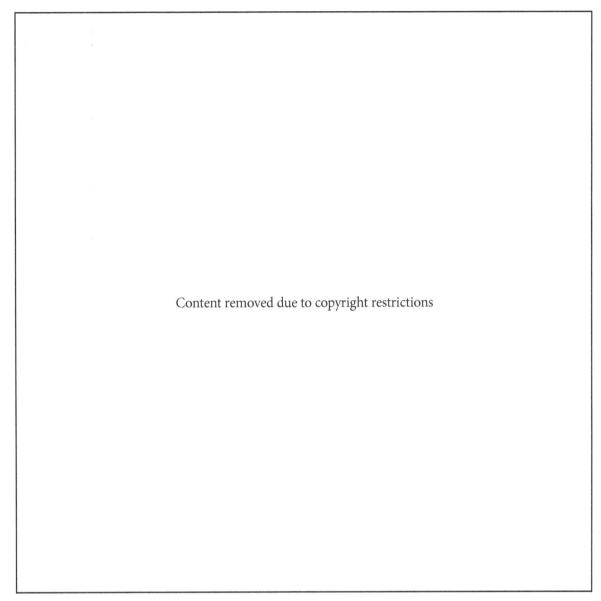

Content removed due to copyright restrictions

FIGURE 6 The world's water cycle. The width of the arrows is proportional to the volumes of transported water.

Freshwater Resources

FIGURE 7 provides estimates of world freshwater reserves. No more water exists on earth than there was 2,000 years ago, but the human population has grown enormously since ancient times.[5]

Here are some facts about water availability[5]: although about 70% of the earth's surface is covered by water, most of this water is unusable ocean water. Approximately 3% of all water is freshwater, of which the majority is unavailable for human use. This water is unavailable because nearly 75% of freshwater supplies are frozen in the polar ice caps and in glaciers. The remaining 1% of readily accessible water comes from surface freshwater; sources include lakes, rivers, and shallow underground aquifers. These readily accessible sources constitute the water supply that is renewed by the hydrological cycle.

Estimates suggest that only 0.01% of the world's total supply of water can be accessible for use by the human population.[5] This amount consists of about 12.5 to 14 billion cubic meters (441 to 490 billion cubic feet), or about 9,000 cubic meters (318,000 cubic feet) for each person on earth. (One cubic meter is approximately 1,000 liters [264 gallons].) Unfortunately, the water supply is not distributed evenly across the world. This unequal distribution is exacerbated by the fact that there may be annual cycles of drought and flooding.

FIGURE 8 shows the earth's distribution of freshwater resources represented by glaciers, surface water, and other reserves. Many of the geographic areas of the world that receive heavy rainfall are located away

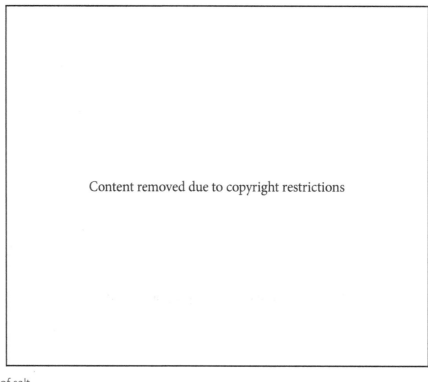

FIGURE 7 A world of salt.

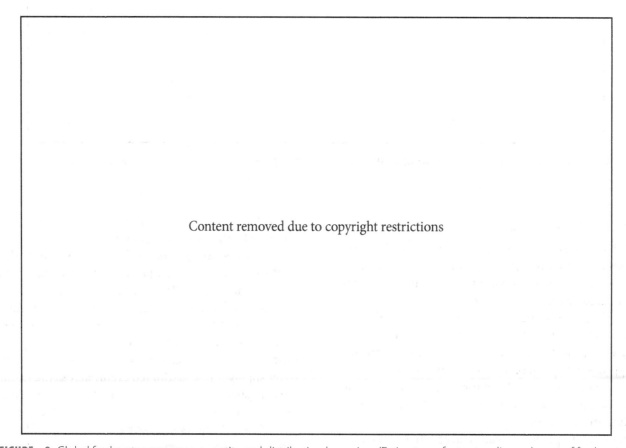

FIGURE 8 Global freshwater resources: quantity and distribution by region. (Estimates refer to standing volumes of freshwater.)

from large population concentrations. The Amazon basin in South America receives nearly one-fifth of the global average rainfall runoff each year. Other areas that receive high amounts of rainfall are Asia, South America, and the Congo River and its tributaries on the African continent. In comparison with other regions, the North American continent has the largest amount of freshwater available to the population. One extreme example of the unequal distribution of water resources is the water supplies of Kuwait versus Iceland. In the former country, the population has only about 75 cubic meters (2,600 cubic feet) per person of available water; in the latter, almost 1,000 times as much is available to the average person. Countries such as Mexico have an uneven distribution of rainwater; 90% of this country is chronically water short. In parts of Asia, such as India, the water supply is affected greatly by seasonal rains. Consequently, during the drier months very little water is available from rainfall.

Water Scarcity and Water Stress

In several areas of the world, the demand for water presently exceeds the available water supply as a result of water scarcity and water stress. (Refer to Exhibit 1 for definitions of water scarcity and water stress.) Ironically, two sections of the world that currently have severe water shortages also are experiencing some of the highest population growth rates in the world. These areas are Africa (sub-Saharan and north) and the Near East, regions that encompass 20 countries. In Saudi Arabia, for example, the supplies of so-called fossil groundwater that exist in aquifers are being rapidly depleted. As a means of supplanting diminishing groundwater sources, several Persian Gulf countries—Bahrain, Kuwait, Saudi Arabia, and the United Arab Emirates—now use desalinization as a method to convert sea water into freshwater.

Presently about 200 million people live in water-stressed countries. For example, water shortages in China affect the northern part of the country, including the capital city, Beijing. Although the United States generally has adequate amounts of water, regional shortages occur from time to time. Some major aquifers in the Midwest are being overutilized and depleted. The western states (e.g., California), with rapidly expanding populations, periodically face water shortages during drought years.

The number of countries that will experience water scarcity is expected to increase as their populations continue to burgeon. Estimates suggest that by the year 2025, approximately 2.8 billion people will live in 48 countries that will experience water stress or water scarcity. These numbers will increase by the year 2050 to 54 countries with a combined population of 4 billion people. The world's population of approximately 6 billion is adding about 80 million members annually. This population increase represents a demand for freshwater that is about that of the entire annual flow of Europe's Rhine River (64 billion cubic meters per year [2.3 trillion cubic feet]).

▶ Treatment of Water for Residential Consumption

Water supplied to the public in the United States undergoes treatment in order to meet quality standards set by the EPA for safe levels of chemical contaminants and waterborne microorganisms. As noted previously, water sources include surface water (lakes and reservoirs) and water from aquifers. Processing of water takes place in water treatment plants, an example of which is shown in **FIGURE 9**. The four stages of water treatment in most plants are as follows: coagulation, sedimentation, filtration, and disinfection. These stages are presented in **FIGURE 10**.

As shown in **FIGURE 11**, after untreated water flows from a storage area into the plant, it first undergoes

FIGURE 9 Purification plant for drinking water.
© jan kranendonk/Shutterstock

131

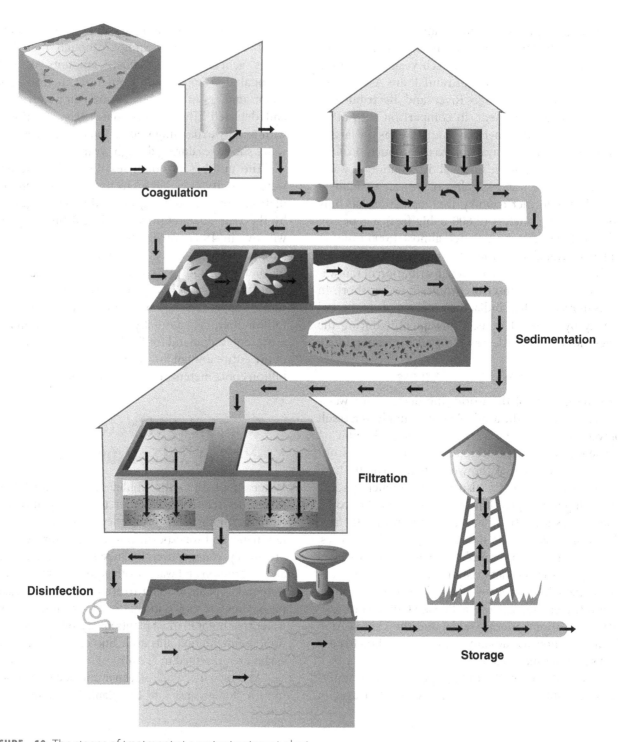

FIGURE 10 The stages of treatment at a water treatment plant.

Modified from Centers for Disease Control and Prevention. Drinking Water: Water Treatment. Available at: https://www.cdc.gov/healthywater/drinking/public/water_treatment.html

coagulation to remove suspended material. Aluminum sulfate is used as the coagulating agent. After the coagulating agent has been mixed with the water, the mixture is transferred to sedimentation tanks similar to the ones shown in **FIGURE 12**. The water then is filtered to remove smaller impurities. The filter is made of progressively finer layers of sand and a layer of activated charcoal. Subsequently, the water is treated with a disinfectant such as chlorine to destroy pathogens. (Refer to **FIGURE 13**.)

Fluoridation of Water

Some communities in the United States add fluoride to public drinking water in order to prevent tooth decay (dental caries). The rationale for this procedure came from the informal observations of dentists during the early 1900s, followed by epidemiologic studies.[7] Dr. Frederick McKay established a dental practice in 1901 in Colorado Springs, Colorado. (Refer to

FIGURE 11 Storage tank for aluminum sulfate used to coagulate solids in water.
Courtesy of Irvine Ranch Water District, Irvine, California

FIGURE 13 On the top is a model of a sand and charcoal filter used in water processing. On the bottom is a chlorinator room for water disinfection.
Courtesy of Irvine Ranch Water District, Irvine, California

FIGURE 12 Tanks used for additional skimming during secondary processing.
Courtesy of Irvine Ranch Water District, Irvine, California

FIGURE 14.) He soon observed that many of his patients' teeth displayed stains, which he referred to as "mottled enamel" or "Colorado brown stain." McKay concluded that high levels of fluoride in the local drinking water probably were the cause of the stains, and also seemed to confer resistance against tooth decay.

Subsequently, dental researchers including Dr. H. Trendley Dean (during the 1930s) further investigated links between fluoride in drinking water and absence of dental caries. Dean used the term **fluorosis** to describe the dental condition in which teeth have been discolored by fluoride. In epidemiologic studies, Dean demonstrated an inverse relationship between the prevalence of dental caries and levels of naturally occurring drinking water fluoride levels. The optimal fluoride level was set at 0.7 to 1.2 parts per million (ppm) of drinking water. This level was thought to minimize the occurrence of fluorosis and confer protection against dental caries.

FIGURE 14 Dr. Frederick S. McKay, one of the pioneers in water fluoridation.
Courtesy of CDC

Water fluoridation as a means of preventing dental caries was tested in prospective field trials in four pairs of cities (one intervention and one control in each pair) beginning in 1945. For example, the intervention city Grand Rapids, Michigan was paired with the control city Muskegon, Michigan. The field trials demonstrated a 50 to 70% reduction in the prevalence of dental caries with no apparent increase in dental fluorosis above what is seen in communities that have low levels of naturally occurring fluoride in their drinking water. Following these successful trials, many communities in the United States added fluoride to public drinking water.

Treatment of Water from Aquifers

Aquifers are a common source of potable water in many communities. For high-quality water from aquifers, minimal aeration, filtration, and disinfection are necessary. In some cases, water drawn from aquifers is free from microorganisms, but undesirable for human consumption because of impurities and coloration that impair the aesthetic qualities of this essential liquid. Such is the case of deep aquifers (present at 600 meters [2,000 feet]) found in some regions of the world (e.g., southern California). This water can be made acceptable through a process of filtration that uses ultrafine filters, as shown in **FIGURE 15**. The

A. Pump

B. Bank of filters

C. Samples of water before and after filtration

FIGURE 15 A, B, and C. Water filtration system for water from aquifer.
Courtesy of Irvine Ranch Water District, Irvine, California

figure shows pumps used to draw the water from the aquifer, banks of filters, and samples of water before and after filtration, in addition to the impurities that have been removed. In this example, the residual impurities removed through filtration are piped to the city's sanitary sewage processing plant.

Drinking Water Contamination

Many consumers in the United States are concerned about the safety of water supplied by municipal water plants. Some dramatic instances of waterborne diseases and the presence of lead and other heavy metals in water from the public water supply have been reported by the media. An instance of lead-contaminated drinking water occurred in Flint, Michigan, in 2014 when the city's water supply was changed from Lake Huron to the Flint River as a cost-saving measure. Despite these unusual instances of drinking water contamination, the public water supply generally is monitored carefully and must adhere to EPA safety standards. Nevertheless, consumers increasingly are adopting bottled water (shall we say "prestige water") as a substitute for tap water (refer to the following text box for a discussion of the relative merits of tap water versus bottled and vended water).

Potable water (drinking water) includes water from wells and runoff from the land's surface. Almost all water in its natural state is impure, because of common naturally occurring and anthropogenic sources of pollution. Naturally occurring sources of pollution arise from the diversity of aquatic animals and plants that inhabit the bodies of water used eventually for

human consumption. In addition to microbial organisms that live in water, fish, aquatic animals, and wildlife produce wastes that contaminate the water. Soils in contact with the water also harbor microorganisms. Decaying tree leaves and branches contribute organic materials. Natural rock and soil formations may introduce radionuclides, nitrogen compounds, and heavy metals such as arsenic, cadmium, chromium, lead, and selenium, as well as other chemicals.

FIGURE 16 demonstrates how human-made pollutants may enter the urban water supply. Water that courses across the surface of the land may incorporate various contaminants, which include the following[8,9]:

- Chemicals and nutrients (e.g., fertilizers and nitrates from agricultural lands)
- Rubber, heavy metals, and sodium (from roads)
- Petroleum by-products and organic chemicals (from dry cleaners, service stations, and leaking underground storage tanks)
- Chemicals used in the home (solvents, paints, used motor oil, lead, and copper)
- Heavy metals and toxic chemicals (from factories)
- Microbial pathogens (from human and animal wastes)

Runoff from urban streets is a growing contributor to water pollution, especially after periods of heavy rainfall. Pet wastes that are washed into storm drains can represent a hazard to human and animal health. As a result, many cities are attempting to curtail this source of water pollution through local ordinances. (See **FIGURE 17**.)

WHICH IS SAFER: TAP WATER, BOTTLED WATER, OR VENDED WATER?

The growing public acceptance of bottled water may be the result of taste and health concerns. Also popular (particularly among Hispanic and Asian populations) is vended water. Here are some facts about the three types of water:

- Residents of communities that fluoridate water may be at increased risk of tooth decay should they drink bottled water exclusively, because bottled water usually is not fluoridated.
- Some bottled water may contain higher bacterial counts than tap water; all public drinking water sources are regulated by the EPA to ensure quality. The opened personal water bottles of school children have been reported to have fecal coliform contamination, possibly as a result of lapses in personal hygiene.
- Water purchased from water vending machines that are poorly maintained may be contaminated with coliform and other bacteria. Vended water comes from an approved source such as tap water; vending machines provide additional treatment to tap water by using carbon filtration and other methods.
- Bottled water, especially luxury brands, is much more expensive than tap water. Often the millions of used water bottles must be discarded in landfills, creating an adverse environmental impact.

Data from Lalumandier JA, Ayers LW. Fluoride and bacterial content of bottled water vs tap water. *Arch Fam Med*. 2000;9:246–250; Oliphant JA, Ryan MC, Chu A. Bacterial water quality in the personal water bottles of elementary students. *Can J Public Health*. 2002;95:366–367; Schillinger J, Du Vall Knorr S. Drinking-water quality and issues associated with water vending machines in the city of Los Angeles. *J Environ Health*. 2004;66(6):25–31; Postman A. The truth about tap. National Resources Defense Council. January 5, 2016. Available at: https://www.nrdc.org/stories /truth-about-tap?gclid=EAIaIQobChMIxan9-KWv1gIVEJFpCh3CswIyEAAYASAAEgJ5fvD_BwE. Accessed September 18, 2017.

Content removed due to copyright restrictions

FIGURE 16 The urban water cycle: humanity's impact on groundwater.

FIGURE 17 In order to prevent water and other pollution, this sign admonishes city residents to pick up after their pets.

In summary, disease-causing agents that may be present in the water supply form four major groups. The first three groups represent agents that sometimes are excreted in feces: parasites (e.g., *Giardia, Cryptosporidia*), bacteria (e.g., *Escherichia coli, Shigella*), and viruses (e.g., norovirus, hepatitis viruses). The fourth group—chemicals (e.g., pesticides, heavy metals)—consists of pollutants that may enter the water from other sources.

Waterborne Diseases and Fecal Contamination

Waterborne diseases are conditions that are "transmitted through the ingestion of contaminated water and water acts as the passive carrier of the infectious agent."[10(p371)] Waterborne diseases are a source of ongoing concern to the residents of the developing world, where waterborne diarrheal conditions take a great toll in morbidity and mortality, and to tourists who travel in these areas. In the developing world, bacterial waterborne diseases are associated with the deaths of newborns and children from conditions such as dehydration. An example of a condition transmitted by water is acute gastroenteritis, defined as an "inflammation of the stomach and or intestines or both."[11] In addition to gastroenteritis, many serious diseases can be spread through the water supply. To some extent, these diseases also affect developed countries including the United States. The text box titled *The Global Importance of Preventing Waterborne Diseases* presents facts about the significance of waterborne diseases caused by bacterial agents.

Despite reassurances by officials about its safety, the public water supply in some areas of the United States occasionally may be responsible for transmitting serious waterborne diseases. When such transmission occurs via the public water supply, it is usually a consequence of a malfunctioning water-processing system (e.g., the 1993 cryptosporidiosis outbreak in Milwaukee, Wisconsin, discussed later in the chapter).

Many pathogens—bacterial, viral, and protozoan—are responsible for waterborne infections. Examples of waterborne diseases are cryptosporidiosis and giardiasis (both caused by protozoan agents), cholera (agent *Vibrio cholerae*), and infection with *E. coli* O157:H7.[10] Other conditions that may be transmitted by water include infections caused by *Legionella pneumophila* and certain viruses (e.g., hepatitis A virus). Symptoms of waterborne diseases caused by bacteria include a form of severe diarrhea that can result in dehydration (as in cholera), fevers and abdominal distress of long duration (as in typhoid fever), and in some cases acute

---

THE GLOBAL IMPORTANCE OF PREVENTING WATERBORNE DISEASES

Waterborne diseases are inextricably associated with poor water quality. A crucial public health measure for preventing waterborne illness is provision of improved water sources.

The World Health Organization (WHO) and the United Nations Children's Fund (UNICEF) in 2000 estimated that approximately 4 billion episodes of diarrhea occurred annually worldwide.[a] These episodes were linked to about 2 million deaths, which primarily impacted children. Bacterial enteropathogens (discussed in text) such as *Salmonella, Escherichia coli*, and *Vibrio cholerae* are associated with diarrheal illnesses. Other diseases from microbial agents carried in unsanitary water include intestinal parasitic infections, trachoma (a cause of blindness), and schistosomiasis.

In 2000 the United Nations (UN) established Millennium Development Goals, which included a target of improved drinking water sources for 88% of the world's population. According to the UN, this target was met in 2010; by 2015 a total of 91% of the global population benefitted from improved water sources.[b] However, about 80% of residents of rural areas did not have improved drinking water sources as of 2015.

[a] WHO/UNICEF Joint Monitoring Programme for Water Supply and Sanitation. *Global Water Supply and Sanitation*. Geneva, Switzerland: World Health Organization and United Nations Children's Fund; 2000.
[b] UNICEF, World Health Organization. *Progress on Sanitation and Drinking Water—2015 Update and MDG Assessment*. Geneva, Switzerland: UNICEF World Health Organization and United Nations Children's Fund; 2015.

---

bloody diarrhea (as in *E. coli* O157:H7). The following is a list of some of the waterborne pathogens:

- Enteric protozoal parasites
  - *Entamoeba histolytica*
  - *Giardia intestinalis*
  - *Cryptosporidium parvum*
  - *Cyclospora cayetanensis*
- Bacterial enteropathogens
  - *Salmonella*
  - *Shigella* (discussed in the chapter on food safety)
  - *Escherichia coli*
  - *Vibrio cholera*
  - *Campylobacter* (discussed in the chapter on food safety)
- Viral pathogens
  - Enteroviruses
  - Adenoviruses
  - Noroviruses (formerly called Norwalk-like viruses)

- Other agents
  - *Dracunculus medinensis*
  - *Legionella pneumophila*

Enteric Protozoal Parasites

Cryptosporidiosis. The infectious agent that causes cryptosporidiosis is called *Cryptosporidium parvum*, a protozoal organism. The symptoms of cryptosporidiosis include watery diarrhea, abdominal cramping, nausea, vomiting, and fever. The condition can be fatal among immunocompromised individuals.[12] **TABLE 1** presents a chronology of cryptosporidiosis in the United States. The first human case was diagnosed in 1976. Since then, several outbreaks have been linked to drinking water sources including public drinking water supplies.

The complex life cycle of the different species of *Cryptosporidium* is shown in **FIGURE 18**. (Note that *Cryptosporidium parvum* is the species of *Cryptosporidium* that causes infections in humans.)

Cryptosporidium oocysts, which are the infectious component for cryptosporidiosis, are excreted in the stools of infected persons.[13] Water used for recreation and drinking may be contaminated with sewage that contains the oocysts of *C. parvum*. Following ingestion by other human hosts, the oocysts (see **FIGURE 19**) reproduce. Resistant to chlorine treatment, infective oocysts may survive treatment by water treatment plants, even modern installations.

The most notorious waterborne outbreak of cryptosporidiosis in the United States occurred in southern Milwaukee in late March and early April 1993. More than 400,000 people were estimated to be affected during this major outbreak.[14] This number actually may undercount the number of affected persons, as the case definition was limited to watery diarrhea.[12]

The outbreak was linked to the Milwaukee Water Works (MWW), the supplier of water for the city of Milwaukee and nine surrounding municipalities in Milwaukee County. Investigators believed that *Cryptosporidium* oocysts (see Figure 19) from untreated

TABLE 1 Cryptosporidiosis (Chronology)	
1976	First human case diagnosed
1984	First well water outbreak
1987	First river water outbreak
1992	Multiple municipal water supply outbreaks
1993	Largest recorded waterborne outbreak in US history (Milwaukee, Wisconsin) Fresh-pressed apple cider outbreak (central Maine)
1994	First outbreak in community with state-of-the-art water treatment (Las Vegas, Nevada)

Modified and reproduced from CDC Public Health Image Library. ID #109. NCID Content Provider. Available at: http://phil.cdc.gov/Phil/details.asp. Accessed September 18, 2017.

Selected outbreaks after 1994	
1997	Children playing in a water sprinkler fountain at a zoo, Minnesota[a]
2007	A splash park, Idaho, 2007[b]
2013	Baker City, Oregon, from municipal water supply contamination[c]

[a] Centers for Disease Control and Prevention. Outbreak of cryptosporidiosis associated with a water sprinkler fountain—Minnesota, 1997. *MMWR*. 1998;47:856-860; [b] Centers for Disease Control and Prevention. Outbreak of cryptosporidiosis associated with a splash park—Idaho, 2007. *MMWR*. 2009(22);58:615-618; [c] DeSilva MB, Schafer S, Kendall Scott M, et al. Communitywide cryptosporidiosis outbreak associated with a surface water-supplied municipal water system—Baker City, Oregon, 2013. *Epidemiol Infect*. 2016;144(2):274–284.

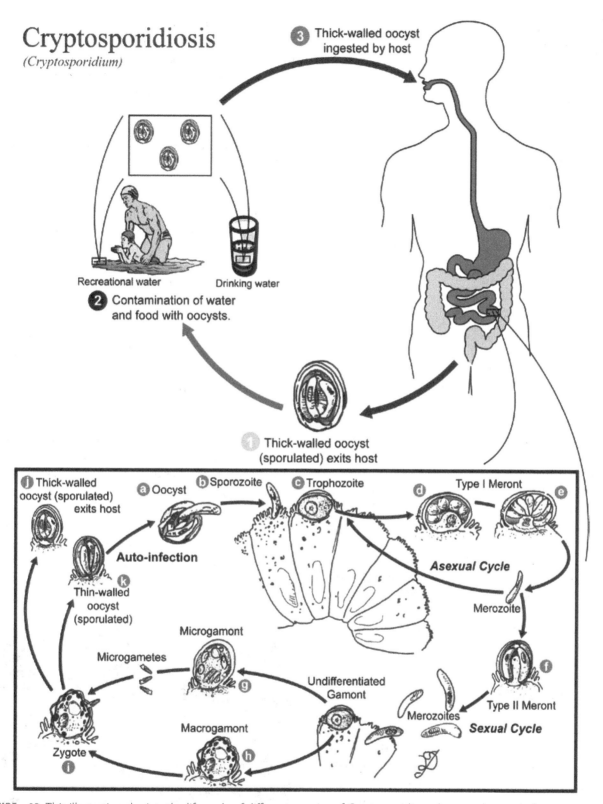

Cryptosporidiosis
(Cryptosporidium)

3 Thick-walled oocyst ingested by host

Recreational water

Drinking water

2 Contamination of water and food with oocysts.

1 Thick-walled oocyst (sporulated) exits host

j Thick-walled oocyst (sporulated) exits host

a Oocyst

b Sporozoite

c Trophozoite

d Type I Meront

e

Auto-infection

k Thin-walled oocyst (sporulated)

Asexual Cycle

Merozoite

Microgamont

Microgametes

Undifferentiated Gamont

f Type II Meront

Merozoites

Sexual Cycle

Macrogamont **h**

Zygote **i**

g

FIGURE 18 This illustration depicts the life cycle of different species of *Cryptosporidium*, the causal agents of cryptosporidiosis.

Courtesy of CDC/Alexander J. da Silva, PhD/Melanie Moser

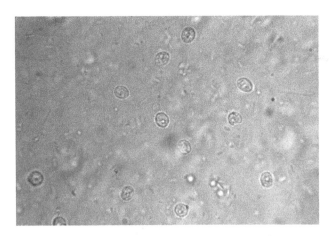

FIGURE 19 Oocysts of *Cryptosporidium parvum*. Oocysts are spheroidal objects, 4 to 6 microns (μm) in diameter.

Courtesy of CDC/ Dr. Peter Drotman

Lake Michigan water were drawn into the water treatment plant. The usual water treatment processes (e.g., coagulation, filtration, and chlorination) were not adequate to remove the oocysts.

Two major rivers flow into the Milwaukee harbor. Along the rivers are slaughterhouses and effluents of human sewage. During a springtime period of heavy precipitation, the rivers may have transported oocysts into Lake Michigan, a source of water for the MWW. Between approximately March 21 and April 5, a marked increase in the turbidity of treated water was noted. On April 7 the MWW issued an advisory to customers to boil their water; subsequently, the MWW closed the plant temporarily on April 9. This massive outbreak in Milwaukee suggests the need to continuously monitor the quality of drinking water (especially for turbidity), to conduct **public health surveillance** of diarrheal illnesses caused by water, and to recognize the hazards that *Cryptosporidium* outbreaks pose for the public.

Contaminated water has been linked to most known outbreaks of cryptosporidiosis in the United States.[15] A study conducted in the San Francisco Bay area evaluated the risk of transmission of endemic cryptosporidiosis by drinking water. The study did not support the hypothesis that drinking water is a risk factor for cryptosporidiosis among the immunocompetent population. Cases of cryptosporidiosis identified by a surveillance system found that travel to another country was a strong and significant risk factor for cryptosporidiosis.

Other sources of *Cryptosporidium* infections are public swimming pools and water parks used by large numbers of diapered children. These settings have been implicated in outbreaks of cryptosporidiosis. It is known that very low doses of *C. parvum* are required for infection. The oocysts are resistant to chlorine treatment; therefore, bathers should avoid drinking water used in public swimming pools. Parents of diapered children should be educated regarding the supervision of their children so that swimming pools do not become contaminated with fecal material.[16]

Amebiasis. Amebiasis is caused by the protozoal parasite *Entamoeba histolytica*, which produces cysts that are carried in human feces.[17] Transmission occurs via the ingestion of cysts that are contained in food and water that have been contaminated by feces. Both asymptomatic and symptomatic illnesses are associated with the organism. The latter include invasive intestinal amebiasis (e.g., dysentery, colitis, and appendicitis) and extraintestinal amebiasis (e.g., abscesses of the lungs and liver). When traveling to a less developed area of the world where sanitary conditions are wanting, tourists should avoid eating fresh fruits and vegetables they did not peel themselves, unpasteurized milk and other unpasteurized dairy products, and food sold by street vendors.[18]

Giardiasis. The agent that is responsible for giardiasis is *Giardia lamblia* (also known as *Giardia duodenalis*), a protozoal organism.[19] (Refer to **FIGURE 20**.) *G. lamblia* produces cysts that transmit the condition via contaminated food and water. The cysts have the ability to survive for long periods in cold water. The incubation period for giardiasis varies from 3 to 25 days, with approximately 7 to 10 days being typical. Symptoms of giardiasis include gastrointestinal effects such as acute or chronic diarrhea; some cases are asymptomatic.[13]

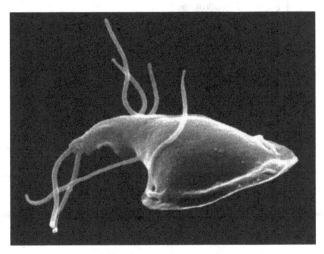

FIGURE 20 The protozoan parasite *Giardia lamblia*, causative agent for giardiasis.

Courtesy of CDC/Dr. Stan Erlandsen; Dr. Dennis Feely

Cyclosporiasis (an emerging parasitic disease).
In common with other protozoal parasites discussed in this section, the causative organism *Cyclospora cayetanensis* is transmitted via ingestion of food and water that have been contaminated with cysts (oocysts) from the organism. Foodborne outbreaks have involved fresh produce (e.g., snow peas and raspberries). During May through July 2007, a cluster of 29 cases of cyclosporiasis, reported in British Columbia, Canada, was linked to imported basil.[20] The protozoal parasite causes watery diarrhea and other symptoms of abdominal distress in addition to low-grade fever.

Bacterial Enteropathogens

Examples of microorganisms in this category are *Salmonella, Escherichia coli* O157:H7, and *Vibrio cholerae. Salmonella* bacteria are associated with a number of foodborne (see the chapter on food safety) and waterborne diseases. The variant (serogroup) of *Salmonella* called *Salmonella enterica* serogroup Typhi (*S. enterica* Typhi) causes typhoid fever, which is transmitted by fecal-contaminated water and food (e.g., sold by street vendors). Typhoid fever is a very acute disease that causes fever, headache, and chills; in severe cases, it may produce confusion, delirium, and death.[21] According to the CDC about 400 typhoid fever cases occur in the United States each year. Globally, typhoid fever causes approximately 21 million cases of disease and 200,000 deaths annually. Historically, there have been many examples of waterborne outbreaks: during 1973, an outbreak of 188 proved or presumptive cases occurred at a migrant labor camp in Dade County, Florida.[22] Another outbreak was reported in 1985 in Haifa, Israel, and involved 77 confirmed cases.[23]

The bacterium *E. coli* may be transmitted through contact with contaminated lakes and swimming pools and via ingestion of contaminated water. The same organism also may be transmitted by contaminated food, as discussed in the chapter on food safety. The following text box describes a waterborne outbreak of *E. coli.*

The bacterium that causes cholera is known as *Vibrio cholerae.* The inhabitants of developed countries such as the United States (annual incidence 0 to 5 cases) have very low risk of contracting cholera, which primarily affects the developing world.[24] A continuing pandemic, lasting for four decades in Asia, Africa, and Latin America, has been a cause of epidemic diarrhea. The underlying factors responsible for cholera outbreaks are an inadequate infrastructure for processing

A WATERBORNE OUTBREAK OF *ESCHERICHIA COLI* O157:H7

In the summer of 1998, a large outbreak of *Escherichia coli* O157:H7 infections occurred in Alpine, Wyoming. [There were] 157 ill persons; stool from 71 (45%) yielded *E. coli* O157:H7. In two cohort studies, illness was significantly associated with drinking municipal water. . . . The unchlorinated water supply had microbiologic evidence of fecal organisms and the potential for chronic contamination with surface water. Among persons exposed to water, the attack rate was significantly lower in town residents than in visitors (23% vs. 50%, p < 0.01) and decreased with increasing age. The lower attack rate among exposed residents, especially adults, is consistent with the acquisition of partial immunity following long-term exposure. Serologic data, although limited, may support this finding. Contamination of small, unprotected water systems may be an increasing public health risk.

Reproduced from Olsen SJ, Miller G, Brever T, et al. A waterborne outbreak of *Escherichia coli* O157:H7 infections and hemolytic uremic syndrome: implications for rural water systems. *Emerg Infect Dis.* 2002;8:370–375.

water and migrations of large numbers of people to urban areas. Although cholera is a treatable condition, the disease has a case fatality rate of as high as 50% when untreated. The symptoms of cholera are vomiting and profuse watery diarrhea that can culminate in shock and death.

Viral Pathogens

Over 100 kinds of viruses are found in human stools and pose a potential for transmission by water.[25] "These viruses are more resistant to environmental conditions and sewage treatment processes, including chlorination and ultraviolet (UV) radiation, than many of the sewage-associated bacteria."[25(p179)] Virus-associated conditions that may be spread through water are viral gastroenteritis and viral hepatitis. "The human enteric virus group, which includes Norwalk virus, rotavirus, hepatitis A virus, adenovirus, and enterovirus, is one of the leading causes of human illness."[25(p179)] The term *enteric* is defined as relating to the intestines. Disease outbreaks caused by enteric viruses have been associated with water and food that were contaminated by virus-laden human stools.

Two causes of viral gastroenteritis are noroviruses and adenoviruses. Infection with norovirus produces nausea, vomiting, and watery diarrhea with cramping.

Symptoms of norovirus-associated gastroenteritis usually continue for 24 to 72 hours. Most patients recover fully and do not have residual medical issues. Young children, elderly adults, and immunocompromised individuals can experience serious illness. Transmission routes for noroviruses include ingestion of contaminated food or water and close contact with those who are infected.[26]

The most common means for spreading adenoviruses are direct person-to-person contact, via the air from coughing and sneezing, and from contaminated surfaces. The stools of infected persons (e.g., on diapers) may carry some forms of adenoviruses. Among the diseases that adenoviruses cause are respiratory illnesses (most frequent outcome) and a range of conditions such as gastroenteritis and conjunctivitis. Less commonly, adenoviruses also are spread by waterborne transmission. Adenoviruses have been detected in swimming pools and small lakes.[27] High concentrations of these viruses have been detected near the mouths of rivers in southern California.[25]

Viral hepatitis A (caused by the hepatitis A virus) can be spread via person-to-person contact (e.g., the fecal-oral route) and by contaminated food (e.g., shellfish, fruits, and vegetables), water, and ice.[13,28,29] Countries with poor sanitation can be settings for the spread of hepatitis A. Infected persons who have deficient personal hygiene can spread the virus as well. Viral hepatitis E (a liver infection with the hepatitis E virus) is also transmitted by the fecal-oral route and is found in developing countries with inadequate sanitation and drinking-water contamination. The most frequent mode of transmission is via polluted drinking water. In order to prevent hepatitis E infection, travelers who visit developing countries with unsafe water supplies, for example, in Asia, the Middle East, Africa, and Central America need to avoid drinking tap water.

Due to the presence of infectious agents and toxins in sewage, workers who come into contact with sewage are at increased risk in comparison to the general population of contracting infectious diseases, such as hepatitis C (another form of viral hepatitis), caused by agents present in fecal matter.[30]

Other Agents

Guinea worm. Although there are several important waterborne diseases in this category, one that is noteworthy for the developing world is dracunculiasis (also called guinea worm disease).[31] As the result of an eradication campaign, the range for guinea worm is confined to rural sections of a small number of African countries. The causative organism is the nematode (a kind of roundworm) *Dracunculus medinensis*, which forms larvae that enter the water supply. The larvae infect small crustaceans in the water that are ingested in unfiltered water. In the abdominal cavity of the human host, the larvae mature into worms. Female worms that range in length from 3 to 6 feet (70 to 120 cm) then migrate to the surface of the skin of the feet where they produce painful blisters. The female worm then erupts from this lesion and, when the victim comes into contact with a body of water, releases larvae back into the water, thus perpetuating the cycle of infection. Refer to **FIGURE 21** for an illustration of the clinical features of dracunculiasis as well as additional information.

Legionellosis. The term *legionellosis* refers to illnesses caused by the Legionnaires' disease bacterium; the condition is classified as a waterborne disease.[13] The two distinct clinical forms of legionellosis are Legionnaires' disease and Pontiac fever (a milder form of legionellosis with pneumonia absent). Legionnaires' disease produces fever, cough, and pneumonia[13,32] and is associated with a case-fatality rate of about 15%. More than 25,000 Legionnaires' disease cases (and over 4,000 deaths) occur annually.[32]

The Legionnaires' disease bacterium known as *Legionella pneumophila* was first identified in 1977 after causing an outbreak of pneumonia that resulted in 34 deaths in 1976 at a meeting of the American Legion Convention—hence the name Legionnaires' disease. Microbiologists now recognize that more than 43 species of *Legionella* exist and that more than 20 of them are associated with human disease. However, *L. pneumophila* is regarded as the causative agent for most cases of legionellosis.[32]

Low levels of Legionnaires' disease bacteria are found in freshwater lakes, streams, and rivers. In the environment, some species of protozoa (e.g., some varieties of amoeba) serve as a host for *L. pneumophila*.[33] The organism can grow in domestic water systems, cooling systems, and whirlpool spas.[13] Transmission of the bacterium can occur when water that is rich in *L. pneumophila* becomes aerosolized and is inhaled or ingested in such a way that it enters the respiratory system. The United States Department of Labor notes that "[c]ooling towers, evaporative condensers, and fluid coolers use a fan to move air through a recirculated water system. This allows a considerable amount of water vapor and sometimes droplets to be introduced into the surroundings, despite the presence of drift eliminators designed to limit droplet release. This water may be in the ideal

A. Portable pipe filters are a convenient method for preventing Guinea worm disease. A young boy uses a portable pipe filter to prevent transmission of Guinea worm disease.

The Carter Center/E. Staub

C. Former U.S. President Jimmy Carter and his wife, Rosalynn, examine a pipe filter in northern Ghana. Since 1986, The Carter Center has led the global campaign to eradicate Guinea worm disease.

The Carter Center/A. Poyo

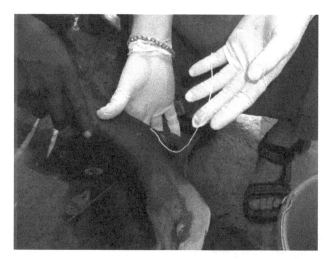

B. Traditional treatment of Guinea worm disease consists of wrapping the two- to three-foot-long (61- to 91-cemtimeter -long) worm around a small stick and extracting it: a slow, painful process that often takes weeks. The figure shows an emerging Guinea worm.

The Carter Center/E. Wolfe

D. Guinea worm disease incapacitates its victims so adults cannot work and children cannot play or attend school. Filters catch the microscopic water fleas that contain infective larvae. This woman is using such a cloth filter.

The Carter Center/E. Staub

FIGURE 21 Guinea worm disease and the use of filters.

temperature range for Legionnaires' disease bacteria (LDB) growth, 20°–50°C (68°–122°F)."[34] **FIGURE 22** illustrates a cooling tower. Because the growth of *L. pneumophila* is possible in some types of cooling towers, proper maintenance of them is essential.

Chemicals in the Water Supply

As previously noted, chemicals enter the water supply from natural and anthropogenic sources. These substances may be present as contaminants in drinking water.

A number of chemical contaminants have been identified in drinking water. These contaminants reach drinking water supplies from various sources, including municipal and industrial discharges, urban and rural run-off, natural geological formations, drinking water distribution materials and the drinking water treatment process. Chemical contaminants for which epidemiologic studies have reported associations include the following: aluminum, arsenic, disinfection by-products, fluoride, lead, pesticides and radon. Health effects reported have included various cancers, adverse reproductive outcomes, cardiovascular disease and neurological disease.[35(pS13)]

Pharmaceutical and personal care products (PPCPs) represent another source of water contamination. These chemicals may be either washed off or excreted from the body; examples of PPCPs that may end up in untreated sewage effluent, surface water, groundwater, and drinking water are analgesics, oral contraceptive agents, drugs for lowering cholesterol, and anticonvulsants.[36] In fact, the term *sewage epidemiology* describes the field of monitoring excreted drugs in the sewer system to assess the level of illicit drug use in the community. The chapters on toxic metals and elements and pesticides and other organic chemicals cover some of the hazards associated with metals, pesticides, and other chemicals. The following section will provide additional information about the effects of chemical contamination of drinking water.

Water Disinfection By-Products (DBPs)

The chemicals used to disinfect water include chlorine, chloramines, chlorine dioxide, and ozone. These chemicals are associated with by-products of chlorination called DBPs.

For example, chlorine is associated with trihalomethanes (THMs), which are among the most common and widely measured DBPs.[37,38] Researchers have probed the relationship between DBPs and several forms of cancer (e.g., bladder and rectal cancer) as well as adverse reproductive outcomes. Several epidemiologic studies have investigated the association between chlorination of drinking water and risk of birth defects; two examples of supportive studies were those conducted by Smith et al.[39] and Hwang and colleagues.[37]

FIGURE 22 Air conditioning cooling tower.

Smith et al. reported an association between exposure to THMs during pregnancy and lowered birth weight; the relationship differed by ethnicity of study participants.[39] The setting for the study was Bradford, a highly diverse city in northern England. Many of Bradford's residents experience social and economic deprivation. Research participants (n = 7,428) were babies from the "Born in Bradford" cohort as well as their mothers. A questionnaire was used to assess each mother's water consumption during pregnancy. Data regarding THM concentrations were provided by the local water company.

Hwang and colleagues examined data from a cross-section of 285,631 Norwegian births in 1993–1998.[37] The results of this cross-sectional study suggested that consumption of chlorinated waters that contained large amounts of natural organic materials was related to increased risk of birth defects.

Nevertheless, at this stage, little is known about the potential adverse health effects of exposure to DBPs.[38] Many researchers who have addressed this topic have been confronted with methodological difficulties, especially with respect to exposure assessment. Typically, studies rely on approximate methods of exposure assessment that do not account for individual variability in patterns of water consumption (e.g., the amount of water consumed, whether water is consumed at work as well as at home, and use of bottled and filtered water).[40]

Solvent-Contaminated Drinking Water

Industrial chemicals may infiltrate the underground aquifers used for public water supplies. An example is contamination of water by a leaking underground solvent tank used by a semiconductor plant in Santa Clara County, California.[41,42] Although the tank held many different chemicals, the chemical solvent trichloroethane (discussed in the chapter on pesticides and other organic chemicals) was present in the highest concentration. Unfortunately, the tank was located near a local water company's drinking water well. The leak was discovered in November 1981; by December 7 the levels of trichloroethane at the well were 1,700 parts per billion (ppb) and in mid-December reached 8,800 ppb. The level of 1,700 ppb exceeded by 8.5 times the level required by the state of California for remediation. Residents of an area affected by the contaminated water supply believed that an excessive number of spontaneous abortions and birth defects were occurring in their neighborhood. An investigation conducted in 1983 showed significant associations between exposure to the contaminated water and adverse pregnancy outcomes (congenital malformations and spontaneous abortions), but was unable to demonstrate a causal connection. A follow-up study suggested that the solvent leak was unlikely to have caused the increased numbers of adverse pregnancy outcomes.

▶ Beach and Coastal Pollution

The final topic in this chapter is pollution of ocean water. The seemingly boundless world's ocean, which covers 70% of the planet, performs essential functions necessary for maintaining life on earth. According to the National Ocean Service (a branch of the National Oceanic and Atmospheric Administration [NOAA]), these actions include production of more than half of global oxygen and regulation of climate.[43] Other benefits include marine transportation, recreation, economic resources, food, and medicine. Alarmingly, sewage, untreated wastewater, and urban runoff endanger coastal areas. Plastics (e.g., plastic bags, disposable drink containers, discarded plastic medical devices, and microbeads in personal care products) wash up on our coasts and drift far out into the ocean where they form gargantuan masses that threaten sea creatures. Other troubling sources of ocean pollution are from drilling oil, petroleum releases from oil platforms, and oil spills from tankers.

Some estimates suggest that half of the world's coastal areas are endangered.[44] **FIGURE 23** shows a number of human activities that lead to coastal degradation. These actions include draining of coastal ecosystems, dredging, solid waste disposal, construction of dams for flood control, discharge of wastes from farms and industries, and logging activities.

The approximately 1 billion people who live near coastal areas cause great stress on coastal ecosystems. Growth rates of populations near coastal regions are estimated to be twice the rate of worldwide population growth.[45] As the population mushrooms, coastal areas are threatened by overdevelopment, poor planning, and economic expansion. Each day the world's coastal regions are the recipients of billions of gallons of treated and untreated wastewater. During heavy rains urban runoff into the oceans degrades the quality of ocean water by adding microbial agents, nutrients, and chemical toxins. The problem of urban runoff is compounded by developments that result in the loss of **wetlands**, which act as natural water-filtering mechanisms. Excessive amounts of nutrients that enter the oceans may cause harmful blooms of algae, resulting in reduced levels of oxygen in the water (anoxic conditions). An anoxic ocean environment can bring about fish kills and damage other forms of ocean life.

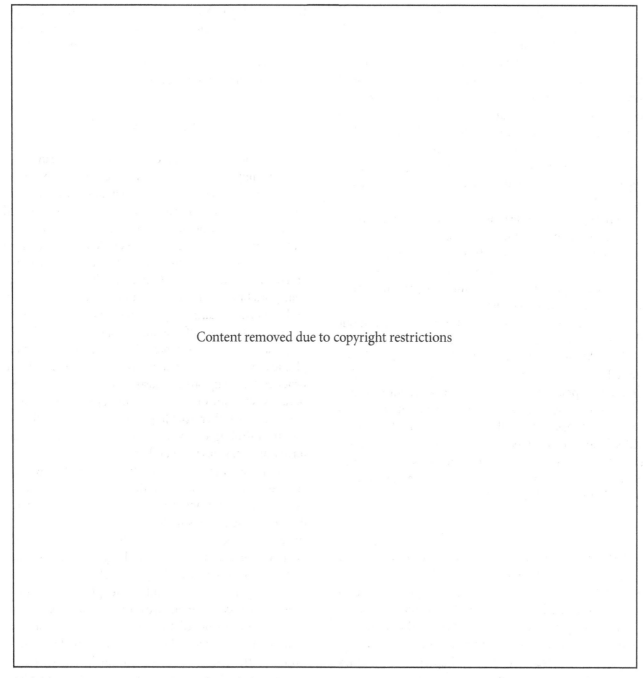

Content removed due to copyright restrictions

FIGURE 23 Human actions leading to coastal degradation.

Urban runoff and sewage contamination of the ocean expose swimmers to waterborne diseases—gastrointestinal, respiratory, skin, and eye infections. As a result of ocean water contamination, beach closings may transpire some parts of the United States, especially after heavy rainfall that creates urban runoff. (See **FIGURE 24.**)

The EPA conducts an ongoing survey of beaches as authorized by the Beaches Environmental Assessment and Coastal Health Act (BEACH Act of 2000.)[46] The EPA surveyed a total of 3,762 beaches regarding advisories (meaning possible risks of swimming in the water) or closings that occurred during the 2012 swimming season and reported that about 40% had one or more advisories or closures. By far, the most frequent cause of beach closings was elevated bacteria levels that exceeded water quality standards. **FIGURE 25** shows the percentage of beaches with one of more notification actions.

Storm water runoff is a leading cause of ocean pollution. Garbage that is discarded carelessly on the street may end up in the ocean or on beaches, as **FIGURE 26** demonstrates. Following heavy rains, visitors to the

FIGURE 24 Beach closing sign. With increasing levels of pollution in some areas, beach closings have become more frequent.

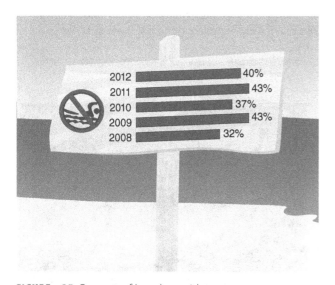

FIGURE 25 Percent of beaches with one or more notification actions.

FIGURE 26 Ocean pollution evident in the harbor at the port town of Cobh, Ireland.

beach are likely to find massive quantities of nonbiodegradable plastics (e.g., Styrofoam cups, rings from beverage six packs, and plastic bags) that are littering the shoreline. In addition to being offensive, these materials endanger birds and fish. Motor vehicle oil and automotive chemicals that are dumped carelessly into storm drains also eventually pollute the ocean.

Petroleum Spills

Oil spills from tankers and offshore drilling platforms can have a devastating impact on the shoreline,

aquatic life, mammals, and birds. One of the worst oil spills in US history was caused by the tanker *Exxon Valdez*, described in the following text box and shown in **FIGURE 27**.

Oil platforms similar to the one shown in **FIGURE 28** have been associated with accidental releases of crude oil. January 28, 1969 was the date of an extensive oil spill off the coast of the city of Santa Barbara, California.[47] The spill originated from an offshore drilling rig known as platform Alpha, operated by the Union Oil Company. This episode, which lasted for 11 days and allowed 3 million gallons (11 million liters) of oil to escape, caused

On March 24, 1989, the tanker *Exxon Valdez*, en route from Valdez, Alaska to Los Angeles, California, ran aground on Bligh Reef in Prince William Sound, Alaska. The vessel was traveling outside normal shipping lanes in an attempt to avoid ice. Within 6 hours of the grounding, the *Exxon Valdez* spilled approximately 10.9 million gallons [41.3 million liters] of its 53 million gallon (200 million liter) cargo of Prudhoe Bay Crude. Eight of the 11 tanks on board were damaged. The oil would eventually impact over 1,100 miles (1,770 kilometers) of noncontinuous coastline in Alaska, making the *Exxon Valdez* the largest oil spill to date [as of 1992] in US waters.

The response to the *Exxon Valdez* involved more personnel and equipment over a longer period of time than did any other spill in US history. Logistical problems in providing fuel, meals, berthing, response equipment, waste management, and other resources was one of the largest challenges to response management. At the height of the response, more than 11,000 personnel, 1,400 vessels, and 85 aircraft were involved in the cleanup. . . .

Concern over oil-related wildlife mortality was intense during the spill. The grounding occurred at the beginning of the bird migration season. The US Fish and Wildlife Service estimated that mortalities directly related to the spill ranged from 350,000 to 390,000 birds, especially common and thick-billed murres, assorted sea ducks, bald eagles, and pigeon guillemots; 3,500 to 5,500 sea otters; and 200 harbor seals. In addition, killer whales may have been affected by the spill as their numbers in the area declined shortly after the spill. Of the 1,630 birds (over 36,000 dead birds were collected) and 357 sea otters that were trapped and treated by the International Bird Rescue Research Center (IBRRC)–run facilities (established in Homer, Kodiak, Seward, and Valdez in response to this spill), the total survival rate was 50.7% for birds, and 62% for sea otters. These survival rates are considered very good for oil impacted animals.

Unlike birds, sea otters had to be anesthetized to be washed, which increases the risk to the animal, and increases the cost of rehabilitation. The sea otter rehabilitation program was complex, with a total of 29 veterinarians, and 9 veterinarian technicians scheduled to provide 24-hour care. The resulting cost of the sea otter rehabilitation program was at least $51,000 per sea otter. The highest percentages of sea otter fatalities (60%) were recorded in the first 3 weeks of the spill.

Reproduced from National Oceanic and Atmospheric Administration. *Oil Spill Case Histories, 1967–1991, Summaries of Significant US and International Spills*. Report No. HMRAD 92-11. Seattle, Washington; 1992.

FIGURE 27 The *Exxon Valdez* oil spill. Upper left: Oil being removed (lightered) from the ship. Upper right: *Exxon Valdez* surrounded by a boom. Lower left: Biologist measuring depth of oil penetration. Lower right: Workers using high-pressure, hot-water washing to clean an oiled shoreline.

Reproduced from National Oceanic and Atmospheric Administration, NOAA's Ocean Service, Office of Response and Restoration. Image Galleries: *Exxon Valdez* Oil Spill. Available at: http://response .restoration.noaa.gov/gallery_gallery_photo.php? Accessed April 5, 2010.

FIGURE 28 Oil platform off the California coast.

an ecological catastrophe. The affected shoreline is an environmentally sensitive area noted for its pristine waters and abundant sea life. As a result of the spill, 3,600 ocean-feeding sea birds were killed. The carcasses of numerous poisoned seals and dolphins had to be removed from the beaches. This catastrophe was responsible for killing an untold number of fish and invertebrates and wreaked havoc on sensitive kelp forests.

In addition to the *Exxon Valdez* and Santa Barbara oil spills, there have been numerous other incidents. For example, the *Sea Empress* spilled approximately 72,000 tons (65,317 metric tons) of crude oil and 360 tons (326 metric tons) of heavy fuel oil when it ran aground at the entrance of Milford Haven harbor near Wales on February 15, 1996.[48] Nearby residents reported strong smells and complained of various symptoms that were associated with the spill. When contrasted with people living in control areas, residents in the exposed area indicated that they had higher rates of physical and psychological symptoms, which were consistent with the known toxicological effects of oil. The *Nakhodka* oil spill, which occurred on January 2, 1997, caused more than 6,000 tons (5,443 metric tons) of oil to be spilled into the Sea of Japan. Most of the oil drifted to the shoreline of the western portion of the island of Honshu, which is Japan's main island. Cleanup of the spill required the use of hand tools such as ladles and buckets because the area was inaccessible to machines. Local residents and those who were involved in the cleanup efforts experienced a number of acute symptoms of exposure, including low-back pain, headache, and effects on the eyes and skin.[49]

The process of extracting oil from petroleum fields has caused significant environmental damage in some areas of the world. The tropical forest areas of the Ecuadorian Amazon hold large oil reserves. As a result of drilling and extraction activities, billions of gallons of untreated wastes and oil have been dumped into the environment in this region. To prevent further damage to this ecologically sensitive area, controls will be needed to stem the flow of pollutants.[50]

On April 20, 2010, an explosion at the *Deepwater Horizon* oil platform and the resulting damage to the wellhead caused the largest marine oil spill in history up to that time. The catastrophe released 5 million barrels of oil into the Gulf of Mexico, from a location that is about 50 miles (80 kilometers) south of the Louisiana coastline. Information about the spill is provided in the following text box. **FIGURE 29** illustrates firefighting efforts at the site. A report of the effects of the oil spill is available from the Institute of Medicine.[51]

▶ Conclusion

Water is an essential element of life on earth—a human being can survive for only about one week without water. As the global population expands and increasing industrialization creates ever-growing demands for water, supplies of this vital commodity have become endangered. Several areas of the world currently face chronic shortages and water stress; often these are the same areas that are experiencing skyrocketing population growth.

Surface water and groundwater are used as the sources of potable water in the majority of the countries of the world. These sources are vulnerable to contamination from human activities such as sewage

THE *DEEPWATER HORIZON* OIL SPILL, GULF OF MEXICO

Background: On the night of April 20, 2010, an explosion followed by a conflagration devastated the *Deepwater Horizon* oil platform, which eventually sank into the depths of the Gulf of Mexico. The drilling rig, owned and operated by Transocean Ltd. under contract with the British Petroleum Oil Company, was located in the Gulf approximately 50 miles (80 kilometers) southeast of the Mississippi River delta. The drilling rig extracted crude oil from a well that was about 5,000 feet (1,524 meters) below the surface of the water. When the platform sank, oil began gushing from the well. The extreme depth of the well challenged efforts to staunch the oil flow.

Dates of the spill: The spill commenced on April 20, 2010, with the explosion on the drilling rig, and ended on July 15, 2010, when the well was finally capped.

Significance of the spill: The *Deepwater Horizon* oil spill was history's largest accidental marine oil spill. By the time the wellhead had been capped, nearly 5 million barrels of oil are believed to have escaped from the well. Although some of the oil was recovered, an estimated 4.2 million barrels of oil were released into the Gulf of Mexico. Initial reports suggested that only about 1,000 to 5,000 barrels of oil per day were spewing from the well, a figure that greatly underestimated the scope of the disaster. Subsequent estimates increased periodically as the full scale of the catastrophe became known. The official tally eventually grew to up to 60,000 barrels per day.

This catastrophe eclipsed all previous marine oil spills that occurred in the United States and anywhere else in the world. The second largest marine release of oil in history also occurred in the Gulf during 1979 in the Bay of Campeche from the Mexican oil rig *Ixtoc 1*. Estimates placed the total from this spill at 3.3 million barrels.

Fate of workers onboard the rig: The platform was staffed by a crew of 126 at the time. A total of 115 crew members were able to evacuate. An additional 11 workers were assumed to have perished at sea and remained unaccounted for despite an extensive 3-day search by the US Coast Guard.

Immediate impact of the spill: Oil slicks from the gushing well covered nearly 30,000 square miles (78,000 square kilometers) of Gulf waters. As oil moved toward landfall, it eventually impacted the coastal areas of Louisiana and the neighboring states of Mississippi, Alabama, and Florida. Crude oil worked its way into the ecologically sensitive marshes at the mouth of the Mississippi River; a substantial die-off of wildlife occurred in Louisiana. The spill had immediate and devastating consequences for the local economy in oil-affected areas. In addition to discouraging tourism, a mainstay of the region, the catastrophe severely curtailed the fishing industry. Government authorities prohibited fishing at the mouth of the Mississippi River and nearby affected areas. An additional concern was the long-term effects of the thousands of gallons of dispersants applied to the floating crude oil upon marine life forms.

Partial data from Robertson C, Krauss C. Gulf spill is the largest of its kind, scientists say. *The New York Times*. August 2, 2010. Available at: http://www.nytimes.com/2010/08/03/us/03spill.html. Accessed September 17, 2017; and The Encyclopedia of Earth. Deepwater Horizon oil spill. Available at: http://editors.eol.org/eoearth/wiki/Deepwater_Horizon_oil_spill. Accessed September 17, 2017.

FIGURE 29 *Deepwater Horizon* fire.

disposal, large-scale farms, manufacturing facilities, and urban runoff. Standard water-processing methods are unable to remove many toxic chemicals and some pathological microbes. In the developing world, where adequate water processing methods are not in place, waterborne infections are a major cause of morbidity and mortality. The world's oceans, which seem to be vast and invulnerable to pollution, are rapidly degrading, especially in the coastal areas. The 21st century will need to become the era for implementing pollution abatement measures in order to protect a finite and increasingly endangered resource—water.

The cost of water to the consumer varies greatly across the globe and depends on local supply availability and demand. In some countries, bottled water accounts for 10% or more of drinking water supplies because water is unavailable or unsafe. Melting of the world's glaciers, which in some regions replenish vitally needed surface water, ultimately may cause further exacerbation of water shortages when the glaciers disappear completely.

Study Questions and Exercises

1. Define the following terms:
   a. Surface water
   b. Groundwater
   c. Hydrology
   d. Hydrological cycle

2. Describe the principal reserves for water. Which areas of the world have adequate supplies and which are facing a chronic shortage?

3. How is the majority of water used in the average household? What are some ways in which households might conserve water and prevent waste of water?

4. Why has bottled water garnered favor in recent years? To what extent is bottled water safer than tap water? What safeguards are in place to protect the quality of bottled water?

5. Explain the four stages of water treatment. How is it possible for waterborne pathogens such as *Cryptosporidium* to contaminate water that has been treated in modern treatment plants?

6. Describe three waterborne diseases and suggest methods for their prevention.

7. What historical observations led to the fluoridation of water? Take a position for or against the fluoridation of water.

8. What are some examples of toxic chemicals that may enter the public water supply? Describe some of the health effects that are attributed to toxic chemicals present in drinking water.

9. Defend or refute the hypothetical statement that the world's oceans, because of their vast size, are invulnerable to pollution from microbial agents and toxic chemicals.

10. Find an article in your local newspaper or other media source regarding local efforts by citizens to clean up the beach at a nearby lake or ocean. What steps can individuals take to prevent water pollution?

11. Arrange a visit to your local water plant to observe how water is processed for delivery to customers as finished water.

12. Based on your reading of this chapter and your own opinions, describe risk factors for oil spills from platforms and oil tankers.

13. Conduct a review of media reports of methods for water conservation. Suggest three methods whereby agriculture and industry might conserve water.

14. State three human actions associated with coastal degradation in highly populated areas. In your own opinion, what can be done to reduce the impact of these factors? (Refer to Figure 23.)

15. Define the term guinea worm disease. What procedures have led to a reduction in the frequency of this condition? (Refer to Figure 21.)

For Further Reading

Water: Our Thirsty World, A special issue of *National Geographic*, April. 2010.

References

1. US Environmental Protection Agency, Office of Water. Drinking water and health: what you need to know! EPA 816-K-99-001; 1999.

2. Tibbetts J. Water world 2000. *Environ Health Perspect.* 2000;108:A69–A73.

3. US Environmental Protection Agency. Safe Drinking Water Act. Drinking water facts and figures. EPA 816-F-04-036; 2004.

4. Holt MS. Sources of chemical contaminants and routes into the freshwater environment. *Food Chem Toxicol.* 2000;38 (1 suppl):S21–S27.

5. Hinrichsen D, Robey B, Upadhyay UD. Solutions for a water-short world. *Population Reports.* Baltimore, MD: Johns Hopkins University School of Public Health, Population Information Program; 1998. Series M, No. 14.

6. United Nations Environment Programme. Vital water graphics: freshwater resources. 2002. Available at: http://staging.unep .org/dewa/assessments/ecosystems/water/vitalwater/05.htm. Accessed June 5, 2017.

7. Centers for Disease Control and Prevention. Achievements in public health, 1900–1999: fluoridation of drinking water to prevent dental caries. *MMWR.* 1999;48:933–940.

8. Tong ST, Chen W. Modeling the relationship between land use and surface water quality. *J Environ Manage.* 2002;66:377–393.

9. US Environmental Protection Agency. *Water on Tap: What You Need to Know.* Washington, DC: EPA Office of Water; 2003.

10. Leclerc H, Schwartzbrod L, Dei-Cas E. Microbial agents associated with waterborne diseases. *Crit Rev Microbiol.* 2002;28:371–409.

11. Centers for Disease Control and Prevention. Norovirus. Available at: https://www.cdc.gov/norovirus/about/symptoms.html. Accessed June 24, 2017.

12. MacKenzie WR, Hoxie NJ, Proctor ME, et al. A massive outbreak in Milwaukee of *Cryptosporidium* infection transmitted through the public water supply. *N Engl J Med.* 1994;331:161–167.

13. Heymann DL, ed. *Control of Communicable Diseases Manual.* 20th ed. Washington, DC: American Public Health Association; 2015.

14. Dillingham RA, Lima AA, Guerrant RL. Cryptosporidiosis: epidemiology and impact. *Microbes Infect.* 2002;4:1059–1066.

15. Khalakdina A, Vugia DJ, Nadle J, et al. Is drinking water a risk factor for endemic cryptosporidiosis? A case-control study in the immunocompetent general population of the San Francisco Bay Area. *BMC Public Health.* 2003;3:11.

16. Carpenter C, Fayer R, Trout J, et al. Chlorine disinfection of recreational water for *Cryptosporidium parvum. Emerg Infect Dis.* 1999;5:579–584.

17. Centers for Disease Control and Prevention. Parasites—amebiasis. Causal agent. Available at: https://www.cdc.gov/parasites/amebiasis/pathogen.html. Accessed June 22, 2017.

18. Centers for Disease Control and Prevention. Parasites—amebiasis—*Entamoeba histolytica* infection. Available at: https://www.cdc.gov/parasites/amebiasis/general-info.html. Accessed June 22, 2017.

19. Centers for Disease Control and Prevention. Parasites and health: giardiasis. Available at: https://www.cdc.gov/parasites/giardia/pathogen.html. Accessed June 22, 2017.

20. Shah L, MacDougall L, Ellis A, et al. Challenges of investigating community outbreaks of cyclosporiasis, British Columbia, Canada. *Emerg Infect Dis.* 2009;15:1286–1288.

21. Centers for Disease Control and Prevention. Typhoid fever. For healthcare professionals. Available at: https://www.cdc.gov/typhoid-fever/health-professional.html. Accessed June 23, 2017.

22. Hoffman TA, Ruiz CJ, Counts GW, et al. Waterborne typhoid fever in Dade County, Florida. Clinical and therapeutic evaluation of 105 bacteremic patients. *Am J Med.* 1975;59:481–487.

23. Finkelstein R, Markel A, Putterman C, et al. Waterborne typhoid fever in Haifa, Israel: clinical, microbiologic and therapeutic aspects of a major outbreak. *Am J Med Sci.* 1988;296:27–32.

24. Centers for Disease Control and Prevention. Cholera—*Vibrio cholerae* infection: sources of infection & risk factors. Available at: https://www.cdc.gov/cholera/infection-sources.html. Accessed June 23, 2017.

25. Jiang S, Noble R, Chu W. Human adenoviruses and coliphages in urban runoff-impacted coastal waters of southern California. *Appl Environ Microbiol.* 2001;67:179–184.

26. Centers for Disease Control and Prevention. Norovirus. Clinical overview. Available at: http://www.cdc.gov/ncidod/dvrd/revb/gastro/norovirus-foodhandlers.htm. Accessed June 23, 2017.

27. Centers for Disease Control and Prevention. Adenoviruses. Available at: https://www.cdc.gov/adenovirus/index.html. Accessed June 23, 2017.

28. Centers for Disease Control and Prevention. Viral hepatitis. Hepatitis A questions and answers for the public. Available at: https://www.cdc.gov/hepatitis/hav/afaq.htm#whatHepA. Accessed June 23, 2017.

29. Centers for Disease Control and Prevention. Viral hepatitis. Hepatitis E FAQs for health professionals. Available at: https://www.cdc.gov/hepatitis/hev/hevfaq.htm#section2. Accessed June 23, 2017.

30. Brautbar N, Navizadeh N. Sewer workers: occupational risk for hepatitis C—report of two cases and review of literature. *Arch Environ Health.* 1999;54:328–330.

31. Centers for Disease Control and Prevention. DPDX. Dracunculiasis. Available at: https://www.cdc.gov/dpdx/dracunculiasis/index.html. Accessed June 23, 2017.

32. US Department of Labor. Occupational Safety and Health Administration. Legionnaires' disease. Available at: https://www.osha.gov/dts/osta/otm/legionnaires/disease_rec.html. Accessed June 23, 2017.

33. Cirillo JD, Falkow S, Tompkins LS. Growth of *Legionella pneumophila* in *Acanthamoeba castellanii* enhances invasion. *Infect Immun.* 1994;62:3254–3261.

34. US Department of Labor. Occupational Safety and Health Administration. Legionnaires' disease: cooling towers, evaporative condensers, and fluid coolers. Available at: https://www.osha.gov/dts/osta/otm/legionnaires/cool_evap.html. Accessed June 23, 2017.

35. Calderon RL. The epidemiology of chemical contaminants of drinking water. *Food Chem Toxicol.* 2000;38(1 suppl):S13–S20.

36. Potera C. Drugged drinking water. *Environ Health Perspect.* 2000;108:A446.

37. Hwang B-F, Magnus P, Jaakkola JK. Risk of specific birth defects in relation to chlorination and the amount of natural organic matter in the water supply. *Am J Epidemiol.* 2002;156:374–382.

38. Nieuwenhuijsen MJ, Toledano MB, Eaton NE, et al. Chlorination disinfection byproducts in water and their association with adverse reproductive outcomes: a review. *Occup Environ Med.* 2000;57:73–85.

39. Smith RB, Edwards SC, Best N, et al. Birth weight, ethnicity, and exposure to trihalomethanes and haloacetuc acids in drinking water during pregnancy in the Born in Bradford cohort. *Environ Health Perspect* 2016;124:681–689.

40. Zender R, Bachand AM, Reif JS. Exposure to tap water during pregnancy. *J Expo Anal Environ Epidemiol.* 2001;11:224–230.

41. Deane M, Swan SH, Harris JA, et al. Adverse pregnancy outcomes in relation to water contamination, Santa Clara County, California, 1980–1981. *Am J Epidemiol.* 1989;129:894–904.

42. Wrensch M, Swan S, Lipscomb J, et al. Pregnancy outcomes in women potentially exposed to solvent-contaminated drinking water in San Jose, California. *Am J Epidemiol.* 1990;131:283–300.

43. National Oceanic and Atmospheric Administration (NOAA). National Ocean Service. Why should we care about the ocean? Available at: http://oceanservice.noaa.gov/facts/why-care-about-ocean.html. Accessed June 24, 2017.

44. United Nations Environment Programme. Vital water graphics: coastal and marine. 2002. Available at: http://staging.unep.org/dewa/assessments/ecosystems/water/vitalwater/38.htm. Accessed June 5, 2017.

45. Hendrickson SE, Wong T, Allen P, et al. Marine swimming-related illness: implications for monitoring and environmental policy. *Environ Health Perspect.* 2001;109:645–650.

46. US Environmental Protection Agency. *EPA's BEACH Report: 2012 Swimming Season.* EPA 820-F-13-014; 2013.

47. Clarke KC, Hemphill JJ. The Santa Barbara oil spill: a retrospective. In: Danta D, ed. *Yearbook of the Association of Pacific Coast Geographers.* Honolulu, HI: University of Hawaii Press; 2002:157–162.

48. Lyons RA, Temple JM, Evans D, et al. Acute health effects of the *Sea Empress* oil spill. *J Epidemiol Community Health.* 1999;53:306–310.

49. Morita A, Kusaka Y, Deguchi Y, et al. Acute health problems among the people engaged in the cleanup of the *Nakhodka* oil spill. *Environ Res.* 1999;81:185–194.

50. San Sebastián M, Armstrong B, Stephens C. Outcomes of pregnancy among women living in the proximity of oil fields in the Amazon basin of Ecuador. *Int J Occup Environ Health.* 2002;8:312–319.

51. Institute of Medicine. *Assessing the Effects of the Gulf of Mexico Oil Spill on Human Health.* Washington, DC: The National Academies Press; 2010.

Ethical Considerations: How They Apply to Air Pollution

By the end of this chapter the reader will be able to:

- define "ethics" and differentiate normative ethics from practical ethics
- describe the Tuskegee Syphilis Study and its impact on regulations covering research on human subjects
- describe the similarities and differences between regulations for animal research and for human research
- create a "Code of Ethics" for public health students

I. INTRODUCTION

Why Bother?

If everyone just got along, respected one another, did not pollute the environment, and lent a helping hand to the needy, this chapter would not be necessary. Yet, human history as well as current events have shown that some regulation of human behavior is necessary for the safety, health, and well-being of the public. In addition, many people believe that nonhuman animals, ecosystems, and the environment are not adequately protected.

Ethical standards are established in a variety of ways. Public laws establish the rules for accepted general behavior. Governmental agencies set the rules for special problems such as construction standards, air and water quality, use of human and animal research subjects, and contaminant emissions from cars, power plants and factories. Professional societies and trade groups establish codes of conduct, including ethics requirements for their members. Local communities, clubs, families, religions, and even individuals also establish written and unwritten rules for behavior.

Thus, the ethical standards related to air pollution derive from many sources. Today, every person, professional group, social group, and business entity has several types of ethical constraints that bear on their activities that influence air quality. In the final analysis, it is the behavior of individuals who decide how to perform their daily activities that really matters.

Environmental laws are based on the public's expectation that the government will provide for safe, and even esthetically pleasing, environments, both indoors and outdoors.

As shown in **Exhibit** 1 environmental ethics has a long history. Air pollution regulations have the force of law, and they are periodically revised. Such standards impact public health and welfare, both directly and indirectly through their economic effects. Because the direct (intended) effects are accompanied by their indirect (unintended) effects, new, or proposed, air quality regulations are usually controversial.

What Does "Ethics" Encompass?

Ethics has both formal and practical aspects. *Formal ethics* is a branch of philosophy that both studies the fundamental principles of moral behavior and describes the rules for acceptable behaviors. Philosophers who pursue ethics examine the history, variety, and basis for normative (i.e., proper) behaviors. They also take a lead in advancing their branch of philosophy, including holding conferences, publishing journals, and proposing changes in prevailing ethical standards. Specialists in ethics, i.e., *ethicists,* can be totally committed to the topic. The activities of ethicists can include analyses and critiques of timely ethical issues, sometimes with the intent of modifying the behavior of others. Ethics also interfaces with the law, and laws defining ethical behavior are continuously evolving. Such laws are examples of *practical ethics,* in that they define and regulate behavior.

One might assume that ethical standards have some firm basis, but it is difficult to identify universal ethical principles or standards. The simplistic concept that something is ethical only if it does no harm is impractical. Both time and place determine what behavior is ethical and what is unethical. Wartime battlefield ethical standards, for example, have little in common with the standards that underlie modern medical ethics: Secrecy, respect for persons, and considerations regarding acceptable risk of harm are worlds apart in these contrasting arenas. It is therefore difficult to identify any universally-accepted basis for defining what is proper and what is not. Even the best decisions usually have some undesirable consequences.

Rewards and punishments are used to encourage conformity with ethical standards. Some of these positive and negative incentives are externally imposed, but there are also internal guidelines. Individuals and organizations can take comfort when they know that they are conforming to high ethical standards and thus have nothing to hide. Success and status are linked to external perceptions of ethical behavior. In short, ethical standards do place constraints on behavior, but conforming to high standards reduces the risk of censure, or worse consequences.

Ethical standards change over time as society evolves, and as technology advances to present new challenges. Practical issues and contemporary concerns influence what is accepted behavior at any given time. In the past century, new areas of ethical concern have emerged including (1) those involving the use of human and laboratory animal research subjects and (2) protection of the environment. Humans and animals are widely used in air pollution studies to gather data for protecting people, domestic animals, wildlife, and ecosystems. Thus, ethical standards for protecting research subjects are relevant to this chapter, as are standards for protecting the general environment.

Exhibit   1 A brief history of environmental ethics.

The foundations of modern thinking about the relationship between industrial civilizations and the natural environment can be traced back over 200 years ago. A British scholar, T. Robert Malthus (1766–1834), argued in an essay that uncontrolled population growth was unsustainable without changes in the growth of food production (Malthus, 1798). According to Malthus:

"Population when unchecked increases in a geometrical ratio. Subsistence increases only in an arithmetical ratio. A slight acquaintance with numbers will shew the immensity of the first power in comparison of the second."

Malthus' simple proposition stressed both the importance of (1) modeling future trends and (2) thinking about the impact of human population growth on human welfare. He was not directly concerned with the impact of population on the environment, but he helped to prepare the foundations for considering such problems.

More recently, thinkers and writers have developed the basic concept of Malthus into an environmental theme that includes the impact that humans have on nature. *Silent Spring,* a widely-read book by Rachel Carson (1963), drew attention to the ability of some useful pesticides (DDT, aldrin, and dieldrin) to concentrate in the environment. Such concentration, Carson argued, could have negative impacts on the environment (including bird populations) and on public health. Paul Ehrlich, a Stanford University ecologist, warned in his popular book *The Population Bomb* (1968) that human population growth has threatened the Earth's life-support systems.

NASA's Christmas 1968 photographic image of a fragile, beautiful Earth isolated in dark empty space made it evident that our planet has limited capacities to sustain life and to deal with environmental pollutants. Shortly after the image was published, the first Earth Day in 1970 and the creation of the U.S. Environmental Protection Agency (1970) firmly established a public commitment to the environment, and thus environmental ethics. The first administrator of the U.S. EPA, William D. Ruckelshaus, wrote in a press release two weeks after the formation of the agency:

"So we shall be an advocate for the environment with individuals, with industry, and within government."

Thus, "the environment" achieved *legal status* and the protection of the U.S. government. Air quality is currently a major aspect of the legal commitment to protect the environment.

Topics related to environmental ethics were presented and debated in books, magazines, and the journal, *Inquiry,* throughout the 1970s. Philosophical issues emerged including whether or not nonhuman life had *intrinsic value* (i.e., was valuable for its own sake), rather than only *instrumental value* (i.e., value only in relation to its benefit to humans), and who might represent nonhuman living things in legal actions.

Publication opportunities were broadened by the founding of the journal, *Environmental Ethics,* by Eugene C. Hargrove in 1979; the establishment of the *International Society for Environmental Ethics* in 1990; the founding of the journals *Environmental Values* in England in 1992 and *Ethics and the Environment* in 1996; and the establishment of a second international association, the *International Association for Environmental Philosophy* in 1997.

For further information, in addition to the above sources, one can visit the *Internet Encyclopedia of Philosophy* (http://www.iep.utm.edu) and *The Stanford Encyclopedia of Philosophy* (http://plato.stanford.edu).

II. ETHICS AS A BRANCH OF PHILOSOPHY

Ethics, also called moral philosophy, is concerned with distinguishing right from wrong and good from bad. *Metaethics* (meaning "about ethics") addresses some of the larger questions such as "Is there any difference between right and wrong?" and "Are all moral standards just arbitrary?" Approaches to metaethics place philosophers into several camps, including the following:

- *Naturalists* maintain that moral concepts are matters of fact and that moral decisions can be based on scientific or factual investigations.

- *Cognitivists* maintain that moral judgments can be either true or false and can, in principle, be subjects of knowledge or cognition as opposed to emotion or volition.
- *Intuitionists* maintain that knowledge of right and wrong is self-evident, not requiring analysis.
- *Subjectivists* maintain that moral judgments are only about approval or disapproval by individuals or societies.

There are other ways to approach metaethics, but when it comes to deciding what should actually be done in a given situation, another branch of philosophy, *normative ethics,* applies. There are several normative theories, but they generally fall into the following two categories:

- *Consequentialist* (also teological) theory maintains that the morality (rightness or wrongness) of an action depends only on its consequences.
- *Nonconsequentialist* (also deontological) theory maintains that it is the motive, or conformity to an ethical rule or principle, that primarily determines the morality of an action.

There are several other normative theories that do not fall easily into these two categories, but nonetheless are used to distinguish moral from immoral actions:

- *Theological* theory maintains that it is the will of God, or divine command, that defines morality.
- *Utilitarian* theory maintains that affording the greatest happiness to the greatest number is the measure of morality of an action. There are debates on inclusion. Should only the happiness of humans be considered, or should other living things, and which ones, be included?
- *Situational* theory maintains that each situation may require a unique analysis of what is, or is not, moral.
- *Egoist* theory maintains that actions are right only if they are in the interest of the person performing the action (self-interest).

As one might expect, arguments about the morality of a given decision leads to invoking one or more of the above theories. There is no agreement on which theory is right or wrong as a measure of whether a given action (or decision) is itself right or wrong. Judgments must nevertheless be made, and there is seldom universal agreement on their correctness. In difficult decisions, precedent and personal and cultural norms are often the basis of judgments.

At times, the interests of one group (e.g., people with cancer) conflict with that of another group (e.g., laboratory animals in cancer therapy studies). This circumstance has been dealt with by a formal ethics review committee using the principle of maximizing the good (for cancer victims) and minimizing the harm (to research animals). In practice, an ethics committee will require adherence to good experimental design, use of the minimum number of laboratory animals to answer the scientific questions, and use of the best techniques for eliminating any pain and distress that might be experienced by the animals. If an independent ethics committee determines that the

"good" significantly outweighs the "harm," the study may be approved, with monitoring and periodic review as the study progresses. For air pollution standards, the interests of susceptible individuals or groups (e.g., people with heart and lung disease) are counterbalanced by the interests of individuals or groups that must sacrifice economically in order to meet the standards.

III. HUMAN AND ANIMAL SUBJECTS RESEARCH ETHICS

From the perspective of this book it is useful to examine the ethical aspects of research with human and laboratory animal subjects. Such subjects are extensively used in toxicology and epidemiology research on the health effects of air pollutants. Air quality standards are dependent on the results of such research. Also, because the ethical standards in such research are highly developed and effectively monitored, they can provide insight on the potential future of the evolving topic of *environmental ethics.*

Historical Background

The late 1800s to the early 1900s was a remarkable period: radioactivity and x-rays were discovered; the practical automobile and airplane were developed; the industrial revolution began; medicine and public health rapidly advanced; the telephone revolutionized communication; and widely-available domestic and commercial electric power emerged. As a result, human life was radically and rapidly transformed, probably like never before. The industrial smokestack became a symbol of progress. The awesome power of science and technology was widely perceived to be in control of the future of humankind. This rapid change in lifestyle also generated a fear that poorly understood, yet powerful new forces were replacing the familiar traditional agents of change. There was concern over the possibility that the negative aspects of the scientific and industrial revolutions might outweigh their promised benefits. Some notable events illustrate this concern.

In 1818 Mary Shelley (1797–1851), young lover and future wife of the renowned poet Percival Shelley (1792–1822), wrote the novel *Frankenstein* while at a retreat with Percival and friends. In her horror story the protagonist, a young Dr. Frankenstein, who was obsessed with creating life, animated a creature (the "monster") made in the image of a large man. The doctor was shocked by and even hated his ugly creation, which led to a series of tragic events. The understandably traumatized monster turned murderous and eventually killed his creator's new wife. The monster fled to escape the nearly-insane Dr. Frankenstein's wrath. On its surface, the tale is one of science and ambition gone tragically wrong. The tale can be interpreted in at least two ways: (1) the horror associated with a parent (or creator) hating their offspring (or creation) and (2) the tragic consequences of the pursuit of science without due restraint and caution. It was the second interpretation that caught the public's imagination. Even the inventor Thomas Edison (1847–1931), who obviously embraced new technologies, produced a film, *Frankenstein,* in 1911. Later the English actor Boris Karloff (1887–1969, who was born as William H. Pratt), epitomized Dr. Frankenstein's monster in popular cinema (**Figure** 1). That, and other films, supported the public's fear of science, progress, and technology.

Fortunately, in the nearly two centuries since Mary Shelley wrote her famous horror novel, science and technology has not led to humankind's downfall. Human lifespans have doubled, infant mortality has declined, and access to mobility has increased. This fortuitous outcome is, in part, due to the basic ethical principles

Content removed due to copyright restrictions

Figure 1 Boris Karloff as Dr. Frankenstein's monster from a 1931 film, *Frankenstein.*

followed by most scientists. These principles include open communication of results, honesty in reporting, and an interest in improving the quality life and the general level of knowledge. There have been exceptions in adhering to these idealistic principles; for example, in cases of scientific fraud, in some corporate behavior, and in the interest of winning wars. Yet, the public's trust in science was still relatively high in the mid-1900s.

Human Research Ethics

Although the public was somewhat sensitized to the potential abuses by scientists by sensational books and films, it was the shock of Nazi experiments during World War Two that proved that such abuses could be a rude reality. So-called "medical experiments" were performed on Jews and other prisoners. Many of the experiments were later determined to be "crimes against humanity." The human subjects were involuntarily subjected to extreme pain and even death. The studies included the effects of cold water immersion, oxygen deprivation, and new vaccines. The scientists (largely physicians) claimed that the studies were justified in that they sacrificed a few to benefit a much greater number. The trials of Nazi scientists at Nuremberg applied a set of principles (**Table** 1) in order to determine the guilt of the experimenters. Several of the investigators, were convicted and sentenced to death by hanging or to imprisonment. Only two of about 30 that were tried were acquitted. Even today, the *Nuremberg Principles* are central for defining "crimes against humanity" and the conditions for conducting ethical research with human and animal subjects. After the trials, the Nazi experiments were seen by many at the time as a bizarre Nazi anomaly that had been properly dealt with, perhaps once and for all time. For an analysis of the ethical aspects of the Nazi experiments, see the article "Too hard to face" by a Professor of Bioethics, Arthur Caplan (2005).

The view that civilized people could not engage in such studies was shattered when the U.S. press in 1973 exposed the infamous *Tuskegee Syphilis Study* see (Cobb, 1973). In October 1932, when the U.S. Public Health Service (PHS) began the study on about 400 Alabama black men, it was not known whether the accepted treatments for syphilis, including the administration of arsenic or mercury, were worse than the untreated disease. There was a perceived need to know the effects of "no treatment" on the course of syphilis. As a result, the subjects were not treated, and instead the

Table 1 The Nuremberg Code.

1. The voluntary consent of the human subject is absolutely essential. The duty and responsibility for ascertaining the quality of the consent rests upon each individual who initiates, directs, or engages in the experiment. It is a personal duty and responsibility which may not be delegated to another with impunity.[A]
2. The experiment should be such as to yield fruitful results for the good of society, unprocurable by other methods or means of study, and not random and unnecessary in nature.
3. The experiment should be so designed and based on the results of animal experimentation and a knowledge of the natural history of the disease or other problem under study [so] that the anticipated results will justify the performance of the experiment.
4. The experiment should be so conducted as to avoid all unnecessary physical and mental suffering and injury.
5. No experiment should be conducted where there is an *a priori* reason to believe that death or disabling injury will occur; except, perhaps, in those experiments where the experimental physicians also serve as subjects.
6. The degree of risk to be taken should never exceed that determined by the humanitarian importance of the problem to be solved by the experiment.
7. Proper preparations should be made and adequate facilities provided to protect the experimental subject against even remote possibilities of injury, disability, or death.
8. The experiment should be conducted only by scientifically qualified persons. The highest degree of skill and care should be required through all stages of the experiment of those who conduct or engage in the experiment.
9. During the course of the experiment the human subject should be at liberty to bring the experiment to an end if he has reached the physical or mental state where continuation of the experiment seems to him to be impossible.
10. During the course of the experiment the scientist in charge must be prepared to terminate the experiment at any state, if he has probable cause to believe, in the exercise of the good faith, superior skill, and careful judgment required of him that a continuation of the experiment is likely to result in injury, disability, or death in the experimental subject.

[A]Projects involving human subjects who are unable to give consent will require legally effective informed consent from guardians/conservators.

Reprinted from *Trials of War Criminals before the Nuremberg Military Tribunals under Control Council Law No. 10, Vol. 2, pp. 181–182*. Washington, D.C.: U.S. Government Printing Office, 1949.

---

natural course of the disease was followed and documented by the PHS physicians. Many believe that the original study was justified with respect to its intent, which was to determine the best treatment, if any, for the disease. The study continued for decades. What the press revealed almost 40 years into the study was shocking. In 1941, penicillin was discovered to be a cure for the disease, but the PHS physicians continued to withhold treatment from most of their research subjects. The decision to continue was based, in part, by concerns over the unknown long-term side effects of the new drug. This decision was widely perceived to be in violation of the Nuremberg Principles. Furthermore, the subjects were not informed that they were in a study without treatment for their disease. For a more thorough description of the Tuskegee Syphilis Study, see White (2000).

The U.S. Congress acted quickly and decisively. In 1974, regulations were instituted that required all government-funded human research to be performed only after approval by an ethics board, the *Institutional Review Board* (IRB). An IRB has specific requirements and responsibilities including:

- It must have at least five members with sufficient expertise and diversity to review research protocols, include more than one profession, include a non-scientist, and have at least one member who is not affiliated with the institution that it serves.
- It must review, require modifications as needed, and approve or disapprove the submitted protocols.
- It must conduct continuing review and monitoring and if necessary terminate or suspend the research.

- It must report to federal and institutional officials any serious non-compliance by the investigators or unexpected serious harm to the research subjects.

During IRB review of research protocols, all of the following criteria must be satisfied prior to approval:

- equitable selection of subjects (to protect disadvantaged populations such as minorities and prisoners)
- minimization of risks
- risks must be reasonable in relation to the importance of the project
- informed consent in the language of the subject is sought and documented
- monitoring, as needed to insure safety of the subjects
- protection of privacy and confidentiality of the subjects (However, a court order can force the release of information.)
- additional protection for fetuses, children, pregnant women, prisoners, mentally disabled, and other vulnerable individuals (Legal guardians or conservators must approve entry of some subjects into a study.)
- furthermore, the *consent form* in the language of the subject must have information on all foreseeable risks; how any injuries will be dealt with; and who to contact in the event of questions, problems, or injury
- a description of the research purposes, duration, procedures, and any benefits to the subject, others, or science
- a statement that participation is voluntary and that refusal to participate (or to withdraw at any time) will not adversely affect any benefits to which the subject is entitled
- a statement, if applicable, as to alternate treatments available to the subject if the study involves an experimental treatment for a disease or medical condition

This very brief description of some of the IRB's basic responsibilities illustrates the ethics review and monitoring considerations for human research. The review requirements have several ethical implications. First, ethical abuses (as occurred in the World War Two Nazi prison camps and in the Tuskegee study) will not be tolerated. Second, human subject rights include protection from unreasonable or unknown harms, access to information about potential risks, and power to refuse to participate in situations where known or suspected risks are involved. And third, the government is willing to establish formal requirements, with monitoring and sanctions to protect research subjects. These principles are more highly developed than those that govern air pollution exposures. People exposed to air pollutants seldom have the option of refusing to be exposed.

Animal Research Ethics

The long-standing relationships between humans and other animals include companionship, servitude (as for working animals), entertainment, herding (for food and other products), and use in science, product safety testing, and medicine. As a result, humans have developed respect and even affection for many species. The protections given to non-human research subjects are very similar to those provided for human research subjects. In several aspects the protections are even greater for laboratory animals.

The legal protection for animals in research predates that for human subjects. In England, antivivisectionists (who favored abolishing all live animal research) were involved in enacting the *Cruelty to Animals Act* of 1896. The act required investigators, who used vertebrate animals who might experience pain, to be licensed. Local laws against cruelty to animals, whether or not they are involved in research, also apply to laboratory animal studies. Animal protection in research, teaching, and testing has evolved significantly in the last 25 years in response to pressure from concerned groups and individuals. In the United States, federally-funded and other research is required to have approval from an *Institutional Animal Care and Use Committee* (IACUC). The IACUC is similar to the IRB (for human studies) with respect to composition and duties. The use of IACUCs to review animal research protocols is supplemented by a voluntary stringent accreditation system for research institutions. *The Association for Assessment and Accreditation of Laboratory Animal Care International* (AAALAC) (http://www.aaalac.org) publishes information including international regulations and resources that aid in promoting humane treatment of animals used in research, teaching, testing and training. Among the many criteria for accreditation by the AAALAC are stringent requirements related to housing, food, environmental quality, transportation, medical treatment, training of care personnel, and for some species, environmental enrichment.

Table 2 Abbreviated principles for the care and use of vertebrate animals in testing, research, and training.

1. The transportation, care, and use of animals should be consistent with the Animal Welfare Act and other applicable Federal laws, guidelines, and policies.[A]
2. Procedures involving animals should be designed and performed with due consideration of their relevance to human or animal health, the advancement of knowledge, or the good of society.
3. The animals selected for a procedure should be of an appropriate species and quality and the minimum number required to obtain valid results.
4. Proper use of animals, including the avoidance or minimization of discomfort, distress, and pain when consistent with sound scientific practices, is imperative.
5. Procedures with animals that may cause more than momentary or slight pain or distress should be performed with appropriate sedation, analgesia, or anesthesia. Surgical or other painful procedures should not be performed on unanaesthetized animals paralyzed by chemical agents.
6. Animals that would otherwise suffer severe or chronic pain or distress that cannot be relieved should be painlessly killed at the end of the procedure or, if appropriate, during the procedure.
7. The living conditions of animals should be appropriate for their species and contribute to their health and comfort. Normally, the housing, feeding, and care of all animals used for biomedical purposes must be directed by a veterinarian or other scientist trained and experienced in the proper care, handling, and use of the species being maintained or studied.
8. Investigators and other personnel shall be appropriately qualified and experienced for conducting procedures on living animals.
9. Where exceptions are required in relation to these Principles, the decisions should not rest with the investigators directly concerned but should be made by an appropriate review group such as an institutional animal care and use committee.

[A]For guidance throughout these Principles, the reader is referred to the Guide for the Care and Use of Laboratory Animals prepared by the Institute of Laboratory Animal Resources, National Academy of Sciences (NRC, 1996).
Data from NRC (1996).

The *National Institutes of Health* principles for animal research (**Table 2**) parallel the Nuremberg Code. However, because animals cannot give consent or withdraw from a study, additional monitoring and attention to relieving pain and distress are required.

In spite of the great progress made in protecting research animals, some advocacy groups still strive to abolish such animal use, as well as other uses of animals that are intended to benefit humans. Those who advocate giving *rights,* as opposed to *protections* for non-human animals are represented by animal rights organizations. In contrast, those who have concern for animal suffering and strive to protect the interests of animals belong to the *animal welfare* camp.

Air pollutants can adversely affect domestic and wild animals. Primary air standards are designed to protect human health, not animal health. Animal protection is included by the U.S. EPA in setting its secondary National Ambient Air Quality Standards (see Chapter 6).

IV. PROFESSIONAL ETHICS

Professional Associations, Societies, and Other Organizations

Professional associations and societies have several functions including:

- defining the qualifications for membership;
- helping to train and certify their members;
- publishing research, news, and other materials of interest to their members;
- holding periodic conferences for exchange of ideas;
- providing recognition of members for outstanding service;
- promoting their goals through public education and, at times, political action; and
- establishing *ethical standards* that must be followed by members in good standing.

It is this last function that will be examined further.

It must first be understood that an *essential* ethical obligation for any profession is to perform its main duties. Physicians must treat and prevent disease. Lawyers must defend their clients. Researchers must advance knowledge. Industrial hygienists must make the workplace safer and more productive. Ecologists must study and protect ecosystems. Engineers must design and maintain devices, systems, and processes that serve their employers, the public, and (in many cases) the environment. Industry and other businesses have a primary ethical obligation to provide jobs and needed goods and services. Professions and organizations also have their ethical responsibilities. The benefits institutions and professions provide to society must not be outweighed by harms that could result from unscrupulous behavior. Therefore, protecting the value of a profession benefits society by the adherence of its members to *codes of ethics*.

Sample Professional Codes of Ethics

The *Center for the Study of Ethics in the Professions* at the Illinois Institute of Technology maintains an extensive collection of about 1,000 codes of ethics (http://ethics.iit.edu). The codes come from professional and social organizations, companies, journals, and governments.

By examining a few codes of ethics (also called *codes of conduct*), one sees that they often include several basic elements:

- *Duty*—to perform one's duties competently and professionally
- *Honesty*—to report facts honestly and without bias, and not participate in deception
- *Service*—to serve individual clients, employers, society, the profession, and often the environment
- *Integrity*—to protect the dignity and prestige of the profession, and not engage in harassment or other disrespectful behavior
- *Confidentially*—to protect privacy, except in cases of illegality or where safety is at stake

Institution of Civil Engineers (http://www.ice.org.uk)

Civil engineers design and build bridges, roads, railways, stadiums, buildings, and other large structures. Their contributions are essential for supporting day-to-day life, and promoting prosperity, environmental quality, and sustainability. The *Institution of Civil Engineers*

(ICE), founded in 1818, publishes numerous technical journals, organizes conferences, has offices in five continents, and has approximately 80,000 members worldwide. Their "Rules of Professional Conduct" have the following six elements:

1. All members shall discharge their professional duties with integrity.
2. All members shall only undertake work that they are competent to do.
3. All members shall have full regard for the public interest, particularly in relation to matters of health and safety, and in relation to the well-being of future generations.
4. All members shall show due regard for the environment and for the sustainable management of natural resources.
5. All members shall develop their professional knowledge, skills, and competence on a continuing basis and shall give all reasonable assistance to further the education, training and continuing professional development of others.
6. All members shall:
   a. Notify the institution if convicted of a criminal offence;
   b. Notify the institution upon becoming bankrupt or disqualified as a Company Director;
   c. Notify the Institution of any significant breach of the Rules of Professional Conduct by another member.

Note that "the institution," under 6 a. above refers to the ICE.

The Ecological Society of America (http://www.esa.org)

Ecology is a scientific discipline that deals with relationships among organisms and their environments. Ecologists not only perform research, but they are also involved in formulating policy that relates to ecosystems. The *Ecological Society of America* (ESA), founded in 1915, has chapters in Canada, Mexico, and the United States. The ESA publishes several scientific journals (e.g., *Frontiers in Ecology* and *The Environment*), and it has over 10,000 members worldwide. Its interest in environmental issues include:

- natural resources and ecosystem management;
- biological diversity and species extinction;

- ozone depletion;
- biotechnology; and
- ecosystem restoration and sustainability.

The ESA certifies and trains qualified ecologists in order to help them incorporate ecological principles in decision making. All members of the organization are expected to observe the following principles when acting professionally:

1. Ecologists will offer professional advice and guidance only on those subjects in which they are informed and qualified through professional training or experience. They will strive to accurately represent ecological understanding and knowledge and to avoid and discourage dissemination of erroneous, biased, or exaggerated statements about ecology.
2. Ecologists will not represent themselves as spokespersons for the Society without express authorization by the President of ESA.
3. Ecologists will cooperate with other researchers whenever possible and appropriate to assure rapid interchange and dissemination of ecological knowledge.
4. Ecologists will not plagiarize in verbal or written communication, but will give full and proper credit to the works and ideas of others, and make every effort to avoid misrepresentation.
5. Ecologists will not fabricate, falsify, or suppress results, deliberately misrepresent research findings, or otherwise commit scientific fraud.
6. Ecologists will conduct their research so as to avoid or minimize adverse environmental effects of their presence and activities, and in compliance with legal requirements for protection of researchers, human subjects, or research organisms and systems.
7. Ecologists will not discriminate against others in the course of their work on the basis of gender, sexual orientation, marital status, creed, religion, race, color, national origin, age, economic status, disability, or organizational affiliation.
8. Ecologists will not practice or condone harassment in any form in any professional context.
9. In communications, ecologists should clearly differentiate facts, opinions, and hypotheses.
10. Ecologists will not seek employment, grants, or gain, nor attempt to injure the reputation or

professional opportunities of another scientist by false, biased, or undocumented claims, by offers of gifts or favors, or by any other malicious action.

Industrial Hygiene Associations

Industrial hygiene is a profession (and also an art and a science) devoted to protecting the health and safety of people in their workplaces and communities. Professional industrial hygienists possess college or university degrees in either engineering, physics, chemistry, biology, or a related physical or biological science. They typically practice their profession as employees in industry, government, and academia, or as private consultants. Industrial hygiene societies are engaged in training, certification, publication, and in making recommendations (for workplace air quality, safety, and stress related to heat, cold, vibration, ergonomics, etc.). Industrial hygienists are often involved in assessing and controlling industrial emission releases into the environment. Several professional organizations, including the *American Industrial Hygiene Association,* the *American Conference of Governmental Industrial Hygienists,* the *American Board of Industrial Hygiene,* and the *Academy of Industrial Hygiene,* jointly support a shared "Code of Ethics." The following eight elements are selected from a larger code of 19 elements (http://www.acgih.org):

1. Deliver competent services with objective and independent professional judgment in decision-making.
2. Recognize the limitation of one's professional ability and provide services only when qualified.
3. Follow appropriate health and safety procedures, in the course of performing professional duties, to protect clients, employers, employees and the public from conditions where injury and damage are reasonably foreseeable.
4. Assure that a conflict of interest does not compromise legitimate interests of a client, employer, employee or the public and does not influence or interfere with professional judgment.
5. Comply with laws, regulations, policies and ethical standards governing professional practice of industrial hygiene and related activities.
6. Maintain and respect the confidentiality of sensitive information obtained in the course of professional activities unless: the information is reasonably understood to pertain to unlawful activity; a court or governmental agency lawfully directs the release of

the information; the client or the employer expressly authorized the release of specific information; or, the failure to release such information would likely result in death or serious physical harm to employees and/or the public.

7. Report apparent violations of the ethics code by certificants and candidates upon a reasonable and clear factual basis.

8. Refrain from public behavior that is clearly in violation of professional, ethical or legal standards.

A Student's Pledge

Ethical codes and pledges are not limited to professional associations. The following was adopted by engineering students graduating from the University of California at Berkeley.

The Engineering Ethics Pledge:

"We, the graduating engineering class of 2004, in recognition of the affect of technology on the quality of all life throughout the world, and in accepting a personal obligation to our profession, it's members and the communities we serve, do hereby commit ourselves to the highest ethical and professional conduct and pledge to use our education only for purposes consistent with the safety, health and welfare of the public and the environment. Throughout our careers, we will consider the ethical implications of the work we do before we take action. We make this declaration because we recognize that individual responsibility is the first step on the path to a better world."

For more on the history of Berkeley's Engineering Ethics Pledge, see http://courses.cs.vt.edu/~cs3604/lib/WorldCodes/Pledge.html.

Comments on Codes of Ethics

The foregoing codes of ethics and student's pledge illustrate the commitment of individuals and their professional groups and other associations to ethical principles. When a company, society, or other group establishes an ethical code and enforces it in its membership, they thereby gain respect. As mentioned previously, adhering to strict ethical principles constrains behavior, however, it is expected of professionals. When encountering an organization for the first time, one might seek a copy of their Code of Ethics. If such a code does not exist, one does not know what behaviors are acceptable by the members.

V. PRACTICAL ETHICS

Ethical Decision Making

A *decision* may be defined as a conclusion, or a formal judgment, that is reached after due consideration. An immediate question raised by this definition is "What must be considered before making the decision?" In an ideal world, *all* of the relevant facts and *all* of the relevant consequences to *all* of those affected by each possible decision would be considered. Even in such an ideal world, certain individuals and/or groups (also called *stakeholders*) might see the decision as unfair. Such disaffected stakeholders could disagree with the relative weighting and interpretation of the facts, with the importance of the various consequences, and even the wisdom and fairness of those who made the decision.

As an example, consider a decision by a regulatory body to significantly tighten a regulation on the permissible air concentration of $PM_{2.5}$ (fine particles). The relevant facts considered by the decision makers might have included epidemiological associations between $PM_{2.5}$ and various health-related outcomes (hospital admissions, mortality rates, etc.), results of the impact of fine particles on climate model predictions, and the costs of installing particle collection devices on cars, trucks, and factories. The decision would likely be applauded by advocacy groups that focus on protecting health and the environment. On the other hand, automobile and truck drivers and some economists might challenge the decision. They might believe that the health-related associations could have been produced by factors other than anthropogenic $PM_{2.5}$ (such as co-pollutant gases, natural particles, and meteorological factors), and that the climate models were not adequately validated (see Chapter 5). The disaffected groups could also point out the adverse effects of the tightened regulations on the cost of goods and services, and even the loss of jobs (factors that also affect public health). No matter what decision is made, some would be pleased and others would be displeased. Regardless of the decision made on the air standard, litigation is very likely to follow. This is the reality of decision making in our world.

Balancing Interests

The foregoing example clearly illustrates that ethical decisions commonly involve a balancing of interests. The interests of those who might suffer adverse health outcomes was contrasted with the interests of those who would be economically affected. In the example, the regulators weighed the potential direct health effects more heavily than the potential indirect health effects (due to the costs of goods and services and the potential loss of jobs). The regulators also accepted the current climate model's long-term predictions and gave them more weight than the immediate economic concerns. Did the regulators make an ethical decision? To the extent that they seriously considered all of the relevant data and all of the significant consequences, the answer would seem to be "yes." The decision still might not be considered to be ethical in the eyes of some stakeholders. One would also need to know if the decision makers had conflicts of interest or external pressures that biased their decision. If that were the case the answer could be, "no." Balancing interests, although an ethical requirement, is a difficult task.

Public Participation in Decision Making

Given that decisions affecting air quality are based on complex scientific data and sophisticated modeling analyses, is there a role for public participation? And if the answer is, "yes," what form should that participation take? There are several models for public involvement in decision making, including:

- *Public comment*—After a tentative decision is made by an authoritative body, a public solicitation is made that invites comments from all interested parties. The received comments are then "considered" prior to issuing a final decision. Governmental bodies such as the U.S. EPA use this model.
- *Public representation*—The decision-making body (e.g., a committee) has one or more voting members that represent the public. Such representatives have access to the information being considered by the decision-making committee, and they participate in deliberation and voting. This model is used by committees that approve or disapprove research protocols involving human and nonhuman research subjects. The final decision is usually based on a majority vote.
- *Public initiation*—The public, usually represented by elected government representatives or advocacy organizations, is involved in formulating a law (which includes ballot measures such as propositions) that is put to a vote. In the case of laws, the vote is conducted by elected legislators. In the case of a ballot proposition, the final decision is made by registered voters.

Each of these models has strengths and weaknesses. The public comment model allows experts to perform an analysis and arrive at what they deem to be an appropriate tentative decision. The published tentative decision will typically have an accompanying discussion of the data and analysis that supports the decision. Thus, the public has the opportunity to analyze the work of the decision makers and to provide informed input. The weakness of this model is that the public input is not binding, and may not be seriously considered prior to issuing the final decision. For this model to work well the public input should be effectively incorporated into the final decision.

The public representation model has the advantage of including public representatives in both the formulation and acceptance of a tentative decision. The representatives can introduce data, analysis, and arguments before a conclusion is reached by the decision-making body. For this model to work well the public representatives must devote the time and effort necessary to have effective input. Potential weaknesses of this model are:

1. That the public representatives may be overwhelmed by the complex data and analyses to the extent that they are not adequately involved; and
2. That their votes are outnumbered by the experts, making them "token" participants.

The public initiation model probably has the greatest potential for maximizing the power of the public in decision making. Professional societies, as well as informed and motivated individuals prepare laws that are presented to legislators. Elected representatives are obligated to represent the interests of their constituents and to accept input from them. After all, they face reelections in which their legislative records will be scrutinized. In the case of ballot initiatives, the voting public makes the final decision. Weaknesses of the public participation model include not only its expense, but also the possible lack of adequate technical input from experts. The final decisions may be made as a result of political deal making (in the case of laws) or biased advertising campaigns (in the case of ballot measures). Also, ballot measures may be approved by a small margin of those who vote, which can adversely affect small groups. This problem is referred to as "the tyranny of the majority."

All of these models, along with others (e.g., the use of focus-groups or public polls initiated by decision makers), permit public input. The success or failure of a given decision with respect to its public support is measured by the level of public approval or protest, and sometimes litigation.

The Common Sense Criterion

The *common sense criterion* (also called the *laughability factor*) refers to the extent to which a decision is or is not obviously fatally-flawed. For example, each year in each large city, a large number of people require emergency medical attention for choking on food. Imagine a panel of experts called together to make recommendations that would eliminate the problem. After considerable analysis they recommend outlawing all solid food—problem solved! However, the solution does not pass the common sense test, and it is even laughable. The banning of all solid food would obviously harm, if not destroy, public health. Similarly, consider air emissions that can adversely affect public health. The problem could be solved by eliminating cars, trucks, factories, electric-power plants, agriculture, animal husbandry, pollen-and spore-producing plants, and microbial life. This solution, although logical, is also laughable, as it would lead to ending all human life.

The examples given are extreme, but they demonstrate some important principles. First, a problem should not be analyzed in isolation. The problem exists in a complex world, and isolating it may not be wise. The problem is that the human brain tends to focus on problems in isolation, which is often useful (e.g., a focus on an imminent threat). Second, even the most well-reasoned step-by-step analysis can lead to a ridiculous conclusion. The scientific method actually encourages such linear stepwise analyses in which the result has been proved to be valid. However, validity and practicality are not the same. Third, and most important is this simple truth.

When a decision is made, all of the consequences will occur, not just the intended ones.

Decisions can be, and are often, made without due regard to their full range of consequences. Wise decisions are those that lead to net outcomes that do more good than harm in the real world.

VI. SUMMARY OF MAJOR POINTS

Ethics has both theoretical and practical aspects. Laws also define accepted ethical behavior. In philosophy, the nature of morality (i.e., ethical behavior) is examined. *Metaethics* deals with the large questions about ethics, and *normative* ethics deals with considerations of what *should* be done from an ethical stand-

point. Should only the consequences be considered (as in teology), or should conformity to values (e.g., honesty and compassion) and principles (as in deontology) prevail in determining moral behavior? Do both teology and deontology have roles in settling air quality standards? In practical ethics, decisions must be weighed, balancing goods and harms, weighing conflicting interests of affected groups (including animals, plants, and the environment), and considering public acceptance (at a given time and in a given culture).

Research with human and non-human subjects is an area in which ethical considerations have undergone considerable evolution. Approval or disapproval of studies are made by deliberative committees with specified diversity and responsibilities. Such committees weigh the importance of studies against pain, suffering, and other risks faced by the subjects. Also maximizing the benefits and minimizing the harms associated with a study is an essential consideration.

Professional ethics are based on the elements of duty, honesty, service, integrity, and confidentially. Specific professional groups identify and enforce their ethical standards by *Codes of Conduct*. Such codes often include protecting the interests of people, animals, and the environment. Such codes exist for professional, social, business, and other groups. A code of ethics reveals what can be expected from those who adopt it.

Decision making can be a complex process that involves many ethical considerations. Balancing interests of individuals and groups that are affected is an aspect of decision making. The make-up of the group that makes decisions, and the process used, are also ethical considerations. Public influence on decision making takes several forms including opportunities to comment, participate in deliberations, and even formulate and make final decisions. The wisdom of a decision must be measured by all of its significant consequences, including the intended and the unintended consequences.

VII. QUIZ AND PROBLEMS

Quiz Questions

(select the best answer)

1. Ethical standards:
   a. are studied in a branch of philosophy.
   b. are enforced by laws.
   c. may change in a given culture over time.
   d. All of the above are true.

2. Research projects with laboratory animals typically:
   a. need not conform to any ethical standards.
   b. are only permitted if done by veterinarian researchers.
   c. are permitted only after an ethical review.
   d. do not require any control of pain or distress.
3. The Nuremberg Tribunal:
   a. established criteria for "crimes against humanity."
   b. was focused on prosecuting physicians that performed the Tuskegee Study.
   c. prosecuted Nazi physicians after World War Two.
   d. Both a. and b. are true.
   e. Both a. and c. are true.
4. Research with human subjects:
   a. must be approved by an Institutional Review Board.
   b. is illegal.
   c. can be conducted without ethical review if the degree of pain and discomfort is not severe.
   d. does not require obtaining informed consent.
5. Which statement is *not* true in metaethics?
   a. Intuitionists maintain that people know right from wrong, so that a formal analysis is irrelevant.
   b. Metaethics involves asking large questions about ethics instead of analyzing the ethics of specific issues.
   c. Metaethics does not differ from normative ethics.
   d. None of the above are true.
6. Utilitarian ethical theory:
   a. maintains that God is the final authority.
   b. maintains that "the greatest happiness for the greatest number" is a measure of the morality of an act.
   c. maintains that an act is moral if it benefits the person performing the act.
   d. None of the above are true.
7. Professional ethics:
   a. only apply to physicians.
   b. are defined by "Codes of Conduct."
   c. are the same for all scientific disciplines.
   d. are established by federal laws for each profession.

8. Members of the "Institution of Civil Engineers" have ethical obligations that include:
   a. taking into account the interests of future generations.
   b. showing regard for the environment.
   c. notifying the Institution of Civil Engineers if they have a criminal offense conviction.
   d. All of the above are true.
9. A member of the "American Industrial Hygiene Association" is ethically obligated to:
   a. provide requested services even if they are not qualified.
   b. report all unprofessional activities of their clients or employers.
   c. protect the safety of employers, employees, and the public in the course of performing their professional duties.
   d. protect the reputations of other industrial hygienists who violate the ethics code unless ordered to testify under oath.
10. The Tuskegee Syphilis Study:
    a. is an example of a study that followed sound ethical principles.
    b. stimulated congressional action to protect human subjects in research studies conducted in the United States.
    c. was conducted by Nazi scientists.
    d. Only b. and c. are true.

Problems

1. List at least five elements that you would include in a "Code of Ethics" for engineers that design and operate air pollution control systems for industry, and discuss why each element is important.
2. Review the "Engineering Ethics Pledge" and discuss how it could be applied to students graduating from your degree program.
3. How do the ethical requirements for research studies using laboratory animals differ from those using human subjects?
4. Discuss the ethical implications of establishing and enforcing air quality standards that result in substantial economic hardship for a community.
5. List the "pros" and "cons" of each of the three models of public participation with respect to establishing a new, more stringent, air pollution regulation.

6. Examine the first five elements of the Nuremberg Code. For each element, replace the concept of "experiment" with the concept of "exposure to air pollutants." Do the principles apply to air pollutant exposures?

7. As in problem 6 above, replace the concept of "experiment" with the concept of "a governmental regulation." Do our air pollution regulations meet the spirit of the Nuremberg Code?

VIII. DISCUSSION TOPICS

1. In following the ethical principle of "the greatest happiness for the greatest number":
   a. Should the happiness of non-human animals be considered?
   b. Could following this principle also lead to actions that would be considered unethical in our culture?

2. Should the ethical principle "do no harm" become law? Why or why not?

3. Suggestions have been made to distinguish "harms" (which should be minimized) from "wrongs" (which should never be permitted). Should such a differentiation be made? Why or why not?

4. Are current standards for air quality based on firm ethical principles? If so, which principles? If not, should the ethical basis be strengthened, and how?

References and Recommended Reading

Caplan, A. L., Too hard to face, *J. Am. Acad. Psych. Law,* 33:394–400, 2005.

Carson, R. L., *Silent Spring,* Houghton Mifflin, Co., Boston, MA, 1962.

Cobb, W. M., The Tuskegee Syphilis Study, *J. Nat. Med. Assoc.,* 65:345–348, 1973.

Ehrlich, P., *The Population Bomb,* Ballantine Books, New York, 1968.

Kennedy, D., Animal activism: Out of control, *Science,* 313:1541, 2006.

Malthus, T. R., *An Essay on the Principle of the Population, As it Affects the Future Improvements of Society with Remarks on the Speculations of Mr. Godwin, M. Condorcet, and Other Writers,* Printed for J. Johnson in St. Paul's Church–Yard, London, 1798.

NRC (National Research Council), *Guide for the Care and Use of Laboratory Animals,* National Academy Press, Washington, DC, 1996, pp. 1–118.

Pitts, M., A guide to the new ARENA/OLAW IACUC Guidebook, *Lab Animal,* 31(9):40–42, 2002.

Sideris, L., McCarthy, C. and Smith, D. H., Roots of concern with nonhuman animals in biomedical ethics, *ILAR Journal,* 40:3–14, 1999.

Silverman, J., Suckow, M. A., and Murthy, S., *The IACUC Handbook, 2nd Edition,* CRC Press, Boca Raton, FL, 2006.

Thomson, J. J., Chodosh, S., Fried, C., Goodman, D. S., Wax, M. L., and Wilson, J. Q., Regulations governing research on human subjects: Academic freedom and the Institutional Review Board, *Academe,* 67: 358–370, 1981.

U.S. EPA (U.S. Environmental Protection Agency), *EPA's Formative Years, 1970–1973,* http://www.epa.gov/history/publications/print/formative.htm (accessed August, 10, 2009).

White, R. M., Unraveling the Tuskegee study of untreated syphilis, *Arch. Intern. Med.,* 160:585–598, 2000.

Zurlo, J., Rudacille, D. and Goldberg, A. M., *Animal and Alternatives in Testing: History, Science, and Ethics,* Mary Ann Liebert, Inc., Larchmont, NY, 1994.

Figure and Table Credits Page

Air Quality

LEARNING OBJECTIVES

By the end of this chapter the reader will be able to:

- Discuss the impacts of historically important air pollution episodes.
- List health effects associated with air pollution.
- Describe potential hazards linked to indoor air.
- Enumerate the typical components of urban ambient air pollution.
- Explain the concept of global warming.

▶ Introduction

This chapter covers the sources and causes of air pollution, the components of air pollution (e.g., gases and particles), and some of the health and environmental effects that have been linked to air pollution, including greenhouse gases and global warming. A theme of the chapter is that clean air is intimately connected with the health of the earth and is a prerequisite for the well-being of humanity. While some may argue that controlling air pollution is too costly, this opinion has not been borne out by the evidence. For example, in the United States the Clean Air Act of 1990 sought to clear the nation's air of damaging pollutants. According to the US Environmental Protection Agency (EPA), by 2020 this act will be responsible for substantial reductions in adult and infant mortality from particle pollution and ozone and lowered morbidity from conditions such as chronic bronchitis, heart attacks, and asthma exacerbations. These benefits to quality of life will greatly exceed the costs of implementing clean air standards.[1]

▶ Overview: Causes and Effects of Poor Air Quality

The causes of poor outdoor air quality and smog include the combustion of fossil fuels by motor vehicles, power plants, and industrial processes. In turn, such combustion releases harmful pollution into the air we breathe. The products of fossil fuel consumption are sulfur dioxide, particles, ground-level ozone, nitrogen oxides, carbon monoxide, and lead. Air pollution is particularly acute in low- and middle-income countries, where 98% of cities fail to meet World Health Organization (WHO) air quality standards.[2]

In the developed world many high-income nations have formulated and implemented air quality standards for safeguarding public health. Nevertheless, in high-income countries more than half of residents of live in cities that do not meet WHO air quality standards.[2] With respect to the United States, the American Lung Association notes that approximately one-half of Americans in 2016 were residents of counties that had unhealthful amounts of particles and ozone.[3] Refer to **FIGURE 1** for

FIGURE 1 Smog in New York City.
© Peter Janelle/EyeEm/Getty

an example of air quality in New York City on a smoggy day; air pollution obscures famous landmarks such as the Brooklyn Bridge. Over the past decades, air quality has improved considerably in most of the United States. However, much needs to be done to protect the gains that have been made and to improve the air in cities that do not have satisfactory air quality.

The potential damaging effects of air pollution are numerous: adverse human health effects (e.g., lung damage) and adverse environmental effects (e.g., acid rain and global warming). Most people who live in urban areas have experienced, at one time or another, the effects of outdoor air pollution. Symptoms can include burning eyes, aching lungs, difficulty breathing, wheezing, coughing, headache, and other symptoms such as an irritated throat and nose.[4,5] In recent years the United States and many other developed countries have made significant progress in improving air quality as a result of measures such as catalytic converters in automobiles, control of emissions from factories, and use of less-polluting fuels. Nevertheless, in the large cities of many developing nations, for example, Beijing, China, and Mexico City, Mexico, air quality has continued to degrade.

Often people refer to air pollution as **smog**. Originally, smog referred to smoke plus fog. Also, smog denotes

… A mixture of pollutants, principally ground-level ozone [discussed later in this chapter], produced by chemical reactions in the air involving smog-forming chemicals. [These chemicals can arise from both anthropogenic (due to human activities) and natural sources.] A major portion of smog formers comes from burning of petroleum-based fuels such as gasoline. Major smog occurrences are often linked to heavy motor vehicle traffic, sunshine, high temperatures, and calm winds or temperature inversion (weather condition in which warm air is trapped close to the ground instead of rising).[6]

The term **smog complex** refers to "eye irritation, irritation of the respiratory tract, chest pains, cough, shortness of breath, nausea, and headache" associated with smog.[4] In our homes, at work, and in other enclosed spaces, we may be exposed to secondhand cigarette smoke, allergens, potentially toxic molds, and hazardous chemicals.

High levels of air pollution can endanger our health and can kill people as well, especially when reactive gases are discharged into the atmosphere and when vulnerable persons are exposed. Health effects associated with air pollution can include some forms of cancer such as lung cancer and skin cancer (from possible depletion of the ozone layer), damage to vital tissues and organs such as the nervous system, and impairment of lung and breathing function. There have been numerous occasions of air pollution–caused mortality. For example, in the chapter on pesticides and other organic chemicals it was noted that during a release of toxic air pollutants in Bhopal, India, large numbers of people were killed by toxic fumes released into the environment. A second incident happened in London, England, where a 1952 great "smog disaster" killed several thousand people. Similar examples will be cited later in this chapter.

Air pollution damages the environment and causes property damage. It reduces visibility in national parks such as the Grand Canyon in the United States and can even interfere with aviation. Environmental damage linked to air pollution includes harm to forests, lakes and other bodies of water, wildlife, and buildings. Visit many large cities of the world and you will see that their structures often are blackened from many years of exposure to smog and smoke. These types of environmental damage are not geographically limited in scope; air pollution is a global problem. One example is shown in **FIGURE 2**, which portrays haze across northern India in a picture taken from a satellite above the earth. Satellites and other technologies make it possible to view similar clouds of air pollution over many parts of the earth.

FIGURE 2 Haze above northern India as seen from a satellite.

FIGURE 3 Boy wearing a face mask for protection against air pollution.

The problem of urban air pollution is continuing to grow more acute in the developing world, where populations are expanding rapidly and fast-paced industrialization is coupled with increasing use of motor vehicles. In the developing areas, the use of fossil fuels has contributed to worsening air pollution. In some megacities, for example, Beijing, Delhi, Jakarta, and Mexico City, poor air quality threatens the health of these cities' inhabitants (see **FIGURE 3**).

▶ Notorious Air Pollution Episodes in History

Major lethal air pollution episodes include those in the Meuse Valley in Belgium (1930); Donora, Pennsylvania (1948); and London, England (1952).[4]

Meuse Valley, Belgium

One of the earliest modern episodes of hazardous air pollution occurred during the first week of December 1930, in the Meuse Valley in Belgium. The Meuse Valley is located near Liege, Belgium, which at the time had a high concentration of steel industry operations (e.g., foundries, mills, coke ovens, and smelters). During an infamous episode of severe air pollution, sulfur dioxide, sulfuric acid mists, and fluoride gases rose to extremely high levels. This noxious mixture was thought to be associated with the deaths of more than 60 persons during the last 2 days of the incident. The resulting mortality was more than 10 times the normal mortality rate.[7] Most of the fatalities occurred among the elderly who had preexisting heart and lung diseases.[4]

Donora, Pennsylvania

During the time interval from approximately October 27 to October 30, 1948, an environmental air pollution disaster occurred in Donora, Pennsylvania, a small town located on the Monongahela River about 30 miles south of Pittsburgh. The disaster was associated with an air inversion (defined later in the chapter) in the valley in which the town was located. In this very severe episode of air pollution, fog combined with particulate matter and industrial and other contaminants. The sources of the contaminants were iron and steel mills, coal-fired home stoves, factories that burned coal, coke ovens, and metal works. This episode caused some form of illness among approximately half of the town's 14,000 residents; about 400 of them were hospitalized, and 20 died before the smog finally lifted at the end of October.[8] **FIGURES** 4 and 5, respectively, show how the town was obscured by air pollution on various days around the time of the smog episode and the locations of people who died.

Although the episode of late October affected a wide cross-section of age groups, those who were aged 55 years and older tended to be the most severely affected. During the incident, persons who were stricken reported respiratory symptoms (cough, sore throat, and difficulty breathing) and gastrointestinal symptoms (nausea and vomiting). Previous histories of heart disease and lung disease were contributing factors to the adverse outcomes of smog exposure.[4]

The Lethal London Fog of 1952

During December 5 through December 9, 1952, a very severe episode of air pollution settled on London, England. Traditionally, London had been known for its foggy climate coupled with smoke caused by the use of coal and other fossil fuels to heat homes, run power plants, and operate factories. At least 1 million coal stoves spewed forth choking sulfurous smoke. As a result, so-called "pea-souper" fogs were well known to the residents of the English metropolis. The consequence of the particularly lethal fog that occurred in December 1952 was a reported excess of 3,000 deaths above normal. Many environmental health experts consider the London fog of 1952 to be a landmark for the study of the health effects of air pollution and a catalyst that has led to research in this field.[7]

The foregoing examples (in the Meuse Valley, Donora, and London) illustrate the growing accumulation of evidence regarding associations between acute episodes of air pollution and increased mortality,

FIGURE 4 Views of Donora, Pennsylvania taken at about the time of the 1948 smog episode.

Zone where 12 of 20 deaths occurred

FIGURE 5 A sketch of Donora made by Charles Shinn for the US Public Health Service in 1949. The circle indicates the locations of more than half of the deaths that occurred during the killer smog.

Data from Davis D. *When Smoke Ran Like Water: Tales of Environmental Deception and the Battle Against Pollution*. New York, NY: Basic Books; 2002. Sketch by Charles Shinn. Modified and reproduced from US National Library of Medicine, National Institutes of Health, Images from the History of Medicine. Available at: https://collections.nlm.nih.gov/catalog/nlm:nlmuid -101450758-img. Accessed June 6, 2107.

evidence that spurred air pollution research and galvanized public health officials.

▶ Sources and Causes of Air Pollution

What is meant by the term **air pollution**? First consider perfectly clean air—which is not found in the natural environment, even in the most remote locations such as up in the mountains far away from human activities. In the laboratory, it is possible to produce clean air artificially by using filtration and other methods. After removing contaminants, we would find that the largest components (by weight) are nitrogen (76%), oxygen (23%), argon (1%), carbon dioxide (0.03%), plus a variety of other gases in lesser amounts and water vapor depending upon the relative humidity.[9]

The normal ambient air—air that we breathe—might be thought of as a kind of soup composed of particles and vapors that arise from natural and anthropogenic sources. Each liter of air may contain thousands of invisible suspended particles and also hundreds of invisible vapors; because these constituents are invisible, we are unaware of their presence.[9] Air pollution refers to the presence, in various degrees, of those substances (e.g., suspended particles and vapors) not found in perfectly clean air.

Numerous sources emit pollutants; these sources can be dichotomized into natural and anthropogenic

sources. The former include volcanic ash, dusts, and organic materials carried by the wind. The latter are subdivided roughly into stationary sources (e.g., power plants and oil refineries) and mobile sources (e.g., on-road vehicles, off-road vehicles, and nonroad vehicles).

The types of pollutants may be classified as either primary or secondary. Primary air pollutants (discussed later in the chapter) are those emitted directly by sources of pollution. Examples are ozone, nitrogen dioxide, and carbon monoxide. Secondary air pollutants are those generated from atmospheric chemical reactions among primary pollutants.[9] An example would be the production of smog (discussed subsequently).

Naturally Occurring Air Pollution

Several natural events produce air pollutants, especially particulate matter. These phenomena include wind storms that spread dust clouds, salt evaporation along the earth's coasts, and production of materials that have a biologic origin (e.g., mold spores, pollen, and organic material from plants and animals).[10] In some areas of the world, raging forest fires emit huge amounts of smoke and ash into the atmosphere. The smoke trails can be seen by satellites hovering above the earth. In some cases, forest fires are truly natural events, such as when caused by lightning strikes. In other cases they are human-made events, for example, when caused by human carelessness, arson, or efforts to clear vegetation from the land.

Volcanic eruptions are another natural source of air pollution. Examples are the dust clouds produced by the eruptions of El Chichon near Mexico City; Galunggung in West Java, Indonesia; and Mount Pinatubo, in the Philippines. In the US state of Washington, the 1980 Mount Saint Helens eruption spewed forth tons of fine ash that descended upon a wide geographic area. (Refer to **FIGURE 6**.) Volcanic dusts often contain free crystalline silica, which is a toxic mineral.[11] The acute effects of exposure to volcanic dusts are irritation of the eyes and upper respiratory tract. Repeated exposure is thought to be a risk factor for the lung disease **pneumoconiosis**, especially when fine particles (less than 10 micrometers in diameter) are inhaled. However, a 5-year longitudinal follow-up study of loggers who were exposed to ash from Mount Saint Helens indicated that the risks of lung diseases such as chronic bronchitis and pneumoconiosis are minimal when exposure is initially high and then tapers off over time.[11]

Anthropogenic Sources of Air Pollution

As noted previously, anthropogenic sources of air pollution include stationary sources and mobile sources.

FIGURE 6 Eruption of Mount Saint Helens on May 18, 1980.
© InterNetwork Media/Photodisc/Getty

FIGURE 7 Electric power plant—example of a stationary source of air pollution.

FIGURE 8 Stationary source of air pollution: oil refinery.

FIGURE 9 Rush hour on the Golden Gate bridge, California.
© Keep Smiling Photography/Shutterstock

Stationary Sources of Air Pollution

Stationary sources include electric generating plants (see **FIGURE 7**), factories and manufacturing complexes, oil refineries (see **FIGURE 8**), chemical plants, and incinerators.

Mobile Sources of Air Pollution

Mobile sources include on-road vehicles (e.g., cars, trucks, and buses), off-road vehicles (e.g., dune buggies and snowmobiles), and nonroad vehicles (e.g., airplanes, ships, and trains).[4,12] According to the US Environmental Protection Agency (EPA), motor vehicles produce approximately half of two major causes of smog—volatile organic compounds (VOCs) and nitrogen oxides (NO_x)—almost 75% of carbon monoxide, and more than half of emissions of toxic air pollutants.[5]

- *On-road vehicles*—The contribution of motor vehicles to air pollution is likely to continue as the number of drivers on the road increases, although technical improvements have reduced emissions from passenger vehicles. (Refer to **FIGURE 9** for a view of rush hour traffic on the Golden Gate bridge in northern California.) The number of miles traveled each year on US highways increased by 178% between 1970 and 2005.[5] During the current century, vehicle miles increase by about 2% to 3% annually. In the United States, most drivers commute to work alone despite the availability of car pool lanes in many locations. Many geographically dispersed regions of the United States do not have convenient public transportation systems in place. This situation contrasts with developed European countries and Japan, two areas of the world that have excellent public transportation systems, which make the use of cars unnecessary or, at least, less frequent. Also contributing greatly to the air pollution problem are buses and trucks, which can cause more pollution (e.g., particle emissions) than automobiles.

- Modern automobiles produce much less pollution than automobiles did in the 1970s. Improvements include low-sulfur fuels, emission control technology, removal of lead from gasoline, and use of alternative fuels. Other innovations to reduce air pollution include electrically powered and hybrid vehicles.

- *Off-road vehicles*—Although their use is less frequent than that of on-road vehicles, off-road vehicles such as dune buggies and snowmobiles can add to air pollution in the areas where they are used. For example, they may be a cause of air pollution in national parks and wilderness areas where their use is permitted.

- *Nonroad vehicles*—Trains, airplanes, and ships also contribute to the burden of air pollution. Regarding the US transportation sector, the EPA has determined that large commercial jets are the third largest contributor of greenhouse gases.[13] These emissions from the jet engines of aircraft imperil human health and have been linked to climate change.

▶ Components of Air Pollution

How do scientists classify air contaminants? According to Phalen, "One classification segregates air contaminants into the broad categories of infectious agents, allergens, chemical irritants, and chemical toxicants (biologic and nonbiologic). Another classification segregates air contaminants into particles, gases, and vapors. . . ."[9(p2)]

As noted, air pollution is composed of a number of components; these include solids and gases.[14] What we see as air pollution (for example, in Figure 13) is actually a mix of contaminants, particularly in the case of smog. Note also that there may be substances present that are not visible to the human eye. As a result of

chemical reactions (described in the section on temperature inversion) that take place in the presence of certain atmospheric conditions, some of the contaminants become visible. Among the constituents of air pollution from motor vehicles (e.g., cars and trucks) are sulfur dioxide, particulate matter, greenhouse gases (e.g., CO_2), carbon monoxide, **hydrocarbons**, and nitrogen oxides.[15] Other polluting chemicals can include heavy metals and toxics such as benzene.

The term **criteria air pollutants** is used to describe "a group of very common air pollutants regulated by EPA on the basis of criteria (information on health and/or environmental effects of pollution)."[6[p45]] Criteria air pollutants are present everywhere in the United States.[16] Criteria air pollutants are ground level ozone, particulate matter, nitrogen oxides, carbon monoxide, sulfur dioxide, and lead.[16] In addition, several other pollutants are relevant to air quality: volatile organic compounds and smog (a mixture of pollutants). **TABLE 1** presents a summary of the names of criteria air pollutants, sources, health effects, and environmental effects. The following discussion presents a detailed examination of these pollutants, with the exception of lead and smog (defined previously). Lead, once a universal component of gasoline, has been phased out or is being phased out in most areas of the world; nevertheless, lead remains an important environmental contaminant that arises from many sources in addition to air pollution. Refer to the chapter on toxic metals and elements for coverage of lead.

Ozone is a gas that is one of the molecular forms of oxygen. The ordinary oxygen gas found in air is a molecule made up of two oxygen atoms bonded together (O_2). Ozone (O_3) consists of three oxygen atoms bonded together into a molecule.[6] Occurring in nature, ozone has the sharp smell associated with sparks from electrical equipment. Ozone is a main component of photochemical smog. Found near ground level, ozone in smog stems from a series of chemical reactions among the products of combustion of fossil fuels (including gasoline) in combination with various chemicals found in products such as solvents and paints.

Previously, in the chapter on ionizing and nonionizing radiation, we considered the role of ozone in protecting the earth from ultraviolet (UV) light as well as the influence of human activities on the environment that are hypothesized to have reduced the ozone layer. The health effects attributed to ground-level ozone include respiratory difficulties such as reduced lung function, exacerbation of allergic respiratory disease, local irritation of the eyes and respiratory tract, and reduction of the ability to fight off colds and related respiratory infections. Besides reducing visibility, environmental effects include damage to forests

TABLE 1 Overview of Criteria Air Pollutants

Name of Pollutant (Symbol)	Example of Source	Health Effects	Environmental Effects
Ozone (O_3) (ground-level ozone)	Variety of oxygen formed by chemical reaction of pollutants	Breathing impairment; chest pain, coughing, throat irritation	Affects vegetation (plants and trees) and ecosystems; main ingredient of smog.
Nitrogen dioxide (NO_2), nitrogen oxides (NO_x)	Combustion of fuels by cars, trucks, and vehicles, and by power plants	Irritates airways; aggravates respiratory diseases, e.g., asthma	Contributes to acid rain, which damages trees and lakes.
Carbon monoxide (CO)	Combustion of fossil fuels by cars, trucks, and other vehicles	Reduction in oxygen-carrying capacity of the blood	Very high levels not likely outdoors.
Particulate matter (PM_{10} and $PM_{2.5}$)	Many, e.g., fires, power plants, industries, vehicles	Airway irritation; lung and heart effects; premature death in people with heart of lung disease	Haze; increased acidity of lakes and streams; forest and crop damage; discolors buildings, furniture, and clothing.
Sulfur dioxide (SO_2)	Burning of fossil fuels	Breathing problems; lung damage; aggravates asthma	Contributes to acid rain; damage to trees and lakes; building damage.
Lead (Pb)	Leaded gasoline, paint, batteries; lead smelters	Can damage nervous system, immune system, and kidneys	Persists in environment; accumulates in soil, sediments; can harm plants and animals.

Data from US Environmental Protection Agency. Criteria air pollutants. Available at: https://www.epa.gov/criteria-air-pollutants. Accessed June 19, 2017.

and plants and oxidation effects that cause damage to certain kinds of fabric and rubber.

Nitrogen oxides (NO_x) refer to gases made up of a single molecule of nitrogen combined with varying numbers of molecules of oxygen. Nitrogen oxides are "produced from burning fuels, including gasoline and coal, and react with volatile organic compounds to form smog. Nitrogen oxides are also major components of acid rain."[6(p46)]

Although clean air is mostly nitrogen, some forms of nitrogen are considered to be major environmental pollutants.[17] Although the primary source of nitrogen pollution is fertilizer used in agriculture, approximately 25% of nitrogen generation (in the form of NO_x or NO_2—nitrogen dioxide) is the product of combustion of fossil fuels, for example, gasoline used in automobiles, as well as other fuels such as natural gas, diesel oil, and coal. Air pollution scientists attribute urban ozone, acid rain, and oxygen depletion of coastal waters to NO_x. Travelers to London and European cities can observe readily the damage to ancient marble-faced buildings, stone structures, and public monuments that has resulted from the acids in air pollution. With respect to human health, NO_2 and NO_x are potentially harmful to the respiratory system.

Carbon monoxide (CO) is defined as "a colorless, odorless, poisonous gas, produced by the incomplete burning of solid, liquid, and gaseous fuels. Appliances fueled with natural gas, liquified petroleum (LP gas), oil, kerosene, coal, or wood may produce CO. Burning charcoal produces CO and car exhaust contains CO."[6(p45)] Exposure to high levels of CO can result in death or serious health consequences. Indoor use of unventilated charcoal barbecues and inappropriate use of ovens (powered by natural gas) for space heating have been associated with fatalities. Smokers are exposed routinely to carbon monoxide from tobacco smoke, although this level of exposure is not sufficient to cause death. Carbon monoxide levels can become dangerous in poorly ventilated mines. On January 2,

2006, an explosion at the Sago coal mine in West Virginia was linked to the deaths of 12 of 13 miners who were trapped deep underground. The sole immediate survivor demonstrated symptoms of severe carbon monoxide poisoning for which treatment was rendered in a hyperbaric chamber. High levels of toxic carbon monoxide impeded rescue efforts at a Montcoal, West Virginia mine, where an explosion on April 5, 2010 killed 29 miners.

Inhaled carbon monoxide aggravates coronary heart disease, as well as circulatory, lung, and respiratory diseases, due to reduced oxygen-carrying capacity of the blood and increased demand on the heart and lungs. Carbon monoxide has more than 200 times more affinity for binding with hemoglobin in the blood than oxygen does. The combination of carbon monoxide and hemoglobin is called **carboxyhemoglobin**. High levels of carboxyhemoglobin interfere with the capacity of blood to transfer oxygen and carbon dioxide.[18] Patients who suffer from carbon monoxide poisoning can experience a range of symptoms, such as visual disturbances and impairment of mental and physical functioning.

Aerosol particles, also known as **particulate matter (PM)**, include dust, soot, and other finely divided solid and liquid materials that are suspended in and move with the air.[6] Particulate air pollution is a worldwide problem, producing—in some cases—what we observe as visible haze. The sources of particles include diesel exhaust from trucks and buses; smoke from incineration of garbage, wastes from crops, and slash burning; industrial activities; and effluents from wood-burning fireplaces. Particulate matter, which has been linked to lung damage, bronchitis, and early mortality, also causes environmental degradation through the deposition of soot on vehicles, clothing, and buildings. Such pollutants are known to irritate the eye, nose, and throat.

Particulate matter refers generically to a mixture of particles that can vary in size. (Refer to **FIGURE 10**). Let's consider as a reference point the thickness of a human hair (about 50-70 microns in diameter) and compare it with two particle sizes that are used as air pollution standards: PM_{10} and $PM_{2.5}$. Particles classified as PM_{10} are larger than 2.5 micrometers in diameter and range up to 10 micrometers in diameter. The $PM_{2.5}$ pollutants include the class of particles that are called ultrafine (diameter of 0.01 to 0.1 micrometers) and fine (diameter of 0.1 to 2.5 micrometers). Both are criteria air pollutants, as noted previously. The general health effects of particulate matter include respiratory system irritation, lung damage, and development of bronchitis. (More information on the health effects associated with PM is presented later in this chapter.)

In comparison with the larger particles, the invisible particles of diameter 2.5 micrometers ($PM_{2.5}$) or smaller have been of greater concern recently. $PM_{2.5}$ particles have the capability to bypass the body's normal defenses and can be inhaled deeply into the lungs where they are deposited; if they do not dissolve, the body's natural clearance mechanisms are unable to remove them efficiently. Some of the fine particles may contain liquid acid condensates and toxic heavy metals. Some researchers have claimed that $PM_{2.5}$ is associated with approximately 60,000 smog-related deaths annually in the United States;[19] not all agree that the figure is this large.

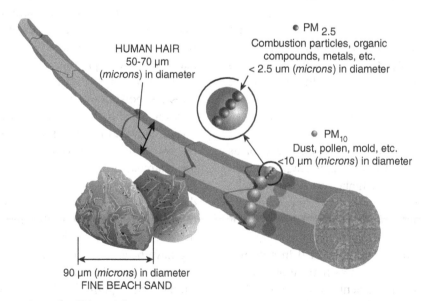

HUMAN HAIR
50-70 μm
(*microns*) in diameter

● PM 2.5
Combustion particles, organic
compounds, metals, etc.
< 2.5 um (*microns*) in diameter

● PM₁₀
Dust, pollen, mold, etc.
<10 μm (*microns*) in diameter

90 μm (*microns*) in diameter
FINE BEACH SAND

FIGURE 10 Size comparisons for PM particles.

Regarding $PM_{2.5}$, the EPA has set a standard of 12.0 micrograms of suspended particles per cubic meter of air ($\mu g/m^3$). This is known as EPA's primary standard for public health protection from airborne particles. Given this standard, let's compare countries with respect to WHO's reports of levels of particulate pollution.[20] WHO reported generally acceptable levels of particulate pollution in the developed regions of the world. However, the same cannot be said of the developing regions.

Based on WHO's data from 2014, the United States, with a mean reading of 8.2 $\mu g/m^3$, met the primary standard. In northern Europe, Scandinavian countries (e.g., Denmark, Norway, and Sweden) had levels that were below 12.0 $\mu g/m^3$. In western Europe, some countries had levels at or close to the primary standard (e.g., France, Germany, and Switzerland). Belgium, Italy, and the Netherlands were examples of countries that slightly exceeded the standard. Some eastern European countries (e.g., Bulgaria, Bosnia and Herzegovina, Hungary, and Poland) exceeded the standard by approximately two to three times. Very high levels of particulate air pollution tended to occur in developing countries. For example, several Middle Eastern countries (e.g., Saudi Arabia and Qatar) demonstrated levels that were roughly nine times the standard. Other developing countries with high levels of particulate pollution were located in Africa and the rapidly industrializing countries of India and China.

Large amounts of PM were released following the collapse of the World Trade Center in New York City after the terrorist attacks on September 11, 2001. Examples of materials that could have been incorporated in the dusts include asbestos, fiberglass, and crystalline mineral components of concrete and wallboard. The Centers for Disease Control and Prevention (CDC) has developed a registry of persons (e.g., nearby residents, workers, schoolchildren, and first responders) who were most highly exposed to the dusts, smoke, and other airborne materials.[21] These individuals will be followed over time to assess whether there have been any adverse health effects associated with their exposures.

Sulfur dioxide (SO_2) is a gas produced by burning sulfur contaminants in fuel, for example, coal. Power plants that use high-sulfur coal or do not have effective emission controls are a source of SO_2. Some industrial processes, including production of paper and smelting of metals, also produce sulfur dioxide, which can form sulfuric acid (H_2SO_4), a strong acid. Thus, SO_2 can play an important role in the production of acid rain.[6] Health effects associated with sulfur dioxide include bronchoconstriction (as in asthma

attacks) and production of excess mucus, which can produce coughing.

Volatile organic compounds (VOCs) refer to a class of chemicals that contain carbon (C), the basic chemical element found in living beings. Essentially all carbon-containing chemicals belong to the group that is called organic. Volatile chemicals evaporate and thus escape into the air easily.[6] Not classified as criteria air pollutants, VOCs are the product of fuel combustion (e.g., diesel fuel, gasoline, coal, and natural gas). Products used frequently in the workplace and at home release VOCs; examples are paints and lacquers, some types of glues, construction materials, and solvents such as benzene and toluene. One of the most significant sources of VOCs is automobiles. VOCs interact with other pollutants to form smog. The impact of VOCs on human health can be serious (e.g., cancers at various bodily sites). Some VOCs are known to be injurious to plants.

Acid Rain

The term **acid rain** occurs "...when sulfur dioxide (SO_2) and nitrogen oxides (NO_x) are emitted into the atmosphere and transported by wind and air currents. The SO_2 and NO_x react with water, oxygen and other chemicals to form sulfuric and nitric acids. These then mix with water and other materials before falling to the ground.[22] Installations such as electric utility plants emit SO_2 and NO_x. (Refer to **FIGURE 11**, which shows the acid rain pathway.) Eventually the

FIGURE 11 Acid rain pathway.

* Numbers shown in figure refer to the pathway for acid rain in our environment.
[1] Emissions of SO_2 and No_x are released into the air.
[2] The pollutants are transformed into acid particles that may be transported long distances.
[3] These acid particles then fall on earth as dust, rain, snow, and other materials.
[4] The acid rain particles may cause harmful effects on soil, forests, streams, and lakes.

Reproduced from US Environmental Protection Agency. What is acid rain? Available at: https://www.epa.gov/acidrain/what-acid-rain. Accessed June 6, 2017.

FIGURE 12 Deterioration of the exterior of a building in Dublin, Ireland. Air pollution, solar radiation, moisture, and cold–heat cycling are contributing causes.

acid rain settles on the earth, creating abnormally high levels of acidity that are potentially damaging to the environment, wildlife, and human health. For example, acid rain is believed to harm forests and certain species of fish, and to contribute to the deterioration of structures. (Refer to **FIGURE 12**.)

Temperature Inversion

The term **temperature inversion** refers to an atmospheric condition during which a warm layer of air stalls above a layer of cool air that is closer to the surface of the earth, as shown in **FIGURE 13**. A temperature inversion is the reverse of the usual situation in which the air closer to the surface of the earth is warmer than the air in the upper atmosphere. Solar radiation causes the earth's surface to become heated and warms the air near the surface. The usual temperature gradient (hot air below and cool above) allows convection of warm air from the earth's surface into the upper atmosphere, thus removing pollutants from the breathing zones of people. During a temperature inversion, pollutants (e.g., smog, smog-forming chemicals, and VOCs) can build up when they are trapped close to the earth's surface. Continuing release of smog-forming pollutants from motor vehicles and other sources during an inversion exacerbates air pollution. A temperature inversion layer as seen from an airplane is shown in **FIGURE 14**.

Temperature inversions contribute to the creation of smog, which is aggravated in cities such

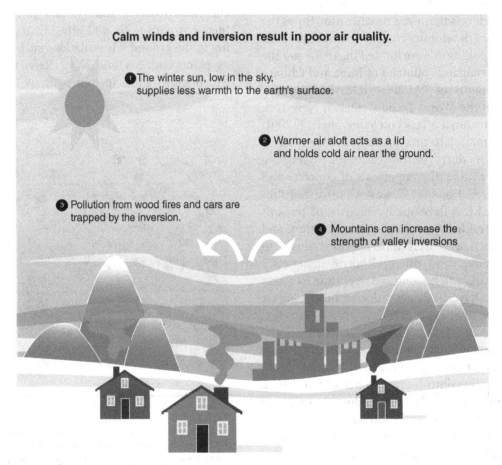

FIGURE 13 Diagram of temperature inversion.

FIGURE 14 Inversion layer as seen from an airplane.

FIGURE 15 Air pollution in southern California on a spring day.

as Los Angeles that have unfavorable topographical characteristics and prevailing winds. In the Los Angeles Basin, under certain conditions, coastal on-shore winds push pollutants farther inland, away from their sources; these pollutants are stopped by nearby mountains, creating higher levels of air pollution than existed along the coast. This concentration of pollutants then may be trapped under an inversion layer; a series of chemical reactions among the pollutants produces smog. **FIGURE 15** shows smog caused by an inversion layer in the Inland Empire region of southern California. You can see that, even on this relatively clear day during spring, air pollution obscures a nearby mountain. The type of smog shown in Figure 15 also is called photochemical smog, which is caused by the interaction of NO_x with VOCs. Ozone near the earth's surface is another major constituent of smog.

Diesel Exhaust

Widespread exposure to diesel exhaust occurs in the general community and in the workplace. A meta-analysis reviewed studies of the possible etiologic role of occupational exposure to diesel exhaust in the induction of lung cancer. The authors reported that across the group of research reports, the pooled risk of lung cancer among workers exposed to diesel exhaust was statistically significantly elevated after controlling for smoking.[23] As a result of researchers' concerns that exposure to diesel exhaust may be linked with elevated risk of lung cancer, public health experts have named diesel exhaust as a probable carcinogen.[24] For example, epidemiologic evidence suggests that in comparison with nonexposed groups, two categories of workers (truck drivers and railroad crews) exposed directly to diesel exhaust have lung cancer incidence rates that are 20% to

40% higher.[25] The level of exposure to diesel exhaust among both types of transportation workers is roughly equivalent.[26] One study reported that some groups of miners were exposed to diesel exhaust levels above recommended standards.[24]

Diesel exhaust, a complex mixture of particles and gases, includes the element carbon, condensed hydrocarbon gases, and **polycyclic aromatic hydrocarbons (PAHs)**, the latter suspected of being carcinogens.[24] Other constituents are hundreds of organic and inorganic compounds, some of which are regarded as toxic air pollutants.[25] Most of the particles in diesel exhaust are very fine and capable of being inhaled deeply into the lungs where they may have a carcinogenic effect. For this reason, lung cancer has been a particular focus of research on the effects of diesel exhaust, which is also thought to contribute to airway inflammation, allergies, and asthma.

When the cost of fuel for vehicles is high and as oil shortages persist, the use of diesel engines will tend to grow in popularity because of their greater energy efficiency and endurance.[25] Even though there have been improvements in diesel engine design that reduce NO and particulate emissions, these newer engines continue to emit higher levels of carcinogenic and toxic substances than do conventional gasoline engines that have catalytic converters.[25] Many of the diesel-driven vehicles (e.g., buses and trucks) in use in the United States are 15 years old or older, indicating that these vehicles do not have the advantages of the latest emissions reduction technology.

Likely to be more vulnerable to the effects of diesel exhaust exposure than adults are children, whose defenses to ward off disease are not as well developed

181

as those of adults. Children who ride in school buses powered by diesel engines are exposed to diesel exhaust. Residents (both children and adults) of urban areas may be exposed to diesel exhaust from motor vehicle traffic. For example, adolescent residents of upper Manhattan in New York City were reported to receive frequent exposures to diesel exhaust from vehicles that travel on city streets.[27] The role that these exposures play in exacerbation of lung disorders needs to be explored more fully.

Despite the supportive findings regarding the potentially carcinogenic role of diesel exhaust exposures, this topic of research remains highly controversial.[28] Some researchers remain skeptical about whether, in fact, a risk to human health exists from exposures to diesel exhaust. Researchers have questioned the validity of data and methods used in risk assessments of diesel exhaust exposure. For example, some of the studies of truck drivers have not controlled adequately for smoking status and the level of diesel exhaust exposure.[29]

▶ Air Quality Standards

This section presents information on the Air Quality Index and National Ambient Air Quality Standards (NAAQS).

The Air Quality Index

The **Air Quality Index (AQI)** is used to provide the public with an indication of air quality in a local area:

> The AQI is an index for reporting daily air quality. It tells you how clean or polluted your air is, and what associated health effects might be a concern for you. The AQI focuses on health effects you may experience within a few hours or days after breathing polluted air. EPA calculates the AQI for five major air pollutants regulated by the Clean Air Act: ground-level ozone, particle pollution (also known as particulate matter), carbon monoxide, sulfur dioxide, and nitrogen dioxide. For each of these pollutants, EPA has established national air quality standards to protect public health. . . . .[30] (summarized in the following table).

Each category corresponds to a different level of health concern. The six levels of health concern and what they mean are:

- ■ "Good" AQI is 0–50. Air quality is considered satisfactory, and air pollution poses little or no risk.

Air Quality Index (AQI) Values	Levels of Health Concern	Colors
When the AQI is in this range:	*...Air quality conditions are:*	*...As symbolized by this color:*
0 to 50	Good	Green
51 to 100	Moderate	Yellow
101 to 150	Unhealthy for sensitive groups	Orange
151 to 200	Unhealthy	Red
201 to 300	Very unhealthy	Purple
301 to 500	Hazardous	Maroon

Reproduced from US Environmental Protection Agency. Air Quality Index (AQI) basics. Available at: https://airnow.gov/index.cfm?action=aqibasics.aqi. Accessed June 7, 2017.

- ■ "Moderate" AQI is 51–100. Air quality is acceptable; however, for some pollutants there may be a moderate health concern for a very small number of people. For example, people who are unusually sensitive to ozone may experience respiratory symptoms.
- ■ "Unhealthy for Sensitive Groups" AQI is 101–150. Although general public is not likely to be affected at this AQI range, people with lung disease, older adults, and children are at a greater risk from exposure to ozone, and persons with heart and lung disease, older adults, and children are at greater risk from the presence of particles in the air.
- ■ "Unhealthy" AQI is 151–200. Everyone may begin to experience some adverse health effects, and members of the sensitive groups may experience more serious effects.
- ■ "Very Unhealthy" AQI is 201–300. This would trigger a health alert signifying that everyone may experience more serious health effects.
- ■ "Hazardous" AQI is greater than 300. This would trigger a health warning. . . of emergency conditions. The entire population is more likely to be affected.[30]

National Ambient Air Quality Standards

Federal standards for air pollution are called the National Ambient Air Quality Standards (NAAQS). The EPA reviews the scientific literature at 5-year intervals and decides whether to revise each standard. Current standards (as of 2010) are presented in the following text box.

NATIONAL AMBIENT AIR QUALITY STANDARDS

The Clean Air Act, which was last amended in 1990, requires EPA to set National Ambient Air Quality Standards (40 CFR part 50) for pollutants considered harmful to public health and the environment. The Clean Air Act identifies two types of national ambient air quality standards.

Primary standards provide public health protection, including protecting the health of "sensitive" populations such as asthmatics, children, and the elderly. *Secondary standards* provide public welfare protection, including protection against decreased visibility and damage to animals, crops, vegetation, and buildings.

The EPA has set National Ambient Air Quality Standards for six principal pollutants, which are called "criteria" air pollutants. Periodically, the standards are reviewed and may be revised. The current standards are listed in **TABLE** 2. Units of measure for the standards are parts per million (ppm) by volume, parts per billion (ppb) by volume, and micrograms per cubic meter of air ($\mu g/m^3$).

TABLE 2 National Ambient Air Quality Standards for Criteria Air Pollutants

Pollutant		Primary/ Secondary	Averaging Time	Level	Form
Carbon monoxide (CO)		Primary	8 hours	9 ppm	Not to be exceeded more than once per year
			1 hour	35 ppm	
Lead (Pb)		Primary and secondary	Rolling 3-month average	0.15 $\mu g/m^3$	Not to be exceeded
Nitrogen dioxide (NO$_2$)		Primary	1 hour	100 ppb	98th percentile of 1-hour daily maximum concentrations, averaged over 3 years
		Primary and secondary	1 year	53 ppb	Annual mean
Ozone (O$_3$)		Primary and secondary	8 hours	0.070 ppm	Annual fourth-highest daily maximum 8-hour concentration, averaged over 3 years
Particule pollution (PM)	PM$_{2.5}$	Primary	1 year	12 $\mu g/m^3$	Annual mean, averaged over 3 years
		Secondary	1 year	15.0 $\mu g/m^3$	Annual mean, averaged over 3 years
		Primary and secondary	24 hours	35 $\mu g/m^3$	98th percentile, averaged over 3 years
	PM$_{10}$	Primary and secondary	24 hours	150 $\mu g/m^3$	Not to be exceeded more than once per year on average over 3 years
Sulfur dioxide (SO$_2$)		Primary	1 hour	75 ppb	99th percentile of 1-hour daily maximum concentrations, averaged over 3 years
		Secondary	3 hours	0.5 ppm	Not to be exceeded more than once per year

Modified and reproduced from US Environmental Protection Agency. Criteria air pollutants. National Ambient Air Quality Standards (NAAQS) table. Available at: http://www.epa.gov/criteria-air-pollutants/naaqs-table. Accessed June 18, 2017.

▶ Health Effects of Air Pollution

The aesthetic impacts of air pollution include reduction in the quality of our lives by obscuring the natural environment, by damaging property, and, in some cases, by being malodorous. This section will focus on the human health effects of air pollution and will present information on methods for the measurement of air pollution in the laboratory.

Measurement of Air Pollution in Experimental Studies

Improvements in air quality in the United States have reduced the levels of pollutants in the air substantially. Consequently, increasingly sensitive techniques are needed to define the current health effects of air pollution. Examples of these sensitive techniques are shown in **FIGURE** 16, which illustrates scientific devices used in air pollution health effects studies, primarily with small animals. Air purifiers are used to create artificially purified air that has known levels of contaminants. Laser particle analyzers are used to quantify precisely the amount of particulate matter in a sample of air. Exposure chambers administer precise amounts of pollutants under controlled conditions to small mammals. Through the use of devices such as these, air pollution researchers are able to measure exposure to air pollution much more definitively than is possible through studies conducted in the ambient environment.

Human Health Effects

Among human populations, air pollution is associated with short-term (acute) and long-term effects. The former can include irritation of the eyes, nose, and throat;

A

B

C

D

E

FIGURE 16 Devices employed in experimental studies of air pollution. The exposure chambers are used with small animals: A. Laser particle analyzer. B. Exposure chamber. C. Air purifier. D. Exposure chamber. E. Exposure chamber.

Courtesy of Dr. Robert Phalen, Air Pollution Lab, University of California, Irvine

aching lungs, bronchitis and pneumonia, wheezing, coughing, nausea, and headaches. Examples of long-term effects are heart disease, chronic obstructive pulmonary disease (COPD), and lung cancer.

Population subgroups differ in their susceptibility to air pollution. Vulnerable groups who are at increased risk of being affected by air pollution include the elderly, persons afflicted with chronic diseases, and growing children. Persons who have low educational attainment or diabetes or who are black appear to be more susceptible to the adverse affects of air pollution and might be particularly likely to benefit from air pollution emissions controls.[31] On the other hand, another viewpoint is that introduction of emission controls could pose an economic burden for small businesses that employ minority groups that have low incomes.

As they grow and develop, children who live in some areas of the world are exposed to air pollution numerous times over the course of their lives. A meaningful question for researchers pertains to the effects of the cumulative impact of air pollution on children over long time periods.[32] These exposures that begin early in life may lead to future cases of asthma and serious lung diseases as well as chronic cough and respiratory irritation.

Three of the major health effects are airway sensitivity disorders (e.g., asthma), lung cancer, and heart attacks. In addition, heavy episodes of air pollution have been correlated with increased mortality rates. The specific effects of air pollution are related to total exposure—duration of exposure (for example, how long one lives in a smoggy environment) and the type and concentration of the pollutant. Other considerations in health effects are environmental and temporal factors—temperature, climate, and timing of exposure.[4]

Anatomy of the Lung and Impact of Air Pollution on the Body

This section will describe how components of air pollution enter the human lung and how they impact the body. (Refer to **FIGURE 17**.) During respiration, air is drawn in through the nose and mouth. The air then passes through the windpipe into the right and left lungs, which have three and two lobes, respectively. Each lobe is supplied with bronchial tubes that branch several times and terminate in bronchioles and alveoli. The lobes of the lungs and bronchi are shown in Figure 17A. Figures 17B and D illustrate the structure of the bronchial tubes, bronchioles, and alveoli; exchange of oxygen between inhaled air and the circulatory system takes place in the alveoli. Figure 17C

(left side) shows the complete structure of a right lung that was taken from a dog.

Consider one of the major components of air pollution—smog. According to animal studies, smog has the capacity to damage the cellular structure of airways (e.g., windpipe and bronchial tubes) to the lungs. In response to ozone exposure, the exposed airways sometimes manifest swelling and inflammation. People who are exposed to smog may experience breathing difficulties and may develop acute or chronic cough.

Other conditions that are believed to be associated with the irritating effects of smog are chronic obstructive pulmonary disease and, among sensitive persons, exacerbation of asthma. Also suspected of being associated with smog and other forms of air pollution are some types of cancer.

Epidemiologic Studies of Air Pollution Health Effects

This section covers the following outcomes that have been studied in relation to air pollution: mortality, coronary heart disease, chronic obstructive pulmonary disease, asthma, and lung cancer.

Mortality

The World Health Organization estimated that 7 million people died from air pollution in 2012. From the global perspective, alarmingly high air pollution levels in cities located in developing countries substantially increase the risk of human mortality. In the United States, researchers have studied relationships between air pollution and mortality. Dockery et al. demonstrated statistically significant associations between air pollution and mortality in a prospective study of 8,111 adults who resided in six US cities.[33] In a study conducted among the predominantly Mormon residents of Utah Valley in central Utah, elevated concentrations of particles (PM_{10}) were associated with increased mortality, particularly from respiratory and cardiovascular causes.[34] Other epidemiologic studies conducted in large urban areas such as New York City have investigated associations between rising air pollution levels and mortality.

One type of epidemiologic study has examined the relationship between daily mortality and air pollution levels. The historically significant extreme air pollution episodes noted previously (e.g., the London fog in 1952) appeared to provide at least anecdotal evidence of the correlation of increased mortality with the times that air pollution levels rose to very high levels. Ito et al. examined London data for the period 1965 through 1972 for levels of air pollution classified

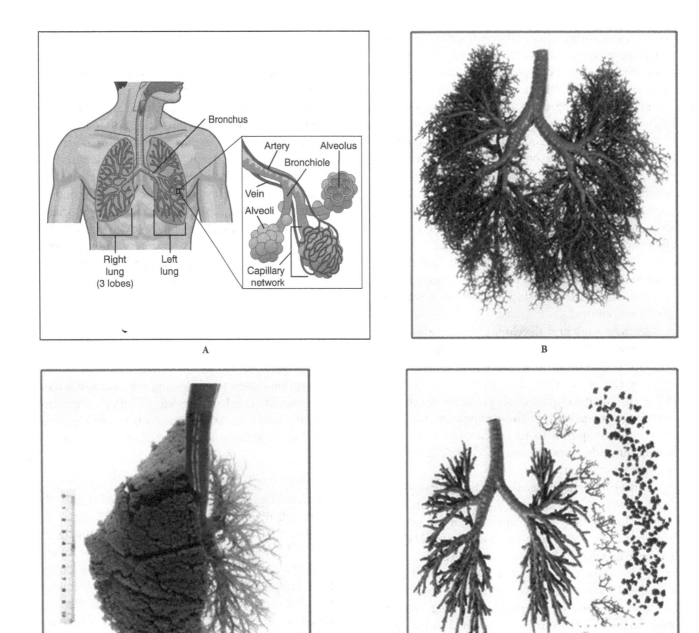

FIGURE   17 Lung anatomy: A. Diagram of the lungs. B. Human tracheobronchial tree. C. Right lung and left tracheobronchial tree. D. The bronchial tree dissected showing (respectively) bronchial tubes, bronchioles, and alveoli.

(A) Reproduced from Centers for Disease Control and Prevention. Basic information about lung cancer. Available at: http://www.cdc.gov/cancer/lung/basic_info. Accessed May 5, 2010. (B, C, and D) Dr. Robert Phalen, Air Pollution Laboratory, University of California, Irvine.

according to type of pollutant.[35] Statistically significant associations were found between air pollution variables and mortality.

Another study that reported a correlation between increases in total daily mortality and increased air pollution (SO_2 and smoke shade) was conducted in New York City.[36] Daily mortality was related to particulate air pollution in St. Louis, Missouri and counties in eastern Tennessee.[37] Researchers estimated the daily mortality rate associated with gaseous air pollution and

particulate air pollution—inhalable particles (PM_{10}) and fine particles ($PM_{2.5}$). For each 100 micrograms per cubic meter increase in PM_{10}, the total mortality was reported to increase by 16% in St. Louis, Missouri, and by 17% in the eastern Tennessee counties. Weaker associations were reported for $PM_{2.5}$; associations between mortality and gaseous pollutants (e.g., SO_2, NO_2, and O_3) were not statistically significant. Another study conducted by Dominici et al. found that daily variations in PM_{10} and daily variations in mortality were positively associated. Cardiovascular and respiratory mortality were more closely related to particulate pollution than were other forms of mortality.[38]

Coronary Heart Disease

Individuals who have preexisting heart or lung disease may be at particular risk for the fatal or aggravating effects of air pollution that lead to coronary heart disease (CHD). People who are afflicted with ischemic heart disease combined with arrhythmias or congestive heart failure may have heightened sensitivity to pollutants from motor vehicle emissions.[39] Cigarette smoking and air pollution may act synergistically to aggravate lung diseases such as emphysema. Extreme temperatures may add to this synergistic effect.

Carbon monoxide arises from cigarette smoke, automobile exhaust, and certain types of occupational exposures. An investigation into the possible association between angina pectoris and heavy freeway traffic found no direct association between myocardial infarction and ambient carbon monoxide. It was hypothesized that there was an indirect association between exposure to carbon monoxide in the ambient air and acute myocardial infarction through smoking, which is associated with elevated blood carbon monoxide levels.[40]

The air of one large metropolitan city exposed pedestrians and persons who worked outdoors to carbon monoxide levels that ranged from 10 to 50 ppm; there were even higher levels in poorly ventilated areas of the city.[41] The recommended standard for carbon monoxide in occupational settings is a maximum of 50 ppm. Pedestrians and workers who have heart problems may be at increased risk of aggravation of their conditions when exposed to high levels of ambient carbon monoxide in the urban environment.

Chronic Obstructive Pulmonary Disease

A major investigation, the Tucson Epidemiological Study of Airways Obstructive Diseases, has tracked the etiology and natural history of COPD.[42] (The chapter on occupational health defines and provides more information on COPD.) Based on a multistage stratified cluster sample of white households in the Tucson, Arizona area, it has generated many important findings, including the effects of passive smoking on children.[43]

Asthma

One of the most frequent chronic conditions in the United States, **asthma** has shown an increasing prevalence since 1980.[44-46] This increase has happened even as air pollution has declined steadily. Currently asthma is regarded as a key public health problem that confronts the United States.[45] Residents of inner-city areas (notably children) seem to be more affected by the condition than are persons who live in other areas.[47] The growing problem of childhood asthma is significant to public health because of the burden of morbidity and suffering that this condition contributes to the lives of children and their parents. Interestingly, in the United States, the prevalence of childhood asthma varies by socioeconomic status and racial and ethnic group. Black children who live in low-income areas have the highest asthma prevalence and morbidity in comparison with other ethnic and racial groups.[48] Indoor air quality and genetic factors may be relevant to the occurrence of this significant respiratory disease. Some facts regarding asthma are the following:

> Asthma is a chronic respiratory illness often associated with familial, allergenic, socioeconomic, psychological, and environmental factors. . . . Although recent reports suggest asthma-related mortality has been declining since 1996, a disparity remains between rates for non-Hispanic whites and those for non-Hispanic blacks and other racial/ethnic populations. . . . Non-Hispanic blacks experience higher rates than non-Hispanic whites for ED [emergency department] visits, hospitalizations, and deaths; these trends are not explained entirely by higher asthma prevalence among non-Hispanic blacks. . . . Other racial/ethnic populations experience higher asthma mortality and hospitalization rates than non-Hispanic whites while also reporting lower asthma prevalence and fewer outpatient and ED visits.[46(p147)]

Symptoms of asthma—difficulty breathing and tightness of the chest—are a response to muscle contractions that constrict the trachea, lungs, and other parts of the airway. Excess mucus secretion also contributes to breathing difficulties. Asthma is believed to have a complex etiology that involves both genetic and environmental factors.[49] Among the triggers for asthma attacks are allergens, pollutants, and viral infections; examples of sources of allergens are vermin (i.e., cockroaches and rodents), dust mites, mold, and household pets (i.e., dogs and cats).[50] Other potential triggers are **environmental tobacco smoke**, cold air, exercise, stress, and aspirin.

Air pollution has been studied as a possible factor in asthma occurrence. Exploration of this association presents methodologic difficulties due to the facts that air pollution contains a complex mixture of substances and asthma has a complex, heterogeneous etiology.[51] Examples of components of air pollution studied in relation to asthma include particles, molds, nitrogen dioxide, ozone, and pollen.

Epidemiologic studies have reported an association between high concentrations of air pollution and asthma prevalence.[52] Among schoolchildren in Japan, incidence rates of asthma were associated with air pollution components such as particles (PM_{10}) and nitrogen dioxide.[52] A Los Angeles study of asthma among black children found that particles and molds were related to respiratory symptom occurrence.[53]

Lung Cancer

Although air pollution is a suspected cause of lung cancer, researchers have had difficulty in establishing a definitive association because of problems in measuring the effects of low-level exposures and problems in measuring air pollution itself. An example of research on air pollution's health effects is that conducted by Henderson et al.[54] Census tracts in Los Angeles were aggregated into 14 study areas that represented homogeneous air pollution profiles. The study reported a correlation between the geographic distribution of lung cancer cases and the general location of emission sources for hydrocarbons.

One of the components of air pollution that may be implicated in lung cancer mortality is fine particulate matter. Pope et al. conducted an analysis of a data set that contained information on risk factors, air pollution levels, and mortality from approximately 500,000 adults who resided in metropolitan areas throughout the United States.[55] These individuals were part of a large, ongoing, prospective study called the Cancer Prevention II study, which was conducted by the American Cancer Society. The investigators concluded that exposure to fine particulate matter over extended time periods was a risk factor for both lung cancer and cardiopulmonary mortality.

In large population studies, the effects of air pollution exposure may be impossible to disentangle from the effects of other exposures, for example, tobacco smoke. A retrospective study conducted in Erie County, New York found that air pollution alone was not associated with lung cancer.[56] However, the same study reported that the risk of lung cancer increased among heavy smokers who had extensive exposure to air pollution.

A Swedish study reported that air pollution from vehicle exhaust emissions may be important for increasing the risk of lung cancer.[57] According to the Swedish group, one of the components of vehicle emissions that may increase risk of lung cancer is NO_2.

▶ Indoor Air Quality

Indoor air that is of poor quality can be a significant factor in the etiology of lung disease and exacerbation of existing conditions such as asthma and bronchitis. A report authored by four leading health and governmental organizations states:

> Studies from the United States and Europe show that persons in industrialized nations spend more than 90 percent of their time indoors. . . . For infants, the elderly, persons with chronic diseases, and most residents of any age, the proportion is probably higher. In addition, the concentrations of many pollutants indoors exceed those outdoors. The locations of highest concern are those involving prolonged, continuing exposure—that is, the home, school, and workplace.[58(p1)]

The indoor environment provides many opportunities for exposure to potentially irritating and harmful substances. Examples are aerosolized chemicals, fumes from gas appliances, components of building materials, and secondhand smoke from tobacco products. Adverse health outcomes that have been linked to indoor pollution include respiratory diseases such as asthma, Legionnaires' disease, the sick building syndrome, hypersensitivity pneumonitis, and multiple chemical sensitivity.[59]

Indoor Air Quality in the Home

Residential indoor air pollution poses risks for respiratory illness of various types.[60] For example, certain environmental characteristics tend to be found in the dwellings of inner-city children who have asthma; these characteristics include the presence of cockroaches, persistent dampness, wall-to-wall carpeting in children's bedrooms, exposure to environmental tobacco smoke, infestations with rodents, and pets that have fur.[47] Other factors that influence the quality of indoor air are effluents from gas stoves and the use of construction materials that contain formaldehyde.[60] Dust mites, molds, and bacteria, all of which are linked with asthma, also may be identified in indoor air.[61] Evidence suggests that children who become sensitized to allergenic indoor air pollutants such as molds and animal fur may incur an increased risk for the development of asthma.[61] Dwellings that have damp, odiferous interiors may be conducive to the growth of fungi, dust mites, and bacterial pathogens, all of which, in turn, tend to be related to respiratory symptoms.[62]

Indoor Use of Biomass Fuels

A frequent cause of indoor air pollution in developing countries is the use of unventilated indoor cooking stoves that burn biomass fuels (wood, animal dung, or cuttings from crops). (Refer to **FIGURE 18**.)

Approximately half the global population uses biomass fuels for cooking and heating; in some areas of the world (e.g., south Asia and sub-Saharan Africa), this figure reaches 80%. Often biomass fuels are combusted in crude stoves or pits that have been dug into the floor. Due to inefficient combustion and the lack of ventilation in household areas used for cooking, the house fills up with smoke. As a result, the persons who occupy the dwelling may be exposed to substantial amounts of pollutants: PM_{10}, carbon monoxide, nitrous oxides, sulfur compounds, and polycyclic aromatic hydrocarbons (PAHs). Some estimates indicate that the level of indoor air pollutants in such homes exceeds US EPA standards by several orders of magnitude. As shown in Figure 18, women who are responsible for cooking receive the largest doses of indoor air pollution, as do infants who may be strapped to the women's backs. Other household residents who may be at risk of the adverse effects of indoor air pollution are the elderly, who spend more time indoors than do other family members. A study conducted in India reported that elderly men and women who live in homes that use biomass fuels have a higher prevalence of asthma than elderly persons who live in homes that use cleaner fuels.[49]

Content removed due to copyright restrictions

FIGURE 18 Woman cooking with an indoor stove.

Sick Building Syndrome and Building-Related Illness

Sick building syndrome (SBS) is another example of a condition ascribed to indoor air pollution.[63,64] SBS

> ...is used to describe situations in which building occupants experience acute health and comfort effects that appear to be linked to time spent in a building, but no specific illness or cause can be identified. The complaints may be localized in a particular room or zone, or may be widespread throughout the building. In contrast, the term "building related illness" (BRI) is used when symptoms of diagnosable illness are identified and can be attributed directly to airborne building contaminants.[65]

SBS is a temporary phenomenon that is relieved when affected persons are no longer inside the building. Symptoms of SBS can include headache, respiratory tract irritation, dry skin, and fatigue; the cause of the symptoms of SBS is unknown. In comparison, **building-related illness (BRI)** describes symptoms of diagnosable illnesses that can be linked to specific pollutants; examples are Legionnaires' disease and hypersensitivity pneumonitis. Possible causes of SBS are inadequate building ventilation, chemical contaminants, and biological contaminants.[65]

A condition that bears similarity to sick building syndrome is multiple chemical sensitivity. The onset of multiple chemical sensitivity is described as the development of sensitivity at about the same time to several chemicals, which are present in the ambient environment at low levels. The onset of the condition occurs in many cases following exposure to indoor air that has quality problems.[59] Also hypothesized as being related to low-quality indoor air is hypersensitivity pneumonitis, an illness "characterized by flu-like symptoms that include fever, chills, fatigue, cough, chest tightness, and shortness of breath."[59(p402)] Causal factors associated with the illness include exposure to molds, fungi, and bacteria found in indoor air.

Secondhand Smoke

FIGURE 19 demonstrates the lungs of two smokers— the lungs on the left are those of a smoker who had quit briefly before succumbing to a heart attack. The lungs shown on the right are those of a smoker who quit for several years. Note that the long-term quitter's lungs show horizontal striping, which corresponds to remaining deposits of carbon from cigarette smoke. The smoker who had quit for only a short period of time had lungs with more extensive deposits of carbon.

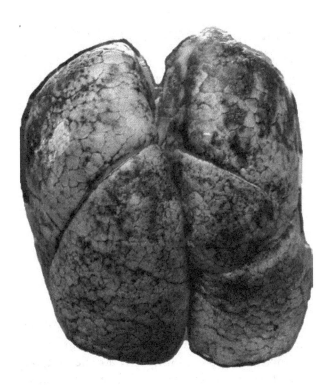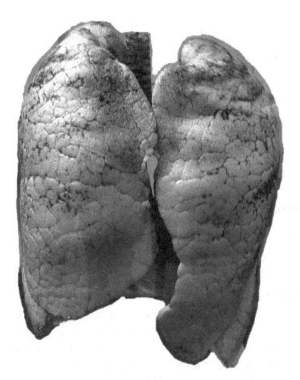

FIGURE **19** A. Dorsal view of the lungs of a male heavy smoker who quit 18 months prior to a fatal heart attack at 71 years of age. B. The lungs of a smoker who had quit smoking for a number of years.

Courtesy of Dr. Robert Phalen, Air Pollution Lab, University of California, Irvine.

The harmful effects of smoking upon smokers have been well known for some time. Some of these harmful effects are lung conditions such as emphysema and chronic obstructive pulmonary disease, heart disease, as well as lung cancer and cancers at other bodily sites. More recently the effects of exposure to environmental tobacco smoke (ETS) have become recognized more clearly. Exposure to ETS is also called "secondhand smoking," "passive smoking," or "involuntary smoking."[58]

The term **passive smoking**, also known as exposure to sidestream cigarette smoke, refers to the involuntary breathing of cigarette smoke by nonsmokers in an environment where there are cigarette smokers present. In restaurants, waiting rooms, international airliners, and other enclosed areas where there are cigarette smokers, nonsmokers may be unwillingly (and, perhaps, unwittingly) exposed to a potential health hazard. The effects of chronic exposure to cigarette smoke in the work environment were examined in a cross-sectional study of 5,210 cigarette smokers and nonsmokers. Nonsmokers who did not work in a smoking environment were compared with nonsmokers who worked in a smoking environment as well as with smokers. Exposure to smoke in the work environment among the nonsmokers was associated with a statistically significant reduction in pulmonary function test measurements in comparison with

the nonsmokers in the smoke-free environment.[66] A 1992 report from the US Environmental Protection Agency concluded that environmental tobacco smoke is a human lung carcinogen responsible for approximately 3,000 lung cancer deaths annually among US nonsmokers.[67] The nonsmoking spouses of smokers are at greater risk of dying than are the nonsmoking spouses of nonsmokers. Eleven studies conducted in the United States have shown an average 19% increase in risk of death among nonsmoking spouses of smokers.[68] Among children, passive smoking is associated with bronchitis, pneumonia, fluid in the middle ear, asthma incidence, and aggravation of existing asthma.

Research on passive smoking presents several methodologic difficulties. Relatively small increases in risk of death from passive smoking are difficult to demonstrate, given the use of questionnaires to quantify smoking by spouses, the long- and short-term variability in exposures to cigarette smoke from sources other than the spouse (e.g., those at work, restaurants, and entertainment venues), and the long latency period between exposure to cigarette smoke and onset of disease. Additional research will be required to improve methods, such as the use of biologic markers, for assessing exposure to cigarette smoke.

Many states (e.g., California, Massachusetts) in the United States have banned smoking in locations such as restaurants where nonsmokers (both customers and employees) may be exposed to secondhand smoke. Smoking is no longer permitted on domestic airlines in the United States. Many foreign countries have begun to introduce smoking bans in public areas including restaurants; an example is Ireland. These steps will help to protect the public's health by reducing exposure to secondhand cigarette smoke.

Global Climate Change and Global Warming

According to one source, the term **global warming** is defined as follows:

> An increase in the near surface temperature of the Earth. Global warming has occurred in the distant past as the result of natural influences, but the term is most often used to refer to the warming predicted to occur as a result of increased emissions of greenhouse gases. Scientists generally agree that the Earth's surface has warmed by about 1 degree Fahrenheit [0.55 degrees Celsius] in the past 140 years.[69]

The use of fossil fuels, including coal and petroleum-based fuels, causes the release of gases, including **carbon dioxide (CO_2)**, methane, chlorofluorocarbon gases, and nitrous oxide. Chlorofluorocarbon gases used in air conditioners have been linked to the depletion of the ozone layer. Reduction of ozone levels in the upper atmosphere produces increased levels of ultraviolet radiation, normally absorbed by stratospheric ozone. The result could be an increased incidence of skin cancers and cataracts.

Gases that arise from natural sources and anthropogenic activities such as the burning of fossil fuels may accumulate in the atmosphere. Sometimes these gases are referred to as **greenhouse gases**, owing to the fact that in sufficient concentrations in the atmosphere, they may have the effect of trapping heat and causing the earth's temperature to rise. This principle is illustrated in **FIGURE 20**.

Have the earth's surface temperatures actually increased during the past century? According to the National Oceanic and Atmospheric Administration (NOAA), the answer is "yes," with some qualifications.[70] Since the end of the 19th century, temperatures at the surface of the earth have increased generally by about 0.74 degrees Celsius (1.3 degrees Fahrenheit), and for the past 50 years the linear trend of increase is about 0.13 degrees Celsius (0.23 degrees Fahrenheit), although some areas (e.g., the southeastern United States and sections of the north Atlantic) have cooled.

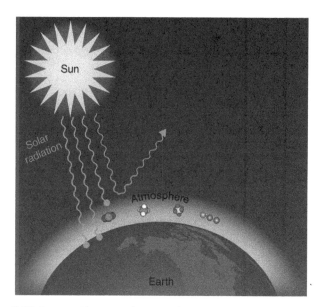

FIGURE 20 The greenhouse effect.

Reproduced from Deluisi B, National Oceanic & Atmospheric Administration. The greenhouse effect. Available at: https://www.esrl.noaa.gov/gmd/outreach/carbon_toolkit/basics.html. Accessed June 6, 2017.

Temperatures in North America and Eurasia have shown the greatest warming trend. **FIGURE 21** portrays global temperature anomalies during the period 1880 to 2016 (anomalies refer to departures from the long-term average temperature during the same time period). The trends shown by the data in Figure 21 suggest that global temperatures have shown an increase of 0.07 degrees Celsius (0.126 degrees Fahrenheit) per decade since 1880.

An international environmental group known as the Intergovernmental Panel on Climate Change (IPCC) has pointed to the likelihood of the role of human activities in causing global warming.[71] Increases in greenhouse gases have been linked with warming of the planet. With continuing emissions of greenhouse gases, models of future trends portend temperature increases of 0.5 to 8.6 degrees Fahrenheit (0.28 to 4.8 degrees Celsius) by the end of the 21st century.

A key issue is whether the increases in global temperature that have been observed during the past century represent natural temperature variability or are the effect of greenhouse gases. Analyses of temperature changes over the past millennium have used data from tree rings and ice cores. These analyses indicate that the recent large temperature increases during the late 20th century are most likely due to anthropogenic activities that have increased levels of greenhouse gases in the atmosphere.[72]

Deforestation

Contributing to the greenhouse effect is deforestation, which decreases the capacity of trees and the

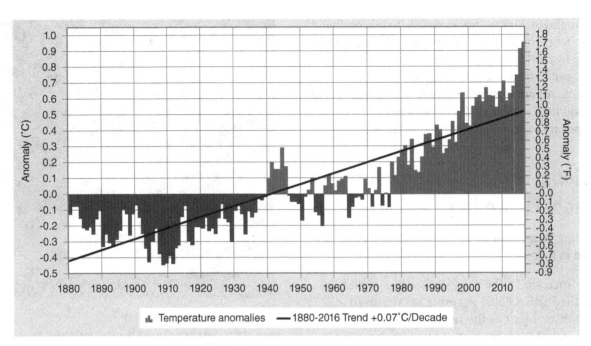

FIGURE 21 Global land and ocean temperature anomalies—January to December.

Reproduced from NOAA, National Centers for Environmental Information. Climate at a Glance: Global Time Series. Available at: http://www.ncdc.noaa.gov/cag/. Accessed August 17, 2017.

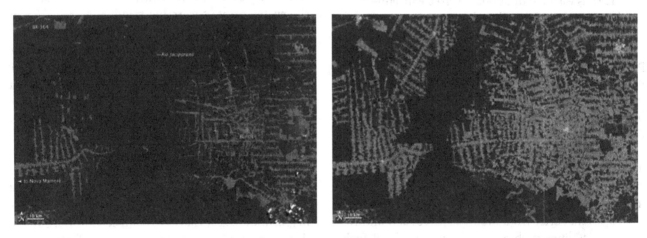

FIGURE 22 Brazilian deforestation of the state of Rondônia.

Reproduced from NASA, Earth Observatory. Amazon deforestation. Available at: https://earthobservatory.nasa.gov/Features/WorldOfChange/deforestation.php. Accessed June 7, 2017.

forest ecosystem to reduce the amount of CO_2 in the atmosphere. When deforestation occurs, biodiversity is reduced, resulting in the loss of plants that some-day might yield valuable medicines and other products. Deforestation often is the result of burning huge swaths of land, further adding to air pollution.

Extensive areas of the world have been affected by deforestation including the Brazilian Amazon jungle, the largest tropical forest in the world (31% of the world's total). **FIGURE 22** provides earlier and later satellite images that show the progress of deforestation during a 12-year period.

Deforestation is not limited to the Amazon region; vast sections of the United States also have suffered from the widespread removal of trees. Forests, which take up about 33% of the land mass in the United States, contribute clean air, water, habitat for animals, recreational opportunities, and valuable lumber. One of the areas that has been affected is the US Pacific Northwest. In this region, logging of old-growth forests by the method of clear-cutting has caused habitat fragmentation, whereby continuously forested areas are segmented into smaller parcels that are separated by nonforested zones. The net result is the destruction of habitat needed for the survival of animals that must leave the protective cover of the forest and traverse nonforested segments in order to seek food and water. (Refer to **FIGURE 23** for an example of clear-cutting.)

FIGURE 23 Deforestation caused by clear-cutting practices in the United States.

Potential Impacts of Global Warming

The potential consequences of global warming include disturbances in the native habitats of plant and animal species. Another possible end result could be the production of an environment that is conducive to the growth of vector-borne diseases, growth of organisms in the ocean that cause foodborne seafood poisoning, and exacerbation of the effects of air pollution. Global warming, which has been linked to extreme climatic conditions such as heat waves, droughts, and monsoons, may cause disruption of the food supply and dwindling of food resources, especially in developing areas. Refer to **FIGURE 24** for an overview of the potential health

effects associated with climate variability and change. Potential health effects shown in the figure range from temperature-related illnesses and deaths to vector- and rodent-borne diseases. Moderating influences involve nonclimatic factors such as population growth, changes in the standard of living, and improvements in health care and the public health infrastructure. Adaptation measures are steps that can be taken to lessen the possibility of adverse health outcomes linked to climate change. Examples of these measures are increasing the protection of populations via public health programs such as immunizations as well as the use of protective technologies (e.g., air conditioning and water treatment).[73]

Changes in the Distribution of Endemic Diseases

As global mean temperatures increase, changes in the ecological system favor the growth of some disease-causing agents (e.g., bacteria and fungi) and disease-carrying vectors. The increases in the prevalence and incidence of emerging and reemerging infectious diseases have been attributed to some degree to climate changes that are occurring in some regions of the world.[74] For example, as the temperature increases, the range of arthropods such as the *Aedes aegypti* mosquito can expand farther north. Normally, freezing temperatures during winter kill off this species of mosquito, which can carry viruses that cause diseases such as dengue fever and yellow fever. Also, extreme weather conditions such

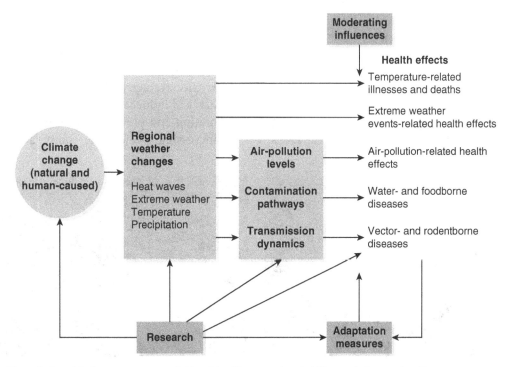

FIGURE 24 The relationship between potential health effects and variability and change in climate.

Modified and reproduced from Patz JA, McGeehin MA, Bernard SM, et al. The potential health impacts of climate variability and change for the United States: executive summary of the report of the health sector of the US National Assessment. *Environ Health Perspect.* 2000;108:368.

as heavy rainfall provide breeding grounds that contribute to the growth of mosquito populations.

Some Canadian experts believe that global warming might cause higher temperatures and longer summers that enable disease vectors to expand northward.[75] Another consequence could be that a warmer climate in Canada would permit the establishment of formerly exotic zoonoses (defined in the chapter on zoonotic and vector-borne diseases). As a result, Canadians would be at increased risk of contracting vector-borne diseases such as arboviral encephalitis, rickettsial diseases, and Lyme arthritis. Increased temperatures might contribute to the contamination of food sources derived from animals due to *Salmonella* and *E. coli* O157:H7. If summers become longer and winters milder, rodents and small mammal species that are reservoirs for zoonotic diseases might be able to breed and survive for longer time periods. Consequently, the human population would be at increased risk of zoonotic diseases such as hantavirus infection and plague.

Retreating Glaciers and Rising Oceans

Evidence of a changing global climate is the retreat of glaciers in high mountain areas worldwide. High-altitude areas on earth that are showing the retreat of perennial snow and glaciers are Glacier National Park in Montana (United States), Mount Kilimanjaro in Africa, and the Alps in Europe.[76] Regions such as these could be completely devoid of glaciers in the future. **FIGURE   25** demonstrates how the Columbia Glacier in Alaska has receded from 1986 to 2016.

Another apparent effect of global warming has been for the average height of the world's oceans to rise gradually as water stored in frozen sources melts. Refer to the following text box.

Particularly at risk of flooding due to a rise in the level of the sea are low-lying areas (especially low-lying coastal cities), deltas, and coral atolls.[77] Rising sea levels

will cause intrusion of salt water and erosion of coastal areas. Countries that would be most affected are Vietnam, Egypt, Bangladesh, and low-lying island nations. According to a mid-range scenario in which the level of the ocean rises by 16 inches (40 centimeters) by the year 2080, as many as 200 million people would be affected by surges in the ocean level. An even greater increase in sea level by 1 meter (3.3 feet) would affect additional millions of people in China, Bangladesh, Egypt, and Indonesia.

Extreme Climatic Conditions

Evidence suggests that global warming is associated with extreme climatic conditions including heat waves and severe rain storms.

Small changes in global mean temperatures can produce relatively large changes in the frequency of extreme temperatures. . . . Higher average ambient air temperatures are likely to induce more vigorous cycles of evaporation and precipitation. Indeed, a trend of increasing climate variability and extreme

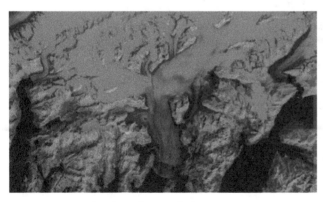

FIGURE   25 Columbia Glacier, Alaska—1986–2016.

Reproduced from NASA, Earth Observatory. Columbia Glacier, Alaska. Available at: https://earthobservatory.nasa.gov/Features/WorldOfChange/columbia_glacier.php. Accessed June 7, 2017. Images by Jesse Allen and Robert Simmon, using Landsat 4, 5, and 7 data from the USGS Global Visualization Viewer.

precipitation events has been observed over the past century, and recent models strongly correlate this trend with anthropogenic production of greenhouse gases.[78(p2283)]

From 1979 to 1995, the United States experienced a total of 6,615 heat-related deaths that were distributed as follows: heat due to weather conditions (2,792), heat due to human-made factors (327), and unspecified heat-related cause (3,496).[79] The major risk factors for heat-related death include excessive physical exertion during high temperatures, alcohol consumption, being overweight, using certain medications, and age. (Refer to **FIGURE 26**.)

Among significant episodes of heat-related mortality, two of particular note occurred: in Chicago, Illinois (US), and in France. The July 12 to July 16, 1995 heat wave in Chicago caused the daily high temperatures to rise to the range of 93°F to 104°F (33.9°C to 40.0°C); the city had a record-high temperature of 119°F (48.3°C) on July 13. The resulting high temperatures were responsible for 465 deaths that were certified as heat related during the period of the heat wave.[80]

Figure 26 presents more recent data on heat-related deaths in the United States, between 1979 and 2014. Heath-related deaths are a significant cause of

mortality in this country. Such deaths may become common as global warming and temperatures become more extreme in the future. From 1979 to 2014, about 9,000 deaths from heat-related causes have occurred in the United States. A peak in deaths occurred in 2006, an extremely hot year in this country.

During August 2003, a blistering heat wave descended on France, causing a death toll of almost 15,000.[81] Many of the deaths occurred among the elderly after temperatures reached the low 100s Fahrenheit (low 40s Celsius) in a country where it is uncommon to use air conditioning. One account indicated that "morgues and funeral parlours coped with an overflow of victims. Refrigerated storerooms were set up; and temporary workers hired to collect bodies from private homes and hotels. Grave diggers worked overtime."[82(p411)]

▶ Controlling Air Pollution and Global Warming

At the beginning the 21st century, the United States was the leading producer of greenhouse gases with 23% of the earth's emissions of such pollutants.[83] The major source of air pollution in the United States is combustion of fossil fuels, particularly by coal-fired electric generating plants and internal combustion engines. With only about 4% of the world's population, the United States is currently the second leading source of carbon dioxide emissions (producing 16% of the global total).[84] China has the distinction of being the world's leader in global-warming pollution and is responsible for approximately 28% of total emissions.

The world's developing nations are increasing their contribution of greenhouse gases as these countries add to their populations and increase their levels of industrialization. A number of steps have been proposed to reduce the emissions of harmful air pollution: technological controls, the climate protocols such as the Paris Agreement, and energy conservation.

Using Technology to Control Particulate Matter

Several mechanical devices that are used to reduce industrial emissions of particulate matter are scrubbers, filters, and electrostatic precipitators. Scrubbers are machines that transfer particles in gases to a collecting liquid. An electrostatic precipitator (see **FIGURE 27**) confers negative or positive electrical charges to particles

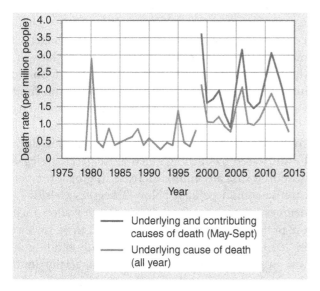

FIGURE 26 Deaths classified as "heat related" in the United States, 1979–2014.

Reproduced from US Environmental Protection Agency. Climate Change Indicators: Heat-Related Deaths. Available at: https://www.epa.gov/climate-indicators/climate -change-indicators-heat-related-deaths. Accessed June 7, 2017. Data sources: Centers for Disease Control and Prevention. CDC WONDER database: Compressed mortality file, underlying cause of death. Available at: http://wonder.cdc.gov/mortSQL.html. Accessed February 2016; Centers for Disease Control and Prevention. Indicator: Heat-related mortality. National Center for Health Statistics. Annual national totals provided by National Center for Environmental Health staff in June 2016. Available at: http://ephtracking.cdc.gov /showIndicatorPages.action.

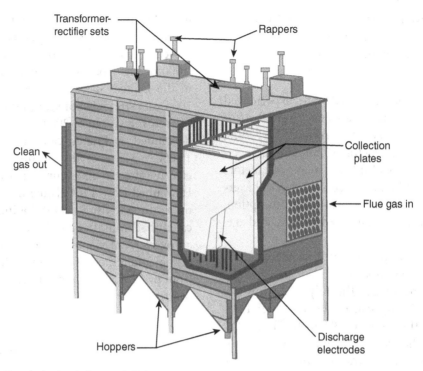

FIGURE 27 Conventional electrostatic precipitator.

Modified and reproduced from US Environmental Protection Agency. Basic Concepts in Environmental Sciences, Module 6: Air Pollutants and Control Techniques—Particulate Matter. Available at: http://www.epa.gov/apti/bces/module6/matter/control/control.htm#precipit. Accessed April 13, 2010.

that are present in gases and collects them on a surface that has the opposite charge.[85]

The Kyoto Protocol

The Kyoto Protocol was an international treaty that addressed climate change.[86,87] Initiated in Kyoto, Japan in December 1997, the provisions of the protocol were a legally binding commitment among the ratifying nations. The purpose of the protocol was to reduce emissions of greenhouse gases believed to be the cause of recent climate changes. The protocol required developed countries to reduce their emissions by targeted amounts. For example, the United States would be required to cut emissions by 7% and European countries (Switzerland, central and eastern Europe, and the European Union) by 8%. The Kyoto Protocol specified that it would come into effect 90 days after it was ratified by a sufficient number of industrialized countries that in combination produce at least 55% of the world's total CO_2 emissions. For some time, implementation of the Kyoto Protocol was stalled because an adequate number of countries, including the United States, had failed to ratify it. By February 2005, 141 nations including Russia had ratified the protocol, meaning that it could be implemented. The Kyoto Protocol went into force on February 16, 2005.[87] The United States, the world's largest producer of CO_2 at the time of the climate change pact, did not ratify the protocol; Australia was the only other developed country that has not signed the agreement.

In December 2009, almost 115 world leaders and more than 40,000 participants assembled in Copenhagen, Denmark to deliberate over climate change policy.[88,89] One of the products of the Copenhagen Climate Change Conference was an agreement known as the Copenhagen Accord, which articulated a political intention for reigning in carbon emissions and coping with climate change. Participants in the Copenhagen climate talks asserted that climate change was a major contemporary environmental challenge that should be addressed by curbing greenhouse gases. Delegates proposed that any future increase in global temperature by should be kept below 2 degrees Celsius (3.6 degrees Fahrenheit) above levels that prevailed during the preindustrial era. This goal was set to be reviewed in 2015. The agreement was not legally binding and was opposed by many countries, especially in the developing world. At the conclusion of the conference, talks became deadlocked. Nevertheless, this international conference ultimately may have had the positive effect of increasing the world's awareness of control of greenhouse gases and related issues.

Paris Agreement

The Paris climate conference in December 2015 culminated with the Paris Agreement.[90-93] A total of 195 countries adopted the legally binding agreement, which had the following features:

- The global temperature rise during the present century is to be kept below 2 degrees Celsius above preindustrial levels.
- Countries would seek to limit the temperatures rise to 1.5 degrees Celsius (2.7 degrees Fahrenheit).
- Parties to the agreement would report periodically on their progress in meeting climate change targets.
- Parties would reconvene every 5 years for a reassessment of their progress.
- Thirty days after, at least 55% of parties that were responsible for at least a total of 55% greenhouse gases officially ratified the Paris Agreement.
- The agreement came into force on November 4, 2016.
- On June 1, 2017, President Trump announced the withdrawal of the United States from the Paris Agreement.

Energy Conservation

From a global perspective, the Kyoto Protocol, the Copenhagen Accord, and similar agreements should be helpful in reducing the emission of greenhouse gases. In the United States, individual states such as California have assumed leadership in addressing climate change. Examples of steps that can be taken to reduce the emission of greenhouse gases and prevent global warming are the following:

- Increase the efficiency of older power plants.
- Develop more renewable and alternative energy sources (e.g., wind turbines and solar panels).
- Use energy-efficient designs in home construction and electrical appliances; try to reduce dependence on such appliances.
- Increase the fuel efficiency of motor vehicles as in the use of fully electric, hybrid gas-electric, and other high-mileage designs.
- Increase the use of public transportation; use bicycles for getting around in cities.

▶ Conclusion

Clean air is an essential element for the survival of life on earth. Air that is polluted can endanger our health and cause damage to trees, wildlife, and property. Sources of air pollution can be subdivided into natural and anthropogenic sources. Natural pollution arises from volcanoes, dust storms, and fires. Anthropogenic sources arise from stationary and mobile sources. The former include factories, oil refineries, and incinerators; examples of the latter are various types of vehicles used on air, water, and land. The health effects of air pollution include increased mortality rates and lung and cardiovascular diseases. As a result of growing emissions of greenhouse gases associated with the consumption of fossil fuels, the phenomenon of global warming is believed to be causing extreme climatic changes and rises in the average sea level. Air pollution and global warming can be reduced through the use of more efficient energy technologies, by limiting population growth, and by conserving energy. Many developed countries have expended significant efforts toward reduction of air pollution. Although these efforts have helped to produce cleaner air, additional steps need to be taken.

Study Questions and Exercises

1. Define the following terms in your own words:
   a. Smog
   b. Air pollution
   c. Criteria air pollutants
   d. Normal ambient air

2. Give examples of how air pollution endangers human health. Include in your discussion a review of the short-term and long-term health effects of air pollution.

3. How does air pollution impact the environment? In what ways can the pollutants NO_x and SO_2 damage structures and monuments over long periods of time?

4. Define the following sources of air pollution and give examples:
   a. Stationary
   b. Mobile
   c. Natural
   d. Anthropogenic

5. Describe how ground-level ozone can be harmful to our health while ozone in the upper stratosphere plays an important role in protecting our health.

6. Explain the adverse health effects attributed to carbon monoxide. Which population groups are likely to be most vulnerable to the effects of carbon monoxide exposure?

7. Define what is meant by a temperature inversion. Explain how temperature inversions contribute to the creation of smog.

8. Explain why environmental health experts are concerned about the possible adverse consequences of exposure to diesel exhaust. Describe one major adverse health effect that has been attributed to diesel exhaust. Name the risk groups that are most affected by exposure to diesel exhaust.

9. Refer to the diagram that shows the anatomy of the human respiratory system (Figure 17, part A, page 257). Which parts of the respiratory system are most likely to be affected by fine particulate matter?

10. Define the term *Air Quality Index*. How does the Air Quality Index aid in protecting the health of the population?

11. Epidemiologic analyses have demonstrated a correlation between an increase in total daily mortality and an increase in air pollution. Give examples of historically significant fatal air pollution episodes that were characterized by extreme increases in air pollution and accompanying increases in mortality.

12. Explain the difference between sick building syndrome and building-related illness. Describe the sources of indoor air pollution that can affect human health adversely.

13. Define what is meant by greenhouse gases and describe how they contribute to the greenhouse effect.

14. Describe three methods for the control of greenhouse gases. Which method, if any, is likely to be most effective?

15. Define the term *global warming* and present arguments for and against the proposition that global warming has occurred during the past century. What environmental outcomes have been attributed to global warming?

For Further Reading

Davis, Devra. *When Smoke Ran Like Water*, 2002.
Gore, Al. *Earth in the Balance*, 1992.
Dawson, Kate Winkler. *Death in the Air*, 2017.

References

1. US Environmental Protection Agency (EPA). Benefits and costs of the Clean Air Act amendments of 1990. Available at: https://www.epa.gov/sites/production/files/2015-07/documents/factsheet.pdf. Accessed June 19, 2017.

2. World Health Organization (WHO). WHO global urban ambient air pollution database (update 2016). Available at: http://www.who.int/phe/health_topics/outdoorair/databases/cities/en/. Accessed June 19, 2017.

3. American Lung Association. *State of the Air 2016*. Chicago, IL: American Lung Association; 2016.

4. South Coast Air Quality Management District (AQMD). Smog and health. Available at: http://www.aqmd.gov/home/library/public-information/publications/smog-and-health-historical-info. Accessed June 16, 2017.

5. US Environmental Protection Agency. *The Plain English Guide to the Clean Air Act*. Research Triangle Park, NC: Office of Air Quality Planning and Standards; 2007.

6. US Environmental Protection Agency. National Risk Management Research Laboratory. *Environmental Curricula Handbook*. EPA 625/R-02/009. Appendix B: Glossary of Terms. Washington, DC: US Environmental Protection Agency; 2002.

7. Bell ML, Davis DL. Reassessment of the lethal London fog of 1952: novel indicators of acute and chronic consequences of acute exposure to air pollution. *Environ Health Perspect*. 2001;109(suppl. 3):389–394.

8. Helfand WH, Lazarus J, Theerman P. Donora, Pennsylvania: an environmental disaster of the 20th century. *Am J Public Health*. 2001;91:553–554.

9. Phalen RF. *The Particulate Air Pollution Controversy: A Case Study and Lessons Learned*. Boston, MA: Kluwer Academic Publishers; 2002.

10. Health Effects Institute. Understanding the health effects of components of the particulate matter mix: progress and next steps. Boston, MA: Health Effects Institute; 2002.

11. Centers for Disease Control and Prevention. Epidemiologic notes and reports cytotoxicity of volcanic ash: assessing the risk for pneumoconiosis. *MMWR*. 1986;35:265–267.

12. California Environmental Protection Agency, Air Resources Board. Glossary of air pollution terms. Available at: https://www.arb.ca.gov/html/gloss.htm. Accessed June 16, 2017.

13. US Environmental Protection Agency. EPA determines that aircraft emissions contribute to climate change endangering public health and the environment. Press release. Available at: https://www.epa.gov/newsreleases/epa-determines-aircraft-emissions-contribute-climate-change-endangering-public-health. Accessed June 20, 2017.

14. National Institutes of Health. MedlinePlus. Air pollution. Available at: http://www.medlineplus.gov/airpollution.html. Accessed June 19, 2017.

15. Union of Concerned Scientists. Cars, trucks, and air pollution. Available at: https://www.ucsusa.org/clean-vehicles/vehicles-air-pollution-and-human-health/cars-trucks-air-pollution#.WkP7pBqo6bM. Accessed December 27, 2017.

16. US Environmental Protection Agency. Criteria air pollutants. Available at: http://www.epa.gov/criteria-air-pollutants. Accessed February 24, 2017.

17. Kaiser J. The other global pollutant: nitrogen proves tough to curb. *Science*. 2001;294(5545):1268–1269.

18. Medical Dictionary. Carboxyhemoglobin. Available at: http://medical-dictionary. The free dictionary.com/carboxy hemoglobin. Accessed June 19, 2017.

19. [No authors listed]. Novel technologies measure ultrafine air pollution in the L.A. Basin. *J Environ Health*. 2004;66(8):51.

20. World Health Organization. Annual mean concentrations of fine particulate matter ($PM_{2.5}$) in urban areas (μg/m3). Available at: http://gamapserver.who.int/gho/interactive_charts/phe/oap_exposure/atlas.html. Accessed June 20, 2017.

21. Centers for Disease Control and Prevention. Potential exposures to airborne and settled surface dust in residential areas of lower Manhattan following the collapse of the World Trade Center—New York City, November 4–December 11, 2001. *MMWR*. 2003;52:131–136.

22. US Environmental Protection Agency. What is acid rain? Available at: https://www.epa.gov/acidrain/what-acid-rain. Accessed June 17, 2017.

23. Lipsett M, Campleman S. Occupational exposure to diesel exhaust and lung cancer: a meta-analysis. *Am J Public Health*. 1999;89:1009–1017.

24. Cohen HJ, Borak J, Hall T. Exposure of miners to diesel exhaust particulates in underground nonmetal mines. *AIHA J*. 2002;63:651–658.

25. Kagawa J. Health effects of diesel exhaust emissions—a mixture of air pollutants of worldwide concern. *Toxicol.* 2002;181–182:349–353.

26. Liukonen LR, Grogan JL, Myers W. Diesel particulate matter exposure to railroad train crews. *AIHA J.* 2002;63:610–616.

27. Northridge ME, Yankura J, Kinney PL, et al. Diesel exhaust exposure among adolescents in Harlem: a community-driven study. *Am J Public Health.* 1999;89:998–1002.

28. Stayner L. Protecting public health in the face of uncertain risks: the example of diesel exhaust [editorial]. *Am J Public Health.* 1999;89:991–993.

29. Steenland K. Lung cancer and diesel exhaust: a review. *Am J Ind Med.* 1986;10:177–189.

30. US Environmental Protection Agency. AIRNow: Air Quality Index (AQI)—A guide to air quality and your health. Available at: https://www.airnow.gov/index.cfm?action=aqibasics.aqi. Accessed June 17, 2017.

31. Levy JI, Greco SL, Spengler JD. The importance of population susceptibility for air pollution risk assessment: a case study of power plants near Washington, DC. *Environ Health Perspect.* 2002;110:1253–1260.

32. Health and Clean Air. Saving the children. *Health & Clean Air Newsletter.* Spring 2003. Available at: http://www.healthandcleanair.org/newsletters/spring2003.html. Accessed June 17, 2017.

33. Dockery DW, Pope CA III, Xu X, et al. An association between air pollution and mortality in six U.S. cities. *New Engl J Med.* 1993;329:1753–1759.

34. Pope CA III. Adverse health effects of air pollutants in a nonsmoking population. *Toxicol.* 1996;111:149–155.

35. Ito K, Thurston GD, Hayes C, et al. Associations of London, England, daily mortality with particulate matter, sulfur dioxide, and acidic aerosol pollution. *Arch Environ Health.* 1993;48:213–220.

36. Schimmel H, Greenberg L. A study of the relation of pollution to mortality: New York City, 1963–1968. *J Air Pollut Control Assoc.* 1972;22:607–616.

37. Dockery DW, Schwartz J, Spengler JD. Air pollution and daily mortality: associations with particulates and acid aerosols. *Environ Res.* 1992;59:362–373.

38. Dominici F, McDermott A, Zeger SL, et al. National maps of the effects of particulate matter on mortality: exploring geographical variation. *Environ Health Perspect.* 2003;111:39–43.

39. Mann JK, Tager IB, Lurmann F, et al. Air pollution and hospital admissions for ischemic heart disease in persons with congestive heart failure or arrhythmia. *Environ Health Perspect.* 2002;110:1247–1252.

40. Kuller LH, Radford EP, Swift DP, et al. Carbon monoxide and heart attacks. *Arch Environ Health.* 1975;30:477–482.

41. Wright GR, Jewizyk S, Onrot J, et al. Carbon monoxide in the urban atmosphere. *Arch Environ Health.* 1975;30:123–129.

42. Lebowitz MD, Holberg CJ, Knudson RJ, Burrows B. Longitudinal study of pulmonary function development in childhood, adolescence, and early adulthood. *Am Rev Respir Dis.* 1987;136:69–75.

43. Lebowitz MD. The relationship of socio-economic factors to the prevalence of obstructive lung diseases and other chronic conditions. *J Chronic Dis.* 1977;30:599–611.

44. Mannino DM, Homa DM, Pertowski CA, et al. Surveillance for asthma—United States, 1960–1995. *MMWR Surveill Summ.* 1998;47:1–28.

45. Mannino DM, Homa DM, Akinbami LJ, et al. Surveillance for asthma—United States, 1980–1999. *MMWR Surveill Summ.* 2002;51:1–13.

46. Rhodes L, Bailey CM, Moorman JE, et al. Asthma prevalence and control characteristics by race/ethnicity—United States, 2002. *MMWR.* 2004;53:145–148.

47. Crain EF, Walter M, O'Connor GT, et al. Home and allergic characteristics of children with asthma in seven U.S. urban communities and design of an environmental intervention: the Inner-City Asthma Study. *Environ Health Perspect.* 2002;110:939–945.

48. Klinnert MD, Price MR, Liu AH, et al. Unraveling the ecology of risks for early childhood asthma among ethnically diverse families in the Southwest. *Am J Public Health.* 2002;92:792–798.

49. Mishra V. Effect of indoor air pollution from biomass combustion on prevalence of asthma in the elderly. *Environ Health Perspect.* 2003;111:71–77.

50. National Institutes of Health. Of air and asthma: air pollution's effects. Bethesda, MD: National Institutes of Health (NIH); 2008.

51. Delfino RJ. Epidemiologic evidence for asthma and exposure to air toxics: linkages between occupational, indoor, and community air pollution research. *Environ Health Perspect.* 2002;110(suppl 4):573–589.

52. Shima M, Nitta Y, Ando M, et al. Effects of air pollution on the prevalence and incidence of asthma in children. *Arch Environ Health.* 2002;57:529–535.

53. Ostro B, Lipsett M, Mann J, et al. Air pollution and exacerbation of asthma in African-American children in Los Angeles. *Epidemiol.* 2001;12:200–208.

54. Henderson BE, Gordon RJ, Menck H, et al. Lung cancer and air pollution in south-central Los Angeles County. *Am J Epidemiol.* 1975;101:477–488.

55. Pope CA III, Burnett RT, Thun MJ, et al. Lung cancer, cardiopulmonary mortality, and long-term exposure to fine particulate air pollution. *JAMA.* 2002;287:1132–1141.

56. Vena JE. Air pollution as a risk factor in lung cancer. *Am J Epidemiol.* 1982;116:42–56.

57. Nyberg F, Gustavsson P, Jarup L, et al. Urban air pollution and lung cancer in Stockholm. *Epidemiol.* 2000;11:487–495.

58. The American Lung Association (ALA), the Environmental Protection Agency (EPA), the Consumer Product Safety Commission (CPSC), and the American Medical Association (AMA). *Indoor Air Pollution: An Introduction for Health Professionals.* Publication 1994-523-217/81322. Washington, DC: US Government Printing Office; 1994.

59. Oliver LC, Shackleton BW. The indoor air we breathe: a public health problem of the '90s. *Public Health Rep.* 1998;113:398–409.

60. Lebowitz MD, Holberg CJ, Boyer B, Hayes C. Respiratory symptoms and peak flow associated with indoor and outdoor air pollutants in the southwest. *J Air Pollut Control Assoc.* 1985;35:1154–1158.

61. Vojta PJ, Friedman W, Marker DA, et al. First national survey of lead and allergens in housing: survey design and methods for the allergen and endotoxin components. *Environ Health Perspect.* 2002;110:527–532.

62. Engvall K, Norrby C, Norbäck D. Asthma symptoms in relation to building dampness and odour in older multifamily houses in Stockholm. *Int J Tuberc Lung Dis.* 2001;5:468–477.

63. Jaakkola JJK, Tuomaala P, Seppänen O. Air recirculation and sick building syndrome: a blinded crossover trial. *Am J Public Health.* 1994;84:422–428.

64. Mendell MJ, Fine L. Building ventilation and symptoms—where do we go from here? *Am J Public Health*. 1994;84:346–348.

65. US Environmental Protection Agency. Indoor air facts no. 4 (revised): sick building syndrome. Available at: https://www .epa.gov/sites/production/files/2014-08/documents/sick _building_factsheet.pdf. Accessed June 17, 2017.

66. White JR, Froeb HF. Small-airways dysfunction in nonsmokers chronically exposed to tobacco smoke. *New Engl J Med*. 1980;302:720–723.

67. US Environmental Protection Agency. *Respiratory Health Effects of Passive Smoking: Lung Cancer and Other Disorders*. EPA publication 600/6-90/006F. Washington, DC: EPA; 1992.

68. Boyle P. The hazards of passive—and active—smoking. *N Engl J Med*. 1993;328:1708–1709.

69. National Aeronautics and Space Administration (NASA). Earth Observatory glossary. Available at: https://earthobservatory .nasa.gov/Glossary/?mode=alpha&seg=f&segend=h. Accessed June 17, 2017.

70. National Oceanic and Atmospheric Administration (NOAA). Global warming. Available at: https://www.ncdc.noaa.gov /monitoring-references/faq/global-warming.php. Accessed June 20, 2017.

71. US Environmental Protection Agency. *Inventory of U.S. Greenhouse Gas Emissions and Sinks: 1990-2015*. EPA 430-P-17-001; 2017.

72. Crowley TJ. Causes of climate change over the past 1000 years. *Science*. 2000;289:270–277.

73. Patz JA, McGeehin MA, Bernard SM, et al. The potential health impacts of climate variability and change for the United States: executive summary of the report of the health sector of the U.S. National Assessment. *Environ Health Perspect*. 2000;108:367–376.

74. McMichael AJ, Patz J, Kovats RS. Impacts of global environmental change on future health and health care in tropical countries. *Br Med Bull*. 1998;54:475–488.

75. Charron DF. Potential impacts of global warming and climate change on the epidemiology of zoonotic diseases in Canada. *Can J Public Health*. 2002;93:334–335.

76. Yohe E. Sizing up the Earth's glaciers. 2004. NASA Earth Observatory. Available at: http://earthobservatory.nasa.gov /Features/GLIMS/. Accessed June 17, 2017.

77. Patz JA, Kovats RS. Hotspots in climate change and human health. *BMJ*. 2002;325:1094–1098.

78. Patz JA, Khaliq M. Global climate change and health: challenges for future practitioners. *JAMA*. 2002;287:2283–2284.

79. Centers for Disease Control and Prevention. Heat-related mortality—United States, 1997. *MMWR*. 1998;47:473–476.

80. Centers for Disease Control and Prevention. Heat-related mortality—Chicago, July 1995. *MMWR*. 1995;44:577–579.

81. CBSNEWS.com. France ups heat toll. September 25, 2003. Available at: http://www.cbsnews.com/stories/2003/08/29 /world/main570810.shtml. Accessed June 17, 2017.

82. Dorozynski A. Heat wave triggers political conflict as French death rates rise. *BMJ*. 2003;327:411.

83. A wake-up call for environmental health. *Lancet*. 2003;362:587.

84. Natural Resources Defense Council. Global warming 101. Available at: https://www.nrdc.org/stories/global-warming-101. Accessed June 17, 2017.

85. US Environmental Protection Agency, Air Pollution Training Institute (APTI). Basic concepts in environmental sciences. Module 6: Air pollutants and control techniques. Particulate matter: control techniques. Available at: https:// www.apti-learn.net/lms/content/epa/courses/re_100/index .htm?cid=2&userID=43049&bookmarks=. Accessed June 21, 2017.

86. ThoughtCo. What is the Kyoto Protocol? Available at: https:// www.thoughtco.com/what-is-the-kyoto-protocol-1204061. Accessed June 17, 2017.

87. United Nations Framework Convention on Climate Change (UNFCCC). Kyoto Protocol Reference Manual. Bonn, Germany: UNFCCC; 2008.

88. United Nations Framework Convention on Climate Change (UNFCCC). Copenhagen Climate Change Conference—December 2009. Available at: http://unfccc.int/meetings /copenhagen_dec_2009/meeting/6295txt.php. Accessed June 22, 2017.

89. *The Guardian*. Climate change talks yield small chance of global treaty. Available at: http://www.guardian.co.uk /environment/2010/apr/11/climate-change-talks-deal-treaty. Accessed June 17, 2017.

90. United Nations Framework Convention on Climate Change (UNFCCC). The Paris Agreement. Available at: http://unfccc .int/paris_agreement/items/9485.phphttp://unfccc.int/paris _agreement/items/9485.php. Accessed June 22, 2017.

91. United Nations Framework Convention on Climate Change (UNFCCC). The Paris Agreement—status of ratification. Available at: http://unfccc.int/paris_agreement/items/9444 .php. Accessed June 22, 2017.

92. European Commission. Paris Agreement. Available at: https:// ec.europa.eu/clima/policies/international/negotiations/paris _en. Accessed June 22, 2017.

93. Shear MD. Trump will withdraw U.S. from Paris climate agreement. *The New York Times*. June 1, 2017. Available at: https://www.nytimes.com/20 17/06/01 /climate/trump-paris -climate-agreement.html. Accessed June 22, 2017.

Index